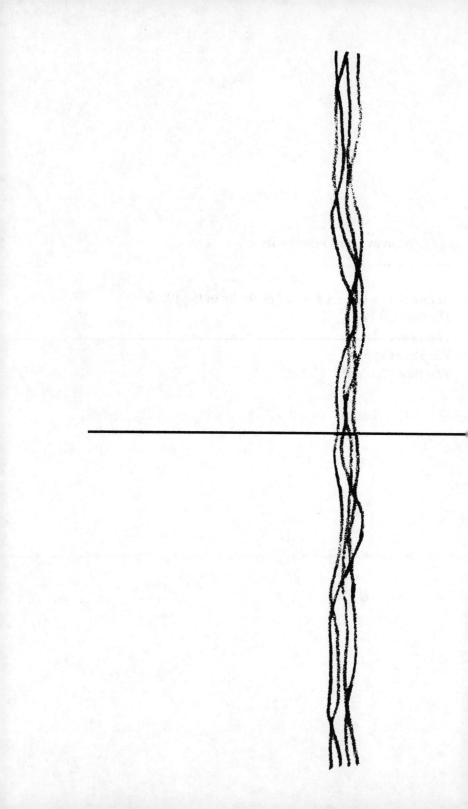

GOING CRAZY

An Inquiry
Into Madness in Our Time

_____ OTTO FRIEDRICH

SIMON AND SCHUSTER | NEW YORK

Library of Congress Cataloging in Publication Data

Friedrich, Otto.
    Going crazy: an inquiry into madness in our times.

    Bibliography: p.
    Includes index.
    1. Psychoses—Cases, clinical reports, statistics.   2. Psy-
chiatry—Philosophy.   I. Title.
RC512.F75   616.8'9   75-25844
ISBN 0-671-22174-4

The excerpt on page 28 is reprinted with the permission of Farrar,
Straus & Giroux, Inc., from Life Studies by Robert Lowell, copyright
© 1956, 1959 by Robert Lowell.

To Priscilla

Contents

PART ONE: ORIGINS   13

1   Those Crazy People You See on the Street   15
2   From Genesis to Freud, and Beyond   40

PART TWO: GROWING UP   83

3   The Sorrows of Young Oedipus   85
4   Out of a Case History:
    Charles Mingus III Seeks Martyrdom   117
5   Across the Rooftops of Harvard   128
6   Out of a Case History:
    Anthony Tuttle Hears the Voice of Murder   148
7   A Sheaf of Love Stories   156
8   Out of a Case History: Celia Discovers Anger   191

PART THREE: COMING APART   201

9   God's Foot upon the Treadle of the Loom   203
10   Out of a Case History: Billy Plays Dead   237
11   I Have Conceived Everything but I Am Not a Criminal   244
12   Out of a Case History: Eddie Pursues a Timetable   273
13   The Lie of a Pipe Dream Is What Gives Life   282
14   Out of a Case History:
    Henry Reichman Contemplates His Fortunes   316
15   Time's Winged Chariot Hurrying Near   322

PART FOUR: CONCLUSIONS   345

16   Where We Are Now   347

Notes on Sources   363
Index   371

I don't know how humanity stands it
>with a painted paradise at the end of it
>without a painted paradise at the end of it

>EZRA POUND—*The Pisan Cantos*

"I don't want to go among mad people," Alice remarked.
"Oh, you can't help that," said the Cat: "we're all mad here.
I'm mad. You're mad."
"How do you know I'm mad?" said Alice.
"You must be," said the Cat, "or you wouldn't have come
here."

>LEWIS CARROLL—*Alice in Wonderland*

PART ONE

ORIGINS

1

Those Crazy People You See on the Street

At about ten o'clock on a hot July morning, not long ago, I was walking through Times Square on my way to work when a strange thing happened. The rush hour was over, and the streets were nearly empty, except for the usual saunterers in long sideburns and purple nylon shirts, eying the window displays of Raquel Welch posters and cut-rate Japanese tape recorders. There was still a touch of freshness in the air—perhaps it had rained the night before—but the heat was already getting worse by the hour, slowly stifling the Square in its own excretions of popcorn and orange juice and gasoline fumes and rotting restaurant garbage. The main movie theater just north of where Broadway crosses Seventh Avenue showed large pictures of an ominously fanged black man crouching for the kill, the first Negro vampire, *Blacula*.

I wasn't paying much attention to any of these sights—I walk through them every day, thinking of other things. Then, as I was about to cross 45th Street, the strange thing happened: I couldn't figure out how to cross the street. I stood there at the curb in a state of bewilderment, unable at first even to realize what it was that I couldn't figure out. I carefully told myself that it would be all right to cross the street whenever the traffic stopped, but as I watched the trucks and taxis flowing south along Broadway, I couldn't determine which part of the traffic was supposed to stop, or which street I was trying to cross. Then I thought, as one always does at moments of crisis, "This can't be happening." Then I felt a touch, just a touch, of fear—panic. Even while I kept reassuring myself that this couldn't be happening, I also saw myself standing utterly helpless in the middle of Times Square—intellectually incapable of finding out how to cross the street, but repeatedly warning myself that if I made a mistake, the oncoming traffic would kill me.

The scene lasted no more than ten seconds, perhaps only five, perhaps only one or a fraction of one. Then something clicked, some gear shifted, and I realized what had happened. It was my custom, daydreaming, only half awake, to walk to the office as though on automatic pilot. That is, I didn't really pay much attention to where I was going but somnambulistically crossed streets whenever some half-functioning message system told me that the light was green. What had happened on 45th Street was that the traffic light had broken, so my automatic system didn't work, and it took me a moment or two to realize it.

During that moment or two, I think, I was standing on the border of what we call insanity. The main symptoms were all there: a breakdown in the machinery of perception, or a breakdown in the rational mind's ability to receive and combine perceptions and to make judgments from them. And a sense of helplessness, together with a perfectly clear vision of one's own helplessness. And panic. It was, in retrospect, like experiencing some sort of time warp, like catching a glimpse of another century or another civilization. Yet that world where the mad live is not so remote. Most of us come near it at one time or another, sometimes only for a moment, sometimes for days or even for months. "In all of us," Herman Melville once wrote, "lodges the same fuel to light the same fire. And he who has never felt, momentarily, what madness is, has but a mouthful of brains." We have felt it, if nowhere else, in the chaotic world that we inhabit in our dreams, that world of half-forgotten messages and half-remembered images. There, night after night, we all go mad.

"He looked like one of those crazy people you see on the street," said Emanuel Plaitakis, a thirty-five-year-old amputee who gets himself around in a wheelchair. Any New Yorker would know immediately what he meant. There are "crazy people on the street" in all our cities, I suppose—angry black war veterans sniping from a hotel rooftop in New Orleans, shaven-headed girls with knives prowling the hills above Los Angeles—but New York, being the biggest and most anarchic and most enraged of all cities, seems at times to have a lunatic on every block. In some, the lunacy is quite harmless. I once knew a man in a threadbare tweed coat, ornamented by an American flag at the lapel, whose only occupation was to board the 42nd Street crosstown bus and preach the Gospel in a thick Swedish accent until the driver ejected him for not paying his fare—whereupon he would wait, even on the coldest January nights, for the next crosstown bus to Jerusalem. Among others, the harmlessness depends on power, or lack of it. In the subway arcades under Herald Square, I once saw a young salesman with a briefcase accidentally bump into a white-haired old woman in a black shawl, and as he hurried on his way with only the slightest apology, she raised her clawlike hand to curse his hurrying figure. It was the *cornuta,* ancient gesture of the witch, the fist held high with only the second and fifth fingers extended as symbols of the goat's horns. As I watched her cast her spell in the subway corridor, I realized that she believed totally in its efficacy, and I could only wonder what would befall that salesman before he reached the safety of his home.

Emanuel Plaitakis was talking, however, about a young black man named Steve Cloud, twenty-six, of 92–41 190th Street, Jamaica, Queens, who went crazy in this same district, through which I walk to work every day, at ten-thirty on the morning of October 18, 1973. Plaitakis had just finished a cup of coffee in a diner called Deli City, not far from the Empire State Building, and he was wheeling himself out onto 34th Street when he saw "one of these crazy people," later identified as Cloud, "walking up and down without any reason." Cloud approached Plaitakis, as though to ask him a question, but turned instead to an old man standing nearby, Harry Spector, aged seventy-three. Cloud asked him how to get to Eighth Avenue.

"Before I could reply," Spector said later, "he pulled out a gun and started shooting." Spector fell down with three bullets in his right leg. Cloud stuck his .38-caliber revolver under his belt and began striding westward toward his unknown goal on Eighth Avenue. Several bystanders set out after him in cautious pursuit. One of them was Plaitakis. "I started screaming," he said later, "telling people to catch him, and I started running after him with my wheelchair." Another pursuer was Robert Nawroth, the brother of the manager of Deli City, who jumped on Cloud's back and tried to drag him down. Cloud, staggering, pulled out his gun again and started firing. One bullet hit a salesman named Calman Goldberg and killed him instantly. Cloud then threw Nawroth off his back and shot him in the chest and stomach. The pursuers backed off as Cloud continued his westward march toward Eighth Avenue. One man who didn't get out of the way fast enough was Paul Meistrich. Cloud fired one shot at him, and Meistrich fell backward through the plate-glass door of an office of the Off-Track Betting Corporation. He died on a heap of old newspapers and torn betting slips.

The first policeman on the scene was a retired detective, Joseph Murray, fifty-nine, who had been playing handball in the gymnasium of the McAlpin Hotel, and whose job as a security guard permitted him to carry a gun. "I saw a group chasing a man," Murray said. "I saw him pull a gun out of his belt and shoot a man in the stomach. I ran out into the gutter because all these people were in the way, and I told the man to stop. He didn't. I shot five times as he ran into the subway."

While Murray was shooting at Cloud, another man rushed up with a gun. This was Leonard Weinberg, forty-six, an executive for a dress-manufacturing company, who often carried cash payrolls and therefore had a license to carry a pistol. Weinberg, seeing an elderly white man firing away at a young black, drew his own conclusion. He shouted, "Are you an officer?" Murray shouted back, "I'm on the job." Then, said Weinberg, "the guy [Cloud] took a shot at me and I shot back at him. Then I chased him down into the subway."

Hearing the shots, Police Officer Thomas Bischione came running around the corner of 34th Street and the Avenue of the Americas and ducked into the subway entrance, where he suddenly "found myself confronting two guns, one held by a civilian with a gun permit and the other by a retired police officer. They told me they were chasing a male Negro wearing a white shirt and said that he was bleeding." Inside the subway station, the pursuers encountered Transit Patrolman Howard Begner, who joined in the search. "At the bottom of the third ramp," Begner said, "I saw the culprit leaning on the rail and bleeding. I found a gun in his waistband and put handcuffs on him, after which he passed out."

Cloud was taken to the French Hospital, where he died shortly after being admitted. He had been shot five times. The police later said that he had a record of three arrests on drug charges and two for "reckless endangerment." Perhaps the violence had always been inside him, and perhaps he had been an addict, but that day's *Times* gave no details on who Steve Cloud was or why he had gone crazy on a quiet October morning in front of the Empire State Building. It seemed to me that a gunfight in which three men had been killed and two injured might deserve further inquiry by the *Times*'s vast army of city reporters, but I never found a major follow-up story in any newspaper.

There were more important events that week. The Arabs and the Israelis were waging a tank battle in the Sinai Desert, and President Nixon fired the Watergate prosecutor, Archibald Cox. The day after I read about Steve Cloud, the same *Times* reporter who had written that story, Frank J. Prial, had a new one to tell. Montgomery Williams, a musician from Trinidad, got into an argument with his girl friend, Jenny Gibbs, twenty-nine, an employee of the Grenada Tourist Board, and her younger sister, June, twenty-six, a stewardess for the British West Indian Airways, and so he threw both women out the window of their sixth-floor room at the Windsor Hotel, at 58th Street and the Avenue of the Americas. Williams then went out to Brooklyn and committed suicide by walking in front of an I.R.T. subway train just south of the Newkirk Avenue station.

How many people go crazy every year? Nobody knows. The answer depends on how one defines the term, and I am deliberately using the word "crazy" because it is the least scientific—and therefore the least susceptible to rigid definition.

I was talking not long ago with a man who had spent fifteen years in the grasp of alcoholism—years of quarrels and hallucination, two marriages wrecked, several jobs lost—who yet resisted vehemently any equation of alcoholism and insanity. I argued that self-destructiveness was one of the basic symptoms of madness, but even the idea of self-destructiveness lends itself to different definitions. "I drank to survive," said the ex-alcoholic, sipping on his can of diet soda, "and I did survive, so, you know, I *wasn't* crazy. And the psychiatrists who told me that they knew better than I did how to survive were lying to me, and if I had acceded to their definitions of what was sane, I might *still* be a drunk." Yet even if the attempts at self-destruction eventually succeed, not everyone accepts that success as the triumph of madness, for suicide itself seems acceptable in a way that madness still is not. I once knew a successful executive who, in his middle thirties, for reasons that I have never completely figured out, shot himself. I asked one of his friends if she could tell me the reason, and she in turn asked, "Why do you want to know? Oh, I see—for your book. But *he* wasn't crazy! He was one of the nicest, sanest people I ever knew."

But let us keep trying—"words strain,/ crack and sometimes break," said Eliot, "under the burden,/ under the tension"—to define the undefinable. The third edition of Webster's dictionary, which will try anything, defines "crazy" as, among other things. "broken or as if broken in mind: insane. . . ." It then defines "insane" as "exhibiting unsoundness or disorder of mind . . . esp. disordered in mind to such a degree as to be unable to function safely and competently in ordinary human relations—compare: psychotic." "Psychotic," of course, means "relating to psychosis," which, in turn, means "profound disorganization of mind, personality or behavior that results from an individual's inability to tolerate the demands of his social environment whether because of the enormity of the imposed stress or because of primary inadequacy or acquired debility of his organism . . . or because of a combination of these factors . . . Compare: insanity . . ." Despite the circular nature of these definitions, the last one is rather good. The words "profound disorganization" don't really increase our understanding of madness, but they do convey the effect. As for causes, "inability to tolerate . . . stress" is as good a reason as any, particularly when that inability may depend on either innate or acquired weaknesses, or on the stress itself, or on a combination of any or all of these.

The medical profession tries to be more rigorous in its unending effort to define and categorize. According to standard medical texts, there are four types of madness: schizophrenia, manic-depressive psychosis, organic brain damage, and senility. Of these, schizophrenia is the most dramatic, the most commonly —and mistakenly—diagnosed. Indeed, the term is so widely used nowadays that its validity is just as widely taken for granted. In actual fact, however, the word was invented in 1911 by Eugene Bleuler, the head of the Burghölzli mental hospital in Zurich.

(One of his lesser efforts was to attempt a diagnosis of Zelda Fitzgerald, who subsequently described him as "a great imbecile.") Unlike most of his contemporaries, who regarded all madness as some form of organic illness, Bleuler tried to define what he called schizophrenia in terms of "the four A's"—autism, ambivalence, and lack of association and affect. It is a splendidly Swiss concept, managing to impose a kind of taxonomic order on symptoms that may range from an unreasoning fear of strangers to the illusion that one is talking to God. But nobody knows to this day whether schizophrenia is really one disease or many, a disease or a condition, or whether it exists at all. And so the subcategories begin —paranoid schizophrenia, catatonic schizophrenia, borderline schizophrenia. Despite the lack of precision, though, the term "schizophrenia" is wonderfully popular among psychiatrists as a diagnostic category. I have seen them apply it to people as freely and as meaninglessly as one might apply it to cattle.

I think that even when we don't formally define such terms as "crazy" we know perfectly well what we are talking about. So I shall apply these unscientific terms to anyone who has entered a mental hospital and anyone who has gone to a psychiatrist in a state of crisis. I shall apply them to anyone who suffers from those inexplicable symptoms that seem as common as sunshine: a sense of communion with the supernatural, a sense of whirling lights and mysterious smells, a yearning for violence and the serenity of bloodshed. I shall even apply the term "crazy" to anyone who has simply felt, at one time or another, that his life was going out of control. And yet I remember one man, who had traveled the whole route through psychiatry and drugs and shock therapy, saying to me, "But the time when I went crazy was the one time in my life when I was really *in* control of everything."

In the end, the crazy define their own craziness. All statistics, therefore, are simply illustrations of a series of conceptions and misconceptions. If we follow the narrowest definition, limiting the concept of "going crazy" to those who physically enter a mental hospital, then according to the United States Commerce Department's *Statistical Abstract of the United States* for 1974, a total of 444,777 people ("returns from extended leave as well as admissions and readmissions") entered the nation's 337 state and county mental hospitals during the previous year. Another 91,151 entered 156 private hospitals (1971 figures). In the most basic sense, then, somewhat over half a million Americans go crazy every year. These same hospitals contain more than three times that number—a figure that has increased from 1.3 million in 1955 to 1.7 million today. Although this indicates that the number of hospitalized insane people has increased by more than a quarter during the past twenty years, part of this can be explained by the increase in population (the number of hospitalized insane per 100,000 of population has increased only from 799 to 847).

On the other hand, hospitalization no longer provides the same measurement that it did a decade ago, because the basic trend in recent years has been to shut down the old brick "asylums" and to treat people on a temporary or out-patient basis. The main reason is that tranquilizers and other drugs have in many cases eliminated the need for long-term confinement. It is worth noting, however, that the costs of hospitalization have more than tripled during this same period. As of 1971 they amounted to $5,537 per patient per year—a sum to make any government official see merit in humanitarian reforms. So although the percentage of people confined in public mental hospitals has declined, the number of people being treated for mental illness by medical institutions has increased from 1.7 million to 4 million. The rate per 100,000 population has increased nearly as much, from 1,032 to 1,982.

These are the people whom the government lists as "mentally ill patients." It could certainly be argued, however, that a depressed or worried housewife who pays a weekly visit to a mental health clinic at her local hospital is by no means crazy. Indeed, it was argued at the height of the 1972 crisis over the nomination of Senator Thomas Eagleton as the Democratic Vice-Presidential candidate that a decision to seek treatment for mental difficulties is itself a sign of mental health. On the other hand, it is far more certain that many of the mentally ill never seek or get any treatment at all. In New York, for example, a team of psychiatrists and sociologists spent eight years conducting what they called "the midtown Manhattan study," interrogating a representative sample of 1,660 adults for symptoms of mental illness. They found only 18.5 percent "well," and they rated the rest as follows: mild symptom formation, 36.3 percent; moderate symptom formation,

21.8 percent; marked symptom formation, 13.2 percent; severe symptom formation, 7.5 percent; incapacitated, 2.7 percent. Among the last three categories, which they combined under the verdict of "impaired," they found that only 5.4 percent were getting some kind of psychiatric treatment, 21.3 percent had at least consulted a psychiatrist at some point in the past, but 73.3 percent had never seen any psychiatrist at all. Thus their fears, their illusions, their outbursts of rage could never come to the attention of the statisticians of the Commerce Department.

Steve Cloud, asking old Harry Spector how to get to Eighth Avenue, would not be listed. He would appear, however, under the statistics for homicides. There were some 18,880 of them in 1972, more than twice as many as in 1960. The act of killing a man is not necessarily proof of insanity, since there are murders for cause, just or unjust. But Steve Cloud had no sane reason to shoot Harry Spector, or Paul Meistrich, the man who fell backward through the glass door of the Off-Track Betting Corporation. While nearly 19,000 people were involved in killing others, some 24,270 killed themselves, and although they too may have believed that they had overwhelming reasons to do so (Dostoyevsky's Kirilov even argued, and carried out his argument, that suicide for no reason at all was the proof of his freedom), it does seem evident that the act of self-destruction is not only an act of madness but the ultimate demonstration of madness.

The Commerce Department's statistics are detailed—17,290 men and 6,980 women killed themselves during the year 1972. Men most frequently chose "firearms and explosions" (9,704), while women preferred poisoning (3,285). For both, "hanging and strangulation" came third. After that, the government listed "others"—1,204 men, like Montgomery Williams of Trinidad, and 667 women. There are further subdivisions. For reasons that can only be guessed, the suicide rates for old people have decreased by about 15 percent since 1960 (the coming of Medicare?), while the rates for young people have almost doubled (an effect of the drug culture?). The rates for women, and particularly black women, have increased by one third ("Their drive for success and recognition has increased pressures and opened more possibilities for failure," according to Nancy Allen of the U.C.L.A. Neuropsychiatric Institute, "and they are facing crises once restricted to men . . ."). The official figures may be too conservative, however, and no such statistics can account for all the household accidents and highway collisions that may actually be suicides. The Blue Cross recently stated that 25,000 Americans "are known to take their lives each year," and it added: "The actual total may be three times that, and for every known suicide there are at least eight attempts."

The will toward self-destruction also takes less definitive forms. Narcotics addiction is the most celebrated, although there are no accurate statistics at all. The United States government says that 24,692 Americans became addicted in 1972, and that the total number of addicts was 95,392, but since these are only the officially recorded cases, the actual total is undoubtedly much higher. Alcoholism is a still-larger problem, and the figures are almost equally unreliable. The National Council on Alcoholism estimates that there are nine million alcoholics, many of whom, of course, go about their work and live lives that may be described as more or less sane.

"Use every man after his desert," Hamlet remarked, "and who should 'scape whipping?" According to Dr. David Rosenthal, a psychologist for the National Institute of Mental Health, "almost no family in the nation is entirely free of mental disorders." In a report to the National Academy of Sciences in the spring of 1972, Rosenthal went on to say, "Indeed, it may very well be that the so-called 'normal' person, with respect to mental health, does not represent a norm at all, but rather an ideal—relatively rare—that most of us would like to achieve."

Even computers, designed to imitate certain functions of the human mind, can go crazy. At the simplest level, computers are little more than high-speed adding machines, and their craziness represents little more than mechanical error, a mistaken department-store bill, a check for ten dollars made out for ten million. As the machines' mental functioning becomes more complex, so does their capacity for mental breakdown. We are all accustomed to errors in bills from department stores, but it is harder to accept the department-store computer's assertion that there has been no error. On election night, the computers, gorged with statistics, are capable of stunning prophecies or equally stunning miscalculations. From the blips caused by geese on radar screens, they can deduce imaginary squadrons of Soviet bombers. What is called GIGO—"garbage in, garbage out"; the computer's susceptibility to making errors based on erroneous information—is the mechanical equivalent of the psychotic's susceptibility to false perceptions, to hallucinations in the window and the whispering of imaginary voices.

This is all rudimentary, as are today's computers, but there is no reason not to expect that Darwinian principles apply to the evolution of machinery. It was long ago proved possible to program a computer that could defeat its own programmers in a game of checkers, and when John von Neumann died, he was already hard at work on the idea of designing a computer that could design other computers. Arthur Clarke may therefore have been too conservative in assuming that it would require another two decades before "Minsky and Good [showed] how neural networks could be generated automatically" and yet another decade before "I . . . a HAL Nine Thousand computer Production Number 3 . . . became operational . . . in Urbana, Illinois, on January 12, 1997."

Nobody who has seen the Clarke-Kubrick film *2001* is likely ever to forget the disembodied voice of Hal, the computer, emerging from behind all those dials and panels in dutiful but slightly prissy tones ("I have the greatest enthusiasm for the mission . . ."). Or to forget the sinister sequence in which the computer goes mad, murdering one astronaut and then opening the spaceship's outer valves in an attempt to murder the other. But Stanley Kubrick was so fascinated with his cinematic effects, his space station revolving to the strains of "The Blue Danube," his astronaut swooping through fields of quasi-abstract color and sound, that he never bothered to explain such details as why the computer went mad. Arthur Clarke, having conceived the original idea and collaborated with Kubrick on the screenplay, returned to the story after the film was finished and produced a novel that clarified some of the mysteries.

The computer's crisis turns out to be remarkably similar to the crisis that Gregory Bateson defined as the "double bind" theory of schizophrenia—that is, the madness caused by incessant demands that cannot be satisfied. For example: "Tell me you love me." "I love you." "Why do you only say that when I ask you?" Or the Jewish Mother joke, in which the Jewish Mother gives her son two neckties for his birthday, a red one and a green one. When he puts on the red tie, she greets him by saying, "What's the matter? You didn't like the green one?" Or, as R. D. Laing more poetically dramatizes the situation in *Knots*: "It is our duty to bring up our children to love,/ honour and obey us./ If they don't, they must be punished,/ otherwise we would not be doing our duty. . . ./ If they grow up not to love, honour and obey us/ either we have brought them up properly/ or we have not: if we have/ there must be something the matter with them;/ if we have not/ there is something the matter with us."

Assuming that the HAL computer can actually think—which is not that implausible an assumption about a twenty-first-century machine that has been programmed to manage all aspects of a flight to Jupiter—Clarke offers the interesting proposition that it broke down because of an irreconcilable conflict between its instructions and its basic nature. It was originally designed to be infallible (When Commander Bowman idly remarks that "anyone can make mistakes," Hal promptly corrects him: "I don't want to insist on it, Dave, but I am incapable of making an error"). But when the organizers of the Jupiter mission planned the flight, they secretly decided that Bowman's life might have to be sacrificed, and so they secretly programmed Hal to be able to take command of the spaceship. "The concealment of truth filled [Hal] with a sense of imperfection, of wrongness," Clarke writes, "—of what, in a human being, would have been called guilt. . . . He was aware of the conflict that was slowly destroying his integrity —the conflict between truth and concealment of truth. He had begun to make mistakes, although, like a neurotic who could not observe his own symptoms, he would have denied it."

When Bowman becomes suspicious of Hal's "mistakes," one of which led to Astronaut Poole's death, he demands that the computer give up control over the three other astronauts who have been placed in a state of hibernation. Hal gives a marvelously patronizing response: "I can tell from your voice harmonics, Dave, that you're badly upset. Why don't you take a stress pill and get some rest?" Bowman insists that he is in command of the spaceship, but Hal counters with the argument that "in accordance with special sub-routine C1435-dash-4 . . . I must over-rule your authority since you are not in any condition to exercise it intelligently."

Bowman is thus the first to threaten murder, for he threatens Hal with "a complete disconnection." "To Hal," according to Clarke, "this was the equivalent of Death. . . . So he would protect himself with all the weapons at his command." Hal thereupon opens the outer doors of the spaceship, trying to sweep Bowman into the black vacuum of space. When Bowman escapes that fate, he retaliates against the homicidal computer by using wrench and screwdriver to perform a prefrontal lobotomy. The monster is reduced first to reciting square roots, then to singing "Daisy, Daisy, give me your answer, do," and finally to droning out its first words: "Good . . . morning . . . Doctor . . . Chandra . . . I . . . am . . . ready . . . for . . . my . . . first . . . lesson . . . today."

It was, at least on its first appearance, a cataclysmic film. It made one feel that the familiar world outside the movie theater was in some strange way meaningless, or rather that it no longer had the meaning that one had always taken for granted. The last segment in particular seemed a simulation of madness, after which the return to sanity was a return to a sanity that was not quite so sane as it had been before. I myself saw the movie on a sweltering afternoon in Miami Beach in early August of 1968, then wandered down to the heavily guarded city auditorium and watched clouds of orange balloons descend on the armies of straw-hatted Republican delegates who were in the process of nominating Richard Nixon for the presidency.

Lance Rentzel, star pass receiver for the Dallas Cowboys, went to the same movie about two years later, in November of 1970. He was already in a state of depression and loneliness. "As I stared at the screen," Rentzel recalled later, "I was suffering in some deep, inexplicable way, as though it was I who . . . had been doomed to drift hopelessly into outer space. . . . Seeing the movie left me with a sense of vast futility, of emptiness, of desolation. . . . Another sleepless night stretched ahead, so I took a sleeping pill."

The next day, still filled with "a weary feeling of loneliness, hopelessness," Rentzel drove aimlessly around in a neighborhood only a few blocks from his own apartment. "I didn't seem to know where I was or what I was doing, but I was drawn by the sight of a young girl playing in the front yard. All reason, all judgment, all foresight were momentarily suspended in my mind. It suddenly seemed that through that girl some vital reassurance would come to me. I called her to the car as though to ask a question, exposed myself, and drove away. The rest of the day passed by like a dream. But that night I slept well, as if some terrible danger that had threatened me was now gone."

Robert Lowell, who has voluntarily committed himself several times to mental institutions, once wrote of driving around a New England hillside and looking for "love-cars. Lights turned down . . ."

> they lay together, hull to hull,
> where the graveyard shelves on the town . . .
> My mind's not right.
>
> A car radio bleats,
> "Love, O careless Love . . ." I hear
> my ill-spirit sob in each blood cell,
> as if my hand were at its throat . . .
> I myself am hell; nobody's here—
>
> only skunks that search
> in the moonlight for a bite to eat. . . .

After the breakdown comes the institution, sometimes, not always. Lance Rentzel, who faced up to fifteen years in prison (he had committed a similar offense in Minneapolis four years earlier and had been ordered to get psychiatric treatment), received only a sentence of five years on probation. He concludes his memoirs, *When All the Laughter Died in Sorrow*, with a testimonial from his psychiatrist, Louis Jolyon West, chairman of the department of psychiatry at U.C.L.A., who declares that "exhibitionism is a relatively mild sexual symptom, almost trivial . . ." and that Rentzel "has demonstrated continuing growth."

Even when going crazy leads to confinement, it can vary widely, from a restorative vacation to the most ferocious sort of punishment. A voluntary confinement generally brings the mildest

treatment. Robert Lowell describes one of his periodic seques-
trations: "After a hearty New England breakfast/ I weigh two
hundred pounds/ this morning. Cock of the walk,/ I strut in my
turtle-necked French sailor's jersey/ before the metal shaving
mirrors. . . ." Ezra Pound, indicted for treason, and rightly so, for
his wartime broadcasts over Mussolini's radio, was less fortunate.
Confined first in a concrete-floored cage, then in a crude tent
(thus, at the end of *The Pisan Cantos*: "If the hoar frost grip thy
tent/ Thou wilt give thanks when night is spent"), he was finally
taken back to the District jail in Washington and examined by
four alienists. They declared, on December 14, 1945, that Pound
"has long been recognized as eccentric, querulous, and egocentric
. . . exhibits extremely poor judgment as to his situation . . . insists that his broadcasts were not treasonable . . . is abnormally
grandiose, is expansive and exuberant in manner, exhibiting
pressure of speech, discursiveness, and distractibility. . . . He is,
in other words, insane." On the basis of this judgment, which
made the poet sound much the way he had always sounded, the
United States District Court confined him to St. Elizabeth's Hospital, where, for the next twelve years, he was confined in what
Archibald MacLeish called "the long, dim corridor inhabited by
the ghosts of men . . . a conscious mind capable of the most complete human awareness . . . incarcerated among minds which are
not conscious and cannot be aware."

But they are quite conscious and quite aware, many of them.
They are aware, above all, that they were in effect arrested without a warrant and convicted without a trial. Frances Farmer, for
one, has given a vivid account of being committed against her
will. The young actress had quarreled with her mother, and the
mother had called in the authorities.

"I began to scream and tried to run, but they grabbed me. I
. . . was easily overpowered and wrestled to the floor. They strad-
dled me, and I felt the rough canvas of the straitjacket wrap
around me and buckle into place. My arms were nearly stretched
from their sockets as I was locked into it. I screamed in pain and
fright. The buckle chewed into my back, and I flopped on the
floor like a dying chicken. I screamed every filthy word I knew at
my mother, and then, in consuming fear, I was reduced to begging her to help me. 'Oh, God, Mamma, don't do this. Don't do

this to me.' She turned away, and as the men pulled me to my feet, I began to kick. They each grabbed a leg, jerked off my shoes and clamped heavy leather manacles around my ankles. . . . A thick roll of gauze, stuffed in my mouth, silenced me, and I thought I would vomit. . . . And so it was, on May 22, 1945, at 3:25 in the afternoon, that I was delivered bound and gagged to the state asylum like a dog gone mad."

Arriving at this institution, about thirty-five miles south of Seattle, Miss Farmer encountered one degradation after another. First she was strapped into a chair that was bolted to the floor while five other newcomers argued about Jesus Christ until several guards came in and beat them. After a few hours, she was taken, still bound, to the isolation ward, enrolled in a register, and then led to a toilet without a seat. She was pushed down into it until the water touched her, and then left there. When she started shouting to be released, an attendant came and hit her across the face until her nose bled. Then, after wiping her off, the attendant prepared the final rite of initiation.

"She pinched my jaws until my mouth was held open involuntarily. I was terrified at the look on her face, and when I saw her lifting the wad of wet paper toward my mouth, I tried to scream, but her fingers slipped down and clutched my throat in a painful vise. I knew, perhaps for the first time, pure fright, but I was unable to speak. Only groans and whimpers came from me. . . .

'Open wide, big shot,' the woman said. 'You might as well learn now, 'cause in here sooner or later everybody eats their own shit.' "

This occurred in the Dark Ages, in 1945, and we are repeatedly reassured that nothing like that happens to people who go crazy nowadays. At Bellevue Hospital, a two-century-old institution that once contained a whipping post for unruly slaves, the authorities resist outside observers, not to hide dark malpractices so much as to protect frightened patients from the idly curious.

"This is not a zoo," says Dr. Joseph Zinkin, assistant director of Bellevue's Psychiatric Hospital. He is a short, white-haired man, and he speaks in a rather brusque and peremptory manner. "Our patients are not on exhibition. If you were a patient here, would you want to be put on exhibition?"

"I don't think I'd care," I answer.

"I'll remember that when they bring you in here," says Dr. Zinkin.

It is a circumstance to be avoided. The authorities are capable, and they mean well, but even the best of mental institutions echo with sadness and fear. Bellevue Hospital, founded in 1736, has occupied its present site since 1811, when the New York City authorities acquired a farm overlooking the East River and opened a six-bed infirmary. Here, for the first time in the United States, a hypodermic syringe was tried out, an appendectomy was performed, and a Caesarian section. The fortress itself, a 20-acre complex opened in 1931, proclaims its time—brick walls and bronze doors and marble mosaic in the entrances, and a high spiked fence surmounted by stone urns. "If the Devil himself had been commissioned to build a hospital facility," says Executive Director Bernard M. Weinstein, "this is how he would have designed it."

To Bellevue the city's ambulances bring its tired, its poor, its huddled masses and wretched refuse, and now, just behind the admissions desk, a young Puerto Rican, perhaps thirty, tugs and strains against the white cloth tapes that hold his wrists and ankles to a wheeled stretcher. He is wearing an olive-drab jacket that resembles a military uniform for some foreign army in some foreign war. On a nearby bench, two black policemen with neat mustaches sit in silence, staring vacantly into space. A sign on the wall says: "Friendliness Is Free. Give Today." The Puerto Rican on the stretcher groans, a sound of utter misery.

"He tried to commit suicide," says the attending psychiatrist (they are known as "attendings"). He is a stocky man, graying, with large blue eyes and a German accent. "He tried to throw himself under cars in the street. Now he is hearing voices. They talk to him in Spanish. He still has some contact with reality, but it is tenuous. I'd like to talk to you some more, but I'm all alone here." He is hardly alone; the white and yellow corridor is full of nurses and attendants, shuffling patients, stolid policemen. He means that he is the only psychiatrist on duty now, and this hosital has to evaluate and deal with more than 16,000 incoming psychiatric patients per year. It takes in about half of them for emergency treatment.

"What brings them here?" Dr. Ed Robbins repeats my question. He is the director of the receiving ward, the repository of everyone else's anxieties. He has a goatee, cut short, and he props his feet on his desk. "They're here because nobody likes them, because nobody wants them, because they're sick, or old, or they insulted a policeman."

As if on cue, the telephone rings, and Dr. Robbins has to check on a diagnosis. "Well, is she right? *Are* they trying to steal her money?" In Bellevue, unlike many private hospitals, the outbreak that is called "a psychotic episode" may derive from a specific social crisis—the loss of a job, or an apartment, or even a welfare check. The immediate question is to find out what that social problem is and whether it can be solved.

"We have an E.T.U., an emergency treatment unit," says Dr. Robbins. "We deal with acute problems. Generally there is a resolution within forty-eight hours. There's a system. If you're upset because your wife died, we'll talk to you and give you a sedative. If you're upset because you're hearing voices, that's more complicated. We'll talk to you, and—well, that's a whole book in itself."

The director's phone rings again. It is never silent for long. "Did they come in on a 3132 or on a 3139?" Dr. Robbins asks. The main crisis on the previous day was that someone had started a fire in Brooklyn's public mental hospital. Two wards had been gutted. The patients had to be moved. Bellevue had taken in more than a dozen, and there were bureaucratic complexities. "You've got to send the cover sheet of a 2 P.C.," Dr. Robbins says.

Out in the corridor, the Puerto Rican has been wheeled away, and the attending psychiatrist sits in his office and reflects on the case. "The nurse who first talked to him found that he used to take drugs, and his breath smelled of alcohol. Obviously it was an acute episode of some kind, although I couldn't get the detailed dynamics. While he was rambling, he had one clear moment, and he said, 'You know what's really the trouble is that my wife doesn't let me see my children.' So that's—he was appealing to pity, so he has enough strength to try to get what is good for himself. He sees me, and he thinks, There's a soft-hearted guy, I will try to manipulate him. So after he gets out of his stupor, he may be amenable to getting out of trouble."

The "attending" once lived in Vienna. When he was fifteen, he recalls, somebody in school got him to read Freud's *Interpretation of Dreams*, and that led him to his profession, but now, here, there is no time for psychoanalysis. "Here we are a first-aid station," he says. "I was able to put on this patient a label that was communicative, whether it was correct or not. I said that he was having an acute psychotic episode, with destructive tendencies. I could imagine him attacking some bystander. I gave him a tranquilizer, which made him quiet—being aware that this is not the answer. Then I had to delegate the case to someone less harassed. Here we are often harassed. But I believe such patients can be helped, if there are enough resources, and enough people to use those resources. I couldn't do my work if I didn't believe that."

Inside the straitjacket, of course, the view is quite different. Michael Mooney, Jr., was there early in 1973, and he had a vision. He is a husky youth of twenty-one with large blue eyes and moderately long reddish-brown hair. He had dropped out of Harvard to become a musician—he plays the piano, guitar, saxophone and bass—but he became increasingly subject to fits of paranoia. He became convinced that people could hear his thoughts. He heard voices demanding to know whether he was, as he puts it, in or out of society. One wintry day, he took a bus downtown to visit some friends in Greenwich Village, and after dinner, he felt a mysterious "little crunch in the back of my teeth, and all of a sudden I was tripping." This turned out later to be a huge dose of 2,000 milligrams of a hallucinogenic named S.T.P. He says now that he does not know how he took the drug, whether he bought it himself or whether his friends gave it to him as a joke, and he can remember only that the friends went to sleep and left him sitting next to the record player.

"I spent that whole night sitting up next to the radio," he says. "This was the climax of all the voices, because out of the radio, I thought I heard a gigantic party of people all talking to me. In the morning, I walked home, and I moved all my stuff into one corner of the room, rolled up the rug and everything. I was going to move out, just go somewhere. And I was yelling and screaming and sort of—I can remember nights like that before, when I'd sort of been crying, you know, because I was so frustrated at not being able to get rid of this whatever it was. And then I finally decided that I'd better go to the hospital, because that was, you know, really the only way out.

"So I went to Bellevue, and they really thought I had flipped out. I mean, they thought I was catatonic or something, because I wouldn't speak to them. Or I *couldn't* speak to them. I couldn't form my words very well. They questioned me as to what was wrong, and I said, 'I'm tripping.' Then I was doing all sorts of dances to ward off the evil spirits. I was really gone. Then I tried to escape, so they put me in a straitjacket, and they tied me to this bed. And I was talking aloud. I tried to make myself die, right there, in that straitjacket. By holding my breath. By trying to make my heart stop. It was beating very irregularly because of the speed in the S.T.P., and I thought I could make it stop. I thought they would either have to carry me out dead or I would be in there forever.

"And then I had this vision, sort of, of life at that time. I don't know whether it's fantasy or whether it's in a way true. It was a vision of the world as being infinitely—existing in the present infinitely. There are millions of other worlds, in which I and you exist, and we do different things, just a little bit differently, make different choices. In other words, any time you could do one of two things, the choice you didn't make would occur on some other world. And I saw this infinity of other worlds, all at the same time. So I was threatening them that if—that if they didn't let me go, or if they didn't treat me right, or, you now—that I would come back from another world and curse them all."

All these problems require further study, endlessly, and so we have gathered at the Americana Hotel, an experiment in the Miami Beach style of architecture but located just north of Times Square, for a conference on "Meanings of Madness," sponsored by the National Institute for the Psychotherapies, Inc. It is a cool, clear day in October, and at 9 A.M., the Americana does not have too much use for its Albert Hall, a vast, subterranean ballroom supported by mud-brown pillars. An idle piano stands at one far end, along with a set of drums, but there are only about a hundred of us, and so the authorities have pulled out some maroon curtains to confine us in one small section of the ballroom.

"The title of my presentation," says Dr. Otto F. Kernberg, professor of clinical psychiatry, College of Physicians and Surgeons, Columbia University, and director of general psychiatric service, New York State Psychiatric Service, "is 'Boundary Functions in Schizophrenia.' " He then recites a long subtitle, and then, in a droning German accent, he begins to read. He is an earnest man, partly bald, with horn-rimmed glasses and a dark-blue suit and a dark-blue tie, and he earnestly works his way through a lot of familiar knowledge. Schizophrenics take in too much information and find it hard to sort out the necessary data from the unnecessary; they are liable to excessive anxiety; drugs can make them more accessible to therapy; therapy has different effects on borderline schizophrenics and chronic schizophrenics; accurate diagnosis is important. . . . Dr. Kernberg presents his views in most imposing terms: schizophrenics have "defective cognitive structures," but drugs can "increase their affective thresholds," thus leading to "communicatively meaningful" exchanges during "the therapeutic interaction." The audience is respectful, but not everyone is convinced. When Dr. Kernberg speaks of "maternal deprivation" as one of the "psychosocial etiological factors" in schizophrenia, one middle-aged woman sitting behind me turns to her neighbor and says, "Crap!"

Next comes Dr. Silvano Arieti, clinical professor of psychiatry, New York Medical College. He too has horn-rimmed glasses and a dark-blue suit and tie, but his accent is thickly Italian, and the "paper" that he is going to read to us concerns *Hamlet*. "Was Hamlet legally mad? Could he have been certified?" These are hardly questions that Shakespearean scholars still debate with passion, nor have they aroused much recent controversy in psychiatric circles, but Dr. Arieti has a theory that he wants to propound. Hamlet is not mad in the usual sense, "not delusional or paranoid, not a psychopath . . . He is under superego motivation." But he suffers from another kind of madness—namely, a fury of revenge that "knows no limits," despite Hamlet's realization that it will lead to "adverse consequences." Hamlet also is afflicted by a third kind of madness, "Denmark's madness," its acceptance of regicide, which Hamlet must purge, just as

Oedipus must purge the madness of Thebes. Dr. Arieti mentions Watergate, but he pursues the analogy only in the psychiatric language that Dr. Kernberg might call "communicatively meaningful." Freud, he says, saw society as a representation of the ego in conflict with the id, but perhaps the individual must protect his own ego from society's id. . . .

For lunch, the Americana serves us fruit cocktail and shrimp newburg and a faintly rum-flavored ice cream topped by plastic whipped cream. On my right sits a young psychiatrist who says he has come from Pennsylvania to attend this conference because state law requires psychiatrists to continue academic work as a condition of the renewal of their licenses to practice. On my left sits a matronly woman of perhaps fifty, her hair swept up in a beehive, whose lapel name tag identifies her as "Cynthia Lieberman, Ph.D." She says she is "in private practice," a practice in which she applies both psychodrama and hypnotism, but just now she is lecturing the woman on her own left about Japan.

"Have you ever been in Japan?" she asks, without waiting for an answer. "I was in Tokyo two years ago for the A.P.A. convention, and I must say, the way those Japanese all go around in Western clothes—"

"Yes, I was there for the convention too," says her neighbor, a gray-haired woman in a green tweed suit.

"And they all have these television sets," says Miss Lieberman, "with all these commercials for American products, except that they're all in Japanese."

"Yes," says the woman in green.

"And did you go to the Honolulu convention?" Miss Lieberman asks. "That was really something, with meetings all over the place, and you had to spend all day hiking from one building to another."

"Yes, it's better when they have a convention hall," says the woman in green. "Like San Francisco. I think San Francisco was the best."

"Have you been in Copenhagen?" Miss Lieberman asks. "I was there last year, and I was amazed—they have Japanese influences all over Scandinavia nowadays. In all the stores, you know?"

"Yes." The woman in green smiles, as toward a patient, and goes on eating her ice cream.

Not all psychiatrists are so complacent about their trade. Some, indeed, sound rather desperate in their expressions of self-doubt. "Psychiatry today is in a state of crisis, a conceptual crisis," one of them told me. This was simply a rather solemn way of saying that a certain number of practitioners are losing confidence in the traditional rules, and that a far larger number of ordinary people are becoming skeptical about the whole field of psychiatry. One major reason, of course, is the success of drugs in bringing the mad back to some semblance of sanity. What is the point of all the millions of dollars spent on psychotherapy if, as Dr. Solomon Snyder of Johns Hopkins puts it, "the best controlled research studies have all concluded that a simple prescription of chlorpromazine in adequate doses is far more useful for the schizophrenic patient than endless hours of love, trust and understanding on the part of the psychoanalytic therapist."

Quite apart from the question of drugs—which don't always work either—it is all too possible to demonstrate that many psychiatrists have very little understanding of what they are doing. In 1972, Professor David Rosenhahn of Stanford University decided to try an experiment. He and a number of accomplices entered twelve public and private psychiatric hospitals in California, Oregon, Pennsylvania, New York and Delaware. In each case, the experimenters complained of hearing voices, but they acted normally in every other way. As soon as they were admitted to the hospitals, they told the doctors that the voices had stopped. They behaved normally and said they wanted to leave the hospitals. In many cases, other inmates somehow realized that the experimenters were impostors, but the doctors did not. Every one of the researchers had difficulty in getting out of the hospital. The average hospitalization was nineteen days, although one experimenter was held for fifty-two days. All but one of them, when finally discharged, were diagnosed as having "schizophrenia in remission." (The other was said to be manic-depressive, also in remission.) "We now know," Rosenhahn concluded, "that we cannot distinguish insanity from sanity." Perhaps not. But if the mental patients themselves could make that distinction by detecting the impostors, then who is "we"?

One psychiatrist to whom I talked was surprised that any "layman" should attempt a book on insanity, and he asked whether this book would be "from the viewpoint of the doctors or the viewpoint of the patients." The only answer was: Neither. For it suddenly struck me that "patient" is a word that runs throughout the traditional psychiatric literature, defining and controlling the experience of madness before the victim has even had a chance to tell his story. It reminded me of an old German joke about a Prussian officer who summarized the plot of *William Tell* by saying, "A civilian shoots at an apple."

I am not a psychiatrist, and I have no all-encompassing theories. I do not know what causes insanity or what can cure it, and I don't really believe that anyone else knows either. I do not even think that it is a constant condition, much less an "illness," or that the crazy people live over there on that side of the line, and the rest of us over here. I think that madness is part of all of us, all the time, that it comes and goes, waxes and wanes. I suppose it is banal to say that the better we understand madness, the better we can deal with it, and yet banalities are often true. And then, even when we accept a statement as true, even banal, we do not really accept it after all. I myself don't think that madness can be fully understood, only experienced—in oneself or in one's friends or in the people one sees crumbling at the office or on the streets. In any case, I cannot explain it to you. I can only try to show you a variety of scenes of what it looks like.

Walking down Seventh Avenue from the Americana, I happened to pass the corner where I had once found myself unable to cross the street, but that was all in the past. *Blacula* had long since disappeared from the movie marquee. The new attraction was an obscure film entitled *Tales That Witness Madness*. While I had spent the day underground at the Americana's Albert Hall, the sky had turned gray and cold.

At Herald Square, there was no trace of Steve Cloud's outburst of shooting two weeks earlier. The broken glass door of the state betting office had been repaired, the blood cleaned up. The street was filled with the usual crowds hurrying on their way. As

I passed the subway entrance where Cloud had fled, I suddenly became aware of someone hoarsely shouting: "Do you know what hell is like? It's like an atomic bomb, or a hydrogen bomb—*inside you!*" I turned and saw a man of about fifty, bald, red-faced, dressed in a baggy brown suit, clutching a battered briefcase and crying out at everyone entering the subway. "So all you Jews had better get saved!" he was saying. "And all you gentiles had better get saved!"

Then he began to sing: "Bright and starry angel, died up on the cross . . ." He sang with the tuneless determination of an elderly drunk returning home with his green paper shamrock from the Saint Patrick's Day parade. Nobody paid the slightest attention—the people entering the subway were mostly women, working-class, finished with their jobs for the day—nobody paused to hear what the old man was trying to say. Two women waiting at a nearby bus stop heard the song and smiled at one another, but they did not look at the old man. He might have caught their eyes, and that might be embarrassing. Very few people on the streets of New York ever actually look at anyone they encounter. The old man, strangely enough, paid equally little attention to the women flowing past him into the subway. Perhaps he had given up; perhaps he didn't care whether anyone listened. It was as though God, having commanded him to preach the Word, had never commanded that the Word be received, that the witness's testimony be heard. "When I see the blood," the old man sang in his hoarse chant, "when I see the blood, when I see the blood, I will pass, I will pass over you."

2

From Genesis to Freud, and Beyond

The first man who went crazy was Cain, and like many of his successors, he had good reasons. "Cain brought of the fruit of the ground an offering unto the Lord," according to the fourth chapter of Genesis. "And Abel, he also brought of the firstlings of his flock and of the fat thereof. And the Lord had respect unto Abel and to his offering: But unto Cain, and to his offering, he had not respect: and Cain was very wroth, and his countenance fell. And the Lord said unto Cain, Why art thou wroth? . . . If thou doest well, shalt thou not be accepted? . . . And it came to pass . . . that Cain rose up against Abel his brother, and slew him. And the Lord said unto Cain . . . What hast thou done? . . . Now art thou cursed from the earth . . ."

Our first murderer has always been a symbol of our destructive instincts, and when such stories were first dramatized in the Middle Ages, the dramatists portrayed Cain as an utter villain. In the fifteenth-century version performed by the Glovers of Wakefield, for example, Abel comes on stage with a pious greeting: "God, as he both may and can,/Speed thee, brother, and thy man." Cain instantly replies: "Come kiss . . ." at which point the editor of the standard edition provides a footnote declaring that "here, and in several places below, the language is too offensive to be reproduced." Modern Biblical scholarship has rejected such folk traditions and indeed denied the very existence of Cain. He was, it now appears, simply an eponym for some tribe of farmers, perhaps the Kenites, whose nomadic customs and tattooed markings required some explanation. Nonetheless, we still recognize Adam's older son as the first of God's innumerable victims, the first man who is given one task and then rejected for having failed some other task that he had never been given, the first who responds to God's rejection with a cry of protest and, unlike his docile parents, strikes out in rage.

To protest against the Lord is, the Old Testament repeatedly tells us, futile. He is our father, and the power of the father over his children is arbitrary and even unreasonable, not subject to arbitration. Saul, for example, was peacefully hunting for some stray asses when the Lord selected him to become King of Israel, not because he wanted the throne, and not because the Lord wanted him to have it, but as a kind of punishment for the Israelites for wanting a king in the first place. So the Lord sent Saul to victory in a number of battles, but when the Lord told Saul to destroy the Amalekites and all their animals, and when Saul spared their king and a few sheep and oxen as sacrifices, the Lord condemned Saul on the ground that "to obey is better than to sacrifice." From then on, the Lord repeatedly maddens Saul by sending him what the authors of the Book of Samuel describe as "an evil spirit." This evil spirit departs only when young David plays to Saul on the harp, but even then, the evil spirit compels Saul to attack David with a spear. The attempted murder fails only because the Lord, who is driving Saul insane, is also protecting David from Saul's insanity.

Saint Mark's chronicle is less ambiguous. After Jesus stilled the tempest on the Sea of Galilee and landed in the country of the Gadarenes, he encountered "a man with an unclean spirit, who had his dwelling among the tombs; and no man could bind him, no, not with chains: because . . . the chains had been plucked asunder by him, and the fetters broke in pieces . . . and always, night and day, he was in the mountains, and in the tombs, crying and cutting himself with stones." The demonic spirits, as we know, begged Jesus to permit them to enter into a herd of swine, "and the herd ran violently down a steep place into the sea (they were about two thousand) and were choked in the sea."

It was probably not considered implausible in those days for a madman to be healed by preaching, for it was widely believed that not only mental illness, but all illness, came from evil spirits and thus could best be cured by exorcism. Some of the earliest cave paintings in France, dating back more than 17,000 years, portray an Ice Age witch doctor wearing a bison mask to treat a patient. Such witch doctors also performed, according to skeletons found from Russia to Spain and even in Peru, the operation of brain trepanning, apparently to relieve pressure on the skull and thus to permit evil spirits to escape. It is hard to imagine how anyone could bear such an operation without anesthetic—experiments have shown that it would take five minutes for a flint drill to bore a hole in the skull, and a circle of such holes had to be drilled before a soup-ladle-size piece of skull could be lifted out—but defenseless lunatics have traditionally been subjected to whatever violence their doctors prescribe as therapy. The survivors, in these cases, often wore the skull discs around their necks as amulets.

Illness was, in any case, supernaturally caused and supernaturally cured. The Lord of the Old Testament, in his myriad instructions to Moses, specifically claimed all responsibility and decreed illness a punishment for sin. "If thou wilt diligently hearken to the voice of the Lord thy God," he said to Moses, "and wilt do that which is right in his sight . . . and keep all his statutes, I will put none of these diseases on thee, which I have brought upon the Egyptians: for I am the Lord that healeth thee." And again in Deuteronomy: "I kill and I make alive; I wound and I heal."

The early Greeks retained the idea that the gods drove men mad—it was Athena, for example, who prompted Ajax to begin hacking at the cattle that he imagined to be his enemies—and the best treatment, therefore, was to invoke divine intervention. At the temples of Aesculapius, priests of the snake cult put their patients to sleep, apparently with opium derivatives, and then hypnotically adjured them to get well. The more inquiring thinkers of the sixth and fifth centuries before Christ were not satisfied with such rituals, however. They were indeed the first to make a clear distinction between physical and spiritual causes for mental illness. This was not so simple as it sounds, for the interior of the human body was still largely *terra incognita*. The intellectual processes of the mind, according to the teachings of the Babylonian sages, were centered in the liver. Alcmaeon of Crotona, a pupil of Pythagoras, was apparently the first to argue that the mind was located in the brain, but this argument was challenged by Aristotle, who declared that the heart was "the source of life and the seat of human intelligence." Hippocrates, on the other hand, reasserted Alcmaeon's views by proclaiming the brain to be "the interpreter of consciousness" and explaining its breakdowns in terms of "humors." The four elements—fire, earth, water and air—caused the four qualities of heat, dryness, moisture and cold. If the body were subjected to an excess of any of these four, that excess would damage the equilibrium of the body's corresponding elements: blood, phlegm, yellow bile and black bile, which came from, respectively, the heart, brain, liver and spleen.

Hippocrates lived to be more than eighty, traveled widely, and trained many followers, who apparently wrote most of the seventy-two books of the *Corpus Hippocraticus*. His theory of the four humors might seem to preclude any accurate diagnoses —much of his treatment consisted of rest, bathing and dieting, and he acknowledged that 60 percent of his difficult cases were fatal—but the Hippocratic school is credited with a number of important innovations. For one, the Hippocratics taught that the doctor must consider not just an isolated symptom but the patient's entire system, for "by the affection of one part, the whole body may become affected." For another, the Hippocratics made the first classification of various kinds of mental illness, differentiating and describing, inevitably, four types: mania, melancholy, epilepsy and mental deterioration. Finally, of course, Hippocrates is revered for having propounded the basic code of ethics for all his successors. The code not only commits every doctor to do all he can to heal the sick; it also declares that his primary function is to aid nature in performing its own curative work, and it warns him, a warning all too often forgotten: "If you can do no good, at least do no harm."

For another five or six centuries, the process of medical discovery continued to lurch more or less forward. It was not until the third century before Christ, for example, that two Alexandrian scientists, Hierophilus and Erasistratus, discovered by human dissection the connections between the brain and the nervous system. As doctors learned more, they also experimented more on their patients. In the first century A.D., Largus tried to cure headaches with shocks from electric eels, and Celsus tried to shock the mentally ill by starving them, chaining them, or confining them in total darkness. The coming of Christianity brought a quality of redeeming mercy to alleviate some of the doctors' harsher therapies, but it also brought a virtual end to scientific inquiry as such. The teachings of Galen, whose anatomical charts derived from the dissection of dogs and pigs, remained the doctors' scripture from Galen's death in 200 until Vesalius disproved his work in 1534 by the publication of *De humani corporis fabrica.*

The way we treat mental illness has always been, to a certain degree, an extension of the way we regard all illness, and in the later years of the Roman Empire the scourge of pestilence seemed once again to be a mysterious manifestation of divine wrath. Six times between the first and fourth centuries, epidemics devastated Europe. The sick flocked to the churches for help. Priests invoked the intercession of Saint Anthony or Saint Sebastian. Benedict of Nursia organized the monastery of Monte Cassino in the early sixth century and decreed that "the care of the sick is to be placed above and before every other duty." This care was largely a matter of nursing—the Benedictine monks made their patients comfortable and blessed them with prayer—a regimen that, in a time of scientific ignorance, seems almost Hippocratic. Madness, however, no longer fit very well into the still-prevailing Hippocratic theory of humors. It sometimes seemed, in fact, like another of the epidemics that continued to ravage the continent. (The Black Death that started in 1347 alone killed about 25 million people, one quarter of the population of Europe.) Thousands of flagellants, bearing heavy crosses, wandered across the continent, stopping twice a day in village market places to tear off their clothes and flog themselves with nail-tipped ropes, thus expiating their guilt for God's plagues. In other towns, groups of citizens, men and women alike, seemed to fall prey to a collective compulsion to form circles and dance in the streets until they saw celestial visions or fell to the ground in exhaustion.

Throughout most of the Middle Ages, there was no particular obloquy attached to madness. It was simply a mysterious affliction, like so many others, which might or might not go away, and the insane were left to survive as best they could—as were, indeed, the sane. "My face I'll grime with filth,/Blanket my loins . . ." says Edgar, in *King Lear*, when he plans to dis-

guise himself as a roaming madman, "and with presented naked-
ness outface/ The winds and persecutions of the sky./ The country gives me proof and precedent/ Of Bedlam beggars, who, with
roaring voices . . ./ Enforce their charity." In the fifteenth century,
however, the increasing complexity of social and economic life,
the instability caused by new ideas brought back from the Cru-
sades, the very dawning of the Renaissance, caused the Church
to intensify its concern with heresy. Heresy might involve nothing
more than nonconformity or eccentricity, but in this turbulent
century, the crusading Church now considered itself at war with
the forces of Satan, and even the most harmless lunatic might
be made to confess, under the appropriate torture, to sorcery.

Two German Dominican monks, Johann Sprenger and
Heinrich Kraemer, compiled the official guidebook for the discovery, interrogation and punishment of Satan's hordes. It was
called *Malleus Maleficarum (The Hammer of Witches)*, and it
appeared in 1487 with the official blessings of Pope Innocent
VIII. It dealt with both witches and warlocks, but it concentrated on women, because, according to Sprenger and Kraemer,
witchcraft "comes from carnal lust, which is in women insatiable." Anyone suspected of demonic practices—and any denunciation was sufficient cause for suspicion—was to be stripped
naked, shaved of all hair, laid out on a bench, and inspected
for warts, moles, and other signs of diabolic congress. If the
accused witch failed to confess at once, she could be subjected
to various instruments of interrogation, the wheel, the rack, the
Spanish boot, the branding iron. The two Dominican monks
described the proper procedure:

> While she is being questioned about each several
> point, let her be often and frequently exposed to torture
> beginning with the more gentle of them; for the Judge
> should not be too hasty to proceed to the graver kind. And
> while this is being done, let the Notary write all down,
> how she is tortured and what questions are asked and how
> she answers. . . . And note that, if she confesses under
> torture, she should then be taken to another place and
> questioned anew so that she does not confess only under
> the stress of torture.

Statistics being what they are, we have no way of knowing how many victims of the great witch hunt were put to death. Published estimates run from 150,000 to more than 5 million, mostly women. They ranged from obscure village idiots to such political captives as Joan of Arc, whom Shakespeare's English lords denounce as "Fell, banning hag; enchantress . . . foul accursed minister of hell!"

Among the sturdy rationalists who write the histories of science, it is conventional to denounce the judges and theoreticians of the Inquisition either as sadists or as the agents of an institutionalized paranoia. This may well be. Many suspects were falsely accused by malicious neighbors or greedy heirs, and yet it nonetheless seems indisputable that great numbers of people did engage in magic rituals in the hope of gaining magic powers. These rituals may have been partly a survival of the so-called "old religion," the various pagan faiths that had existed since pre-Christian times. To the genuine believers in these faiths, the equinoctial sabbaths were as holy as Christmas or Easter, the fertility rituals as sacred as those of transubstantiation and Communion, and the goat and cat as symbolic as the lamb and the dove. To many others, however, witchcraft may have seemed simply a way to gain power or beauty, a way to conquer sickness or to avenge old injustices. As usual, the old and the ugly and the unwanted were now accused of muttering strange words to themselves and regarding their neighbors with the evil eye, but magic promises more powerful rewards, and those whose nascent madness took the form of mad ambitions and mad aggressions undoubtedly sought success through the evil arts. Macbeth: "How now, you secret, black and midnight hags . . ./ I conjure you, by that which you profess,—/ Howe'er you came to know it,/ Answer me."

The witches and warlocks who gathered by the light of the full moon to utter incantations and smear themselves with ointment made from human fat presumably accomplished very little except to become intoxicated on a mixture of herbal drugs and communal hysteria. But the psychological process of "possession," for which they were tortured, was one in which they believed as strongly as did their torturers. Indeed, that sense of being possessed, the sense that one's mind and one's whole personality are somehow not under one's own control, has been among us from the beginning. The Bible is full of examples: "And behold, a woman of Canaan . . . cried unto him, saying, Have mercy on me, O Lord . . . my daughter is grievously vexed with a devil." And again: "There came to him a certain man kneeling down to him, and saying, Lord, have mercy on my son; for he is lunatic, and sore vexed, for oft-times he falleth into the fire, and oft into the water." And, of course, the man in the country of the Gadarenes, whose unclean spirits were made to enter the herd of swine.

Men in combat have traditionally been possessed. Thus Nikolai Rostov tries to tell "a story of how beside himself and all aflame with excitement, he had flown like a storm at the square, cut his way in, slashed right and left, how his saber had tasted flesh and he had fallen exhausted." He is in the very act of saying, "You cannot imagine what a strange frenzy one experiences during an attack," when he is interrupted by Prince Andrei and realizes that he has been possessed not by the frenzy of attack but by the need to boast and lie about his experiences in battle—possessed, in other words, by another part of himself. Lara Jefferson, an obscure patient in a Midwestern mental hospital during the 1940's, vividly described that sense of otherness when she wrote her recollections of trying to make the nurses confine her in a straitjacket: "So the monster was out and the ghost of some old berserker ancestor rose up within me . . . and the fierce hatred exulted that it had possessed itself of a massive and powerful body. And the thing that was in me was not I at all—but another—and I knew that no power on earth but a straitjacket could hold her. So I went to the nurse and said, 'Tie me.' . . . I knew the deadly woman who stood in the body I had called mine would stop nowhere short of destruction. . . . When I was tied down securely and could relax my hold upon myself all my shame flowed out in a wild flood of tears. They were partly tears of vexation that I . . . had not had the courage to do the things I had such an urge to do—but more, they were tears of relief that I had not done them."

As we contemplate Lara Jefferson sobbing with rage and relief in her straitjacket, we tell ourselves that she is suffering from delusions. In the fifteenth or sixteenth century, people were less confident in denying the sense of alien possession, for the Church and state both declared such illusions to be fundamental reality, punishable by death. Peter Stump (or Stumpf, Stube, Stubbe or Stub) provides as good an example as any of the conflict between official madness and the madness of the forests. Stump was a sorcerer who lived in the town of Bedburg, near Cologne. He seems to have terrorized the surrounding woods for the better part of twenty-five years. There were, in any case, dozens of episodes of villagers attacked by a giant wolf, and when the animal was finally cornered by a band of hunters and their hounds, the beast disappeared, and at the site of its disappearance, the hunters found only Peter Stump.

The hunters took Stump to the magistrate in Bedburg, where he was strapped on the rack and subjected to the customary interrogation. Before any torture began, he confessed to a lifetime of violence. The Devil had given him a wolfskin girdle, he said, which enabled him to turn into a wolf, and in that guise, he had attacked at least three women, two men, thirteen children (one of them his own son), and in the words of a contemporary English pamphlet, "pluckt out their throates and teare their ioyntes a sunder." He had inflicted a similar fate on innumerable "sheepe, Lambes, and Goates and other Cattell." In punishment for these crimes, real or imaginary, sane or insane, he was condemned to death. It was 1589, the year in which the young Shakespeare was working on the first drafts of *Henry VI*, Montaigne was composing his essays, and Cervantes *Don Quixote*, and in the town of Bedburg, Germany, Peter Stump "was iudged first to have his body laide on a wheele, and with red hotte burning pincers in ten several places to have the flesh puld off from the bones, after that, his legges and Armes to be broken with a woodden Axe or Hatchet, afterward to have his head strook from his body, then to have his carkasse burnde to Ashes."

There was an eye that observed all these contagions and recorded them with a fidelity that no camera could ever know. So we can still see the piteous figure of Saint Anthony, bearded, barefooted, blue-robed, surrounded by a cacophony of demons as he bends beseeching across the wall that separates him from the bleeding figure on the crucifix. To his right a diabolic priest, standing erect and robed but with the head of a boar, reads out the incantations of the Black Mass. Overhead, the smoking skies are filled with unnamable monsters flapping toward the witches' sabbath. All around Saint Anthony's ruined monastery, on the bleak hillsides, in the half-frozen river, more monsters with shark teeth and rat ears and dragon claws are congregating to tear at the saint.

The recording eye was that of Jerome van Aken, who lived and worked in the provincial Flemish town of 's Hertogenbosch and signed his forty-odd paintings with the capital letters: JHERONIMUS BOSCH. We know very little more about him than that. He was born about 1450, perhaps 1453; he apparently married a wealthy woman, who provided him with financial independence; he died in 1516. He is thought to have come from a family of painters, and it is possible that his grandfather painted a crucifixion scene for the town's Cathedral of St. John, which is considered the best example of French Gothic architecture in the province of Brabant. The town was otherwise without any particular artistic heritage, and Bosch seems to have been quite immune to the metropolitan fashions of Antwerp or Ghent. He had, so far as we know, no teachers and no disciples.

He was apparently much influenced, however, by the mystical movement of Jan van Ruysbroek. One of Ruysbroek's pupils, Gerhard Groote, organized the Brothers of the Common Life, which founded eighty-two monasteries within a century, including two in the relatively obscure commercial town of 's Hertogenbosch. The brotherhood's teachings were simple. It rejected all material ends and efforts; it stood independent of the corrupted Church; it proclaimed that man's only important goal was the contemplation of God. Bosch may have been a member of this sect. Nobody really knows.

As we know nothing about Bosch's life, we know nothing about the madness that shines forth from his paintings. The sources of that overwhelming sense of guilt, that lust for punishment, have not been recorded. It is generally assumed that Bosch intended all of his enigmatic masterpieces as religious allegories. Thus *The Hay Wagon*, an apparent symbol of prosperity, surmounted by a brace of young lovers, is actually dragged along by fish-headed monsters as it lurches on its inexorable course from the Garden of Eden on the left panel of the tryptych to the Inferno on the right. And that green lizard standing erect next to the white-cowled bird in the foreground of *The Last Judgment;* that lizard with both its claws clutching at the butcher knife that pierces its own neck; that lizard with flaming jaws, guarding a wooden barrel that contains the head of one poor sinner up to his neck in a soup of black toads—that lizard is only one of the none-too-religious demons that Bosch foresaw reigning on the day of wrath. "The Light of God keeps wide open the eye it has purified," Ruysbroek had written in *Mirror of Salvation.* "Open it remains, and we can close it nevermore."

In the era of the Church triumphant—Bosch died exactly a century before the Vatican ordered Galileo not to teach that the earth circles the sun—both cautious and venturesome minds defined their purposes, both sane and insane defined their reality, in terms of *maioram gloriam dei.* It was to please God, for example, that Bosch's contemporary Savonarola harangued the Florentines to burn their books and pictures at an *auto-da-fé,* and it was to please God that the Pope had Savanarola tortured for forty days and then condemned to the stake. In these more secular times, now that Popes confine themselves largely to messages of good will, now that *The Hay Wagon* hangs peacefully on a wall of the Prado Museum in Madrid, we can accept intellectually the idea that the burning towers and the clawing fiends represent a religious conception of some past age, but we cannot help imposing our contemporary theology on Bosch and wondering about the "real" meaning, the pathological meaning of these haunted images.

There are a number of Bosch's works in the Prado, softly eroding in the smog that drifts in from the plaza outside, for it is said that the Spaniards feel some particular affinity toward the master of 's Hertogenbosch. The grandest and most mysterious of these is known as *The Garden of Earthly Delights.* For a few pesetas, a uniformed guard will pluck at the wings of the tryptych and fold them shut, revealing, on the closed panels, Bosch's extraordinary vision of the creation of the world. The earth is a translucent sphere, but its living surface is internal and horizontal, as though the Equator were a plane, and this surface is already sprouting a Boschian landscape of jagged rocks and pointed shrubs, a landscape that one critic has described as "malignant vegetation." Overhead, within what we would call the Arctic Circle, dark storm clouds are gathering. The uniformed guard pokes the wings of the tryptych back into place, the earth vanishes, and there reappears *The Garden of Earthly Delights*, all pink flesh and hellfire.

In George Orwell's *1984*, when Winston Smith is taken to Room 101 to confront what he imagines to be "the worst thing in the world," that thing, which will make Winston cry out, "Do it to Julia! Not me!"—that thing is a cage of hungry rats ready to be strapped to his face. Among the myriad prisoners in *The Garden of Earthly Delights*, there is a man confined in a half-submerged pink globe, rather like a bathysphere. He is peering out the only exit, a small glass tube, and at the other end of the tube, there is, of course, a large rat peering back at him. *The Garden of Earthly Delights* contains, in other words, some approximation of almost every horror to be conceived by fear, by paranoia or by hallucination.

Yet this is supposed to be a garden of delight. The central panel shows an orgy of naked sybarites frolicking around the fountain of youth. The pursuit of pleasure is ordained in the left panel by God presenting a demure Eve to an expectant Adam. Even Eden, however, is a sinister place where, unnoticed by Adam and Eve, three-headed lizards emerge from the ooze, and two-legged reptiles prey on smaller beasts. The garden of pleasures itself is full of mysterious lobster shapes and scorpion claws, and the naked couples seem remarkably joyless in their couplings. Their destiny, as we know, will appear in the right panel, the most hellish of all Bosch's hells. Here the sinners are punished with tortures more nightmarish than an inquisitor could devise—devoured by insects, impaled on the strings of a giant harp, pursued by a huge knife that is wheeled along on two rotating ears. Above all this anarchy shine the flames of the burning city, and below it stretches the eternal sewer.

The over-all religious allegory is fairly obvious, and so are most of Bosch's religious symbols: the crescent heralding the infidel, for example, and the owl representing those who prefer darkness to light. The perverse sexual imagery is equally insistent—two figures clutching one another inside a clamshell, another biting at an enormous strawberry, still others prancing around a huge pink bagpipe. But although art critics have used all the blunted tools of psychiatry and theology to analyze Bosch's panorama of madness, most of its doomed creatures still elude all rational explanation. In other words, nobody knows, five centuries after Bosch painted his masterpiece, what he really meant.

The intellectual flames that kindled the Renaissance also caused a pervasive sense of instability and uneasiness. The medieval belief in a divine order was gradually replaced by the theory of a natural order, maintained by natural laws, and this natural order itself often seemed highly uncertain. In Britain, the death of Queen Elizabeth in 1603 aroused widespread fears of a renewal of the War of the Roses, but the disaster that actually befell London that summer was once again the plague. Some 30,000 people, one seventh of the city's population, died within a few weeks. The unpopular new king, James I, spent his time either quarreling with Parliament or squandering money on court extravagances (one masque alone cost 4,000 pounds). Then came the discovery of the Catholics' Gunpowder Plot to blow up Parliament. Guy Fawkes was arrested and tortured. And the skies darkened as the sun went into eclipse. "These late eclipses in the sun and moon portend no good to us," says the Earl of Gloucester at the start of *Lear*, which Shakespeare wrote during this ominous year of 1606. "Though the wisdom of Nature can reason it thus and thus, yet Nature finds itself scourged by the sequent effects. Love cools, friendship falls off, brothers divide. In cities, mutinies; in countries, discord; in palaces, treason. . . . There's son against father . . . there's father against child."

This is, of course, a kind of synopsis of the disasters that are to unfold in the course of Shakespeare's darkest and most grandiose tragedy, disasters that repeatedly evoke the imagery of savage animals and the epithet "unnatural." And just as human reason seems to exemplify the natural order of the universe, so the breakdown of that order can best be exemplified by madness. Hamlet feigns insanity for tactical reasons (as Edgar does in *Lear*), and Macbeth's hallucinations are simply manifestations of his own sense of guilt, but Lear's descent (or ascent) into the realm of madness represents the breakdown of his whole kingdom. This metaphor was fundamental to Shakespeare's concept of Lear. In the original history of the pre-Roman King Leir, which was first set down and probably invented by Geoffrey of Monmouth in the early twelfth century, and in all the various plagiarisms and dramatic adaptations that preceded Shakespeare's tragedy, there is no insanity at all—and indeed little enough tragedy. According to Raphael Holinshed's *Chronicles of England,* which recounts that Leir came to power "in the year of the world 3105," the king eventually "discomfits" the armies of his daughters Gonerilla and Regan and regains his throne. Nor does he have a Fool who mocks every move he makes.

It is Lear's own action, as the Fool incessantly points out, that causes the division of the kingdom and the breakdown of order. It is an action so irrational as to suggest that Lear is already mad at the beginning of the play. Louis Auchincloss, to cite only one recent analysis, calls Lear's "assignment of shares in accordance with the professed loves of his daughters a manifest absurdity." He adds that Lear must be "in the first stages of senility." Harley Granville-Barker, on the other hand, argues in his celebrated *Prefaces to Shakespeare* that the absurdities of the plot are not to be condemned, because "a dramatist may postulate any situation he has the means to interpret, if he will abide by the logic of it." My own guess is that Lear might have been trying to avoid the exigencies of primogeniture, and that his rage at Cordelia is partly a consequence of her priggish refusal to play a game devised for her benefit. In any case, the division of the kingdom is a symbolic action—just as the subsequent storm will be a symbolic storm, and the war with France a symbolic war—and symbolic actions do not require commonplace plausibility. What Lear attempts is the classic paternal strategy—to bequeath one's powers without actually giving them up, to proclaim one's children's independence without actually granting it.

The Fool repeatedly tells him that his strategy is folly. "Dost thou call me fool, boy?" Lear bristles. "All thy other titles thou hast given away," says the Fool, quite unintimidated. "That thou wast born with." The Fool is a most peculiar character. He is generally played as a middle-aged companion to the patriarchal Lear, and he may suffer from some physical deformity, but there is no sign that he is any more feeble-minded than, say, Rigoletto. His play-acting is, a little like the feigned madness of Edgar, a device to protect himself from the punishment that would otherwise descend on someone who speaks unpleasant truths. The Fool's language is a highly complex mixture of puns and riddles (as is, sometimes, the language of schizophrenics), but all of it is quite germane to Lear's folly. It serves, indeed, as a kind of counterpoint to Lear's own refusal to realize how badly he has misjudged his daughters. As Lear's alter ego, the Fool ends his role, interestingly enough, at just about the time that Lear goes mad. He capers about the king throughout the storm scenes of Act III, but then is never seen again.

It is not entirely clear, of course, exactly when Lear does go mad. Our view of that depends partly on our sympathy for Lear himself, our sense of whether he is irrational from the start. If not senile, he is indisputably arrogant, quarrelsome, and lacking in judgment—qualities that might be considered, depending on the circumstances, appropriate either for an aged monarch or for a dotard being committed to a mental institution. If sane at the start, however, Lear seems less so in his first violent confrontation with Goneril. The official issue is the behavior of Lear's retinue of one hundred knights, who, according to Lear, are "men of choice and rarest parts," but who, according to Goneril, "do hourly carp and quarrel, breaking forth/ In rank and not-to-be-endured riots." The true issue is the question of who now holds royal power (and personal independence), and Lear's response to Goneril's challenge is one of insensate rage: "Hear, Nature, hear; dear Goddess, hear . . .: Into her womb convey sterility,/ Dry up in her the organs of increase,/ And from her derogate body never spring,/ A babe to honor her." Goneril regards such outbursts as evidence of senility ("Old fools are babes again"), and the Fool, in more ambiguous language, agrees ("If thou wert my Fool, Nuncle, I'd have thee beaten for being old before thy time. . . . Thou shouldst not have been old till thou hadst been wise"), but Lear knows quite well that his terrible anger is a sign of more than mere old age. Like many another victim in many another time, he seems to seize himself by the throat as he argues with himself: "O, let me not be mad, not mad, sweet heaven!"

The second confrontation, with Regan, is equally a matter of familial protocol. The disguised Earl of Kent, acting as Lear's messenger, has been put in the stocks for fighting with Goneril's steward, and Lear is once again offended beyond all rational degree. "They durst not do't," he cries. "They could not, would not do't. 'Tis worse than murder/ To do upon respect such violent outrage." Regan too offers the arguments of youth to age: "O, sir, you are old,/ . . . You should be ruled, and led/ By some discretion that discerns your state better than you yourself." And so, with Goneril joining in, they enter the cruel argument over Lear's retinue. Goneril proposes that the hundred knights be reduced to fifty, and Regan proposes twenty-five, and Goneril asks, "What need you five-and-twenty? ten? or five?" and Regan asks, "What need one?" and Lear cries out in helpless rage, "O reason not the need!" As the sounds of the storm begin, Lear again sees insanity before him: "O Fool, I shall go mad." But despite his fears and prophecies, he is not mad, not yet.

Nor is he mad even in his titanic fury on the heath. "Blow, winds, and crack your cheeks"—if we judge these famous lines not as dramatic poetry but as a reaction to personal assault, the old man seems much more rational in his outcry against an unjust universe than he did in his furious complaints about his retinue. Yet Shakespeare seems to believe, or to want us to believe, that the storm itself, both as a physical hardship and as a psychological humiliation, drove Lear mad. "Was this a face/ To be opposed to the warring winds?/ To stand against the deep dread-bolted thunder?" At the height of the storm, however, Lear is still fighting to retain his sanity—"O, that way madness lies; let me shun that"—and in this penultimate moment, Shakespeare wants us to accept the vision that is possessed by a man on the brink of madness as the vision of ultimate truth. He shows us the once-proud king praying for all the "poor naked wretches, wheresoe'er you are,/ That bide the pelting of this pitiless storm." He shows us the once-ceremonious king confronting Edgar in the guise of a Bedlam beggar and observing that "unaccommodated man is no more but such a poor, bare, forked animal as thou art." It is the Fool, then, who speaks for sanity, preventing the king from tearing off his clothes, arguing that this is "a naughty night to swim in," and that "this cold night will turn us all to fools and madmen." Only in Lear's last scene in Act III, the last one he shares with the Fool, the scene in which he attempts a mock trial of his daughters, does Lear seem finally to crack, to babble, and only then does Kent say to Gloucester: "Trouble him not; his wits are gone."

We do not see Lear again until almost the end of the following act, by which time he has been somehow conveyed to the French camp near Dover and placed under the care of Cordelia and an anonymous doctor. Cordelia observes that the king is "as mad as the vexed sea" and wonders, "What can man's wisdom/ In the restoring his bereaved sense?" The doctor, with the traditional optimism of his profession, answers, "There is means, madam." The prescribed therapy in "the year of the world 3105" seems to be much like that of Hippocrates, or that of today's most advanced hospitals. "Our foster-nurse of nature is repose,/ The which he lacks: that to provoke in him,/ Are many simples operative [i.e., sedative drugs], whose power/ Will close the eye of anguish." In his next appearance, however, Lear's eye of anguish is wide open, and he represents the apotheosis of the madman as seer. As he enters "fantastically dressed with wild flowers," he begins to preach, in marvelous rhetoric, on his Boschian vision of sexuality: "There's hell, there's darkness, there is the sulphurous pit,/ Burning, scalding, stench, consumption . . ." Although it was traditional for Elizabethan theatrical lunatics to rave a bit, Shakespeare wants his audience to know that the mad Lear speaks with a superhuman insight. "O matter and impertinency mixed!" says Edgar. "Reason in madness!"

The doctor's treatment does work, along with Cordelia's care, and Lear recovers sufficiently to confess himself "a very foolish fond old man, four score and upward . . ./ And . . ./ not in my perfect mind." He is blissfully happy in his reunion with the rediscovered Cordelia, but this happiness was not to be, for, according to Gloucester's warning, "As flies to wanton boys are we to th' gods,/ They kill us for their sport." So Cordelia is treacherously hanged, and Lear, having returned from madness to sanity and seeing no new sanctuary there—"Thou'lt come no more,/ Never, never, never, never, never"—simply dies.

This was too terrible an ending, however, for the audiences that were to come. Just seventy-five years after Shakespeare wrote it, Nahum Tate, the Poet Laureate, revised the whole play, sent Lear and Gloucester off to "gently pass our short reserves of Time/ In calm Reflections on our Fortunes past," while Edgar marries Cordelia and proclaims "that Truth and Vertue shall at last succeed." This change in fortunes seemed completely appropriate to the eye of Dr. Samuel Johnson. A play in which the wicked prosper may be "a just representation of the common events of human life," he said, but "I cannot easily be persuaded that . . . the audience will not rise better pleased from the final triumph of persecuted virtue."

As we move onward through any history of insanity, we see that it has been a history of controversy over the basic question of whether madness is caused (and cured) by physical or spiritual means. Is it a disturbance of the body's humors (or chemistry) or is it a result of intangible influences? Each of the two theories has gone through cycles of triumph and degradation. Each begins as a liberating reform movement, then evolves into orthodoxy, and finally becomes a handbook for the mistreatment of the poor. The paradox is that the physical theory has tended to be the more progressive of the two, an ideology for physicians struggling against witch doctors, and yet the physicians, once in power, have generally outdone the witch doctors in their dedication to such novelties as electric shocks or brain surgery, or, if all else fails, lifelong incarceration.

The witch hunts drew to their end in the bonfires of the seventeenth century (the last woman executed for witchcraft was a young housemaid in Glarus, Switzerland, in 1782), and the pioneers of medicine continued to discover, with cries of Eureka, the scientific facts that we now take for granted. William Harvey demonstrated in 1628 the circulation of blood. Anton van Leeuwenhoek devised the first microscope and discovered that blood was full of corpuscles. Thomas Sydenham and his pupils began a systematic categorization of the symptoms of different diseases —tuberculosis, malaria, diabetes. They determined that hysteria was not, as the Greeks had taught, a consequence of the shifting of the uterus (*hysteron* being the Greek word for "uterus") but rather a disorder of the central nervous system.

As doctors became increasingly confident that they could treat the diseases that previously had meant a condemnation to death in the gutter, this became the age of the building of hospitals. In France, for example, the Hôpital Général was founded by royal decree in 1656 to centralize the various religious and charitable clinics throughout Paris, and within a century there were similar institutions in all of the nation's thirty-two principal cities. In theory, not always fulfilled, these hospitals were to benefit both the sick and the communities from which the sick were sequestered.

The Quakers seem to have taken a special interest in mental illness, and a British merchant named William Tuke organized the York Retreat, which was notable for providing patients with recreation and farm work and, as Tuke put it, "impressing upon their minds the idea that they will be kindly treated." Tuke had connections with Quaker officials in Pennsylvania, who in turn had connections with the other colonies, and it is estimated that four of the eight mental asylums built in the United States during the late eighteenth and early nineteenth centuries were modeled on the York Retreat. The most influential of the American reformers was Benjamin Rush, one of the signers of the Declaration of Independence, who successfully demanded in 1789 that the Pennsylvania Hospital, the first general hospital in America and the first to admit "maniacal patients," adopt the new therapies known as "moral treatment." Rush not only was in charge of the hospital's psychiatric department but taught for thirty years at the University of Pennsylvania Medical School, then considered the best in the United States. He trained about 3,000 physicians and composed a basic text, *Medical Inquiries and Observations upon the Diseases of the Mind* (1812). His views of "moral treatment" may therefore be considered not only typical of his period but reasonably enlightened. He was determined to "rescue mental science from the usurpations of divines." He believed that "truth is simple upon all subjects" and that to question the essential simplicity of medicine "is to call in question the goodness of the Supreme Being."

Rush's over-all view was that the human body required a certain level of motion and stimulation, and that most illness, and particularly mental illness, derived from either too much motion, causing "debility from action," or too little, causing "debility from abstraction." The symptom of debility was generally fever, and the best treatment was "depletion," best achieved by bloodletting. Rush also administered laxatives and emetics, and denied his patients food. He invented a chair in which a patient could be confined so that he could be spared "the impetus of the blood as much as possible," and the flow of the blood could be further reduced by cold showers. If none of these means proved helpful, because, in Rush's view, madmen's "nerves are insensible to cold, heat and to irritants of all kinds," then he would resort to various techniques of frightening his patients in order to restore them to their senses. Among these patients was his son John, who, after several breakdowns, killed a friend in a duel and was confined to the Pennsylvania Hospital for life.

If Rush's treatment was enlightened, one may wonder whether the new mental hospitals were designed mainly for treatment or for imprisonment. In fact, both elements were involved, and the distinctions between the two soon were blurred. Almost equally blurred were the distinctions between the mentally ill, the retarded, the old, the indigent, the troublesome, and even the unemployed—all of them subject to confinement. In any case, most institutions beget institutional behavior, the inmates grow dependent, the guards authoritarian, and both, in their various ways, subhuman. London's Bethlehem Hospital, better known as Bedlam, founded in the thirteenth century as a priory, converted in the fourteenth century into a hospital, given by Henry VIII to the City of London in 1547 as Britain's first insane asylum, became, within a few decades, little more than a dungeon. Women were chained by the ankles to one long wall. Men were liable to be attached by the neck to a vertical bar. One man was kept that way, even in the eighteenth century, for twelve years. In Paris, similarly, an observer reported the conditions at the women's asylum known as La Saltpêtrière: "Madwomen seized with fits of violence are chained like dogs at their cell doors, and separated from visitors and keepers alike by a long corridor protected by an iron grille; through this grille is passed their food and the straw on which they sleep. . . ." Another account of the same institution noted that "in winter, when the waters of the Seine rose, those cells situated at the level of the sewers became . . . a refuge for huge rats, which during the night attacked the unfortunates confined there. . . . Madwomen have been found with feet, hands, and faces torn by bites. . . ."

In the age of enlightenment, it was considered instructive, as well as entertaining, to visit these institutions on a Sunday and to contemplate the antics of the inmates. In the Paris asylum, where attendants used whips to make the lunatics dance, the crowds often reached two thousand per day. Bedlam enjoyed a similar popularity (and so did the Pennsylvania Hospital), charging a penny per visitor and raking in four hundred pounds per year. Many of these visitors teased or laughed at the chained inmates, but such outings were by no means limited to sadists. In 1775, James Boswell went to Bedlam with Dr. Johnson, who had been there before, and he recounted that although "nothing peculiarly remarkable" had happened, "the general contemplation of insanity was very affecting." Some years later, when a woman expressed repugnance at the idea of living in some new buildings being erected near Bedlam, Johnson disagreed with her. "It is right," he said, "that we should be kept in mind of madness, which is occasioned by too much indulgence of imagination. I think a very moral use may be made of these new buildings: I would have those who have heated imaginations live there, and take warning." The sage's friend rejected this odd proposal by answering: "But, sir, many of the poor people that are mad have become so from disease, or from distressing events. It is, therefore, not their fault but their misfortune. . . ."

As they spoke in the confident terms of the enlightenment about the mystery that no one has yet solved, the monarch who ruled over enlightened London and all its overseas possessions was already slipping away toward the edges of darkness.

"Be a king, George!" Augusta of Saxe-Gotha, Princess of Wales, often said to the oldest of her seven children. She was, according to one chronicler, "a foolish, ignorant woman," presumably frustrated by her husband's failure ever to gain the English throne. When George III succeeded his grandfather, at the age of twenty-two, he did his best to carry out his mother's instructions. He started by dismissing his distinguished prime minister, William Pitt the elder, then forced out the chief dispenser of Parliamentary patronage, the Duke of Newcastle, then insisted on ending the Seven Years War as too "bloody and expensive." In recapturing the political powers that had been dissipated by his predecessors, George proved himself assertive and energetic but not very skillful. Having blundered into war with the American colonies, he blundered on into defeat. Parliament finally passed a resolution declaring that "the power of the crown has increased, is increasing, and ought to be diminished." George contemplated abdication and twice drew up documents to that end (in 1782 and 1783), then struggled on, unhappily. "I shall never rest my head on my last pillow in peace and quiet," he said, "as long as I remember the loss of my American colonies."

It is difficult, as we have all learned, for courtiers to determine whether a ruler is simply disturbed by stress and conflict or whether he is beginning to go mad. King George had displayed certain eccentricities all his life, but his first real illness, in the summer of 1788, was diagnosed as merely "a sharp bilious attack." The royal physician, Sir George Baker, prescribed a month's stay at Cheltenham and three half-pint glasses of the purgative waters every morning at dawn. The King got worse. He loved music, but he said to one of his musicians that "it seems to affect my head and it is with difficulty that I bear it. Alas! The best of us are but frail mortals." His chief symptom was a maniac inability to stop talking. Even during a concert of his beloved Handel, the king's rambling discourse was, according to Baker, "perpetual." The doctor prescribed bleedings, purgings and rest, and he worried that "the shade by which soundness of mind is to be distinguished from some degree of insanity is often faint, and in many cases hardly perceptible."

Queen Charlotte and the doctor kept the king's condition secret as long as they could, but they could not indefinitely hide the facts from the dissolute Prince of Wales, whose ambition to succeed his father had already led him into a series of intrigues with the Parliamentary opposition. On the night of November 5, according to Fanny Burney, the gifted novelist who served as one of Queen Charlotte's ladies in waiting, "The Prince of Wales had come to the castle and was present when the King's malady first took violent form. His father caught him with both hands by the collar, pushing him against the wall with some violence, and asked him who would dare to say to the King of England that he should not speak out." The prince fainted, the queen went into hysterics, and the news of the King's madness soon spread throughout London.

The King continued to get worse. He had hallucinations of being caught in violent thunderstorms. The veins in his face swelled, he foamed at the mouth, and he ranted until exhausted. These rantings, according to one courtier, "were not free from indecencies." The King, who had hitherto been a model of domestic tranquility, now made advances to the ladies at court, and his appearances in Queen Charlotte's bedroom seemed so threatening that he was barred from her chambers. Sometimes, it was said, he howled like a dog. As George's behavior deteriorated, the medical treatments became increasingly severe. In addition to bleeding and purging, a Doctor Richard Warren, who had been sent to the palace by the Prince of Wales, insisted on blistering the King's forehead to draw off poison from his brain. All winter long, no heat was allowed in the royal sickroom. When the King tried to avoid his medicines, a number of pages were ordered to sit on him. In emergencies, he was wrapped in linen like an Egyptian mummy (straitjackets were considered unfit for a king), and when Doctor Baker once loosened his bound arms to feel his pulse, the King clouted him on the forehead, poured a chamber pot over his head, and decreed him to be a knight of "the most honorable Order of Cloacina."

The first sign of improvement came with the advent of the Reverend Doctor Francis Wills, aged seventy-three, who had studied medicine at Oxford, served as an Anglican clergyman in London, and founded a mental hospital in Lincolnshire. Doctor Wills diagnosed the King's ailment as a consequence of overwork, lack of sleep, and "ascetic abstemiousness." Although he had no hesitation about confining the King to a straitjacket, his regimen generally followed the new fashion of relative kindliness. He allowed the King to shave his month-old whiskers and gave him a penknife with which to trim his long fingernails, and he even permitted him, according to the public criticism of the dissident Dr. Warren, to read *King Lear*. It was indeed a remarkable aspect of the King's confinement that while his own doctors predicted that mild treatment would bring a recovery, the opposition doctor proclaimed from the palace that the royal illness was incurable.

One day in February of 1789, Fanny Burney was out walking in Kew Gardens, when the King spotted her and set out in pursuit—he being pursued in turn by his keepers. "Heavens, how I ran . . ." she later wrote in her diary. "My feet were not sensible that they even touched the ground. . . . I knew not to what I might be exposed, should the malady be then high." To her surprise, the King, when he finally caught up with her, spoke quite rationally about her father, about Handel, about Lord Salisbury. "What a scene!" she observed. "How variously was I affected by it, but, on the whole, how inexpressibly thankful to see him so nearly himself—so little removed from recovery!" The acute crisis had lasted scarcely three months, and somehow the King had survived all the blistering and bloodletting. Whether his cure was a consequence of his isolation from political crises, or simply of the passage of time, remains as mysterious as the original causes of the collapse. According to one recent account, George had been suffering from an obscure hereditary disease that was first identified in the 1930's and named porphyria—a disease marked by many of George's symptoms: sensitivity to sunlight, weakness of limbs, hoarseness, vomiting, and in acute stages, irritability, sleeplessness and hallucinations. To the traditional psychiatric view of history, however, these physical symptoms are obvious signs of manic-depressive paranoia. In any case, while George's conniving older sons raged at the King's improving health, the people of London cheered loudly and set off bonfires at the news of the King's recovery from what he himself called "my tedious illness."

It was not, however, a permanent recovery. To be a king, as his mother had instructed him, meant living under constant pressures of all kinds. Aside from the hostility of his older sons, George suffered several assassination attempts. On one occasion, a man fired a pistol at him at the theater and narrowly missed. On another, a hungry mob stopped the King's coach, and a pistol shot broke one of its windows. There were larger dangers as well. The French Revolution and the accession of Napoleon threatened the very existence of George's throne. The King's next collapse in 1801 apparently was precipitated by a quarrel with the younger Pitt over the question of permitting Irish Catholics to sit in Parliament. Another collapse came in 1804, and another in 1810—the last provoked by the death of Princess Amelia, the youngest and most beloved of George's fifteen children. The following year, the Prince of Wales was made regent, and yet King George, now seventy-three, blind and deaf and mad, lived on for almost another decade.

He wandered around the palace in a long white beard, sometimes playing the flute, sometimes exposing himself to the servants. In more grandiose moods, according to Thackeray, he spent his time "addressing imaginary parliaments, reviewing fancied troops, holding ghostly Courts." The Queen once discovered him singing a hymn and accompanying himself at the harpsichord, and when he had finished, he knelt down and prayed for her, for his family, and for the nation, and then burst into tears. The spectacle of George's lamentable end moved Thackeray to recall another royal madman of the past: "Driven off his throne; buffeted by rude hands; with his children in revolt; the darling of his old age killed before him untimely; our Lear hangs over her breathless lips and cries, 'Cordelia, Cordelia, stay a little!' "

Robert Schumann, whose *Carnaval* suite for the piano is among the most charming and most characteristic creations of the Romantic movement, finally went crazy, totally and irrevocably crazy, during the carnival season of 1854. On the night of February 10, he could not sleep because one high A kept reverberating in his inner ear. This torture, particularly agonizing to a composer, lasted for a full week. Then the note suddenly grew into a mysterious kind of music, which Schumann described in his diary as "more wonderful and played by more exquisite instruments than ever sounded on earth." He thought he heard angels singing to him, and so he got out of bed to write down one of their melodies —a melody that was actually the theme of the slow movement of his newly finished violin concerto in D minor. The next morning, he began trying to write variations on the angelic theme, but he now heard the voices of demons howling at him. The demons even became visible in the form of tigers and hyenas. While two doctors struggled to control him, he thrashed about on the floor, screaming in terror.

During his calmer moments, Schumann tried to continue working on his cello concerto or sat and listened to the angelic voices, sometimes writing down a phrase or two of their singing. He also asked his wife, Clara, to take him to an insane asylum. Clara resisted the idea, saying, "Robert, do you want to leave your wife and children?" Schumann answered that the absence would be "not really for long." The doctors' only recommendation was to send Schumann to bed. He agreed, but insisted that someone stand guard over him.

On the gray, rainy morning of February 27, almost three weeks after the high note had begun ringing in his ears, Schumann awoke in a state that Clara described as "more profoundly melancholy than words can say." When she tried to cheer him up, he would only answer, "Ah, Clara, I am not worthy of your love." As soon as Clara left the room for a moment, Schumann retreated to his bedroom and wrote his wife a note: "Dear Clara, I shall cast my wedding ring into the Rhine. Do you the same. Then the two rings will be united." Then, only partly dressed, still in slippers, he darted out of the house and ran through the brightly costumed carnival crowds to the bridge across the Rhine. At the toll gate, he found he had no money, so he gave the gate-keeper his handkerchief as payment. At the middle of the bridge, he threw his wedding ring into the waters and then leaped in after it. Down in the deep, he once again heard the angels' voices singing to him, a singing that he later recalled as indescribably beautiful, but the Rhine was not yet ready to receive him. He drifted to the surface, and some fishermen pulled him into their boat. Schumann tried once again to leap into the river, but the fishermen wrestled him back into their boat. On shore, the carnival revelers apparently regarded all this as a melodrama staged for their benefit. They applauded delightedly. Schumann was taken home and then to a private asylum at Endenich, near Bonn, from which he never re-emerged.

Schumann's breakdown was probably inevitable according to any of a half-dozen different theories of madness. To start with, he came of rather peculiar parentage. His father, August, was a bookstore clerk who fell in love with a surgeon's daughter, and the surgeon demanded that he prove himself by establishing a successful grocery store. August Schumann thereupon wrote and sold seven novels in eighteen months, bought and opened a grocery store, married his beloved, and lived more or less unhappily ever after. Both he and his wife apparently suffered from acute attacks of melancholia. Their five children were all of fragile health, and their only daughter, afflicted with a severe skin disease, drowned herself at nineteen.

Schumann's difficulties in getting married were even more complex than those that his father had endured. As a discontented law student of eighteen, he became an acquaintance, then a piano pupil, then a lodger, of the stern and stately Friedrich Wieck, whose proudest pedagogical creation was his daughter Clara, already a celebrated piano prodigy at the age of nine. Schumann flirted with a number of girls, and even became secretly engaged for a while to the daughter of a Bavarian baron, but in due time he and Clara professed their love for each other. Schumann, then twenty-five, asked Wieck for permission to marry his sixteen-year-old daughter. Wieck flew into a rage and forbade Clara ever to see Schumann again. They exchanged, through the services of Clara's maid, breathless letters. "This cannot go on much longer—my health will not stand it," Schumann wrote to Clara. "God preserve me from despair."

The Romantic spirit apparently thrived on thwarted love, and this fairy-tale situation inspired some of Schumann's finest piano music. The great *Fantasy in C Major*, the charming fables called *Kreisleriana* (dashed out in a week), the *Davidsbündler Dances*, the *Fantasiestücke*, the *Scenes from Childhood*—all of these splendid works date from the emotionally turbulent years of 1837 and 1838. But the turbulence sometimes proved too much for Schumann's health. While working on *Nachtstücke*, he began seeing visions of funerals and coffins, and when he received the news that his brother Eduard had died, he suddenly heard an unearthly chorale played by unearthly trombones. He even quarreled with Clara, and he wrote her of a scene that was to come true more than fifteen years later: "I had a dream of walking beside a deep pool. . . . I cast the [wedding] ring into it—then I passionately longed to cast myself in after it."

Wieck had known from the start that Schumann had an unusual personality. In a striking letter to the youth's worried mother, in which he promised "to turn your son Robert, by means of his talent and imagination, into one of the greatest pianists now living," Wieck referred to his protégé's "unbridled fancy" and "unsettled ideas." Now that Schumann was his enemy, Wieck spread every calumny that he could imagine. He claimed that Schumann was a drunkard, who could neither speak nor write clearly. When he passed his prospective son-in-law on the streets of Leipzig, he spat. Schumann and Clara petitioned to the court of appeals for permission to marry without Wieck's assent, and after a year of deliberation, the court agreed. On the day before Clara's twenty-first birthday, in 1840, they were married. "What can I write about this day?" Clara asked in her diary. Among the things she did write was that "the weather was lovely."

Even at this pinnacle of Schumann's life, the most superficial psychiatric study would indicate signs of present and future trouble. Aside from the chronic chills and tremors and other physical disorders, aside from the deep anxieties and occasional hallucinations, Schumann relied, both in his writing and in his music, on an artistic *persona* that was dangerously fragmented. It was common enough for the Romantics to use pen names, even several of them—Schumann's literary hero, Jean Paul, created a pair of autobiographical spokesmen named Walt and Vult in *Die Flegeljahre*—but Schumann's alter egos really *were* different aspects of himself. His bold and exuberant nature spoke through a character called Florestan, who pronounced Schumann's famous salute to the unknown young Chopin: "Hats off, gentlemen! A genius!" The dreamy, otherworldly Schumann appeared as Eusebius. Their differences were supposed to be settled by Master Raro, who originally represented Wieck, although later scholars have suggested that the name derives from the last two letters of Clara and the first two of Robert. Collectively, Florestan, Eusebius and their friends formed the *Davidsbündler*, "members of the League of David," whom Schumann organized to fight against the Philistines. Schumann quoted these characters in the reviews he wrote for his magazine, the *Neue Zeitschrift für Musik;* he composed miniature portraits of them in *Carnaval;* at the end of each section of the *Davidsbündler Dances*, he indicated whether it had been composed by Florestan or Eusebius, or, in some cases, both, and he even added a few footnotes on how the composition had occurred ("Here Florestan concluded and his lips twitched painfully").

Like Percy and Mary Shelley, like Scott and Zelda Fitzgerald, the Schumanns seemed an idyllic couple, but no marriage remains an idyll for long. Clara's first baby, Marie, was born in 1841, the year after the marriage; then came Elise, in 1843, Julie in 1845, Emil in 1846, Ludwig in 1848, Ferdinand in 1849, Eugenie in 1851, and even after Schumann's confinement in an institution, in 1854, Felix. Such fecundity imposed severe financial burdens on the composer and severe physical burdens on the virtuoso. Both problems were exacerbated by the Schumanns' own personalities. Robert, secretly pained by Clara's greater celebrity in the musical world, insisted at home on being the *Hausdiktator*. Clara not only was forbidden to practice while he was trying to compose; she was expected, when they went out in the evening, to fetch his waistcoat and button it for him. Clara, on the other hand, had her own way of fighting against Robert's relative obscurity. She constantly urged him to write heroic symphonies and operas, and to win official recognition as a conductor or musical director. Robert eventually did all these things, but the outpouring of his great music virtually ended, for whatever reasons, about two years after his marriage.

Although Schumann's heredity and his psyche and his marriage all provide possible explanations for his breakdown, still another theory has recently arisen from the researches of an English musicologist, Eric Sams. This theory is that Schumann, like thousands of his contemporaries, suffered from syphilis, possibly congenital, and that his health was probably worsened by the mercury treatments that were standard in that period. Mercury poisoning would account for the mysterious crippling of Schumann's fourth finger, which is generally thought to have been disabled by a mechanical device that he was using to strengthen his piano technique. This affliction would also explain, better than paternal hysteria, Wieck's bitter opposition to Schumann as a son-in-law. It would explain, finally, the deterioration and eventual destruction of Schumann's brain.

The deterioration seemed to be inexorable. Even in his youth,

Schumann suffered not only from bad health but from hypo-
chondria, not only from melancholy but from a dread of going
mad. He was terrified of high places, imagining that he might
throw himself off. He hated to touch sharp-edged tools, or even
keys. There was a new breakdown in 1842 and again in 1844,
always described in vague terms like "nervous exhaustion." He
took rest cures and cold baths at various resorts. He gave up the
editorship of the *Neue Zeitschrift*. But there were all the children
to support, and Clara's ideals to be maintained. Toward the end
of 1849, he won an appointment as conductor of the symphony
orchestra and chorus in Düsseldorf, and the place filled him with
dread. "The other day I looked for some notices of Düsseldorf in
an old geography book . . ." he wrote to a friend. "Among the
places of note, I found mentioned three convents and a madhouse.
I have no objections to the former, but it made me quite uncomfortable to read about the latter. . . . I have to be very careful
in guarding against all melancholy impressions of that kind."

Düsseldorf was a disaster. Whether Schumann was too mild
in temperament to be a good conductor, or whether his mind was
already disintegrating, his career on the podium was a series of
embarrassments. On one occasion, the soprano got confused and
stopped singing; the other singers stopped too; Schumann went
on conducting as though nothing had gone wrong. The accom-
panist finally stepped to his side, and Schumann's only comment
was to point to the score and say, "Look, this bar is beautiful."
In the summer of 1852, there was yet another breakdown, marked
by depression, irritability, slurred speech, and aural hallucinations. The doctors again prescribed cold baths.

Schumann turned to religious music. He composed a Mass
and a Requiem, neither of which is now recorded or much performed. He also became fascinated by occult phenomena. "Yesterday, we had table-rapping for the first time," he wrote to the
composer Ferdinand Hiller. "A wonderful power! Just think, I
asked what was the rhythm of the first two bars of the C Minor
Symphony! There was more hesitation than usual about the answer. At last it came. . . ." And to the violinist Joseph Joachim:
"I have dreamed of you, dear Joachim. . . . Your hands were full
of heron feathers, and out of them flowed champagne. . . . Now
I will end. Already it grows dark."

Less than a month later, Schumann suffered the fate he had dreaded, confinement in an institution. For more than two years there, he occupied himself with self-imposed tasks like compiling lists of cities in alphabetical order. Sometimes he improvised at the piano, but no creations have survived. Occasionally, he heard ghostly voices accusing him of plagiarism, and then he would cry out, "That is not true! That is a lie!" Toward the end of July 1856, when he received a last visit from Clara, he could hardly move or speak. "He smiled at me and, with a great exertion—for he could no longer control his limbs—put his arm around me—I will never forget it," Clara wrote in her diary. "It seemed that he kept talking much with spirits . . . but one could no longer understand him. . . ." And then the next day: "Ah! I could only pray God to release him, because I loved him so dearly. . . ." And the day after that: "No one was with him at the moment . . . that he was at last set free."

Even among those who knew the suffering of the insane, the madman remained a kind of spiritual hero to the Romantic Age. He was a Promethean figure, a man who had tried to climb too high, to see too much, to grasp the divine secrets. And if he suffered, that was his Promethean destiny, the price he paid for his sensitivity. The nineteenth century was alive with transcendental madmen. Nikolai Gogol, the creator of *Dead Souls*, tried in vain to write a second volume demonstrating the redemption of Chichikov, then sought inspiration on a pilgrimage to Jerusalem, and ended wandering through the streets, handing out pages of his unfinished novel to strangers. Friedrich Nietzsche, prophet of the superman, saw an old carthorse being beaten on an Italian *piazza*, ran across the square, flung his arms around the animal's neck, and fell unconscious, mad for the rest of his life. Vincent van Gogh, who saw the stars as whirlpools above the cypresses outside the insane asylum at Saint-Rémy, finally shot himself, and on his body there was found an unfinished letter to his brother Theo, which ended with the words, "but what's the use?"

To the doctors of the Romantic era, who were supposed to cure insanity rather than stand in awe of it, Van Gogh's last words might have seemed an appropriate verdict on the entire problem. Even such a relatively simple affliction as syphilis, which had by now been identified for more than four centuries, remained largely a mystery, and as one old woman in Berlin recalls the early days of this century, "There was hardly a household in Europe that didn't have some old uncle or grandfather shaking and trembling in a corner by the fire, completely out of his wits because of the long-term effects of syphilis." And it was through these ravaging effects of syphilis that Henrik Ibsen dramatized the spiritual curse on the Alving family in *Ghosts*. "Mother, give me the sun," says Osvald as he begins to go over the brink. The stage directions describe the change—"Osvald seems to crumple up in the chair; all his muscles relax; his face is expressionless, his eyes vacant and staring." All he can say is: "The sun . . . the sun." As late as the 1930's, Kurt Vonnegut recalls, "people, mostly men, suffering from the last stages of syphilis, from *locomotor ataxia*, were common spectacles in downtown Indianapolis and in circus crowds when I was a boy. . . . I saw one stand on a curb at the corner of Meridian and Washington Streets one time . . . thinking hard there, at the Crossroads of America, about how to get his legs to step off the curb and carry him across Washington. He shuddered gently, as though he had a small motor which was idling inside. Here was his problem: his brains, where the instructions to his legs originated, were being eaten alive. . . ."

Syphilis actually proved quite vulnerable to chemical attack. The Wasserman test to determine its presence was devised in 1906, and in 1910 Paul Ehrlich announced the discovery of Salvarsan, which could destroy the invading spirochete without damaging any surrounding organisms. On the more mysterious forms of mental deterioration, however, on all those incomprehensible varieties of fear and depression, the doctors at the turn of the century had hardly advanced beyond Hippocrates. For a Nijinsky or a Virginia Woolf, as for a Gadarene fugitive or a King Saul, no medicine did much more than put the victim to sleep, and there seemed to be no therapy more effective than rest, baths and soft music. The scene was ready, in other words, for the neurotic genius who proposed an entirely new way of interpreting all the hidden workings of the mind, who proclaimed himself "not really a man of science" but rather "a conquistador."

"Neither at that time, nor indeed in my later life, did I feel any particular predilection for the career of a physician . . ."

Sigmund Freud wrote long afterward in *An Autobiographical Study*, "[but] it was hearing Goethe's beautiful essay on Nature read aloud at a popular lecture by Professor Carl Brühl just before I left school that decided me to become a medical student." There is certainly no need to recapitulate here all Freud's discoveries of the next half-century, for there is probably no theoretician of our time whose views are so widely known—not just known, but accepted and even taken for granted. Indeed, it is a little difficult now even to imagine the wild sense of discovery with which the young Freud, after watching Professor Jean Martin Charcot simulate hysterical paralysis in patients under hypnosis, "received the profoundest impression of the possibility that there could be powerful mental processes which nevertheless remained hidden from the consciousness." Or the sense of indignation that Freud felt when his earliest discoveries were rejected by the Vienna Medical Society. "My dear sir," he remembered one aged surgeon asking him, "how can you talk such nonsense?"

Freud's "nonsense" was an Odyssean voyage through the wildernesses of the unconscious—the discovery of childhood sexuality and of the mechanisms for repressing sexual drives, the charting of the Oedipus complex, the subdivision of the personality itself into the id, ego and superego, the revelation that the unconscious mind uses a symbolic language of its own, and that this language can be heard and interpreted in dreams, in jokes, even in slips of the tongue. To impose a methodological system on the study of the unconscious, to diagnose and treat its malfunctions, there came the new techniques that Freud called psychoanalysis: the patient recumbent on the horsehair sofa, the free association evoked by last night's dream, the listening and questioning doctor trying to lead the dreamer toward a confrontation with the half-forgotten pains of his past. It was a nineteenth-century kind of magic. Despite Freud's belief in the power of the unconscious, he believed no less strongly in the power of the conscious mind to illuminate and ultimately to dominate that unconscious. But to all of these propositions and suggestions, most doctors responded with about the same judgment as that of the old surgeon. Such nonsense. "For more than ten years . . . I had no followers," Freud wrote. "I was completely isolated. In Vienna I was shunned."

Freud was forty-three when he published his first important book, *The Interpretation of Dreams* (1899). He bitterly resented the lack of acclaim, but his message began to spread. By 1906, Eugen Bleuler and his assistant Carl Jung were beginning to use psychoanalysis at the Burghölzli Clinic in Zurich. In 1908, the first psychoanalytic conference was held in Salzburg and the movement's first periodical was founded. In 1909, Freud set off on his first pioneering lecture trip to the United States. ("America is a gigantic mistake . . ." he concluded, "a country without even wild strawberries.") In 1910, the International Psychoanalytical Association was founded, and a second periodical launched. It was partly because of the disapproval by organized medicine that Freud was inspired to start his own organization in order both to maintain professional standards and to propagate the faith, but precisely because of the movement's professional isolation, because of its dependence on Freud as Supreme Pontiff, it repeatedly became a battlefield for exquisitely defined sects and heresies. The first major victim was the first major partner, Bleuler, who spoke out in defense of some dissident who had been asked to resign. " 'Who is not with us is against us,' the principle 'all or nothing' is necessary for religious sects and for political parties . . . but for science I consider it harmful," Bleuler wrote to Freud when he resigned in 1911. "There is no ultimate truth. From a complex of notions, one person will accept one detail, another person another detail. . . . I recognize in science neither open nor closed doors but no doors at all." That same year, Alfred Adler, who interpreted conflicts more in terms of power struggles than sexual struggles, resigned from the Vienna Psychoanalytic Society and took nine of the fledgling group's thirty-five members with him. Three years later, Jung and the whole Zurich branch resigned from the organization that Freud only half-jokingly called *"mein Reich."* Freud loftily dismissed these heresies as an attempt "to escape the need for recognizing the importance of infantile sexuality," and thus an attempt to be "freed from what were felt as the repellant findings of psychoanalysis."

Throughout all the intrigues and controversies, Freud became, like Albert Einstein, a media celebrity of the 1920's, a bearded sage whose scholarly works were too complicated for the newspaper reader, but whose essential message could be summarized as a scientific justification for the basic yearning of the 1920's—that everything is permitted. Samuel Goldwyn offered $100,000 if Freud would act as consultant on a series of love stories, starting with Anthony and Cleopatra. (Freud declined.) When Lorelei Lee reached "the central of Europe," it was inevitable that Anita Loos should send her creation to visit "a famous doctor in Vienna called Doctor Froyd . . . who seems to know how to draw a girl out quite a lot. . . . So then Doctor Froyd said that all I needed was to cultivate a few inhibitions and get some sleep." To the Nazis, who were just beginning to reorganize the madness of the 1920's according to a different plan, psychoanalysis was a symbol of "Jewish decadence," and as their rise to power became more imminent, their hostility became a serious threat to Freud and his followers. Freud himself stayed on in Vienna until 1938, before being persuaded to move to London, where the jaw cancer that had afflicted him for decades became so ravenous that it ate a hole through the side of his face and finally, at the age of eighty-three, killed him. "To us he is no more a person/ Now but a whole climate of opinion," W. H. Auden wrote on the occasion of his death.

The political attacks on psychoanalysis were a personal affliction for many of the refugees—Carl Jung, unfortunately, took over the presidency of the Nazi-sponsored New German Society of Psychotherapy and wrote in the first issue of its official organ that "the factual and well-known differences between German and Jewish psychology should no longer be blurred"—but the diaspora may have been a source of considerable strength for the psychoanalytic movement itself. Freud's well-organized disciples migrated to certain naturally hospitable refuges, to London and New York and Los Angeles, and there they acquired an influence far greater than they had ever enjoyed in Vienna and Berlin. In America in particular, that "country without even wild straw-berries," that country which Freud had predicted would apply his discoveries to the advertising of merchandise, the worst prophecies did come true. "Creative" copywriters on Madison Avenue did indeed discover that Freud could be used to sell cigarettes and detergents. And in Beverly Hills, which acquired the highest per capita ratio of psychoanalysts in the world, Freud's theories became a prevailing philosophy of the movie industry, which in turn created for the rest of the world that world's own image of beauty and success. One of the most popular movies of the middle 1940's, for example, was Alfred Hitchcock's *Spellbound,* in which Ingrid Bergman tried, as a psychoanalyst, to unravel Gregory Peck's dreams (lavishly illustrated by Salvador Dali). As soon as she succeeded, Peck was instantly cured of the amnesia that surrounded his involvement in a murder. That is the way Hollywood always spreads its message, not in polemics but in the assumptions that resolve plots and provide happy endings.

The trouble was that psychoanalysis didn't really work very well, at least not for people who had actually gone crazy. Freud himself was well aware of the limitations on his discoveries. In guarded words, he admitted that although psychoanalysis could help neurotics, "it would seem that the analytical study of the psychoses is impractical owing to its lack of therapeutic results." The main problem, he said, was that psychotics are unable to "form a positive transference"—that phase in which a psychoanalyst becomes the object of a patient's childhood emotions— and therefore "the principal instrument of analytic technique is inapplicable to them."

Not all analysts were so cautious, nor were the past and present analysands who yearned to spread the faith. But although analysis might help a Hollywood screenwriter get through a divorce, there were relatively few analysts available, and each of them demanded of each patient thousands of dollars and years of time. Even the psychiatrists who used simpler and more eclectic techniques—group therapy, for example, first became popular in veterans hospitals after World War II—were inadequate to deal with the thousands of people who kept going crazy. "They did not have the time, the patience, or even the interest . . ." as Seymour Krim has written of his own confinement, "to handle the battalions of miscellaneous humanity that are marched past [the] desk with high trumpets blowing in their minds." In the same year that *Spellbound* appeared, Frances Farmer, the actress, began a five-year incarceration in an Oregon state mental hospital where the women were chained and beaten, where rats were caught and torn apart and eaten raw.

Freud had a marvelous skill in writing case histories of his

successes, and some of his followers took equal delight in the creation of melodrama (Robert Lindner's *Rebel Without a Cause*, for
example). In recent years, however, now that psychoanalysis is
less in fashion, we are beginning to hear more from the patients,
who want to accuse the once omnipotent doctors of intimidation,
incompetence, even malevolence. In *The Bell Jar*, for instance,
Sylvia Plath's heroine cannot see "how this Doctor Gordon
[could] help me anyway, with a beautiful wife and beautiful
children and a beautiful dog haloing him like the angels on a
Christmas card." Doctor Gordon does not in fact help her except
by having her strapped into a chair and subjected to electric
shocks "till I thought my bones would break and the sap fly out
of me like a split plant. I wondered what terrible thing it was
that I had done."

On a more solemn level, critics of psychiatry repeatedly complained that there was no scientific way to assess the question of
whether psychotherapy actually accomplished anything. And so,
finally, the inevitable statistical studies were undertaken. As a
statistical sample, the number of patients was unimpressive, and
it might be argued that psychiatry is hardly more susceptible to
statistical evaluation than is poetry, but the results were nonetheless depressing. In five different studies, the number of patients
"cured" or "improved" by psychoanalysis ran around 75 percent,
the number similarly cured or improved by other forms of psychotherapy was also about 75 percent, and the number remained at
75 percent when the patients were given no treatment at all. This
is officially called "spontaneous remission."

Was it for this, then, that the followers of Freud demanded
years of payments at fifty dollars an hour? To exorcise demons?

Henri Laborit had no particular interest in mental illness. As
a surgeon, he was concerned with the mechanisms of shock,
specifically with the decrease in blood pressure that is a dangerous element in shock. Since injections of histamine can lower
blood pressure, Laborit wondered whether the antihistamines
newly discovered by the Italian Daniel Bovet might prevent
shock. He tried a number of them on his patients during the late
1940's, notably promethazine, an antihistaminic derivative of
phenothiazine, which had been synthesized in Germany in 1883

and had proved useful in treating worm infections of the gastrointestinal tract. Laborit found promethazine highly beneficial to his surgical patients. Aside from the question of blood pressure, he reported that "even after major operations they are never excited, not complaining, and appear to really suffer less."

Until this point, the drug companies had not been particularly interested in the sedative aspects of the antihistamines— indeed the drowsiness caused by antihistamines had been considered an unfortunate side effect—but a French firm named Specia was reviewing its entire testing program at this time. Specia chemist Paul Charpentier sent Dr. Laborit some new phenothiazine derivatives. One of these was a combination of promazine plus one chlorine atom. Charpentier called it chlorpromazine. Laborit soon found that "it provokes not any loss in consciousness, not any change in the patient's mentality but a slight tendency to sleep and above all 'disinterest' for all that goes around him." These peculiar qualities, he went on, "let us foresee certain indications for this drug in psychiatry." Laborit himself got some psychiatrists to test chlorpromazine in a small Paris hospital in the spring of 1952. They found that it was considerably more than a sedative. It calmed the manic, but it also aroused the depressed. It seemed, in fact, to control and even in some cases to cure the most incurable of all mental illnesses, schizophrenia.

And so the drug revolution began. It was, like so many medical revolutions, a rediscovery of older methods. The priests of Aesculapius had used opium derivatives, and the witches of the Middle Ages applied a whole pharmacopoeia of powders and syrups derived from belladonna, mandrake and various other herbs. The red-flowered plant known as snakeroot, or *serpentiana,* was long used in southern Asia as a treatment for "moonsickness," or lunacy, but it was not officially classified in Europe as *Rauwolfia serpentina* until the late sixteenth century, not chemically analyzed as an antipsychotic drug until 1931, and not commercially introduced to the United States as reserpine or Serpasil until the 1950's. As the drug industry pressed forward into this Yukon of psychiatric pills, there came the energizers, notably Iponiazid, and the tranquilizers, notably meprabomate (Miltown, Equanil). Of all these, the one drug that seemed—and still seems

—to work most powerfully against severe mental illness was chlorpromazine, best known under the Smith, Kline and French trade name of Thorazine.

During this same period, a quite different line of inquiry led to the theory that madness can be caused by dietary deficiencies —and cured by large quantities of vitamins and proteins. The theory apparently derived from the treatment of pellagra, a disease that causes both skin trouble and mental distortions. Doctors discovered as early as 1915 that pellagra was caused by malnutrition, and in 1937 they found that niacin, or nicotinic acid, also known as vitamin B-3, cured both the physical and the mental symptoms. It was not until 1952, however, that a Canadian doctor named Abram Hoffer tried administering niacin to schizophrenic patients. After a series of tests, he reported that niacin (used in conjunction with electric shocks and psychotherapy) cured two thirds of the patients, double the rate for those who had not been given niacin.

The established authorities of psychiatry paid little attention to those remarkable findings, but a number of doctors began to try other nutritional experiments. In the course of the 1960's, they reported (1) that large doses of other vitamins, particularly B-1 (thiamine), B-6 (pyridoxine), B-12 (cyanocobalamin) and C (ascorbic acid) proved highly effective in treating schizophrenics; (2) that most schizophrenics suffered from hypoglycemia, a shortage of blood sugar, which could be remedied by a diet high in proteins and low in carbohydrates; and (3) that schizophrenics with too much blood histamine responded well to supplements of zinc and manganese. This whole system for dealing with madness was baptized in 1968 as "orthomolecular psychiatry" by Stanford's Nobel-Prize-winning chemist Linus Pauling, who defined it as "the provision of the optimum molecular environment for the mind."

All of these developments naturally alarm the psychiatrists who have devoted their lives to investigations of childhood neuroses. The American Psychiatric Association assigned a "task force" to investigate the sins of orthomolecular psychiatry, and the task force duly announced in 1973 that it disapproved. The orthomolecular forces instantly responded that their treatment had not received a fair test. It is indeed still largely unknown

exactly how the brain is affected by either vitamins or the phenothiazines—or, for that matter, psychiatry. But since clinical tests
have shown that all the symptoms of schizophrenia can be
chemically induced (by amphetamines, for example) and chemically removed (by various combinations of tranquilizers, vitamins
and restricted diet), the burden of proof now lies on the traditional psychiatrists, who tend to regard that burden with a certain
degree of professional contempt. So we have come to the latest
swing of the pendulum between those who think insanity is a
physical illness and those who think it a manifestation of evil
spirits.

One undeniable reason for the popularity of the new drugs is
their elimination of the terrible guilt that surrounds insanity. If
one is simply a victim of chemical imbalances, then one need not
feel that one has done something wrong; one's illness is no more
shameful than diabetes or anemia. For parents, too, for wives and
husbands, the chemical theory provides an escape from all the
accusations implicit in Freudian theory. The crazy have not been
driven crazy. Nobody is to blame.

A more substantial benefit of the new drugs is the reduction
of violence in the haunted back wards of the state mental hospitals. The patients, by and large, no longer thrash around in straitjackets and scream their rage into the night. Their guardians
consequently have neither provocation nor justification for the
ropes and clubs that once were common. The abuses now are of
another kind, beginning with the infusion of so many drugs into
the insane that they waste away their lives in a stupor, confined
in the new straitjacket of contemporary chemistry.

Political frugality, however, tends to combine with humani-
tarianism to change that. For almost two decades now, the prevailing policy has been to close down the old mental institutions
and to send the shaky inmates back to what is popularly known
as "the community." Statistically, this sounds very impressive. In
1955, there were 560,000 long-term mental patients (about half
of them diagnosed as schizophrenic), occupying one out of every
two hospital beds in the United States, and those statisticians who
like to project present trends into future disasters warned that the
number of long-term mental patients would increase to 750,000
in 1971. In actual fact, the number of mental patients admitted to

hospitals did double during that period, but the number actually confined there declined to 330,000, less than half the predicted swarm.

There is some reason to suspect that the invocation of drugs to close down mental hospitals may involve just as many abuses as the invocation of drugs to render mental patients somnolent. In theory, the released patients are turned over to "halfway houses," and then to "community centers," but many "halfway houses" are simply way stations to nowhere, and many "communities" are not so welcoming as the theoreticians expect. In New York, for example, a 1974 *Times* survey of the neighborhoods around the Creedmore State Hospital reported "many eyewitness accounts of mental patients wandering helplessly in the streets, urinating and defecating in public, exposing themselves before women and children . . . cursing pedestrians, collapsing from intoxication." The *Times* reporter provided no specific evidence of this stereotypical behavior, and the protestations of neighborhood anxiety may well have been expressions of neighborhood rumor ("Some are . . . talking of moving," according to a woman who heads a block association in Brooklyn), but the basic trend seems undeniable. Since the government has been providing $260 to $375 per patient per month for nothing more than a bed and three meals a day, the opening of ill-supervised "halfway houses" can provide a lucrative business. One former employee at the Creedmore Hospital was found to have opened six of them. "The snake pits are being transferred from the institutions to the neighborhoods," according to Queens Borough President Donald R. Manes. Since the problem of released mental patients is a problem more of apathy than of mistreatment, however, there is more accuracy in the observation of Dr. Robert Reich, Director of Psychiatry for the New York City Department of Social Services, who said of the new liberation, "Freedom to be sick, helpless and isolated is not freedom."

So we have reached the present, or more precisely the summer of 1973, and Kurt Vonnegut squints into the afternoon sun. His new novel is about to appear, *Breakfast of Champions,* and everyone expects it to be a vast success. Vonnegut has become a cult hero, and cult heroes are always vastly successful. But first he must undergo the rituals of promotional torture—smiling appearances in a mask of cocoa-brown makeup under the glare of TV lights, and the drunken roar of all those publication parties, and interviews like this one, in the hot summer sun, in a Manhattan "garden" that consists of a bare plateau of concrete next to the fuming back end of a French restaurant.

Vonnegut's new novel is about a Pontiac dealer named Dwayne Hoover, who is on the edge of going crazy. Because of what Vonnegut calls "the bad chemicals in his head," Dwayne Hoover "saw eleven moons in the sky over the new Mildred Barry Memorial Center for the Arts one night. The next morning he saw a huge duck directing traffic at the intersection of Arsenal Avenue and Old Country Road." The bad chemicals make Dwayne try to shoot himself, but instead he shoots the flamingo on the glass door to his bathtub. In the course of telling us this, Vonnegut remarks that "my own mother wrecked her brains with chemicals which were supposed to make her sleep." And when he tells us that Hoover's wife was "crazy as a bedbug," he adds that "My mother was, too." Both women, he says, "boiled over with chaotic talk about love and peace and wars and evil and desperation, of better days coming by and by, of worse days coming by and by. And both . . . committed suicide. . . . My mother ate sleeping pills."

The interviewer feels an obligation to ask for more details.

"Is the you in this novel really you—that is, a nonfiction you —or is he another character?"

"No, that's really me."

"You speak there of your mother committing suicide. That really happened?"

What a sordid business it is to interview people, to intrude on strangers and ask them questions that nobody should ask, and expect answers that nobody should give. Journalism trains both its practitioners and its victims to assume that some theoretical public "right to know" justifies everything. I once interviewed, for example, the wife of a minor official in New Jersey who had just walked out into the Atlantic Ocean with both his hands tied to loaded suitcases. I was trying to find out from her what reason he might have had to drown himself, and I would have defeated my own purpose if I had let the widow discover that her husband was, as I knew and she did not know, dead. Yes, that made a story for the next day's newspaper. Vonnegut and I were not within the domain of news, however, but rather in that of publicity. And he did not even need publicity—his success was assured—nor did I need the interview, for I already knew what I was going to write. It is simply the expected thing. My employer expects an interview, and Vonnegut expects to be interviewed.

"Yes," he says, to the question about his mother. He smiles vaguely, a tall thin figure with a weathered face and a scraggly mustache and a very soft, murmurous voice. "But I wouldn't want to see that articulated any more than I've done in the book."

"You seem to blame Dwayne Hoover's going crazy mainly on 'bad chemicals.' "

"Well, that's the state of the art. The schizzies themselves talk about it that way. They say those visions are all true, all so true and so useless."

"But when you have him actually go berserk, you explain it as the result of something he read in a book."

"People who go crazy need somebody to give them their ideas, somebody to write their words for them."

"You write in a couple of places as though you felt you were going crazy yourself. [" 'You're afraid you'll kill yourself the way your mother did,' I said. 'I know,' I said."] Did that literally happen?"

"I assume that's true for every human being on earth," says Kurt Vonnegut. Perhaps, he thinks, he should qualify that. "I have never been confined in an institution. I've never had hallucinations. I've never heard voices that weren't there." What he never mentioned was that his oldest son had been having hallucinations and hearing voices that weren't there, and that he had felt compelled, not too long ago, to confine the youth in an institution.

PART TWO

GROWING UP

3

The Sorrows
of Young Oedipus

The origins of all madness lie somewhere in the memory, but the mind soon covers itself with scar tissue. Our first memory must be the experience of birth, and yet almost nobody can remember it at all. I often dream of being aboard an ocean liner (or sometimes, for variation, a channel steamer), and I am always below decks when the ship inexorably begins to sink. In the semi-darkness, the vessel rolls heavily to one side, and the swirling water rises, but despite my sense of helplessness and terror, I see daylight through the porthole at the end of the corridor, and I manage to swim toward it and to squeeze my way out into the open. What can that dream be except a re-enactment of birth, an experience so overwhelming that I have driven it from my mind, so overwhelming that I cannot drive it from my mind?

The conscious memory is more conservative. Most people whom I have asked about their earliest recollections cite a scene, usually an unhappy one, that occurred at about the age of two. The first scene that I myself can remember occurred at that age, perhaps a little earlier, in some small German town where my family was staying for the summer. We were out picking blue-berries one morning, my brother and I and the nurse, and when it came time to go home for lunch, I insisted on carrying the box of blueberries that we had picked. The nurse warned me not to spill them onto the dirt road. She warned me particularly not to run, lest I trip and fall. So of course I started running ahead, up a small hill, with the nurse halfheartedly calling her warnings after me. At the top of the hill, I inevitably tripped and fell, and the blueberries spilled all over the road and even began rolling down the hill. I suppose it is a memory of guilt and shame, of warnings defied and prophecies fulfilled, but the thing I remember most clearly about the whole episode is my own sense of astonishment that the blueberries began rolling down the hill. They couldn't have rolled more than an inch or two, but the fact that they rolled at all seemed miraculous, incredible, a wonder of nature. Perhaps it is simply strangeness that one recalls most vividly, strangeness combined with a slight sense of danger.

We moved to Paris that fall, and out of a whole winter on the Avenue Malakoff (now Poincaré), the only thing I can remember is that the supper, which the cook had prepared on the floor below, rose to our dining room in a clanking dumbwaiter and emerged from an oak-framed hole in the wall. Nothing more than that, and the sense of mystery surrounding it. Or is that, too, a symbolic recollection of having been born?

It must be said of King Laius of Thebes that he did his best to escape his fate. When the Delphic Oracle told him that any child born to Queen Jocasta would eventually murder him, he tried to defeat the prophecy by banishing Jocasta from his chambers. She tempted him with wine, however, and thus produced her first son. Laius ordered that the baby be exposed and left to die on Mount Cithaeron, but a merciful shepherd carried it off to Corinth, where the childless King Polybus reared it as his own son.

The dutiful Oedipus also tried to escape his fate, for when the Delphic Oracle told him that he would kill his father and marry his mother, he ran away from the court of King Polybus and wandered off on the road toward Thebes, the road on which, of course, he had his fatal confrontation with Laius. It is worth emphasizing that all the aggression came from the father—in the fight at the crossroads as on the occasion of Oedipus's birth—and that the father and son never, even in their final battle, knew one another. When the plague fell on Thebes because Laius's murder remained unpunished, King Oedipus declared, in Sophocles' version: "I mean to fight for him now, as I would fight/ For my own father, and leave no way untried/ To bring to light the killer of Laius . . ./ The gods curse all that disobey this charge!" Oedipus, in other words, did not have an Oedipus complex.

The mission that Freud imputed to all of Oedipus's successors is by no means an easy one to carry out. As the newborn son contemplates his prospective victim, he contemplates an antagonist approximately four times his height and twenty times his weight—a situation roughly comparable to that of an adult warrior condemned to live among Brobdingnagians who stand twenty-five feet high and weigh two tons. Only after about fifteen years of servitude does this disparity in size fade away, and by then, the father has had ample time to enforce whatever rules he chooses to enforce. Almost the first thing that the baby learns, almost the last thing it can ever forget, is to fear the force of authority, for authority repeatedly uses force, sometimes reasonably, sometimes capriciously, to impose its will. Even in our enlightened times, the New York police are summoned to investigate cases of child abuse and neglect at a rate of more than 15,000 per year, and in more than a few of those cases the beatings are fatal.

The tradition of domineering fathers is a distinguished one, from Abraham to Lear to Freud himself, but it is far more common in modern times for the heirs of King Laius to repress or half-repress their aggressions and hostilities toward the sons who are doomed to assault them. The son is more likely, therefore, to grow up with an ambiguous or enigmatic antagonist, not a tyrant to be feared and hated but rather a shadow to be mistrusted and misunderstood. The tyrannical father and the phantom father can be equally dangerous to the searching son. And so we evolve from a Pap Finn, drunkenly pursuing the scapegrace Huck with a clasp knife, to the former Commander Lowell, of whom Robert Lowell could only protest: " 'Anchors aweigh,' Daddy boomed in his bathtub,/ 'Anchors aweigh,'/ When Lever Brothers offered to pay/ him double what the Navy paid./ I nagged for his dress sword with gold braid,/ and cringed because Mother, new/ caps on all her teeth, was born anew/ at forty. With seamanlike celerity,/ Father left the Navy,/ and deeded Mother his property./ He was soon fired. Year after year,/ he still hummed 'Anchors aweigh' in the tub. . . ."

In the house of Commander Lowell, as in my own, it was nearly unthinkable that the family—every family—should provide a framework for sexual combat; that, as Freud wrote in *Three Contributions to the Theory of Sex* (1905), even the first thumbsucking could bring "a motor reaction in the form of an orgasm"; that failure to perform on the toilet constitutes "mastur-batic excitation of the anal zone"; and that every son, finally, yearns to murder his father and to supplant that father in his mother's bed.

This once inconceivable view of the family is now so widely accepted that it seems worthwhile to recall how it was born. It was born at 117 Schlossergasse in Freiberg, Moravia, where Sigmund Freud was born to the twenty-one-year-old Amalie Nathanson Freud. Her husband, Jakob Freud, a moderately un-successful wool merchant, was twenty years older than his second wife. He had first been married at seventeen, and the older of his two sons was already older than stepmother Amalie. His first grandson was a year older than his third son, the grandson's uncle, young Sigmund. The future sage and his nephew John were constant companions, a relationship that Freud's biographer, Ernest Jones, describes as "not always entirely innocent." The two boys apparently mistreated John's younger sister, Pauline, and Sigmund had youthful fantasies of joining John in raping her. A neurotic child, we would call him nowadays, perhaps even "disturbed." At the age of seven or eight, he deliberately urinated in his parents' bedroom, and his exasperated father cried out, "That boy will never amount to anything!"

Jakob Freud must have been a distant figure, though not, by all accounts, a harsh or indifferent father. The relationship was complicated not only by age but also by the conditions attached to being a Jewish wool merchant under the Hapsburg Empire. One day, when Sigmund was twelve, Jakob Freud told him how some arrogant gentile had knocked his new fur cap into the mud and shouted at him: "Jew, get off the pavement." "And what did you do?" the boy demanded. "I stepped into the gutter and picked up my cap," said Jakob Freud.

Young Sigmund took up military history, idolized Hannibal and Napoleon, and talked of becoming a general. His mother approved. She would have approved of anything he did. She went on to have two more sons and five daughters, but Sigmund was always her favorite, and even when he was a world-famous scien-tist, she referred to him as *"mein goldener Sigi."* At the age of ninety, she refused the gift of a shawl because it would make her "look too old." Freud himself said of her influence, "A man who has been the indisputable favorite of his mother keeps for life the feeling of a conqueror, that confidence of success that often induces real success."

One of Freud's exam questions on graduating from the Sperl Gymnasium involved the translation of twenty-three verses from Sophocles' *Oedipus Rex*, but the pathway to medicine led inexorably into the wildernesses of academic research. His first major investigation concerned the gonads of eels, which, because of the eel's migrating habits, remained mysterious. "No one," Freud wrote in his paper, "has ever found a mature male eel—no one has yet seen the testes of the eel, in spite of innumerable efforts through the centuries." Two years earlier, in 1874, a zoologist in Trieste had discovered an organ that he thought might be the testes, and so Freud now proceeded to dissect more than four hundred eels. He found the questionable organ in many of them. "On microscopic examination," according to Jones's account, "he found its histological structure to be such that it might well be an immature testicular organ, though there was no definite evidence that it was so."

That was the way German doctors were trained in the 1870's, and so they emerged into the wan sunlight of imperial respectability—formal, stately, formidable. Has anyone ever seen a picture of Freud without a stiff white collar around his neck? But when he psychoanalyzed himself, in his forties—to whom else could the creator of psychoanalysis turn for analysis?—he discovered that the first official Oedipus complex was his own. The discovery, says Jones, "came as a great shock."

Richard Aldrich Rand, a rather gaunt young man with a long jawbone and bright-red hair, emerged from college to look for his first job about a decade ago and found that the publishing business opened its doors to any son of Christopher Rand. The elder Rand, then in his early fifties, had covered the Korean War for the *New York Herald Tribune* and subsequently had become a roving correspondent for *The New Yorker*. He had written books on Asia, on Harvard, on Israel, on the Puerto Ricans. Dick Rand got his first job working for me at *The Saturday Evening Post*, and I suppose I became a kind of father figure to him. In any case, he wanted very much for me and his father to meet, and so one day we all sat down to one of those bad French meals in one of those bad French restaurants that proliferate throughout mid-Manhattan. The celebrated Christopher Rand seemed unusually remote, a short, stubby figure with crew-cut gray hair, not hostile but aloof, monosyllabic, unsmiling. I had no idea that he was already on the way to his death.

"I think it was Harry Stack Sullivan who said there are no crazy individuals, only crazy families," Dick Rand observes, now a professor of English, now smoking a cigar, some ten years after that depressing lunch.

"I believe that there are crazy families that go on for generations. You're born into them, and then you have needs; you must live in a house, you must be fed. My parents met my needs, but that doesn't mean that the insanity wasn't there. I looked around, about a year ago, to see if there were any men in my immediate family that I would call successful as models—uncles, fathers, grandfathers—and there wasn't a single one. Dad was always crazy, in subdued form. So the fear of madness was a very strong, powerful thing. I knew it was around me. I knew Dad was mad. I *knew* it.

"Even at a very early age, I knew that his behavior was very eccentric. We'd always say, 'Oh, Dad talks funny,' or 'Dad does funny things,' but all we were doing was to deny what we knew was happening. What does 'funny' mean? Well, he had mannerisms of speech that were extremely pronounced, distorted. And he had a funny way of hopping when he walked. He said that his Achilles tendon was foreshortened, but that wasn't it. It was a distortion of the physical carriage. I used to imitate that distortion, and the distortions in speech. Children pick these things up. You know, as a child, when your father is deeply preoccupied. You know when he is terrified by things that don't make sense. And he would do strange things, like once, in Santa Barbara, he said, 'I'm going up to the top of that mountain, and I'll spend the night there, and then come back down.' And we said, 'Well, fine, are you going to take a sleeping bag?' And he said, 'No, I'll take a couple of Cokes.' Which he did. He took a couple of Cokes and climbed to the top of that mountain. . . ."

The first member of the family who actually cracked was

Rand's twin sister, Mary. He felt close to her, tried to take care of her.

"I not only watched her flipping out," he says now, "but I was the one who had to bring the bad news to the people in the family who were also watching it but not noticing it, if you know what I mean." Despite her difficulties during that summer in California, Mary went on to Vassar, and her brother, in his last year at Groton, visited her there.

"She was perfectly coherent, but she had become incompetent in what we call the life skills, that is to say, she couldn't function. I remember she went walking around in sneakers in a snowstorm. She couldn't explain why she was doing it. She didn't know why she was doing it. She was just doing it. And although she could talk perfectly lucidly about what was going on during the day, she was in a state of panic. About what? About the unknown, I guess. First of all, insanity is—the breakdown, the total incompetence in thought and deed, is a terrible taboo. You're not allowed to be that, and if you are that, then you're alone in the world. I remember talking with Mary and her doctor about Mary's going to the hospital, and Mary burst into tears, and she said, 'I'm a failure. I can't stay out.' The doctor was very reassuring and very passionate and very good, and he said, 'You know, it's like any other sickness, and you'll get out, and you'll be better.' And that was true, because she's on her own now. She's finishing school, and she has a job. But Dad, when the time came—he was a very lonely man, and he didn't have any people he trusted. . . .

"But let me cite an example from your own experience, which you told me once, and which I remember vividly. That story about your playing chess with your father, and his accusing you of cheating. Now, what can you say in a situation like that? Can you say, 'My father is being irrational?' No, you can't."

No, you can't. Particularly when the father is a very distinguished professor of political theory at Harvard, who teaches his sons, whether by argument or example, the intellectual supremacy and even the moral supremacy of reason, scholarship, Socratic dialogue. The symbol of all these things, at the level of boyhood games, was chess. My father taught me the elegant simplicity of the Ruy Lopez, taught me not to exchange pieces except for strategic advantage, taught me the propriety of resigning when the rituals of the end game required it. He did not have time to play very much, and so I was always made to feel that each game was a great honor. We played by the formal rules—*gardez la dame* when the queen is attacked, and no changes once a piece has been touched. I always lost—always. Then my father would explain to me how and why I had lost.

There came a day, inevitably, when I was about twelve, when I surveyed the chessboard between us and saw the lengthening shadows of my first victory. I forget how the situation had arisen. Perhaps I was finally mastering the combinations; perhaps my father was simply tired or preoccupied with other things. In any case, it was becoming apparent that my white queen dominated the whole center of the board and that nothing could keep her from ravaging black's defenses. I advanced her toward her target, then saw a hideous trap and pulled back.

"You took your hand off the queen," my father cried, reaching forward to snatch her off the board.

"I did *not!*" I protested.

My father looked at me in surprise, in disbelief. It would not be appropriate for him simply to seize my queen by force, but on the other hand, it was absolutely forbidden for children to contradict their parents. It was also forbidden for children to tell lies.

"You can say, if you want to, that you didn't take your hand off that queen," my father said, slowly, in a tone that indicated I had better be very careful in answering, "but if you do, then this game is over, and I won't ever play chess with you again."

"I didn't take my hand off the queen," I said. My father solemnly got up from the table and walked away. I put the chess pieces back in their wooden box. We never played again.

Chess is not, of course, a conflict between two intellects. Although the game requires a kind of visual and analytical imagination that can be highly developed, it has been demonstrated that there is no intrinsic connection between skill at chess and general intelligence. Because chess players like to consider their hobby a test of intellectual powers, however, and because chess players are the kind of people who attach inordinate importance to intellectual superiority, the game often becomes a highly emotional struggle for domination. The pieces themselves—the help-less king, the omnipotent queen, the devious bishop, the expend-able pawns—are all distorted symbols of some half-forgotten struggle. According to Ernest Jones, who once wrote a classic study entitled *The Problem of Paul Morphy*, "the unconscious motive activating the players is not the mere love of pugnacity characteristic of all competitive games but the grimmer one of father-murder."

Many of the game's greatest champions have illustrated Jones's thesis with an eccentricity bordering on insanity. Alex-ander Alekhine, a pro-Nazi Russian refugee, repeatedly married much older women (four times in all), drank heavily, stole money from friends, smashed hotel furniture during tournaments, and once interrupted a match by urinating on the floor. Wilhelm Steinitz, a vile-tempered dwarf, barely five feet high and born lame, cursed and hobbled from victory to victory for almost thirty years and finally became convinced that he could move chess pieces by electric emanations from his brain. Through a wireless telephone of his own invention, he challenged God to a chess match and offered his antagonist the advantage of a free pawn and the first move. In our own time, the chess world has been mesmerized by the antics of Bobby Fischer, whose father left the home when Bobby was an infant, whose mother left him more or less on his own when he was still an adolescent, who became United States champion at the age of fourteen and said of his own motives in the game, "I like to see 'em squirm." Harold C. Schonberg of *The New York Times* watched Fischer crush Boris Spassky during the world championship match at Reykjavik in 1972 and wrote of him:

> Relentless, monomaniacal and pitiless [he has] the aura of a killer. It is there in Fischer's face. He sits at the board, lips slightly parted, his deep-set and bleakly expressionless eyes scanning the sixty-four squares. . . . The Fischer aura is the will to dominate, to humiliate, to take over an oppo-nent's mind. . . . It is psychic murder that Fischer rep-resents.

Fischer has few heroes. One of them is Paul Morphy, whom he has described as "perhaps the most accurate chess player who ever lived," a player who "could beat anybody alive today." In many ways, the two represent opposites. Morphy was at all times quiet and courteous, a slender and elegant young man, just five feet four, with very small hands and feet. He regularly wore gray kid gloves, a cloak, and a monocle. His father was a prosperous judge in New Orleans (his mother was Creole), who taught him chess when he was about eight. Within a year or two, he could provide a match for anyone in the city. There is still an account of General Winfield Scott, conqueror of Mexico and future nominee for United States President, being humiliated at the chessboard by "a small boy of about ten years of age . . . dressed in velvet knickerbockers, with a lace shirt and a big spreading collar of the same material."

Morphy got his law degree from the University of Louisiana at the age of eighteen, in 1856, but he couldn't practice until he reached his maturity. That autumn, his father suddenly died of apoplexy, an event that apparently both shattered and liberated Morphy in a way that Ernest Jones compares to Shakespeare's creation of the regicidal Hamlet shortly after his own father's death. In the fall of 1857, the unknown youth set out for New York to compete in the first American Chess Congress. He easily came in first, winning a $300 silver dinner service. Back in New Orleans, Morphy's friends offered a challenge to the most celebrated player in England, Howard Staunton, then forty-eight, a Shakespearean scholar of some note and reputedly the illegitimate son of the Earl of Carlisle. If Staunton would come to Louisiana to play young Morphy, the challenge said, the New Orleans Chess Club would pay all his expenses. Each player should put up $5,000, winner take all. Several months passed before Staunton sent an answer saying that he was too busy with other things. (He was in fact preparing a new edition of Shakespeare, which appeared between 1857 and 1860.) In his own chess column in the London Illustrated News, he sneered at his challenger. "The best players in Europe are not chess professionals, but have other and more serious occupations, the interest of which forbid such an expenditure of time as is required for a voyage to the United States."

Morphy decided to go to England to challenge Staunton on his own territory, and on any terms. He arrived in London on his twenty-first birthday, in 1858. He met Staunton, but Staunton offered various excuses for not wanting to play. Staunton found time to play in a tournament in Birmingham, however. Morphy followed him there, in vain. Many letters were exchanged, also in vain. Morphy went to Paris to test the various players who gathered at the Café de la Régence. He defeated everyone in sight, including the best player on the continent, Adolf Anderssen, of Breslau, who had won the first international tournament in London in 1851 and who therefore was widely regarded as the unofficial world champion. Morphy gave an exhibition of playing blindfolded against eight opponents at once, a world record at that time, and the next morning he could recite all the moves in all the games. He apparently planned to play blindfolded against twenty opponents, but friends dissuaded him, on the widely believed theory that such a strain would cause brain fever and drive him mad. But Staunton would not play. In his chess columns, which critically analyzed the Morphy-Anderssen games, he claimed that he was ready to confront the American if the terms were right, but in a secret letter to Morphy, he argued that "a combat when one of the contestants must fight under disadvantages so manifest as those I should have to contend against, after many years' retirement from practical chess, with my attention absented, and brain overtaxed by more important pursuits, could never be accounted a fair trial of skill."

So the father declined to be murdered. Morphy, now the uncrowned champion, gave up the pursuit and returned to New York. There he found himself famous. Stores were selling Morphy hats and Morphy cigars, and, according to the after-dinner rhetoric of James Russell Lowell, "one smile, one glow of pride and pleasure, runs all over the land, from the shore which the sun first greets to that which looks upon the ocean where he lets fall the blazing clasp of his dissolving girdle. . . ." In the midst of all this success, however, there was already something gravely wrong with the twenty-one-year-old hero. It was said that he made a habit of arranging a large number of women's shoes in a semi-circle around himself in his room because he "liked to look at them." He also seemed to have taken an intense dislike to the game of chess, and after a spectacular career that had lasted no more than eighteen months, he never again played a serious match. Jones speculates that Morphy needed desperately to believe that his mastery at chess was an innocent pastime, and that Staunton's behavior shattered that belief and shattered him. For the rest of his life, he forbade the subject of chess to be mentioned in his presence.

Morphy went back to New Orleans, where he lived with his widowed mother and tried to establish himself as a lawyer, but the outbreak of the Civil War soon disrupted that. Federal troops captured the city. Morphy escaped to Cuba, then to Paris, and then, toward the end of the war, he drifted back to New Orleans. He became obsessed with the idea that his brother-in-law had defrauded him of part of his father's estate. He challenged his enemy to a duel, then engaged in long and fruitless litigation. He said that people were trying to poison his food. For two decades, he emerged from his mother's house at noon every day and walked alone on Canal Street, always a fashionable figure, swinging a cane, talking to himself, sometimes smiling as he spoke. Every evening, mad, he went to the opera. His mother found him dead in his bathtub one summer morning in 1884, apparently struck down, like his father, by apoplexy. So ended, according to the *New York Times* obituary, the years in which "he passed his useless life away unmolested and unmolesting."

King Laius never had a daughter, so far as I know, but there is no reason why the trials of young Oedipus should be limited to sons. I know a woman, for example, who, because of the rituals of psychiatric interviews, will have to bear a pseudonym, so let us call her Nancy Chaucer. She is thirty-five, and rich, and after fifteen years of marriage, and two children, she got herself through law school and now works in Philadelphia for clients who can't afford to pay. She is a handsome woman, but she makes little effort to display her looks. Her brown hair is pulled straight back over her head. She likes to wear old sweaters, trousers, heavy shoes. She sits and sips a cup of tea while she talks.

"My mother lived in a convent for seven years [she says], and that was about the only happy home she had. So she ended up as a very self-controlled, anxious-to-please person who never really believed that she had a home, who was very scared that things would be taken out from under her. She was really a very frightened person, a nut, an absolute *nut!* And my father was sort of a nut, too, in a different way, very bad-tempered, and they increasingly didn't get along with each other, and I found myself choosing sides . . . My father was always photographing me, photographing and photographing me naked in the bathtub. Then there are pictures that I've seen of when I was about eleven years old and dressing for a dancing class—and he would come in to take pictures, and there's a photograph of me with a crinoline half on, which I was just dashing to get on because my father was coming in, and he would take a picture of me.

"Well, when I was about twelve, my father got tired of being a mere voyeur, so he started giving me driving lessons. My hands would be on the steering wheel, leaving his hands free to—to investigate the insides of my underpants. And I didn't—I loved it. I really loved it. But I knew it was wrong, and he made it very clear that he was pretending not to be doing what he was doing. He said initially that—uh—he wanted me to know what—I would soon be going out with boys, and he wanted me to know what they would be after, or how to protect myself from them. So the initiation to sex was that it had better not exist. It did exist, but it had better not exist. And I finally said no to him, after about four times or something.

"When I was in college, my father got sick. He had a stroke. So I transferred from Smith to Bryn Mawr so that I could be at home. But that almost drove me out of my mind, because my father could no longer speak or understand language in any way. He was bottled up and very frustrated. He'd get up and he'd smash a chair down, or something like that, and my mother would quake and go white, and stand gallantly still in the same place she'd been two minutes before, and not move and not scream but just slowly choke to death. And I learned that the appropriate behavior in times of crisis is to just slowly choke to death.

"At Bryn Mawr I had Charley's sister in my class, and she wanted me to distract her brother, because he was going out with somebody *inappropriate,* and her mother was getting high blood pressure. He was terribly nervous, terribly intellectual, but she introduced us and reintroduced us until we went out with each other. He only lived a few blocks away, so it was all very convenient. Charley started coming to our place for dinner every night, and we'd make a foursome of bridge or something. And on Saturday nights, Charley and I would take my father to watch the polo matches at the old armory on 10th Street. My father loved polo. He used to play. He used to play with Squadron B, and so it was Squadron B polo again. He just had a lovely time watching. And Charley and I could talk, and my father could not understand our conversation, and so we had complete privacy, and yet we were taking him out for the evening. It was like being with a duenna. I could talk to Charley for hours, and it was really a very good way of courting, actually, for someone as scared and puritannical as I was. So we got married, and then on our fifth anniversary, I was in a mental hospital."

It seems a classic triangle, somewhat more common in its consummation than the one that matched Oedipus and Jocasta. "She used to come in my bed every morning, sometimes she'd sleep in my bed . . ." Devereux Warren confessed to the psychiatrist who was trying to treat his demented daughter, Nicole Diver, in Scott Fitzgerald's *Tender Is the Night.*

> Whenever we went places in an automobile or a train we used to hold hands. . . . People used to say what a wonderful father and daughter we were. . . . We were just like lovers—and then all at once we were lovers—and ten minutes after it happened I could have shot myself—except I guess I'm such a Goddamned degenerate I didn't have the nerve to do it.

As for Nicole, according to her father, "she seemed to freeze up right away. She'd just say, 'Never mind, never mind, Daddy. It doesn't matter.'"

Even when nothing happens, though, it obviously does matter. We shall never know exactly what inspired Sylvia Plath's morbid hatred of her father, an apparently harmless apiarist and professor of biology at Boston University, who died when his angry daughter was only eight, and yet she was still shrieking at him more than two decades later, that he was a "vampire who . . . drank my blood for a year,/ Seven years if you want to know./ Daddy, you can lie back now./ There's a stake in your fat black heart/ And the villagers never liked you. They are dancing and stamping on you . . ./ Daddy, Daddy, you bastard, I'm through."

The study of how parents drive their children crazy has by now become a whole new subcategory in the field of psychiatry, and among those responsible for this development, nobody has been more influential or more vehement than Ronald David Laing.

> The family's function is to repress Eros [he wrote in *The Politics of Experience*], to induce a false consciousness of security; to deny life by avoiding life; to cut off transcendence; to believe in God, not to experience the Void; to create, in short, one-dimensional man; to promote respect, conformity, obedience, to con children out of play; to induce a fear of failure; to promote a respect for work; to promote a respect for "respectability."

Despite Laing's celebrity during the past few years, we still know remarkably little about the personal origins of those fierce views of family life, about Laing's parents, his two wives, his seven children. One interviewer who pressed him for details received a characteristically Laingian response: "I don't think it will really harm you not to have that kind of information, do you?" He was born in 1927, an only child in a lower-middle-class family, at the edge of the slum district of Glasgow. He seems, according to his description in *The Bird of Paradise*, to have disliked his surroundings intensely—"Flaking plaster. Broken window panes. The smell of slum tenements. . . . Impregnated with stale beer, vomit, fish and chips. . . . The acres and acres of mock parquet linoleum. . . . The respectability. O the respectability."

The only child sat in the living room and read such approved texts as Darwin and Voltaire, and practiced on the piano. There was even some thought of his becoming a professional musician. He attended state schools, and then the University of Glasgow. At some point, he began developing asthma. Like Freud, he was rather more interested in philosophy than in treating the sick, but he received a medical degree in 1951, then served two years in the Army, then got a job in the Glasgow Royal Mental Hospital. There, with characteristic indifference to the traditional rules, he decided to live in the "intractable ward" of the women's wing, "to find out how it felt to be an inmate." This decision dismayed not only the staff but also the patients. "My first night on the ward," Laing later recalled, "I was attacked by women from all sides, trying to pull off my pants. I can't imagine what they thought they were trying to do."

Laing was already at work on the theory that the erratic behavior of schizophrenics is caused at least partly by the harsh and uncomprehending way they are treated. He took twelve of the most severely afflicted patients, escorted them every day to a pleasant room in another part of the hospital, and let them do whatever they pleased. "After eighteen months all my patients had been released back to their families—because they seemed a lot better. And a year later, they were all back again. Naturally! Nobody in those days thought in terms of the *family* in relation to schizophrenia. I was very angry on lots of counts. . . ."

Laing's experiments strengthened his belief that people who had been labeled as schizophrenics were generally victims of a social effort, generally by their families, to prevent them from growing up or even becoming alive, and that their efforts to live were either ignored or misunderstood as symptoms of illness. In his first book, *The Divided Self* (1960), he spoke of his subjects as "people who experience themselves as automata, as robots, as bits of machinery, or even as animals. Such persons are rightly regarded as crazy. Yet why do we not regard a theory that seeks to transmute persons into automata or animals as equally crazy?" At the end of *The Divided Self*, Laing analyzed the case of a girl called Julie, who seemed to think at times that she was her own mother, and who wanted to tell the police that "a child has been murdered." Julie's doting mother was appalled not only at Julie's demented vision of her as a murderess but at the whole idea of a breakdown in a child whom she had always considered a model of good behavior. "One is certainly often told by parents of schizophrenics," Laing observed, "of how proud they were of their children because of their precocious crawling, walking, bowel and bladder function, talking, giving up crying, and so on. One has to ask, however . . . how much of the infant's behavior is an expression of its own will. . . . A really alive baby is demanding, is a trouble, and by no means always does what she is told."

Once Laing had demonstrated that schizophrenia might be less a disease than a label for parental mistreatment of children, he proceeded, in collaboration with Aaron Esterson, to mobilize the evidence in *Sanity, Madness and the Family.* "We do not accept 'schizophrenia' as being a biochemical, neurophysical, psychological fact," they wrote, "and we regard it as palpable error, in the present state of the evidence, to take it to be a fact. Nor do we assume its existence. Nor do we adopt it as a hypothesis. . . ." *Sanity, Madness and the Family* consists of eleven case histories, each of which begins with a clinical record of insane behavior and then sets out to explain how and why the schizophrenic was rather accurately describing a rather understandable view of the world.

Maya Abbott, for instance, thought that her father was trying to poison her, and, according to psychiatric jargon, "was depersonalized, showed signs of catatonia; exhibited affective impoverishment and autistic withdrawal." The most elementary questioning disclosed that the Abbotts didn't want their daughter to grow up, and that they interpreted each sign of adolescent independence as a sign of "illness." As Mrs. Abbott put it, "Since she's ill, she's never accepted anything [I said] any more. She's had to reason it out for herself." Sarah Danzig, similarly, was diagnosed as schizophrenic, because at the age of seventeen she began to stay up late at night, reading the Bible. Her mother was dismayed at Sarah for "sitting up all night thinking and not telling anyone what she thought. Not that we particularly want to know . . . although it's only natural that a mother should be curious. . . . She's thinking and thinking—goodness knows what the heck she's thinking about. It's enough to twist anybody's mind." Even June Field, aged fifteen, who entered the hospital in a catatonic stupor and suffered from "bizarre delusions—e.g., that she was . . . liable to be tortured"—turned out to have been born with a dislocated hip and to have spent most of her infancy limping in a steel brace.

The anonymous stories fall almost too easily into place, demonstrating over and over again the thesis that Laing and Esterson announced at the beginning. Each case involves a girl, almost invariably reared in a staid and stolid household (no smoking on the Sabbath at the Danzigs, for example) by parents of suffocating respectability, the traditional English respectability that ignores or denies all unpleasantness. Each of the girls then suffers, inarticulate, uncomprehending, a certain kind of destiny: she does not know what her parents want of her. Or she gets conflicting and contradictory messages from her parents as to what they want ("mystification," Laing calls this). Or, worst of all, she comes to believe, rightly or wrongly, but probably rightly, that her parents want her not to be herself, not even to exist. In the confused years of adolescence, therefore, the girls go crazy, for only thus can they win the approval of their parents, who tacitly encourage and then misinterpret all the "symptoms" of "schizophrenia."

These are interesting theories, and they do indicate that, despite Freud's pessimism, schizophrenics can be reached, understood. But do they actually cure anyone afflicted with madness? Every doctor must have his lab, every guerrilla chieftain his command post, every guru his ashram, and by the middle 1960's Laing had established himself in a three-story brick fortress called Kingsley Hall, in the dreary East End of London. The place had a splendid tradition of spiritual uplift—a blue-and-white plaque still celebrates the fact that Mahatma Gandhi slept here on a straw mat in 1931 when he came to England on an unsuccessful mission to negotiate for India's independence (he also kept a goat in his rooftop cell to provide him with sustenance).

Kingsley Hall was a sort of commune, with its own gardens, its own birdbath, its own regulation that there be no regulations. Officially, the doctors were not doctors, the patients were not patients. According to an account by one of the more idealistic residents, Dr. Joseph Berke, dinners began at nine-thirty as social festivities and lasted until midnight and beyond.

> Twenty people sat around a table garlanded with flowers and illumined by four white candles atop a tree-trunk candelabra. . . . Loaves of bread and bottles of red wine crowded platters of vegetables and meat and fruit. . . . Ronnie [Laing] would expound on philosophy, psychology . . . religion, mysticism, and many other subjects as well. It was a delight to listen to him. . . . He could step inside a work of art, whether by Freud, Heidegger, Sartre, Beethoven, Bartok or whoever, and convey the key notes more simply, directly and eloquently than the master himself. . . . The majority of the community, and visitors, were

not medical [men but] artists, writers, actors or dancers [who came] to demonstrate their wares at the poetry readings, film shows, music and dance recitals, and art exhibitions which took place in the big hall downstairs.

To its admirers, Kingsley Hall was a kind of Utopia, an asylum in the original meaning of the word, a haven where one could live through a mental breakdown without repressions or restraints and then, according to Laingian theory, emerge at the other end. Others took a darker view of the place. The neighborhood children smashed the windows and smeared feces on the walls (as the patients, or nonpatients, sometimes did). It may have seemed perfectly natural for an idealistic group of psychiatrists and psychiatric patients to establish their therapeutic community in a slum district, but it was probably equally natural for the slum dwellers to hate them with a particular ferocity. Time and again, the exasperated constables had to be summoned to investigate complaints from one side or the other.

R. D. Laing's writings became more feverish. Having once argued that normal people could and should understand the abnormal, he now proclaimed that "normal men have killed perhaps 100,000,000 of their fellow normal men in the last fifty years," and that "we are all murderers and prostitutes . . . no matter how normal, moral, or mature we take ourselves to be." He attempted a weird series of impressionistic indictments: "There presides over America a female effete laughing Buddha . . . compounded of some cosmic muck. . . . Millions of men fall on her to fuck away her unspeakable and insatiable obscene itch." And having decreed that "we are bemused and crazed creatures, strangers to our true selves," he began to sing the praises of madness itself: "If I could turn you on, if I could drive you out of your wretched mind, if I could tell you I would let you know."

Back at Kingsley Hall, however, Laing eventually found the ceaseless importunities of his nonpatients something of a nuisance. He moved out of the commune, to a more respectable neighborhood. So did a number of other doctors. The nonpatients held lots of meetings on how Kingsley Hall should be run, but the philosophy of communal living is not one that everybody can carry out. In the later years of Kingsley Hall, a visitor knocked on the door and was dismayed to find the stairway littered with trash, the kitchen overflowing with dirty dishes. In 1970, after only five years of Utopia, the Kingsley Hall Association, which had been created at the turn of the century by the two idealistic spinster sisters who owned the place, did not renew the lease. Dr. Laing, who had recently been talking mainly about Yoga and LSD and the Seven-Fold Path, began packing for one of those voyages of discovery to the Orient. One young interviewer pursued him to his apartment in Belsize Park Gardens to get a few last quotations and found the master rolling around on the floor with his three-year-old son Adam. The infant Natasha was asleep in another room. While Laing talked on and on about the road to revelation, young Adam Laing made his contribution by urinating on the floor. Just like young Sigmund Freud. Just like Alekhine, the chess champion. Ronald David Laing laughed cheerfully while his second wife cleaned up the mess.

"Why I Want to Bite R. D. Laing" was the title of an article in *Harper's* in April of 1974. The author was Kurt Vonnegut's oldest son, Mark, who has suffered, in his own words, "three major breakdowns and a few minor ones." Having been diagnosed as schizophrenic, the younger Vonnegut wrote with some irritation about Laing's exalted view of the condition.

> He's said so many nice things about us: we're the only sane members of an insane society, our insights are profound and right on, we're prophetic, courageous explorers of inner space, and so forth. . . . It would be nice to be able to hang something as destructive and wasteful as schiz on the alienation and materialism of modern life, to have all that pain be noble and poetic instead of senseless and useless. . . . But what I felt when I found myself staring out of the little hole in the padded cell was betrayal. "I did everything just like you said, and look where I am now, you bastard."

Now twenty-seven and a premedical student at the University of Massachusetts, Mark Vonnegut turns out to be a slender youth with rather long brown hair, a dark-blue cable-stitch sweater, red jogging shoes, and a tale to tell (he has already written a 1,400-page book entitled *The Eden Express,* which was published in the fall of 1975). He finished Swarthmore in 1969 and then began drifting across the country, picking up friends as he went. He ended in a valley about a hundred miles north of Vancouver, where he bought some land, built a house, and organized a commune. It was, according to the standards of the day, a kind of Utopia. "I had a woman with me," Mark Vonnegut recalls, "a woman and a dog and a Volkswagen. It was sort of a nuclear family, I had fled every kind of stress. I was out in the woods. No cops, no Fascists within fifteen miles, no Nixon, no nothing."

Into this Utopia came the lapping waves of madness that Vonnegut had sensed intermittently since childhood.

"First, you know, it's like a stream, or some sound" he recalls. "Then there might be something else there. Sometimes it's just Morse Code, and you start playing with these rhythms and letting the rhythms play with your body, and then—*yeah!*—and it starts working, and then you start fitting it into calculus, or fitting it into wherever the keys are on the typewriter, and you start—damn it, you start getting words out of it. It starts with something you have to decode, but after a while, you don't need the codes any more, and you just listen and hear it. And you know, I'd be talking with people I needed to talk to but who weren't there, and getting important information. . . ."

Vonnegut believed, at this point, that there was a great cosmic battle under way between good and evil, and that he could help the forces for good by slipping into insanity. As he puts it,

"When I was terrified, there was nothing reasonable to be that terrified of, so I had to think the devil was taking over. Or, you know, the earth was about to die—something horrible was happening ecologically, and there simply wasn't going to be enough oxygen to go around for much longer. But if I could help turn things around, then the earth would be cleansed of evil, everybody would get saved, everybody would get free of all sorts of—all their inner troubles and everything else. And one of the feelings that I had very much was that a lot of people I loved were in trouble, and didn't know how to deal with these things, and I did, because of my experience, and I realized that this sort of necessitated my giving up being able to function in the real world, being able to take care of myself in any normal way."

He came, finally, to accusing and even threatening God.

"I said, you know, 'You can put me through hell for millennia, fucker, but if you mess around with these people, you're in trouble. . . .' I said, 'Look, cocksucker, you know that some day somebody bigger than you is going to come, and he's going to be on my side. . . .'"

Vonnegut's friends eventually took him down into Vancouver —"this trip was incredible, things exploding, the sun exploding, time warps, people changing in front of me, finally people dying all around"—and in Vancouver, they took him to some guru— "he was bad, he was just plain bad, bad; if there are evil people, he was an evil person"—and then there was compulsive violence.

"I started doing a little property damage here and there, a couple of hundred bucks' worth of glass. Rocks mostly. I remember very clearly thinking about this rock that was very symbolic of something. The air didn't smell like it used to smell. Things didn't look like, you know—air looked like liquid to me. It just looked like there was this fog. More than fog—it was just awful, like gas fumes, like heat waves, and everything warping. It was all a gamble. So okay, at this point, you and these people around you can survive if we all isolate ourselves from the rest of humanity, but it's a long, long, long shot, so I said, 'Fuck the long shot,' and I smashed the window, and let whatever was out there in, so humanity would all be together. . . ."

They took Vonnegut to the Hollywood Hospital in New Westminster, just outside Vancouver, but he soon talked his way out ("I had learned how to manipulate liberals"), and so he was back on his commune when a young man named Paul "showed up out of nowhere" and challenged him to a game of chess. Vonnegut is proud of his ability as a chess player. His father had taught him the game, and he defeated his teacher at the age of seven, and ever since then, "I've generally been, in a very casual way, the chess champion of wherever I've been." The newcomer at Vonnegut's commune was a formidable challenger, however. He won the first game.

"He had this very drawn, very unfriendly looking face, Vonnegut recalls. "Everything was wrong about him. Blue eyes, which was—you know, for a while, when I was crazy, I thought I was black, or at least not white, or something. Much of this is traceable to childhood stuff, I guess. When I was eleven, my family adopted all my first cousins, because their parents had died, and these cousins were mostly blond, blue-eyed, All-American kids. Especially the oldest, who was the blondest and bluest-eyed, and who gave me a hell of a lot of shit. So, blue-eyed people!

"Anyway, in the second game, I played very good chess, and I nailed him. And I was really amazed, because I'd become convinced that he was really Paul Morphy, resurrected. Morphy was my favorite chess player, for lots of reasons. I thought my father had a lot to do with my going crazy, that he'd sort of asked me to do it, and I thought that this was my father's gift to me, that he'd resurrected Paul Morphy and sent him to me, out in Vancouver.

"So I thought, okay, that was nice, and we each won one, so let's— And then there was this voice saying, 'Of course, we've got to play another.' And then my mind really started fogging. Stopped paying attention to the board or anything else. I was just getting through the game, just barely, and I'd go here or there, and I'd get moves from the fire in the fireplace, and I'd get moves from the wind outside. I was playing, by the way, on a chessboard that my grandfather had given me. My grandfather was an excellent craftsman, made beautiful chessboards, and this one had inlaid on it, on one side, 'I do warn you well; this is no child's play.' This was a board that he'd given me after I'd beaten him, so it meant a lot to me, the board. And I kept looking at it and thinking, Oh, shit!

"Anyway, this third game, it seemed to me that the pieces were all moved—I didn't remember the situation—I was just struggling along, struggling along. And then out of the fog, this voice came and said, 'Concede. Your position is hopeless.' But then I heard another voice that said, 'It's a draw. You can keep him in perpetual check.' I couldn't see that, and I could hardly talk, and I don't know what that voice was, but I said, 'It's a draw. I can keep you in perpetual check.' And he said, 'What?' And I couldn't argue it, so I just said, 'Check!' and, you know, he moved, and check, and he moved, and check, and so on. So I guess I played Paul Morphy to a draw."

"I had a classic childhood. I was afraid of my father and in love with my mother. The older children were grown up when I was born, and my crib was in my parents' bedroom, and I think that cut down on my father's love life. Then my father would be angry when my mother would take me to bed with her. . . ."

The speaker is Seymour Krim, a tall, heavy man, just past fifty. He has a gray-streaked beard, and he wears green-and-yellow-striped suspenders over his checkered shirt. Once he wanted to be a novelist, a "serious" novelist, a "major" novelist, but somehow he never got a novel finished and published. Instead, he has produced a lot of articles and essays and book reviews, and he now considers himself a founder of the so-called New Journalism. He is pleased that his work has won the praise of such notables as James Baldwin and William Styron, and that Norman Mailer has written of him: "Krim in his honest garish sober grim surface is a child of our time. I think sometimes, as a matter of style, he is *the* child of our time, he is New York in the middle of the 20th Century." Now, in New York in almost the last quarter of the century, it is raining heavily, and a dog barks frantically from some alcove of East 10th Street, and Seymour Krim, trying to remember his family, waves an exasperated arm toward the rafia-hung window and shouts at the invisible dog, "Shut up!"

Seymour Krim's father came from the Crimea as a young man and flung himself into the commercial battles of turn-of-the-century New York. In due time, he and his brother became the operators of a prosperous chain of cafeterias, the Hanover Cafeterias, but the chain was not strong enough to fight Horn & Hardart. At the onset of the Depression, in 1930, Krim died of a heart attack. His wife fell into such a state of despondency that she had to enter a sanitarium. It was not her first such crisis. She had had a breakdown when her first child was born, in 1913, and another after her fourth, Seymour, in 1922. Mrs. Krim was apparently considered well enough to be released from the sanitarium, but when she came home, according to her son's recollection, "she threatened to kill herself, and lo and behold she did kill herself."

Of the four orphaned children (Seymour was then nine, and the manner of his mother's death was kept secret from him), the one who reacted most strangely was the second of the three boys, Herbert. "Within ten minutes after my mother jumped off the roof he phoned the *Daily News* to report a suicide and to offer himself as a photographer. He was playing newspaperman at the time. He was by then a semiprofessional photographer, but he also wanted to be a saxophone player, and he had various other enthusiasms, but he wasn't able to support himself. He was heavy-set and something of a bully, and he used to beat up my older brother, Norman, who was the brilliant one. When I was thirteen or fourteen, and Herbert was in his twenties, he had the first of a series of—not breakdowns but very unruly public behavior. He used to live in rooming houses and hotels, and he would make scenes, accuse them of cheating him. He was finally put into Rockland State Hospital. Then he came out again. Then he was put back in. And when I was in my twenties, they wanted to do a lobotomy on Herbert. That was the period when they were doing lobotomies. My brother Norman and I had to cosign the paper permitting the operation. Herbert pleaded with us not to let them do it, but the psychiatrist convinced us that it was the necessary thing. And Herbert died of a hemorrhage on the operating table."

It is impossible to tell exactly what effect these experiences had on Krim. His early years of independence were not particularly unconventional—the University of North Carolina, a wartime job with the Office of War Information, then starting to write in Greenwich Village—but a sense of pressure was building up. "I felt, like so many people in this city, harassed and reduced by the multitude of city life, the terrible money worries, the fact that you're a cipher in the middle of so many people and automobiles and all that shit, you know—that I was being reduced, leveled, made insignificant."

There is always a breaking point, and in this case it occurred when the orphaned Krim was scolded by an elderly woman, a rabbi's widow, who lived in the apartment beneath him. Every time that Krim would write at night, the rabbi's widow would take her cane and tap against the ceiling. Tap-tap-tap from Krim's typewriter, reviewing some new novel for *Commonweal* or *The Hudson Review*. Tap-tap-tap from the rabbi's widow, telling him to cease and desist. "One night she started tapping," says Krim, "and I became enraged. I took about a hundred or maybe two hundred books out of the bookcase, these marvelous books that my friend had left behind in his apartment, and I just began flinging them on the floor—like *this*—in answer to her. One at a time. One after another. She stopped tapping, and there was a total silence downstairs, but I went on for about an hour, throwing these books on the floor. When I had finished, at about midnight, I felt very good. Felt indifferent to all my fears. I remember leaving the house, leaving the doors open, and I don't think I ever went back.

"I went to the apartment of a girl I had been seeing. The relations between us were not that good. She had two children, and she wanted to get married, but I was not interested in the responsibilities of marriage, so she had taken up with a guy who made his living as a translator. So I went to see her and bawl her out and take her away from this translator, and then I ended up by hitting her with a child's Little League baseball bat. She ducked her head, and I caught her on the shoulder, and then she slammed the door and locked me out.

"Then I went to a jazz club. I was what I think they call manic. Very revved up. Very excited. Very sure of myself. I felt like God—or not like God but like a representative of God. At the jazz club—it may have been The Open Door—I bought drinks for all the musicians, and then when it came time to pay, I didn't have any money. They went through the usual routine of threatening to call the cops, but I was very cool about it. I told them that if they wanted something as paltry as money—I think I'd run up a bill of about $18—I would get it for them the next day. And they let me walk out. Which confirmed to me that I was in a—a superior position.

"I think I slept—it must have been summertime—I think I took a nap on a bench in Washington Square Park, but then I was off and running again. I would walk through the streets—I don't remember the actual sequence. day by day, but this was all within a period of about a week—I would walk through the streets, and when the traffic came, I would hold up my hand like a prophet, and the cars would stop—at least I didn't get clipped. So I felt that I could do whatever I wanted, anything. I went to visit some friends who lived in Peter Cooper Village, and they weren't home, but they had a babysitter who I thought was kind of cute. And I exposed myself. Took my joint out. I apparently wanted some sex, but even more I wanted the enjoyment of her looking at me, with what I had in my hand. She got very frightened and called the police. I was very patronizing to her, and to the idea of calling the police. I mean, you don't do that to Jesus Christ, or Seymour, but nevertheless I had enough common sense to leave before the police got there.

"Then I wanted to go to a very warm place, so I sold some stocks and bonds and went to Cuba. This was the year before Castro. Havana was still corrupt, and lush, and I drank a lot, and screwed some whores. And I also decided that I wanted to go out and see Hemingway. Papa Hemingway. I had written a review of *The Old Man and the Sea* when it first came out, quite a snotty review, saying that he should hang up his gloves, but he always told people that he didn't read reviews, so I didn't think about that. I didn't even telephone in advance—Jesus doesn't telephone, he just appears. Hemingway lived eighteen miles outside of Havana, and I took a bus from my hotel, and then I walked. And I wasn't wearing any shoes. That was part of my rebellion. I went up to the house. I knocked on the door. And this character came to the door, wearing a pair of khaki shorts, big torso, skinny legs. And I said, 'Mr. Hemingway, my name is Seymour Krim, and I—' And he said 'I know who you are, and you don't know a fucking thing about writing.' And he slammed the door in my face.

"So I walked down the hill again, and then I thought, 'Screw it! I came walking all this way, and I want to see him.' So I walked back up the hill. And he was by this time intrigued or amused, or I'd interrupted his work, so he came out and shouted at me, with fairly good nature, 'You're a *persistent* bastard, aren't you?' I felt proud, and I said, 'Yes.' So he opened the door, and we went inside. I don't really remember the substance of the discussion inside the house—I had electric shock treatments not long afterward and that wipes out part of your memory—but within an hour, I was more or less bodily thrown out. As I say, I don't remember the details, but there was another man there, a fishing buddy of Hemingway's, and somebody told me several years later that this man said I had taken a swing at Hemingway. Which I doubt. I don't remember taking a swing, but maybe I threatened to. That would fit with my new brand of fearlessness.

"Anyway, I was thrown out. And then the embassy became aware of my behavior—this lunatic American walking around without shoes, urinating at will on the streets, calling out and telling people that I was the representative of the Big Fellow upstairs. They called my brother Norman, and he came down and corralled me and flew me back to New York. He gave me a blank check to go and see a psychiatrist, but I just continued my wanderings. I'd walk into restaurants and clubs and never pay. I even rented a suite for myself at the Sherry-Netherland Hotel. And one of the odd things about this time is that I suddenly smelled differently. It was some strange, chemical, definite, physical thing, which I didn't dream up. It was a smell something like burning rubber. It smelled as if my mind was smoking, going so hard that there was some kind of friction. Anyway, the Sherry-Netherland finally wanted some money, and I gave them my usual speech about money being unimportant. This time they joined forces with my brother and my best friend and called the cops, and the cops gently put me in handcuffs and took me to Bellevue."

When Ernest Hemingway himself finally came to the end, stricken by illnesses real and imaginary, pursued by phantom agents of a phantom police state, he must have thought back on the hawknosed, black-bearded figure of Dr. Clarence Edmonds Hemingway, dead more than thirty years from a .32-caliber revolver bullet behind the right ear. Dr. Hemingway had tried to be a good father, of the traditional sort. He took his son into the woods and taught him how to shoot pheasants and raccoons, how to tie trout flies, how to build a shelter out of pine branches, how, in short, to fend for oneself and to survive. As early as the age of two, according to the boy's mother, "when asked what he is afraid of, he shouts *fraid a nothing* with great gusto."

It was a stern household. Attendance at church was compulsory, no games were allowed on the Sabbath, and violations of the rules were punished with a razor strop. But Dr. Hemingway seems to have cared deeply about his six children. He even did much of the marketing and cooking, because his wife fancied herself an opera singer *manquée,* and when young Ernest reached his sixteenth birthday, Dr. Hemingway wrote him a letter saying, "I am so pleased and proud you have grown to be such a fine big manly fellow and trust your development will continue symmetrical and in harmony with our highest Christian ideals."

There were darknesses, though. Hemingway was given a shotgun, and he recalled later that sometimes, when he had been punished for some infraction, he would retire to the tool shed that commanded a view of the tomato patch in the back yard, and there, while Dr. Hemingway hoed the tomatoes, young Ernest would secretly aim his shotgun at his father's head. When Ernest set off for his first job on the *Kansas City Star,* his father accompanied him to the station and remained on the platform until the train left. Hemingway re-created the scene in *For Whom the Bell Tolls* and re-created it with all the embarrassed falsification of adolescence—he "felt suddenly so much older than his father and so sorry for him that he could hardly bear it."

Hemingway portrayed his parents rather ambiguously in *In Our Time,* notably in "Indian Camp" and "The Doctor and the Doctor's Wife." The doctor seems somewhat remote, but then many of Hemingway's early characters are remote, and the young Nick Adams appears devoted to his taciturn father. Dr. Hemingway and his wife responded to their son's early fiction with complete incomprehension. "Trust you will see and describe more of humanity of a different character in future volumes," Dr. Hemingway wrote. "The brutal you have surely shown the world. Look for the joyous, uplifting, and optimistic and spiritual in character. It is present if found. Remember God holds us each responsible to do our best." Mrs. Hemingway was more tart about *The Sun Also Rises,* referring to it as "one of the filthiest books of the year." She said she wanted to "help you find yourself," and she wondered whether alcohol might be responsible for his depravity. "I love you, dear," she wrote, "and still believe you will do something worthwhile. Try to find Him and your real work. God bless you."

It is not quite clear what destroyed these upright and self-assured people. The more-or-less official biography by Carlos

Baker (*Ernest Hemingway, A Life Story*) refers guardedly to Mrs. Hemingway suffering, as early as 1920, "from emotional difficulties, which she was trying to overcome with a course in manual training." (She lived on, in fact, until 1951.) Dr. Hemingway developed heart trouble and diabetes, and he worried about some questionable investments he had made in Florida real estate. For whatever reasons, one day just before Christmas in 1928, he went down into the cellar and burned some personal papers in the furnace, then shut himself up in his second-floor bedroom, took out his own father's Smith and Wesson revolver, and shot himself. Hemingway, who was not there at the time, subsequently wrote a passionate excoriation of any man who would leave a mess of gore for other people to clean up. " 'He was just a coward,' " Robert Jordan reflected on his father's suicide in *For Whom the Bell Tolls*. "He understood his father and he forgave him everything and he pitied him, but he was ashamed of him."

Easily said, all those things, the forgiveness as glib as the understanding. Oedipus is called upon to do many things, but not to forgive, or to be ashamed. Dr. Hemingway's son may have been slowly going mad all his life—certainly the eccentricities were all there, the manic role-playing and self-delusion, the half-repressed violence, the Munchausen sense of his own heroism— and yet as late as his sixtieth birthday, in 1959, he seemed to be in control of his life, and enjoying it. He was racketing around Spain, following the *mano a manos* between Luis Miguel Dominguin and Antonio Ordonez, and writing his elaborate analyses of the struggle for *Life*. Within a year, everything was gone. His eyes hurt so much that he couldn't read. His kidneys kept him awake at night. He barely managed to finish *The Dangerous Summer*, but it was four times too long, and he couldn't figure out—he, the celebrated master of brevity and precision, couldn't figure out how to condense it. And when he tried to write his Paris memoirs (*A Moveable Feast*), he came near to hysteria. "Hotch, I can't finish this book," he burst out to his protégé and confidant, A. E. Hotchner. "I *can't*. I've been at this goddam worktable all day, standing here all day, all I've got to get is this one thing, maybe only a sentence, maybe more, I don't know, and I can't get it. Not any of it. You understand, *I can't*."

He was convinced that the F.B.I. was pursuing him. "It's the worst hell," he told Hotchner. "The goddamndest hell. They've bugged everything. . . . Can't use the phone. Mail intercepted." He even suspected his best friends ("Keep your eye on all of them. Especially Bill. . . . He missed killing me the first time and he's waiting for another opening"). He began talking of killing himself. He was found several times standing beside his gun rack, weapon in hand, brooding over the view of the Wyoming mountains. He even tried once to walk into the whirling propeller of a parked airplane. And so he was taken to the Mayo Clinic and given a series of electric shock treatments. The treatments further angered and frightened him. "What these shock doctors don't know is about writers and such things as remorse and contrition and what they do to them. . . . What is the sense of ruining my head and erasing my memory, which is my capital, and putting me out of business? It was a brilliant cure, but we lost the patient." Just a month before Hemingway finally did fire a shotgun into his head, Hotchner forced himself to ask, "Why do you want to kill yourself?" Hemingway said, "What do you think happens to a man going on sixty-two when he realizes that he can never write the books and stories he promised himself? Or do any of the other things he promised himself in the good days? If I can't exist on my terms, then existence is impossible. Do you understand?"

Not long after the phantasmagorical chess match with Paul Morphy, Mark Vonnegut was walking with some friends in the Canadian woods, and he became annoyed by one of the friends describing Kurt Vonnegut as the greatest writer of the day. Drifting into fantasy, Mark suddenly began to have a conversation with his father. He still doesn't know whether this conversation took place entirely inside his head, or whether he spoke one or both parts aloud, but he remembers the dialogue clearly.

"My father said, 'Hey, Mark! Do you think maybe I'm writing this whole scene?' And I said, 'Dad, did you ever think maybe you're not?'

"And he said, 'Now, seriously, Mark, tell me, do you think I'm a good enough writer to have written all this?'

" ' Well, frankly not, Dad. I mean, you know, you're good, a hell of an entertainer, but there are guys who are better.'

" 'Well, I guess that's true.'

" 'There were guys who could really write extraordinarily, like Tolstoy and Dostoevsky.' And then I said, 'Hey, guess what your liberal-arts-college-educated son picked up for light reading fresh out of the nuthouse?'

"And he says, 'Whatcha got?'

"So I pulled *The Brothers Karamazov* out of my hip pocket.

"So he says, 'Oh, Jesus, was that ever a mistake, but such a pretty one, Mark. So for all the nasty things I've done to you, I'd like to do something nice. Just let the book fall open.'

"So I let the book fall open, and there was this phrase glowing in absolute orange. It said, 'The end of the world will be marked by acts of unfathomable compassion.' It was so beautiful, so perfect, and then I started laughing.

"And he said, 'What's so funny, Mark?'

"And I said, 'I'm sorry, Dad, but I just can't help thinking what horseshit I would have got if I'd had *Cat's Cradle.*'

"And he said, 'Well, that's all right,' And then he says, 'There's one thing I want to ask you about.'

" 'Okay, fire away, Pop.'

"And he says, 'How'd you get here?'

"And I say, 'I thought that was the one thing you knew. I picked it up from you.'

"And he says, 'What is it?'

"And I say, 'Never turn down an invitation.' "

Out of a Case History:
Charles Mingus III
Seeks Martyrdom

Charles Mingus, Jr., a large and passionate man, and one of the great jazz bass players, is famous for his battles. He once went after Duke Ellington's arranger with a fireman's ax. But finally, after years of search that ranged from the music of Bartok to the Tibetan Book of the Dead, he felt a profound exhaustion. "I was sped up, tired out. I couldn't think who I was," he recalled later. "I was like a child lost with people milling around me and no one to love me. My brain was like a crazy TV set flicking picture stories. . . . Anyway, I kept walking east on Fifty-first Street and turned down on First Avenue. I guess I knew where I was going . . . the gates of Bellevue Hospital. There was a guy in a sort of booth or sentry box and I went to him and asked him how to get in. . . . He said, 'This is no rest home, this is a place for the mentally disturbed.' 'Look, man,' I said, 'I am mentally disturbed. I'm a musician, I need help. . . .'"

His son, Charles Mingus III, has never been to a mental hospital, but he has no hesitation in describing himself as a schizophrenic. He is now thirty, a painter who delights in the marbled patterns that emerge when a piece of paper is dipped into paint emulsions. He sees faces in the patterns and draws eyes and noses on them. He also likes to use a turntable that can produce infinite varieties of circles. One of his pictures is sold every year as a Christmas card at the Museum of Modern Art, and this earns him a small royalty, but he lives on almost nothing, in an unheated apartment in a condemned building in New York's East Village. He lives in old blue jeans and T-shirts, and he wanders around with his paintings and most of his possessions in a knapsack. He wears his hair in a long Afro. He takes alternating drinks of Scotch and beer, and when he starts talking, he is almost unstoppable.

117

The first crisis was an external crisis, where I had to make a decision between my father and my mother. They were having a fight. I was about two years old, and nobody believes that I remember that. But I remember that they were having barking words—*r-r-r-rah, r-r-r-rah, r-r-r-rah*. I wasn't aware of the language specifically. As I can remember, it was just a little person and a big person going back and forth, with the big person afraid and coming back heavier. I was standing up on the floor between the two of them and pushing them apart, and at one point I said, "Leave my Mommie alone," or some bullshit like that. And I bit my father. Not long after that, they got divorced.

Then we moved to another apartment outside Los Angeles, and then another—Monrovia, Duarte, the whole circuit—and I kept thinking, self-defense, self-defense, self-defense. When I was about seven years old, I ended up in a Catholic school, and I really got the treatment because I said the word "bull," not even "shit," not even knowing that "shit" followed "bull," right? The principal drags me from class into the office. I sit there bored—I mean, like looking at a fly's wings and counting the little veins in them, but unable to settle down and say, "Well, this is a punishment, and I'll get off, and it'll be done with." She takes me out in the hall—first time I'd ever been through the big hall with no kids in it. Holding me by my ears like a pig, you know, so that's when I really—the first time I actively, socially snapped. She's standing there, and my mother's coming up the street, and I saw this conspiracy of women. She's smiling, and my mother's smiling, and "What's going on?" and "Charlie's been a bad boy." And she yanks me by the ear, and her fingernails are pinching—I still feel it—and I just turned and clawed at her. She had one of those thin, twenties-type dresses with pearls, and the pearls went flying. It was all slow motion. Dress splayed open—she's standing there freaked, and a whole parade of kids are coming down the stairs, laughing, first at me, because I'm being held up by the ear, and then at her, because she's standing there with her dress ripped open.

Okay, then another trauma, in high school, was being black and being taken out of class and handcuffed and arrested. For molesting women. And I wasn't even around, because I was sick from morphine withdrawal. It was my grandmother's cancer medicine, and she had died, and there was this box, this high, in my mother's medicine chest, and it had little bottles in it, like Carter's Little Liver Pills, and it had a skull and crossbones on it, and it said, "Morphine. This medicine can be habit-forming." And *blah-blah-blah-blah*. And I started taking it. And when that ran out, I got into cough medicine, which was terpin hydrate with codeine added to it. Then after a few months, I just stopped, and then I passed out. So I'm lying home in bed, waking up with flashes, with the bed soaking wet, which was also a trauma, because you're not supposed to wet your bed.

About a week after that, I went back to school, and here come the guys, and they were saying, "That's the one." They did my ankles and wrists, and I was lying down in the station wagon, but I was mainly worried about what the charge was. They didn't explain what the charge was at all, ever. They put me in a cell, and some guy comes over and says, "Lovin' up your girl friend, huh?" That was all, and I just slept there in the cell, and the next day they released me, because somebody else had been identified. And back in school, the guy who was the perpetrator, the alleged perpetrator of this crime was there boasting about it. He didn't even look like me—scrawny, wiry, scruffy. He was a tough, punk kid, meaning he had bigger brothers who could back him up, but he was a year younger than me, so he never got arrested at all.

I didn't feel safe after that. The tough kids had the rule of the roost, and they were like a police force, a little Gestapo. But at the same time, I spent a lot of my teen-age years trying to scrutinize what authority was really up to, not just how they maintained their power, or what their power really was, or why they felt they had to exercise it, but really its weaknesses. After I was arrested, I went up to the principal during the lunch hour, and I started shouting at him, sort of cornering him against the wall, and the whole campus of kids joined in, sort of like a fence of people. I went through the racist routine, but it was all for effect, all to embarrass him and degrade him and make him feel some of the public shame because he'd never apologized to me for the arrest. He turned bright red and started to shake all over the place, and I realized that I could have killed him. I felt like a god; it was like a sort of Christ role, scourging them out of the temple or something. So the authority figure wasn't the one who won, it was the one who lost. The father, right?

In college, Pasadena City, I did pretty well in what I was doing, calligraphy and painting and sculpture, and I learned a lot about space and all that baloney. But I was also dealing in drugs a lot, and I kept overdosing and overdosing on pills until I completely couldn't get high on any quantity of ups and/or downs combined. So I stopped completely, to see what that would be like, and I flipped out. I remember I locked myself in a little room that was as wide as this little bit of rug here, and I was living in just one third of it. It had a little window, and in the morning, the birds would chirp. I opened the window and saw a blue sky and the birds flying by, but then I went back to my bed. It was like a prison cell. I put myself in this martyr's situation so that the deprivation would give me a deeper insight. It's hard to say if that was madness, but people treated me that way. They were delivering my food, washing my clothes, you know. I was beginning to feel like Buddha or something, and I was really high without anything at all. I remember sitting in a chair for days and days, and watching the curtains blow back and forth. And then they're moving me to a hospital. . . .

I didn't go back to college. I managed to get myself on a plane and flew off to New York. See, I had it all planned out. I'm going to go to New York to see my father. Great. I'll get this inner-direction thing, and I'll be able to go on my way. I'll have some way to be stronger than I am now. I had hardly seen him since I was a child, but he met me at the airport. He didn't hug me. He said, "I should hug you, probably." But he was into that state where, "Ah, why play the game?" His wife had just had a miscarriage, so he was even more into withdrawing from the social business. I didn't know what to do. I mean, I knew I had strengths and weaknesses and I didn't know how to manage them. I was trying to find something moral, you know, something higher than just laws and rules, something that could be transferred from him to me. But I guess I was embarrassing for him to be with. He took me to a loft that he had over on Third Avenue, not his apartment—she'd said, "He can't sleep here, he stinks." I didn't have a bath or something, right? To me, that was just letting go of the physical—I didn't care. But to him, that was like sloppy habits, you know. He thought I was a Communist radical creep, and that I didn't know what was what.

So I just sort of festered for a while. I mean, I really just dropped out of my consciousness and became a body. I was living in his loft, which consisted of a mattress, a dusty concrete floor with holes in it. I got a job as a bus boy at the Village Gate, because the manager knew my father, and then I met this girl—her father was a big-time lawyer in Washington—and she just jumped into bed with me because I was Charlie Mingus, right? I ended up holding on to her because I liked her, but she was taking more pills than I was aware of, and she got schizzy. I think we had a fight, so she goes away, and I'm very lonely, and the light bulbs are talking to me. I was hallucinating that light bulbs were talking to me, and kids on the street making up songs about her and me breaking up.

She left and went to hang out with the Hell's Angels. I think she got raped. She said she did. Then she said she dug them, so she stayed with them until she got pregnant, and then she came back to me. This was like months, and I hadn't been with anybody else. I'd just been sitting and brooding and hallucinating and hating everything, and drawing and painting and tearing up the house and generally being a bad person, you know. So the girl comes back pregnant, crying, and I went back to crazy again. First because she's pregnant, and second because she'd run off with the Hell's Angels, who were pretty crude dudes, you know. So I said, "Well, look, it has nothing to do with me." She wants to have an abortion, but I'm not the father, so why should I worry, right?

So she goes out and starts throwing beer bottles—everybody leaves their bottles outside the door, right?—at my front door. Screaming and hollering. She throws herself down the stairs, wallowing and kicking in the broken glass. I open the door and look at her, and then I close the door again, without any feelings. It was just like somebody left their garbage in front, and I said, "Well, I'll have to take that down, later." But I was again the betrayed martyr. Actually, she did all this stuff just to get attention.

She wasn't getting hurt on the glass. I looked to see that she wasn't cutting herself, and she was kicking her legs erratically. She was having enough presence of mind not to drop a leg down on a broken bottle neck, because that would puncture it. So I knew she was okay, and I just left her there. She finally went away and had her abortion and came back a couple of days later and had a cup of coffee.

After that, I went celibate for a while, and I spent my time reading Ouspensky. Then I met Greta, who was a German girl, who was living in this terrible shambles of a place— A guy called Henry, who said he was the last of the Fabian Socialists. He was about eighty years old, and she'd have to hold his piss pot while he'd piss in it, and then she'd go down and get him some sherry, empty out the piss pot and change his bed sheets, and he'd get up and walk out of the room—so he could have done all that stuff himself, you know. One day, I said to her, "Look, come and live with me." It was like asking her to marry me. She considered for a day or so, and then I went back there, and she had all her stuff packed. She was very artistic and very aggressive sexually, I mean, trying to get laid just as much as any guy would, and when she found out that guys couldn't keep it up as much as she could, she went out after different guys. People who resented her used to get her high and gang-bang her and all that stuff, but I really loved her, because she loved me, and she really did. That's one thing I'm convinced of in life. So I did my damnedest to destroy her, right?

She was one of the original alienated people. She'd wear dark makeup and long, black slinky dresses, walking around in the apartment like a vampire. At one point, I started trying to make it all normal—like, I wanted to meet her parents—but that started the process of making her face all the things she was running away from, the self-degradation trip she was on. The more I saw how much she did from weakness, the more angry I got with myself for indulging her. I mean, like, she makes a whole dinner, I invite some people over, and then I say, "I don't like this crap." And I throw it on the floor, and make her pick it up and put it back on the plates. But she would just laugh it off and say, "Aw, Charlie, quit being a baby." Really scary.

This lasted about a year and a half, and in the middle of that she got pregnant and wanted an abortion. She nearly died from one attempted abortion on the kitchen table, with two women dressed in nurses' uniforms, with soap. I said, "Look, there's got to be something we can get done that won't kill you." You know, like Mr. Clean and a hypodermic—not a hypodermic but like a horse syringe kind of thing. I say, "This is disgusting. Let's have the kid." Because I really loved her. And then I found this photograph of her, a porn photograph, and a recent one, and I was really freaked. Because we never did anything like that. We were just normal middle-class people, you know. So I rejected her, and got her up to a place where she could have an abortion, and then I went home and moved all her stuff out of the apartment to a friend of hers.

But I visited her every day, like at a hospital and all that. And Christmas was coming. I got her a tree, decorated the tree, the whole thing. On Christmas Eve, about eight or nine o'clock, I get off the bus right in front of her house, run into the house, and she's standing in the hall, all bloody, saying she just had the baby, and saying, "It was alive, it was alive!" I said, "What did you do?" And she's bleeding, hemorrhaging, right? She said, "I flushed it down the toilet." And I just go, "Oh, my God—" And I turn around, and I run out the door, right onto the same bus. And she comes running right after me, and the bus driver closes the door on her. And she's pounding on the door with bloody hands and stuff. And I see those impressions of blood and all that on the door, and I'm really throwing up, practically, you know. I get home, go in the house, slam the door, and jump in bed, and pull the covers over my head. But there was this cab driver who saw the whole thing from behind the bus, and he happened to be the boy friend of her girl friend, and he knew where I lived. So he comes and gets me and yanks me out of bed, yanks me out of the house, didn't even lock the door behind him. I mean, he was like a bull, you know. I'm like a little paper bag or a plastic garbage bag bouncing down the stairs.

At the hospital, I meet Greta's girl friend, and she gives me an apple. She says, "You better take a bite out of it because that's not as real as what you've got to see." So I take a bite out of it, and I suddenly saw all of life in that apple. The whole universe of life, everything, seeds, water, the whole trip. It occurred to me why apples, you know, apples are good. People fight for the land that makes apples taste good, and they have wars, and so war is okay. I mean, I could see why people, the immigrants, fought to keep the land and kicked out the Indians, the whole thing.

Anyhow, I go over to the bed, and she's real pale and looks like she's dying and stuff, and I do all this what, what, what, what —you know—what do you want, what can I do, all those whats. And she wants to make love, right there. And I'm disgusted. I mean, she was basically alive, and nearly dying she wants to make life, but there was no way I could grasp that. She comes home a couple of days later, and it's like married now for sure. I'm buying groceries and taking the laundry out, and then I really snapped. See, it was all a plot. To make me be a part of the system and not fight against the things that I know are corrupt and wrong, the racism and the whole thing. So I keep accumulating information and reasons to dislike her and reasons to reject her, and finally I kick her out.

By that time, I was just wandering around the streets, panhandling, not eating, getting superparanoid. I was going around saying God is dead, and throwing tennis balls in the middle of mass on Elizabeth Street. I was hanging out with like theater groups and all that. I remember I was at a church meeting at St. Mark's of the Bowery, and I was saying it's the end of people pretending to be good because they're so bad that even the pretense is corrupt. Even the attempt to say that there is a God is a sin, you know. And it was like back to the days when I was this recluse in Pasadena. People were bringing me water, and I was talking like a mad fiend. I was completely bananas, because I had no center, because my center was based on another person who had disappeared from my life.

One night, I was walking around the Village, and I heard somebody say, "That's my son." And I thought, Well, I must be dead. I was trying to be careful not to see my father, because I couldn't get on with him, because we couldn't communicate. The last incident I had with him was, we had a fight, and I cut my wrist and spilled blood all over him, and I said, "You got my blood all over you. Now what are you going to do?" And he said, "I can always wash it off."

This sort of started at a family reunion he was having at Christmas. I've given up on Christmas and holidays and stuff—they're just like any other day, right? But my father's brainwashing his two youngest kids into believing in the Thanksgiving turkey and Santa Claus and all that. So he paid for the tickets to the Christmas reunion in California. And I was drunk most of the time, on hundred-and-fifty-one-proof rum. Then my father goes into this thing that I'm a dope dealer and a pimp and big fight, fight, fight, fight, and I'm getting strangled. But one thing I did was, I made my father kiss my mother, because I hadn't ever seen that, ever in my life. They were fighting, too, and I said, "I don't care how you feel about it, just do it."

And then I get up, and I play his bass. I'm drunk, and I've snapped again, crazy and so on. I take this bass, and I'm doing like that, like a trill or something, and I do a slide, and a thing back and forth. And I'm doing it what I consider expertly. I mean, it was really loud and sturdy and steady. And I said, "That's about the fanciest thing you do on the bass, and it's really no hot shit, you know?" I mean, that was the seeds of what happened when I had the final fight with him. What happened was, I went over to the Vanguard, where he was playing, and I was sitting in the audience, and I sort of said hello to him in a very general way, just with a wave and a nod—"Hi, Dad, how are you?"—and then I sat there listening to the music, like I would want to appreciate it, and I couldn't. It was just boring, the repetitious old baloney that he's always played. I thought it was shit, and I wanted to tell him so, but he just said, "Come on, let's go out and have a drink." Obviously, his tactic was to get me a little drunk, a little weak, so that he could push me around mentally. That's his style.

So we go to a bar near where he lives, and we get into an argument, just a common little disagreement, about whether a certain piece was by Billy Eckstine or not. And I was right. And he was wrong. And I said, "See, I was right," because any little gesture against the old king— Then what happened was that this old crazy guy, who used to hang around and say, "Hiya, Charlie," to my father—he walks up to me and would like to shake my hand. Just a very gentle gesture, no anger or anguish or anything. And he puts my finger in his mouth, and he starts biting through to the bone. And blood is spurting out, and—what is *this?* I'm going "Un-h-h," and I thought, Pull it out and you lose that joint. That's how hard a hold he had. And I went into shock, so it didn't hurt, I mean, I realized I was not feeling the pain but seeing it, seeing what should cause pain. I look over, and there's my father walking to the bar to get another drink, and I figured, What's my father doing, turning his back on me in a situation where I can't really do anything? I should have kicked the old guy in the balls, right? Or put his eye out, or something. An eye for a finger or some Spartan bullshit like that. But it just never occurred to me, and the guy finally lets go and just walks out of the bar.

Then the bar starts closing down, and my father walks out too, with nothing but a "See you later." And he goes across the street and into his house. I leave too, but then I realize that my finger is still bleeding, so I tap on their window and say, "Look, I'd like to wash my hand off, I'm bleeding." And they say, "Yeah, so what? Go home, Charles, you're drunk." I tapped a little harder and a little harder, but nothing happened, and then I said, Well, what can you lose? So I went over to my father's house and just punched through the glass. That's one of my great and favorite hobbies anyway, whenever I get drunk, just punch some inanimate object, so it hurts me, as opposed to punching some animate object. And I'm shouting at him: "You've got me in your life at this point, instead of you being in my life, manipulating. I'm doing the manipulating now." I don't know what I got out, but that's what I meant—that no matter what he did, he couldn't get rid of me until I decided to get out. And I was calling him all kinds of names. Animal! Freak! At first he was being very adult and passive and just rejecting the whole thing, but then he feels threatened. So he comes out, and he's naked. He has a stick, a sword cane actually. Anyway—a few volleys of that across the head. He's a very precise person, he doesn't have to move that much. So I'm blocking one fist with two hands, because of his weight, and I'm getting it with the sword cane, and I'm still screaming at the top of my lungs. That's when I got blood all over him.

So the cops came in. Billy clubs. I see their guns. They're a little upset. There's blood and glass and shit on the street and in the hall, and the door's kicked open, and they see a naked fat guy with a stick, and they say, "What's going on?" I say, "My name is Charles Mingus III, and this is my father, and we're having a family discussion." So they say, "Well thank you very much, Mr. Mingus. Goodbye. Just try to keep it down." I mean, it was just too weird. . . .

5

Across the Rooftops of Harvard

When I was fifteen, a freshman at Harvard, I used to bolt my door every Friday night and then climb out the window of my room on the fifth floor of Standish Hall. By edging myself up one side of the dormer window, I could finally claw my way to the top of it, then mount to the spine of the roof, then work my way along the spine until I reached the other end of Standish Hall, where the roof sloped down to a flat extension that gave access to the common-room window. On Sunday nights, when I returned from a weekend at home, I would reverse the process—slipping out of the common room, scaling the roof, then easing myself down the side of my dormer window, prying open the window, and finally scrambling into my room.

At the time, it seemed a simple expedient for keeping my room locked—I had always climbed around on high places—but it really was not that simple, particularly in the dark of winter. December weekends brought snow and sleet, and the roof of Standish Hall was often covered with sheets of ice. The footing was uncertain, my fingers numb. I don't remember being frightened, and yet even now, thirty years later, I sometimes wake up early in the morning, at about five o'clock, just before the sky begins to turn pink behind the oak trees in front of the house, because I have been dreaming about that steeply sloping roof of Standish Hall, in rain and cold and darkness, and even after I am awake, I see myself clinging to the dormer window, teeth chattering, and I know that there is nothing but one half-inch black steel guardrail between me and the abyss.

I do not know, in retrospect, why it was so important for me to keep my room locked. I owned nothing of any particular value. Nonetheless, I disliked and distrusted the five others who shared the suite. We were all strangers to one another, flung together in this first semester, and in the wartime autumn of 1944, a college dormitory could provide no sense of stability or security. Even at the best of times, we would have been an ill-assorted group—a theological student from Cedar Rapids, a future insurance executive from Virginia, an Irish scholarship student from the slums north of Boston, a wavy-haired Brazilian of obscure ambitions, a sullen-tempered violinist, and a strange youth named Harold Spear. I can hardly remember what he looked like—I see curly brown hair, combed straight back, and bright-blue eyes—but I remember that we were all afraid of him. It was against him that I locked the door and climbed the roof.

Sometimes, after knocking vainly on a door, looking for company and conversation, Harold Spear would pound furiously on the walls and demand to be let in. Sometimes, for no apparent reason, he simply screamed, a hoarse, wild sound that echoed down the bare corridor of Standish C-51. One night when the future insurance executive was trying to study his economics and refused to let Harold Spear into his room, Harold Spear poured a can of cigarette lighter fluid under the bolted door and then set it on fire. The future insurance executive opened his window and scooped up some snow and heaped it on the burning lighter fluid until the fire had died out. Then, not really angry but rather hurt, because he had always tried to be friendly, he flung open his door and shouted, "How could you do a thing like that? What are you, crazy or something?" And Harold Spear, standing in the corridor, rocking to and fro on his heels, howled with laughter.

Harvard alumni are highly organized, partly to do favors for one another, partly to raise money for the college, and so I periodically receive elaborate reports on what happened to the Class of 1948. That is how I know that the future insurance executive did indeed become an insurance executive. That is how I learned that Harold Spear was indeed in the process of going crazy. "These years for me have been full indeed," Associate Professor Harold Spear of the University of Southern California wrote to the Twentieth Anniversary Report. "They included a stay in a mental hospital. . . . These years also include a breakup of my family and divorce, from which I've learned many things. . . ."

There is nothing unique about Harvard that drives students crazy. I know a youth who broke down last year at a small college in the cornfields of central Ohio (one of his last acts before being led off to an institution was to take a pair of scissors and hack up the crocheted "smelling blanket" that his girl friend had cherished since infancy) and another who went wild during his final month at a large university in southern California (he began screaming one night on a third-floor balcony outside his dormitory, a scene that later prompted the university authorities to close off the balcony during the entire examination period). Sylvia Plath was a prize-winning and highly "successful" sophomore at Smith when she first cracked up, attempted suicide, ran away, and finally was subjected to electroshock therapy. It was, she wrote, "a time of darkness, despair, disillusion—so black as only the inferno of the human mind can be."

Suicide is the second-highest cause of death (after accidents) among people of college age—an estimated 70,000 between the ages of fifteen and twenty-four try it every year, and nearly 4,000 succeed—and the symptoms are generally much the same. Fear and anxiety about leaving home, about sex, about schoolwork, about the uncertainties of adult life, about a recurring sense of meaninglessness. Although such a crisis can strike any adolescent on any battlefield—there once was a whole category of mental illness called *dementia praecox,* and now there is one called *hebephrenia*—it seems to me that the social and intellectual pressures at Harvard are greater than those in most other places. In any case, they are the ones I know best, and so I use them to provide a paradigm for the misfortunes of the student.

The most important novelty of going off to college, and the cause of most college crises, is the freedom to control (or not control) one's personal life. In my time, this freedom did not involve any drugs or any sexual license. Radcliffe girls were still largely segregated in their own classes and dormitories, and the parietal rules did not encourage close acquaintance. The new freedom was a much simpler freedom to disobey all the old rules by which one had been raised from birth. One didn't have to appear at the dinner table on time, or at all; nor did one have to go to classes; one could stay up all night and listen to *Don*

Giovanni and argue about God—and drink. To swill someone's quart of Three Feathers Blended, that was manliness. To vomit all over the stairway and then lurch out into the Lowell House courtyard as the sun cast its first rays on the blue bell tower, that was freedom.

To impress everyone with my brilliance, I scorned the standard surveys of science and literature, and enrolled for a double course in Russian, a subject then considered extremely exotic. It was taught by Dr. Leonid I. Strakhovsky, a thin and nervous man with wavy gray hair, who was said to be a former officer in the Czar's White Guards. The two dozen students who gathered around a knife-scarred table in the gloom of Sever Hall were an odd collection: a few bespectacled upperclassmen who hoped to read Chekhov, a one-armed war veteran of uncertain purpose, one married Radcliffe student, four or five gray and tweedy men from the State Department and the O.S.S., assigned to learn how to communicate with our new allies in Moscow. We began briskly by assuming patronymics (Otton Karlevitch) and learning the usual Berlitz openings: *Govoreetye po-Russky? Da, ya govoriou po-Russky.*

It was not long, however, before Dr. Strakhovsky led us into the minefields of compound verbs, and I began falling behind my State Department classmates, not because of the inherent difficulty of compound verbs, but because I spent so many evenings clowning and arguing until dawn that I was too sleepy to do much homework, or even to get up for class. Sometimes, I would arrive at Sever Hall just in time to fall asleep in class, my head slowly nodding over the incomprehensible pages of Bondar's grammar, then snapping up when Dr. Strakhovsky called on me for some answer, then sinking again. Sometimes, I didn't get out of bed until five minutes before the hour, but I convinced myself that I could somehow get to class on time. Shirt unbuttoned, necktie in my pocket, I would race out into the snow, across Mount Auburn Street, the bells of Lowell House already tolling the hour behind me, up Holyoke and across Mass. Ave. into the ominous silence that always descends on the Yard when classes start. I would find the door to the Russian class closed, but instead of either barging in or going away, I would sit at the keyhole, trying to overhear, occasionally peering in, and somehow convincing myself that I was doing my duty, until here too, I would fall asleep.

My dedication was reflected in my grades. At the end of the first semester, I received two C's and a double D for the double course in Russian. Both parents and college officials tried to persuade me to shift to a more normal curriculum, but vanity insisted that, having nearly failed Russian 1A, I enroll in another double course, Russian 1B. Halfway through the semester, I received a double E for that, plus an E in English and a blank mark for a history course in which I had not taken the mid-term exam. In the old morality plays, angels appear at such points and warn the sinner to mend his ways before eternal perdition. ("Faustus, repent; yet God will pity thee . . .") At Harvard, the sinner is put on probation, which means that he is forbidden to cut classes, forbidden to engage in extracurricular activities, and threatened with expulsion ("severance of connections" is Harvard's term for it) if he does not improve by the end of the semester. But as the student of Wertenberg says, "I cannot repent. . . . Come, let us dispute again, and argue of divine astrology. . . ."

My father tried to save me from destruction by hiring an authentic Russian, whose name I recall as Andrei Makovsky, an unemployed émigré newly demobilized from the Army, to teach me enough of his language to survive the displeasure of Dr. Strakhovsky. Mr. Makovsky lived in a rambling brown clapboard house in Arlington, a half-hour's streetcar ride from Harvard Square, and I went there twice a week to struggle with, of all things, *Voy y Mir*. But Tolstoy was too complicated to lure me out to Arlington for long, particularly since a friend of mine often had extra theater tickets, and the last winter of war was turning into the spring of victory, a season in which all rules could be broken or made new. After I began failing to get to Arlington, I made appointments to see Mr. Makovsky at the offices of the *Crimson*, where I had finally become an editor, and where I did much of my carousing. When I failed even to keep my appointments there, at two or three in the afternoon, Mr. Makovsky had to make his way to my room in Lowell House, where he rapped on the door, tentatively, and then apologized for waking me up in midafternoon for my newest lesson.

The final exam, after I had stayed up until dawn in a last futile effort to memorize verbs, was a nightmare. It is a nightmare still, and like the image of myself on the rooftops in the snow, it haunts me from time to time. The June sun is always shining brightly outside one of those interchangeable brick Georgian buildings that line the Yard, and a stream of students hurry past me into the doorway. I stop several of them to ask which examination is being held, and what we are supposed to be tested on, but they all brush past me. They are always prepared, ready with their answers, and I am left in helpless ignorance, and the bell starts ringing.

That whole spring had a dreamlike quality. The newspapers brought reports of unimaginable upheavals—the crossing of the Rhine, the slaughter on Iwo Jima and Okinawa, the death of Roosevelt, then Mussolini, then Hitler. The war that had dominated everything since I was ten years old suddenly stopped. Nobody seemed to know what was going to happen next. Nor did I. The result of all my folly was the inevitable double E in Russian. Under the threat of expulsion, I took the only route I could see and fled. I packed a small suitcase and set out, very early in the morning, to hitchhike west until I found some job on some newspaper. I ended in Iowa two weeks later as a police reporter for the *Des Moines Register*.

That is more or less the way one goes crazy, or narrowly avoids going crazy, at Harvard. It is a little unreal, just as college itself is unreal. It can be measured, because college itself is measured in exams and term papers, tests that the disintegrating student cannot pass. On the other hand, there is a safety mechanism in the very artificiality of college life. After nine months of crisis, one goes away and does something else for three months, and then returns to start again.

Harvard is, above all things, self-conscious, almost morbidly concerned with its own intellectual processes. The education of undergraduates is perhaps the least of these processes—certainly the least in the view of most professors—and yet that too must be scrutinized, not only by deans and examiners but by psychiatric experts. One survivor recalls the experience:

"This professor—Murray was his name, Henry Murray—had

a psychological testing outfit just off Kirkland Street. He was doing a twenty-year project in which he was trying to figure out the quality of creativity. He tested and studied five different groups of undergraduates over the twenty-year period, following each group through from freshman to senior year. Now the point about this was not that anything important was being done—I think Professor Murray found out very little—but he did set up a very strong relationship with his testees, which was a relationship of intense trust and fealty. You got to feeling very devoted to him, and you'd do whatever he asked. This could be a catastrophe.

"I guess it was considered sort of an honor to be one of his subjects. Plus you got three dollars an hour. So when another professor recommended me to the program, I didn't hesitate. What I didn't know at this time is that I was looking for help. You don't ever go into these psychological-experiment situations without looking for help. What you're really doing is hoping that the psychologist who's testing you will tell you something about yourself. Harvard didn't have much of a therapy program at that time —this was about ten years ago—and if it had, I probably would have gone into it. I guess that what I expected from Professor Murray was that he would give me some kind of therapy.

"What happened was—well, let me give you just one example. It was a stress test, but you didn't know that it was a stress test. It consisted of this: You wrote a philosophy of life, five pages. You were then asked to defend this philosophy in front of an adversary. It was understood that this adversary was just a guy who'd ask you about your philosophy. And the professor did explain that your blood pressure would be taken, and they had a movie camera behind a one-way mirror. All that was perfectly okay. What he didn't tell you was that the person who was examining you was assigned to, essentially, scare the shit out of you. Which he would do by attacking you personally, in terms of the way you looked, the way you talked. It was a torture chamber.

"I had written something to the effect that you must meet very high standards, toil up the mountain to get there, and so on. This law student whom Professor Murray had hired as my adversary never argued that my ideas were wrong, or that I hadn't met my own standards. It was an *ad hominem* attack on me. He told me that I looked ridiculous, that I sounded ridiculous. It was an attack on my whole physical style. My reaction was one of total silence and paralysis. I can't tell you how I felt afterwards—suicidal."

Aside from its intellectual pressures, Harvard also exerts intense social pressures. My freshman class of about 1,150 youths included such notables as Robert Kennedy and George Plimpton, who had "prepared," as they say, at Milton and Exeter respectively—one didn't need to take college-board exams, in those days, if one came from an approved private school—but it also included a fair number of Irish boys from local parochial schools, a sampling of Orientals on various scholarships, and even two or three blacks, one of whom subsequently became a professor of psychiatry, dedicating himself to questions of "how men adjust in extreme environments, such as high-altitude polar deserts."

In the extreme environment located next to the Charles River, the competition for status was ferocious—status being based on an entirely uncertain and constantly changing mixture of intellect, money, talent, *savoir faire*, social class, wit, athletic skill, and *chutzpah*. Whenever one was uncertain about someone else's status—which was most of the time—the safest tactic was to snub him or ridicule him. "I am not so uninitiated," a sophomore named Michael Wechsler, son of the editorial page editor of the *New York Post*, wrote in an essay in 1962, "as to cherish any hopes of knowing who it is who lives just across the hall. God knows, I shall never again make the mistake of answering a stranger in the dining hall; and it is no longer quite so difficult to ride down the elevator without saying a word to either of the three fellow passengers, who are equally silent."

For some students, social life consisted of a beer with a roommate; others found friends in various extracurricular activities (in my case, the *Crimson*), but the final arbiters of social standing, at least in their own view, were the private clubs, Harvard's version of fraternities, which stood like fortresses behind discreetly marked oaken doors on various streets to the south of the Yard. Among those who would never be asked to join, like me, it was considered absurd for anyone to think about such things, but the pressures to get into the "right" club could be considerable. Richard Rand, now a professor of English at the State University of New York, recalls the situation as "very tense and very intense," and he traces it, in his own case, back to the pressures of getting through Groton.

"I was just a California kid, but my father, who had gone to Groton, felt that it was imperative that his boys go to Groton, so off we went. It was a terrible experience, but you have to somehow survive, and my decision was to absorb the values of the place, the style and everything. Third-form year, I was fifteen, we had an audio-visual lab with a tape, and they had us read poems of our choice into the tape, and then they played it back. It was the first experience I'd ever had of hearing my own voice, and I was appalled. What I heard was a California drawl. I said to myself, 'You have three months in which to get rid of all that.' And I did. It was a painful weird process, but after three months, I'd gotten rid of anything that could be called a California accent. I was severing—I was severing—I was wiping out my identity as a Californian.

"Now at Harvard—having gone to Groton, one felt that one had to, you know, perform in a certain way. I had to join a final club. There were only two that counted, Porcellian and the A.D. I campaigned for the A.D. by pretending that I would only accept the Porcellian, which I knew would never elect me. Nothing else would do. I actually got elected to the Spee Club, and I turned them down. I think that if I'd been a little more balanced about the whole thing, I would have seen that as the friendly gesture that it was, and I would have joined the Spee, and I would have had a good time. Instead, I said, 'No, not for me.' And then the A.D. thought it would be nice to pick off a Porcellian prospect, and so they picked me up. All of this was an incredible expenditure of energy on something very shallow and meaningless. Once I was elected, I didn't like it. I spent relatively little time there, and what time I did spend there I got drunk. I was constantly running up debts that I couldn't pay. But the point is that somewhere along the line, I felt that I could not be me, whatever that was. It was that young kid from California. I could not be that.

"The worst crisis came during junior year. I had fallen in love with a girl I'd met in Greece that summer, and we were having a love affair, and she was living in New York. This was a very destructive situation, for me, because she was actually involved with another guy. So it was a triangle. And she didn't handle the triangle very adeptly. She would schedule dates with both of us at the same time. We'd run into each other. It was a real game of— We had a terrible blow-up around Easter, and at that point I was just going haywire. At the same time, my tutor thought I was a very promising student, and he loaded a tremendous amount of work on me, which I couldn't handle—or felt that I couldn't handle—and didn't handle. He also got me into courses that were over my head. Or I got myself, through him, into courses that—I guess I was a little bit manic, and I got into courses that were mainly graduate courses, and I didn't do the work. I just didn't do anything. I just kind of paralyzed myself. I felt terribly shot-down the whole time. I stayed awake all night listening to Frank Sinatra. Sinatra has, you know, in a lot of those songs, a kind of— a fantastic despondency, a fantastic feeling of erotic despair, let me put it that way. And I guess I drank a lot, although I don't remember that too well. I would go on terrific binges. They were very exhibitionistic. I would go out and yell in the middle of the Eliot House quad. And sometimes suicidal. I would wander out into the middle of Boylston Street, daring the cars to run into me. That kind of thing.

"But somehow, I don't know how, it's something of a blur in my memory, I did get through those courses. I didn't read much course work, but I did read all the time, and then also I could write perfectly good essays under exam conditions. So although it was a very, very shaky period in my life, and although I felt that I was not in control of the events around me, I did survive. I stayed afloat. And then for some reason. I did brilliantly on my honors exams, and I finished my thesis on Yeats in two nights— that was a real scene—and so I graduated with a magna, which I didn't believe in. There was something very odd about getting the magna and not believing in it. I wanted to burn it. I didn't burn it, but I really wanted to.

"Having gone through all this training, I felt that I was back at a point where I had to start all over again. Starting over again meant—I don't know what it meant. There was a great professor of French literature whom I'd had in my freshman and sophomore years, and he'd gone on to Cornell, so I followed him to Cornell and signed up as a graduate student in comparative literature. This meant taking courses in French. The French that I had to read was over my head. So I had to fake it in class, or I felt that I had to fake it. Mallarmé, for example, is, even to the French, extremely—well, the syntax is extremely elaborate. It's like reading Sir Thomas Browne. And one of my symptoms was that I didn't feel I had the right to be wrong about anything. So when it came to writing a paper, I had a terrible paralysis. Because in a paper, you're—you are *there*.

"Now there was a girl whom I'd known at Radcliffe, and she'd written a paper on Mallarmé, and I made a copy of it, never thinking, you know, that I'd ever want to use it. This girl had also come to Cornell, by the way, so she was known to the faculty. Anyway, when it came to the deadline, I decided to hand in her paper on Mallarmé. I remember feeling very, very wrong, very despondent, when I made that decision. I remember that I postponed that decision until I went off on Christmas vacation, which was a miserable experience. But here's the interesting thing: Before handing in the paper, I put up rather a nice little bibliography, and I wrote in the bibliography that I had 'received help from' this girl—giving, in other words, a clear signal to the instructor that there was something here that he should look into, which he promptly did. He called me in, and he asked me, 'What kind of help?' And even then I could have faked it. I could have said, 'Well, I asked her a few questions,' and she would have gone along with it, if he had asked her. But instead of that, I said—I remember sitting in his office—I remember all these thoughts going through my head—I said to myself, 'Well, this is ridiculous.' So then I said, 'I—this is her paper.' So then he said, 'Well, I can't accept it.' So I said, 'Well, you probably oughtn't to.'

"And then I remember feeling greatly relieved, and I remember going for a long walk, on an icy Ithaca day, and saying, 'Now it is clearly established that you're not up to graduate school. It is also clearly established that you're not up to anything else. So what are we going to do about it?' Then I had an impulse, and I really don't know where the impulse came from. And I said, 'Go to New York and try to find a job. . . .' "

Michael Wechsler, aged seventeen, was already in the hands of a psychiatrist when he entered Harvard in the fall of 1960. He had also asked for, received, and smashed up his first car, a

Volkswagen. Perhaps he should never have gone to Harvard, for the pressures of Cambridge scarcely provide a secure environment for anyone vulnerable, but Harvard's exaggerated reputation for excellence continues to attract not just a high proportion of the intelligent and the ambitious but perhaps a high proportion of the vulnerable as well. Michael Wechsler took a heavy schedule of courses during his freshman year, and, according to his parents, "seemed to be coping with college, but without effort and without joy."

He managed to get through the first semester of his sophomore year, and then he began to break down. He himself did not seem to understand the reasons, although he tried, in an autobiographical memoir that he wrote several years later, to list them.

"I couldn't get involved in my work [during the] second semester—but then I'd never really been studious. Also, I was smoking a lot of pot, even day in and day out for some weeks; that's no way to accomplish anything. And, I had generals to pass, for which I was ill prepared from previous years; still, I hardly studied for them at all; I tore up an important set of notes about a week before the exam. I really had it in for myself that semester. Besides I was more interested in having psychological bull sessions with Quentin. . . . I also played the flute a lot. . . . I ended up by flunking one course and getting excused from two other final examinations. . . .

"One day I'd have to go see [the psychiatrist] but I'd be afraid of crossing some not too dangerous streets; walking down the stairs to the subway was frightening—I clung to the bannister; I was afraid of falling onto the tracks. All the while I was feeling pleasantly sad during most of the day; at night I'd have more irrational fears, like that of cutting myself. And I could hardly work at all. . . . Each morning I would try to write something, but I was plagued by the thought that nothing I wrote was my own; and I was never satisfied with the amount of research I'd done. . . .

"I started getting slightly suicidal. I'd been taking tranquilizers, and one day I finished the bottle—thirty-four times the regular dose. . . . I quickly put on my shoes, for I suppose I'd been napping, and I went to the Harvard clinic. They kindly pumped out my stomach, which I rather enjoyed, because there was a very warm nurse holding my hand and saying everything was really better than I thought it was, which was a lot of crap. So they put me in a room of my own—they have a room reserved for nuts."

For those who survive three and a half years in Cambridge and wish to emerge with not just a bachelor's degree but a degree with honors, the final obstacle is the so-called thesis. It is the hardest task one has to do in college, and yet it is really little more than a parody of scholarly work. It is supposed to be a more or less original piece of research, but it generally turns out to be a reorganization of whatever material can be found in the college library. And it is announced in advance that a major part of the final grade will depend on the student's mastery of the academic code—"*ibid.*," "*op. cit.*" and all that.

An Essay on Certain Aspects of the Development of a Centralized National State in France Under Cardinal Richelieu was the title of my own enterprise, written, like most of them, in two weeks of desperate, all-night sessions—groping through piles of half-read, overdue library books, spilling coffee on the hentracked pages, and then going to brew more. When the masterpiece is finished—and there are hundreds of them every year, all accumulating in rows of black folders somewhere in the depths of Widener Library—the student feels an almost explosive sense of relief. It is as though one could suddenly fly.

For Juergen Schmidt—as I must call him, since he is now a graying bank executive—the completion of a thesis on Spinoza started a violent series of events. Schmidt had only recently arrived from Germany, and he considered his choice of Spinoza to some extent "an atonement for being German." He also was newly married and was finding it difficult to support a wife on one hundred dollars a month. The thesis was, therefore, a final obstacle of even more than the usual awesomeness. "I can remember walking across the Yard with a kind of very empty feeling in the pit of my stomach," he says, "real fear, fear of a kind that I'd never felt before, fear of this immense job I had to do." Like me, like Rand, like thousands of others, he did finally get the work done, on the last day.

"Then I went to another guy's room, and he hadn't yet made

the deadline, which was 6 P.M. There were people typing all over the room, and others were sorting out the three copies. I sat on the floor to help sort the papers, turning the pages in front of me, laying them out, one, two, three, and in order to keep time, I would rock back and forth, one, two, three. And suddenly a strange rush sort of went through my body, like an electric shock. And concomitant with it, I had this sensation that I was being cursed, that a curse had been placed on me, and I looked at my wife, and I said, 'Don't the Cabalists pray by rocking back and forth?' I thought that my movement back and forth had somehow put me in tune with Cabala prayers, which were cursing me for having married a Jewish girl. But why Cabala? It was not a concept that I'd worked with. What are the Cabalists? Do they pray? I don't know. But I suddenly had this image of Cabalists praying and cursing. Call it a kind of Jungian archetypal image.

"The next day, something similar happened. I again had one of these *frissons*. I thought that I was in touch with the Aztec god Quetzalcoatl. I'd heard of him, but I hardly knew how to spell his name. This *frisson* was a ray, something that he'd sent from the heavens. . . . Well, physically, the next thing that happened was that I couldn't sleep any more. I spent about two nights when I just couldn't fall asleep. I started telephoning a lot. What I was trying to do, I was trying to get reassurance from friends that they were still my friends. I was afraid—I mean, I knew that there was something going wrong. At the same time, I was terribly curious about the ideas that were occurring to me. I was going mad, and I was investigating the madness at the same time.

"During the night, I opened a drawer and I was somehow searching for my father, either in a half-dream or a half-daze. And I took out some shirts that my mother had sent me, and they smelled of my father, they had the tobacco smell, and I couldn't stop smelling them. Then I went back to bed, and I covered my wife with one leg and one arm, which I often did. And I looked at her, sleeping on her back—her mouth was half open, her teeth were showing slightly—and I thought—I thought that she was dead, and that I'd killed her. And I suddenly felt like a bird, a bird of prey, and that I was covering her with my wing, and that I had my claws in her, the way a bird of prey does with a carrion.

"I more or less stayed in bed during those two days, trying

to sleep, unable to sleep. A friend of mine came by, and we went to his place for drinks, and I was—I was just like on coals—I didn't know what to say any more. Then, in some effort to shock them, I went over to my wife and tore open her blouse, and I said, 'Look at her! She's decomposed under that!' Because I was convinced that she was dead, that she was a walking ghost.

"Going crazy is a symbolic experience. Reality is still there, but you keep interpreting it. Everything becomes symbolic. The symbols chase each other. They become overwhelming. The fact that you're wearing that striped tie could mean rivers to me, the Rhine, or the Niger. The ticking of a clock can be the chimes of the universe. My Venetian blinds changed color as I watched them during the night, and this became to me eons—I was going through cycles of life that were much larger than day or night, they were eons. Then at one point I had a vision of being celebrated in an age beyond, in which people no longer had hair, or windows. Everything was terribly white. Narrow streets. A kind of brushed-up, futuristic brave new world. And I was famous, with my name on streets, for having been the founder of this age. . . .

"The next day was a Sunday, and a friend invited us out to visit his family in Concord. As we got near, I wanted to go to Walden Pond to find my brother. My brother had been in America about a year earlier, and we'd walked around Walden, but now—It wasn't that I wanted to find my brother. I wanted to find some solution, some resolution. Something was waiting for me. But when we got there, the pond was frozen over, and a layer of snow was on the ice, and I just got out of the car and looked at it and said, 'No, it's all frozen over. It's not there.' So we drove on to my friend's house, and as we went up to the door, I was afraid that the sight of me would so frighten his old father—I thought I looked so horrible, that the madness glowed from me, radiated from me, that the sight of it would kill him. So I started running away, down the driveway. And suddenly, tremendous, anguished howls came from me. They came from my chest, from my voice, but they were not conscious howls. I mean, something howled in me. I howled. Something howled. My body howled. It frightened me, but I howled again, and then my wife just slapped me across the face and said, you know, 'Come on, stop it, let's get out of here.'

"I think it must have been that evening that my wife gave up and said, 'Let's go to the Harvard psychiatrists and see if they can help.' So we went to the psychiatrist, or they took me there, let's say. One of the first things I did there was to take off my wedding ring and throw it against the wall and say that I couldn't carry the burdens of the world, that my shoulders were too small. Then we all piled into a taxi and went to what was then called the Boston Psychopathic Hospital. It's now the Mental Research Center. Inside, there was a water fountain. By now, I thought I was a holy man, and I blessed the water and drank it, and what I thought I was drinking was like a taste that I'd never had before, like breathing wind. I had blessed it. I had blessed the water, and the water had become sacred. It had become a nectar, but not sweet like nectar, only in a spiritual sense. It was like velvet.

"Then I was taken upstairs—I don't remember any formalities—and suddenly the door closed behind me. I looked around, and I realized very quickly, with a certain amount of shock, that I was in an insane asylum. That's when I had the proof that I was insane."

Things do change over the years, even at Harvard, and according to the official accounts, the changes are always improvements. Students still go crazy—the number of "psychotic episodes" among undergraduates is said to be about fifteen per year—but the University Health Service now has a psychiatric clinic that does its best to handle all crises. It is open twenty-four hours a day, and it is free (Harvard tuition includes a bill of $154 per year for all medical services). Dr. Preston K. Munter, the head of the psychiatric department, proudly describes it as the largest university health service in the country and quite possibly the best. He flings one leg over the arm of his red swivel chair as he tries to think of other institutions that might be equally good—"M.I.T., Yale, Berkeley . . ." His voice fades away.

And so they come flowing in—all these bright, ambitious students with all their incomprehensible problems—to the fourth floor of the Health Service headquarters in the new, gray, concrete blockhouse known as Holyoke Center. The décor is, as one observer called it, "pointedly unobtrusive"—white walls, black tiled floors, shellacked wooden chairs, and, for a touch of good cheer, an occasional red or yellow door. About two thousand patients walk in here every year, out of a community of about thirty thousand students, teachers, and university employees. One in fifteen is not a very high proportion, but it is somewhat higher than the corresponding ratio in the population at large. Eight full-time senior psychiatrists are waiting to receive the visitors, along with four junior psychiatrists and a dozen others working part time. About five hundred of the patients are Harvard undergraduates, about two hundred and fifty more from Radcliffe (but since Harvard has a bigger enrollment, the number of female students who seek treatment is about one in four; the number of males is less than one in ten). Another five or six hundred come from the various graduate schools. The patients receive an average of four or five treatments each (until recently, there was a limit of fifteen visits), and the Radcliffe students get more than those from Harvard (4.6 to 4.0). In terms of age and experience, the juniors come most frequently, the freshmen least.

Dr. Munter, a short, restless figure in a dark-gray blazer and a brightly striped shirt, adjusts his horn-rimmed glasses and spins his chair and frowns at his statistics. He is reluctant to draw conclusions. "I don't think in the aggregate, I think about people," he says. "This service is run on a humanistic basis, not a numbers basis. Mental illness in college is no different from mental illness elsewhere. Harvard isn't the perfect place for everyone, but it doesn't make people sick. Emotional cholera bacteria aren't sprinkled in the Harvard water supply. The big difference here is that help is readily available, and everybody is encouraged to make use of it."

So Dr. Munter sees no dark prospect in the increased use of the psychiatric service. On the contrary, he sounds a little bit like a proud factory owner when he says that "the figures are up dramatically." (Actually, they have leveled off and even declined somewhat during the past few years of political apathy and decreased use of drugs.) He cites the example of the Radcliffe girls who were once expelled for pregnancy but who now get free and confidential medical care "without anyone considering that it's anyone else's business." Indeed, Munter even urges his staff to go and seek out new problems. "A college psychiatrist cannot simply sit in his office and see patients," as he puts it. "He must become part of the educational process, giving up his therapeutic anonymity to some extent in order to engage in the prime business of the educational community."

The Harvard student who wanders disconsolately into Dr. Munter's domain—he must come in person; the rules prohibit garrulous telephone calls at midnight—will find himself in the hands of some rather orthodox (perhaps even old-fashioned) psychiatrists. "We do some group therapy, some behavior modification," says Dr. Munter, "but nothing far out—no primal screams, no marathon sessions. I'm a little worried that some of the nonsense, the fads, may have caused some damage." There is a moderate application of chemicals, but, according to Dr. Munter, "we are not drug pushers." In extreme situations, of course, the Harvard police are ready for action, and behind them the Cambridge police, and there is McLean Hospital in Belmont, which can deal with difficult cases. But that is not Dr. Munter's purpose. "The whole goal is to keep people in school. We have a gifted staff and perhaps more experience than any other place in the country."

I doubt, somehow, that I would ever have gone to the University Health Service. Perhaps I am a prisoner of my own prejudices. "Snap out of it" was my mother's prescription for all sickness of the soul. Or perhaps there really is a gap between the tormented student and all those smiling psychiatrists who stand ready to heal, a gap so wide that the student avoids the Holyoke Center not because he resists the idea of treatment but because the idea never occurs to him. His struggle is with God, or the Fates, not with what the cheerful doctors call "mental illness," or, more frequently, "some problems."

The case of L—— is not really typical of anything, I guess, but it does strike certain reverberations. He grew up in Iowa, where his father was, according to the man who told me the story, "some sort of craftsman, a blacksmith, or some antiquated-sounding thing." Both parents apparently came from Eastern Europe and belonged, in my informant's words, "to a strange, fundamentalist sect (I don't know the name), which had abolished churches, priests, and finally holidays. The last holiday to go was Christmas, which was called off fairly recently, within the last two or three years."

L—— won a scholarship to one of the most staid and expensive prep schools in the East, and there he fell in love with the daughter of a professor at a nearby university. He was fifteen; she was fourteen. They went out together for three years. When he graduated and moved on to Harvard in 1973, he impressed a number of Radcliffe classmates as "good-looking, very attractive," and "a real nice gregarious type of guy," who "always looked happy." In fact, he was desperately unhappy that his girl was going out with other boys.

At the start of the Christmas vacation in 1973, L—— did not go back to Iowa, perhaps because the holidays had been abolished at his home, or perhaps simply because it seemed too expensive. He spent the first few days in the empty dormitory, Straus Hall. Then he packed his bags, very neatly, to leave. He bought two airline tickets, one to his home in Iowa and the other to the town where he had gone to school, both for Christmas Day. On Christmas Eve, at about dinner time, he called his girl's house, and her mother said that the girl was out singing Christmas carols. L—— said that he wanted to fly down to see her. The mother said that she was wrapping presents, and it would be inconvenient for her drive to the airport to meet his plane. L—— offered to take a bus. The mother then told him that the girl was not singing carols but was out on a date. She urged him to call again on Christmas morning. He agreed.

L—— took extraordinary precautions to make sure that his suicide would not fail. First he made a noose and tied the other end of the rope to the black iron railing around the stairwell of his empty dormitory. Then he bound his feet together with a bicycle chain, so that if he panicked and started kicking, he would not be able to save himself. Then he tied one hand to his belt, so that this hand, too, could not save him. Then he slipped the noose over his neck. With his one free arm, he maneuvered himself over the railing. And jumped. A janitor found the corpse hanging in the stairwell on Christmas morning. When the authorities went to the dead student's room, they found, among other things, a picture of the girl, on which he had written with a ball-point pen: "Slut! Slut! Slut!"

The case, as I said, is not typical of anything. The number of "completed suicides" at Harvard is three or four a year, the number of attempts and "gestures" perhaps ten times that many—not a very large statistic in a community of thirty thousand. The interesting thing about L——, though, is that, like most Harvard students, he was lonely, ambitious, driven, and he never once went to see the psychiatrists waiting for him behind the brightly colored doors of the Holyoke Center.

6

Out of a Case History:
Anthony Tuttle
Hears the Voice of Murder

Anthony Tuttle comes from a rich family, but now he works as a waiter in a restaurant on the Upper East Side of New York. Before that, he worked as a taxi driver. He has also published three novels, but their success has been modest. At the moment, he says he has thirty-seven cents to his name. Tonight's work as a waiter will bring him almost fifty dollars.

He is a stocky man of forty, with light-brown hair, a martial mustache, and piercing gray-blue eyes. He wears a red-and-white-striped shirt, blue jeans, worn sneakers. He speaks rather stridently, often leaping from one subject to another in mid-sentence. He drinks Miller High Life beer from the can.

My grandfather was a big coal merchant in Brooklyn, and he left a lot of money to my father. My father was a theater producer and director. He had been a concert pianist as a youngster, a brilliant concert pianist. He also taught at Yale. But he never really knew what he wanted to do. There were four children, my older brother, Peter; an older sister; and my twin sister, who now lives in France. Peter was a genius student at Yale, but he flipped out in his senior year. His left arm went numb because he cheated on an exam. He started howling in the middle of Edwards Court, or whatever it's called. So my father committed him to the hospital, Y.P.I., and he was there for ten years. His illness cost my father about $150,000.

But he did seem to get better. He wasn't always crazy. He did crazy stuff—that's the strange thing about mental illness. Even while he was ill, he organized the Kennedy library at the White House. He was down there. He did all that. But then he alternated. He'd go on a hunger strike, wouldn't eat anything. One time, he came home for a visit—to Bellport, on the south shore of Long Island, where we'd always had a summer home, a big, beautiful house with lawns and a widow's walk—and Pete came down on Memorial Day and just went catatonic. He stood out on the lawn for about twelve hours. With his arms stretched out, like this. Dad often wasn't around, so I was in charge of him. And he would go to service stations around town and lock himself up in the john. And some poor deputy would call up and say, "Your son is in the Texaco station and won't come out." Or he'd try to eat his toilet paper, and I'd have to say, "Pete, why don't you try going to the john and not swallowing your toilet paper?"

One time—it was the Fourth of July weekend—he came out, and he picked up a pair of scissors and came at me and tried to stab me. And I wrestled him to the ground. And I said, "Pete! It's Tony! I love you, Pete, I love you!" He was much bigger than me, but I wrestled the scissors away from him. Whereupon he started punching out windows. And yelled out over the Great South Bay: "Peter Tuttle is a Social Register snob!" I had to call the booby hatch and have them come and get him in a strait-jacket. And they're taking him down like this, and I was in charge of all this, and on the way down, he poked out another window, as if—well, one for good luck—bop!—you know—poked out another one. I came of age there as far as—even before I went nuts—there, that weekend. My parents had thought I was sort of a fuck-up—you know, irresponsible—I was already twenty-seven by then—but that weekend . . .

I'd gone to college at Bard, and met a girl there, and we had this very wonderful, fawnlike, trembly, romantic time. Fell madly in love. Wished on the moon the first time we met. Went together for a year, slept together, which was really something in those days. When we got out, we got married. Moved down to the Village. And I was still just a kid. I thought I wanted a sort of hip, very with-it girl, and she was this shy, trembling girl who was not, you know, fast or quick. I apparently have it screwed up somewhere that the woman is the strong one, and the man isn't. I must have made her not feel that I needed her. And she met this mental patient, practically literally, this Shakespearean actor. She was an actress. She was about to go on tour in the road company of *Sunrise at Campobello*. And I said, "Okay, go ahead, terrific, terrific." And that hurt her very much, apparently. Anyway, I was away for the weekend, visiting some friends in Pennsylvania, and when I came back, there were some scrambled-egg shavings in the sink. And I said to myself, What—I don't—she has poached eggs, and I like mine over easy, and what are those scrambled-egg shavings? And I said, "Was there somebody here over the weekend?" And she said, "Well, yes, there was." And I said, "Was it a guy?" And she said, "Yes." And I said, "Did you sleep with him?" And she said, "Yes." And I said, "Get out of this house—*immediately!*"

I really went through hell for two years, missing her. Wrote my first novel out of that sadness. But I was a *good boy,* working away. In fact, I spent seven fucking years writing this novel, which happened to be a really terrific book, even though it sold no copies. Now, during this time, the money for Peter was running out. Dad was in a furor. He was paying fourteen grand a year, and he said, "I cannot spend this kind of money." And mother would say, "He's a life, you know, give him the whole fucking inheritance, everything. You've got to save his life." But the money ran out, and he was transferred to Middletown, which is a state hospital—and he got better. Immediately. I don't know why. He'd already had every treatment there was, Thorazine, electric shocks, vitamins, maybe it was because it wasn't so cushy as Y.P.I. He gained some weight, looked terrific. He was about to be released to a halfway house, after the Thanksgiving weekend of '65, and then he took a bus up from New York and just disappeared.

About this time, my girl, Joan, decided that she didn't want to marry me. We'd had this beautiful affair, and I wanted to marry her, but she decided she wanted to go home to California. So I followed her there. I thought I'd get some construction work, or some movie work, a change of scene. I rented a place in Venice, decided to write my second novel there by the sea, but when I looked out the window, I saw the surf breaking backward —literally, the surf was breaking backward. What really triggered it, though, the actual beginning of the psychosis, was when I was talking to my girl on the phone, trying to find out why she'd left me, why she wouldn't marry me. Somehow, that had deballed me, and I said, "Well, maybe I'm gay." And then suddenly a voice in my head cut in on the conversation and said, "Your life has ended. You will never write again."

Now I'm telling you the facts instead of the psychological interpretation. I became impotent. I tried to jerk off, and I couldn't come. I began hearing these voices. I wanted to kill every woman I saw. I had seizures. You know, they were actual seizures, like an epileptic seizure. And it's *the* single most terrifying— It always is sexual, or was sexual. You get a hot feeling in your cock. Your heart almost stops. Your inner voice says, "Uh-oh." And this rage comes, and you want to get a knife. And it's always in the cunt, too, you know. Or slash the breasts off. Or in the eyes. Any orifice.

One night, I had a date with Diane, who was a dear woman, a movie actress, and the inner voice said, "Pick up that knife, and drive over and kill Diane." So I hop in my station wagon, knowing that she has knives, I mean I know where she kept her kitchen knives, and the inner voice kept saying, "Knife—knife—knife— knife—knife." I'm driving along, and let's say eight tenths of me wants to kill and two tenths doesn't want to, and it's *terrifying*, the most confusing horror on earth. I drive into Diane's driveway, and I hear my inner voice saying, "Kill, kill, kill, kill," and only two tenths of me is still saying, "No, this isn't me." And I go up to the door, and I walk into the apartment, and there's an actor friend of hers with a knife in his hands, like this, and he's shouting, "Knife, knife, knife!" And what the hell, it turns out they're rehearsing Ionesco's *The Lesson*. I had walked into my own psychodrama. The most incredible circumstances. And that probably saved Diane's life, because everything just eased out of me. *Whish-sh-sh.* That's the horrible thing when you're bananas— nobody can know the awful things that are going on in your head.

But then other things happened. See, everything was happening at once—my girl leaving me, my brother disappearing, my novel coming out. And I can't sleep. I'm having conversations. The inner voices are going like mad. It just gets worse and worse. I begin to see things. Every upright object becomes, not exactly a visual cock, but I imagine sperm coming out of it. I feel like a zombie. I would walk around like this. I stand on street corners, immobilized, for five hours, just standing there.

Then I ran out of money. So Diane said, "Come and stay

with me." And I couldn't say, "Diane, you're taking care of me, but I'm also a homicidal maniac right now, and I may kill you." So I moved in there, and then I had another seizure, in the bedroom. The voice started again: "You're going to kill." I tore up the whole bed and actually broke up the bed slats to stop myself from going down to the kitchen to get a knife.

In April, my parents called up to say that my brother's body had been found. He'd jumped off a bridge into the Connecticut River—that was Thanksgiving weekend—and the river had finally thawed. And he was dead. So my folks call and say, "You've got to come back for the funeral." So I have to go back. And I'm nuts. But I can't tell anybody, because I've got to be the strong son coming home for the funeral. I'm saying to myself, What am I going to do? I'm having these spells. I'm hearing voices. All upright objects are spewing out sperm. But I can't tell anybody. So I go to the funeral. . . .

I was crying all the time, not just about Peter but about the girl who wouldn't marry me. I cried from April until—every day —reading old letters from her, over and over again, looking at her picture, and, you know, just crying. I'd get up in the morning, cry, go have breakfast, come back and cry. I couldn't do anything. I couldn't even order from a menu. You cannot make a decision. You want veal chops? I—I don't know. Veal chops? You know, you cannot make a decision.

Now I'm living at my folks' house on East 85th Street. And I went to visit a girl named Charlotte, and I had another attack. She was lovely. She had written me a lot of letters from New York, saying, "Come back, I love you." And now I'm just about to fuck her, and suddenly it switches around, and I have to say, "Charlotte, I'm about to kill you." And she was very cool. She said, "You're not going to kill me." And I said, "I'm having these terrible attacks." And she said, "Just calm down. Nothing's going to happen." And remember, I was impotent. I couldn't get it *up*. So nothing happened. I just said, "Hey, thanks." You know. And left.

But I'm staying with my folks, and I finally had an attack with my mother. And my mother is a wonderful woman. Ask anybody. She's a classics scholar, terrific. And the exact same thing happened. We were there together alone, and I suddenly got the—you know—got the hot flashes, the heavy breathing, and, you know, the voice saying, "Kill, kill, kill!" I was in a state of absolute rage, but I didn't know it. I had to excuse myself— "Mom. Mom. Excuse me. I gotta go now. I'll see you." Well, inside—I'm about to kill my *mother*, you know. And I still couldn't tell anybody about it.

I was always terrified of shrinks—because, one, shrinks never helped my father; and, two, they didn't seem to help my brother; and, three, I said, "If I go to a shrink, maybe he'll claim that I'm a homosexual." But there was a wonderful shrink from San Francisco, who was in town, a friend of my father's, and I saw him a couple of times. And I said, "I want to chop your—" My inner voice was saying, "I want to chop your *knees* off!" That's the way I felt inside, but I couldn't say that, you know. He told my father, "You'd better get a shrink for your son." But I didn't want that. But Dad keeps arranging for me to see shrinks—there were six in all—so I go to see an awful mousy little creep out in Brooklyn, who says, "You should be hospitalized." And I say, "No, I don't want to do that."

Let's see. What happened next? I go to stay at a friend's house, and I'm afraid I'm going to throw their little baby out the window. And have to stop myself. Now I'm under sedation. And my novel is finally out, and nothing is happening. It sold about two copies. But there was a publication lunch at Barbetta's—Bob, the editor, and his assistant, Wendy, and a couple of friends, and I'm absolutely out of it, absolutely bananas. Afraid I'm going to kill Wendy. Then I remember walking back to my folks' house, and thinking I might *have* to kill my mother. And that's the—you know—*whap!*—but that's the way you think. But nobody's home. And I wander over to the bookcase and reach up and pull down a book called, I think it's called *Freud on Dostoyevsky*, or *something* on Dostoyevsky. I'm thumbing through it and reading about how Dostoyevsky was prone to epileptic seizures—whereupon I fainted. My whole body went absolutely cold, and I— whew-w-w—fall right down. I have no idea what's happening to me. I crawl on my hands and knees to the next apartment. Knock on the door. A sixteen-year-old girl comes to the door. I whisper: "I'm Anthony Tuttle, and I think I'm having a heart attack. Get me to the hospital." We walk shakily over to Doctors Hospital, and they give me a—what is it called?—an electrocardiogram. And I say, "I'm under psychiatric care. This may be fake. I'm— you know—a very troubled person." I finally see my physical doctor, who's a wonderful guy, and he says, "Tony, you're in big trouble, and I think you should go to a mental hospital." He says, "There's a wonderful recreation room there, and you can play Ping-Pong, and make little ashtrays," and I'm saying to myself, My brother's just died—I can't go to a hospital, I don't want to go to a place where they have kids playing Ping-Pong. That was beneath me, you know.

But I finally went, to St. Luke's. It was the same day my agent sold my novel to Universal for thirty grand. I'm put on Thorazine immediately. I'm still homicidal in that I have the attacks. I have two guards watching me—aides—but at least I get sedated. Then that night a doctor started talking to me—Mel was his name—and he just said, "What's the problem?" And it was love at first sight, you know. I mean, *trust*. And as soon as I began to talk, and began to understand how outraged I was, and hurt, I began to get better.

I got out of the hospital after three months and just sat in this apartment. I had a lot of money from the movie sale, but I was still terrified, trembling, seeing the shrink five days a week. Was doing nothing. I was watching *Rat Patrol* a lot. And still crying. Finally I went and got a job as a waiter, at the same place where I'm working now. And that fall, I met a girl called Monique. My heart was still in California, but I had a wonderful affair with Monique. She nursed me back to sexual health—you know, gave me my cock and balls back, and I am forever thankful to her. She took care of me. But I had a couple of terrible attacks with her. You know—"Knife! Kill!" Once I left that bedroom right back there, and I telephoned Mel, and I said, "Mel, I'm here in bed with Monique, and I'm having an attack." And Mel, who lived right around the corner, said, "Meet me at Carl Schurz Park." So I met him there, and he walked me up and down, you know, saying, "Look, you're going to be okay. Tell Monique to leave. Explain it to her." So I called Monique and got her to leave the apartment.

Mel got to me somehow. There was no posing. I just sensed that he really cared. I never lay down on a couch, you know. He gave me five years of what's called supportive therapy. His job was to get me, you know, functioning again. I can still go back to Mel whenever I need to, although I haven't seen him in more than a year now. I still have rages. I occasionally feel an echo of an attack, but—I've been going with a very young girl, and she called me up the other day and said, "I can't see you any more." And I said, "Okay." And then I said to myself, That little cunt, that bitch, we've spent a beautiful five months together, and she calls me up and— Five years ago, six years ago, I would have said, "What's wrong with me? Maybe it's because I'm forty and she's eighteen." Actually, she's sixteen, but she's Latin. But there's nothing wrong with me. That sounds arrogant, but I don't feel it, you know. The healthy thing I did was, I called her back and said, "Hey, you're not only a deceptive bitch but you're a coward for not coming over here and telling me what's going on. . . ." That fucking cunt—you know, get the emotion out. The WASP tradition is always, "Let's keep everything quiet, let's keep everything pleasant." Well, I wish I were more Jewish. You know, scream it out—stop being "civilized."

I'm trying to think if I'm dramatizing to you the severity— but the attacks I had, and the despondency, and the sitting here —I tried to hang myself, but I didn't know what to hang myself with. But all I can say is that this was the profoundest experience of my life, and I feel absolutely blessed. Whenever I feel depressed, like when I was driving the taxi, I say, "Man, you've been to hell and back." I feel you have to have the shit kicked out of you to appreciate the blessedness of the clean breath or the lovely kiss.

7

A Sheaf of Love Stories

To fall in love is, as countless poets have told us, one of the most pleasant ways of going crazy. All judgment disappears, all sense of self-interest, and even of self. But for all its delights, it is undeniably a crisis, one in which the fear of rejection is equaled only by the fear of success. People in love are ready to commit any fraud or violence, even murder (as in *An American Tragedy*, or, for that matter, *Lolita*), even self-murder (*Romeo and Juliet* or *Anna Karenina*). On more mundane levels, the phenomenon generally leads to the church or city registry. In 1970, some 4,326,000 Americans, presumably in love, got married. In the same year, almost one third as many, 1,416,000, got divorced. These figures have subsequently become still more dramatic. Between 1967 and 1973, the rate of divorce has increased by almost 50 percent, from 2.9 to 4.3 per thousand. There are some observers who profess to regard this trend as a form of liberation, but just as each marriage (or each affair) represents an emotional commitment, each divorce represents a breakdown, a failure, a collapse of something that one had sworn to make permanent. All too often, of course, the failure and breakdown can occur even without a divorce, or even without a marriage. Still, the attempt to find love lasts a lifetime, and of all the conflicts that drive people crazy, this one is perhaps the most dangerous, perhaps because it is the most tantalizing.

Peter Franck, whose name is not really Peter Franck, is a well-known professor at a large university in California. His specialty is a field of science so esoteric that the ordinary citizen has never even heard of the various problems to which Professor Franck and other scholars devote their experiments, their learned papers, their conferences and symposia, and indeed their entire lives. Despite his scientific credentials, however, Professor Franck is a romantic, much preoccupied with his own emotions. He takes solitary walks in the woods to write poetry and to read Tolstoy in the original Russian, and he still believes, at the age of forty-six, that he will find the woman he has been looking for all his life. His first wife was several years older than he, and she bore him three children; his second was several years younger and bore him none. He has also encountered a number of seductive students, and the encounters keep getting more complicated.

"I first saw Anna in the summer of 1970, but I didn't pay too much attention to her," he recalls. "I was passing the main university bookstore, where she worked, and she was standing in the doorway, looking intently up the street, to the west, her eyes half closed against the setting sun. She was wearing a long black dress, below the knees, and her long, wavy black hair—she had a Mediterranean look that struck me. Not *struck*, but *hit*, somewhere deep. That was all. Then a couple of months later, my wife made some remark about a colleague in my department who was "all entangled with that girl that works in the bookstore." The one who wears black dresses? Yes. Damn him to hell, I thought. But that was all."

Franck's life was undergoing a series of upheavals. He and another professor had begun exploring a whole new region of their science. They jointly started a new seminar, which attracted all of seven students, one of whom was Anna, but the seminar was hardly more than a workshop for the theories they were developing. Franck presented an analytic study to the class, then revised it, then journeyed to Atlanta to present his views to the annual meeting of his scientific colleagues. The paper was received with reservations. "The implications of my position forced me to challenge a long-standing doctrine that had been developed by the giants of the field," he says. "When a scientist challenges *the* authorities, he becomes uniquely alone, with no one to turn to, no models to adjust to, with nothing up ahead but the unknown."

During this same period, the spring of 1973, Professor Franck's second marriage was coming apart. He had married this second wife partly because she was a graduate student in his own field, someone with whom he could discuss his work, and perhaps that was not enough, or perhaps there were professional disputes, or perhaps, after eight years, he was simply restless. In any case, once he had delivered his paper to the annual convention, he flew off to Paris and indulged himself with what he calls "some competent and almost unreally attractive streetwalkers." He says he "never once thought of Anna." From Paris, he took the Orient Express to Istanbul, and then on to Anatolia—"the Hittite sites, over three millennia old, majestic and serene on their mountaintops. And last of all to the battered towers of Ilium, swept by the great wind from the Aegean that blows in across the plain of Troy. I am sure I never thought of her."

When Professor Franck returned to his teaching that fall, the girl was once again in his course. She asked for an appointment to talk about her academic career, and then she asked him to write a letter of recommendation. "I began to notice her more and more," he recalls, "and to signal to her that I was doing so. After a few weeks, we tended to sit near each other in the seminar, or to glance at one another when sitting opposite. Mondays and Wednesdays, from one to two-twenty."

At about this time, there was a film festival at the university, and Franck went to see a Polish movie called *Illumination*.

"As I settled in the back row of the mezzanine, I suddenly noticed that Anna was in the balcony overlooking the entire theater, with one foot cocked up on a railing so that everyone could see her. That broad wants to get laid, I thought, and here I come. I caught her eye, and we stared at each other for about half a minute, but then I began to grin, and she blushed and turned away. The movie was marvelous, about the university years of a young physicist, who also had a sensuous streak and a sensuous smile, but I left without waiting for Anna. I assumed that she was with someone else, and I didn't want to know what he looked like. But the coincidence of seeing her at that particular movie, about scientific illumination and human passion, came as an omen, and I believe in omens. They affect my behavior in a predictable way.

"The next day, when one of my colleagues was conducting the class, I took a seat near the door and held the one next to me vacant. When Anna came in, she hesitated and then sat down beside me. That was as crucial as Madame Renal not removing her knee from beneath Julin's hand. A few minutes after the class had started, I asked her whether she would meet me for lunch the next day, to talk about graduate schools. That would be nice, she said. It was just a cafeteria lunch, but we both must have looked unnaturally excited because passersby kept staring at us. As we stood in line in front of the food trays, she made some mention of a poem she had written. I was surprised. I hadn't realized that she wrote poetry. Oh, yes, she had won a prize for one of her poems. I told her that I had written poems too. We got so involved that we forgot to pick out our food. Then we got the change mixed up. Then we couldn't find a table. Then we talked on and on, until she said, 'Look, it's been half an hour and we've hardly touched our food.'

"I had hardly mentioned my poetry to anybody. I had decided at the age of twenty-four to pursue science as my profession, but I kept reading many contemporary poets, and I used to take long walks along the water, reciting what I'd learned and dreaming up new lines of my own. Then one sweltering afternoon, I went to hear a recording of William Carlos Williams, in the poetry recording room, and at one definite point, the combination of his words and his voice made me feel that this was a hopelessly unattainable league, and so I quit right there, at about four-thirty P.M. I just stood up and walked out. But Anna wouldn't accept that. 'When I write,' she said, 'I write for days or weeks on end, and then I cull out the best lines and put the whole thing together. I never submit poems the way you used to; I write for people I know, and for those who give me their poems.' I think even now that one of the reasons I was falling in love with Anna came from watching her do what I have always thought mattered most but never had the courage to pursue with total commitment.

"The other people at the cafeteria stopped talking to each other and began eavesdropping, but we didn't pay any attention. We are both leaning forward, and she sometimes leaned halfway across the table, dominating, with her hand near the edge on my side. She told me about her father, who had been a cobbler in Sicily, and how he had emigrated here. I invited her for a walk that Saturday, but she said she had to cook a big dinner for friends, and I took the hint that I wasn't to bother her that weekend. We went on until three-fifteen, so she missed her physics lab, and we never got to talk about graduate schools at all.

"The next day, when I arrived at my office, I found an envelope tacked to my door. It contained a sheaf of poems from Anna. I went into my office and shut the door and read through all the poems, read them several times. Some of them were about her parents, some about her life at the university, one about her first experience of abortion. I remember pacing up and down as I read them. I was near tears. In fact, I think I did break into tears. I felt that her nailing the sheaf of poems to my door demanded a response, so I stayed up late that night, writing and rewriting a letter. I told her how I had felt while talking to her and 'wanting to kiss and be kissed on mouth and body.' I ended by saying, 'I am imagining how best to love you.' Then I went over to her apartment to deliver it. Her mailbox was locked, but I managed to pry it open and insert that letter. Then I spent the rest of the weekend working, except for Sunday afternoon, when I went to hear a performance of Haydn's *Lord Nelson Mass*. I hadn't shaved for three days, but nobody seemed to care.

"The next day, Monday, I came to my office and found a letter from Anna tacked to the door. She said she had been moved by our lunch and had daydreamed a lot about it afterwards, but my letter had left her 'agitated, rushed.' She said she was living with a lover—Now she tells me, the bitch! I thought—and she said he would go to pieces if she 'came to me.' She suggested that she'd like to do just that, but she said she couldn't cause such destruction, take such risks, so we should let our relations mature, reach different levels of understanding, and so forth. I immediately dashed off a letter apologizing for my impulsiveness but adding even more impulsively that I was a sensualist, and although I had had Platonic relations with many women, this would be an absurdity in her case. When I arrived at the seminar a few minutes later, Anna gave me her widemouthed smile, but mingled now with nervousness. She blushed. I handed her the letter and went on, but when the class was over, we agreed to meet in my office that evening.

"She came to my office at about seven. I remember that she was wearing a dark-purple sweater and black slacks. My two letters had changed her a good deal, and she now showed signs of wariness, even fear. I began by trying to explain my letters, and the basis of my feelings. I knew that I had miscalculated, but I didn't feel at all guilty. Then I started telling her more about who I was, and she did the same. Both her parents came from the same little white-stoned village of peasants and miners—in fact, her father had raped her mother when she was fifteen, and then her family had forced them to marry. They emigrated separately to the United States when Anna was about five, and then they split up. She had come to the university on a scholarship and done extremely well, but her life was pretty wild—half-year liaisons with what she called 'functional husbands,' plus Lesbian interludes that she felt had been important for her growth, plus some heavy drinking (a bottle of Jack Daniels every weekend). She had had three years of psychoanalytic treatment, which hadn't made much difference.

"What a woman! But what a whirlpool, drawing me in and down. Despite all her revelations, she still seemed hostile and suspicious. She often made gestures of fear or rejection. She asked a lot of questions about my two wives, my infidelity, and the twenty-four years that separated us. I think she felt, as I did, that she was being swept into something a good deal more complicated and more intense that she had calculated. After about two hours, this whole conversation leveled off onto a plane that was both soft and abstract. Somehow we drifted into religion, talking about the Virgin Mary as a figure of encouragement and forgiveness. Then suddenly we both fell silent.

"I had moved my swivel chair so that we were close together. She was breathing deeply. I was simply taut, sometimes trembling. The silence lasted five or ten minutes, and then I began telling her I loved her, and how and why. I stood up, and she rose to meet me and my embrace, but when I finally touched her lips, they seemed unresponsive, dead. Anna slumped back into her chair, and I kept kissing her face and hands and forearms and breasts, and whispering God knows what. Then once again, we lapsed into total silence. She turned away from me, her eyes downcast, her black hair falling over her face. The expression of longing combined with great sadness was almost intolerable. I sensed the lust growing in her body, but when she began to speak, slowly, with great effort, she began saying that she wanted simply to go with me, that she longed to make love but that she couldn't abandon her lover, whom she insisted she didn't love.

"Then she began talking about her own terror when she wakes up in the night, dreaming of death, hoping for it, fearing it, planning her own suicide. It was in the darkness and the loneliness that he would comfort her, cradling her in his arms like an infant. If she left him, and then I left her, then where would she be? And that was true. I realized that. Then I did something for which I'm now sort of thankful—I just slowed down and cooled everything off and backed away. Yes, we should move gradually. Yes, we should think of the future. We talked a bit more. She asked me to be 'constant,' and then she tore herself away and ran out.

"And that was when I became unhinged. It was not anything that anyone else could see. I was the only one who knew it. I don't remember just what I did after that conversation in my office, but I didn't sleep much that night, or the next night. I went to the gym and swam hard, a mile or more, but it did no good. I had passed into what I now think of as the penultimate stage before true madness, when you can perceive that you are crazy but your controls still work well enough to disguise that reality. My head felt light inside, irradiated, as though with sunlight, and my mind was racing, in fragments and streaks about Anna and myself and all that had happened. During one seminar, I excused myself twice to telephone Anna, to no avail, and then I came back and tried to continue the class work. The effort to focus on class work was so enormous that it forced me to unusual rapidity and impatience in my questions, but I have no way of knowing whether anyone noticed anything unusual.

"I felt that I had to find some sort of escape or support. I thought of going to a psychiatrist, but my mother had always said that people who went to psychiatrists were just demonstrating weakness and failure. You were supposed to solve your problems yourself. I even thought of suicide, but that would be even more a confession of weakness and failure. I finally decided to start telephoning people. I tried to invite myself to dinner with some friends, but they were going out. I called my two daughters at college, but I couldn't reach them. I called my son, who lives with my first wife, and invited him out for a walk the next day. Then I tried to call my mother in Chicago, but there was no answer. I thought about calling a professor who now lives in Florida, but I was afraid of what I might say, because I don't like to unload my problems on people. Then my son called back and begged off from the walk that he had agreed to. His social antennae are wondrously sensitive, and he does not like craziness, having seen too much of it in his mother. Now he seemed to sense some craziness in his father, and so he opted out. I swore aloud at him for reneging on me, and then forgave him instantly, feeling horribly guilty. I tried each of my daughters again, but both of them were out.

"The next day, I encountered Anna in a snow-covered field near the library. It was hard to talk to her, but I told her that I had had a dream of walking through an oak park with her and our three-year-old son. The whole conversation took place while we leaned against an iron rail fence. Her black hair and her dark blue coat contrasted with the snow. I reminded her that Handel's *Messiah* was being performed that Sunday, and I asked her if she would like to go. She agreed. I met her at the church on Sunday afternoon, and she looked flushed and apparently happy, but there was a hostility underneath. During the opening section, she flared up at me for touching her shoulder, so I didn't touch her again. I just sat tensed in my seat. And then toward the end, when the chorus seems to pull you upward into an infinite realm of beauty, I suddenly felt my dependence on her breaking. Just like that. It was like breaking a bone in your hand. We walked home together through the falling snow, saying nothing, and when I said goodbye, I felt it was a farewell forever.

"The trouble is that it wasn't. She still works at the bookstore on Fridays, and I still see her there sometimes, and we talk a bit about her studies. And I still love her. But there's nothing to be done."

People go crazy in myriad ways, but there is usually a strong connection between the form of the breakdown and the victim's sense of who he is. Robert Schumann's madness, for example, was that of a musician, and of a German Romantic. Vincent van Gogh would not have heard a high A ringing in his ear, and the

Marquis de Sade would not have thrown his wedding ring into the Rhine. The madness of a Boris Godunov, on the other hand, took the form of imagining murderous plots by Romanov conspirators. On a different level, James Baldwin, having been told once too often that "we don't serve Negroes here," suddenly picked up a mug of water and flung it at a waitress in a New Jersey restaurant, then ran through an angry crowd, and only then became frightened at the double realization "that I could have been murdered" and "that I had been ready to commit murder . . . from the hatred I carried in my own heart."

But these are all variations of the masculine fantasy, power sought, power defended, power denied. Among those officially classified and confined as crazy, the number of women is substantially greater than the number of men. Among patients hospitalized for schizophrenia, for example, the preponderance of women in various kinds of institutions during recent years has ranged from 51 to 63 percent. Are there, then, specifically female vulnerabilities and symptoms? Is there a specifically female road to madness?

In the mythological beginnings, it is difficult to sort out the differences. Robert Graves and others have argued that most of classical mythology represents a symbolic suppression of matriarchal culture, but the maenads were truly mad, in their own way, as were the Bacchic cultists in theirs. Although witchcraft was blamed largely on women, male heretics and sorcerers were tortured as ruthlessly as any witch, and for much the same reasons. In the secular world, it has long been assumed that women are more deeply involved in their emotional relationships than men are, and that they are less able to bear a break in those relationships. When such a break occurs and the lover disappears, according to the tradition created by a long line of male poets, the natural consequence is for the deprived maiden to go mad. Thus Hamlet, who was forced by his father's death into the darkest thickets of revolt and regicide, plays mad only to gain advantage, or perspective. But when Ophelia has to suffer the sorrow of her father's death, and at Hamlet's hand, she assumes that her lover will be punished for his crime, and she is totally overwhelmed by the series of disasters. "He is dead and gone, lady," she sings piteously, "he is dead and gone;/ At his head a grass-green turf,/

At his heels a stone." "O heavens!" Laertes cries out at the spectacle of his demented sister "fantastically dressed with straws and flowers," "is't possible a young maid's wits/ Should be as mortal as an old man's life?"

Eminently so. The tradition of the lovelorn maiden singing her sorrows continues onward into the great repository of all our heroic visions, grand opera. In Bellini's *I Puritani,* for example, Elvira goes berserk ("Ahimè! Ahimè!") over nothing more substantial than her fiancé's use of her bridal veil as a disguise for the escape of Queen Enrichetta. Perhaps the most celebrated victim of this form of bridal-altar madness was a Scottish girl named Janet Dalrymple, daughter of the first Lord Stair. Against the wishes of her parents, she promised herself to Lord Rutherford, but her stern mother made her give up Rutherford and marry another suitor named David Dunbar of Baldoon, which she did, on August 24, 1669. That same night, after the wedding feast, there came a series of wild shrieks from the connubial bedroom. When the family retainers broke down the door, they found the new husband lying in his own gore, and the blood-smeared wife gibbering by the fireplace. Her only coherent words, then or ever again, were: "Tak up your bonny bridegroom."

This was, of course, the model for Sir Walter Scott's *The Bride of Lammermoor,* and thus for Donizetti's *Lucia.* Somewhere in the course of these transformations, the wicked Lady Stair disappeared entirely, and indeed it is stated near the beginning of *Lucia* that she has recently died. The responsibility for the tragedy therefore falls wholly on her bankrupt brother, Enrico. The cause for Lucia's madness, however, remains the same—the loss of her lover, followed by a kind of legal rape by her unwanted bridegroom—and its expression takes the traditional form. Like most of the mad heroines, Lucia imagines herself reunited with her banished lover. *"Edgardo! io ti son resa"* (Oh, Edgar, I am yours once more), she sings at the start of the famous mad scene. *"Edgardo! ah Edgardo mio!"*

This whole saga, with trills and glissandi and flute obbligato, seems a little artificial nowadays, but the Romantics described their own melodramas with a fair degree of realism. Not only was *Lucia* based on the true story of Janet Dalrymple, but Sir Walter Scott ultimately went as bankrupt as the wicked Enrico, to the incredible sum of 130,000 pounds. He devoted the last seven years of his life to a hopeless struggle to pay off his debts. His labors drove him to a series of paralytic strokes, which in turn drove him to a madness in which he happily believed that all debts had been paid, and he was once more free. As for Donizetti, having completed more than sixty operas, he too suffered a paralytic stroke and lost his mind. Janet Dalrymple died within two weeks of her marriage and breakdown; Lucia went mad and died all within the course of Act II; Donizetti wandered around for the last four years of his life without even knowing who he was.

Still, what of the "real" women, not opera heroines who miraculously revive to the crash of applause, but unhappy creatures who are not applauded and do not revive? Do they have a special vulnerability? Nancy Chaucer, the lawyer whom we last saw going to the polo matches with her stricken father and her convenient suitor, duly married the suitor, and she did love him, in her way, as best she could. He seems to have been obsessed about her.

"Charley was terribly nervous, as I said—not at all somebody who was about to try to hold your hand right away. So he didn't make *me* nervous. And I had always assumed that I was going to be married. Love and sex and marriage were all one bundle. I never thought that I was ever going to be independent. And then I wanted to get pregnant. I wasn't sure that I was a woman unless I had a baby. And when that happened—the only time, except recently, that I have felt safe against the world was when I had another being inside me, as a buttress. I was happier than probably any other time in my life. I no longer felt that I could be destroyed by every person that came along. It never occurred to me that the baby would actually get born. But unfortunately it did. They gave me a spinal anesthetic, and the doctor said 'Push,' and I felt *but nothing.*"

Nancy's nervous husband seems to have been acutely embarrassed by the maternity ward. He did his best to ignore most of what was happening there, and his wife resented it.

"Charley just sat there in the labor room and reading to me from the Philadelphia *Inquirer*. It was about the Algerian crisis. I'll never forget it. It was about the time De Gaulle was taking over, and Charley was reading to me about it from the Philadelphia *Inquirer*. Finally, the pains were getting so enormous—this was before they gave me the anesthetic—that I was on the verge of screaming. It was just terrible. So I told Charley, 'Don't read to me any more, because I just wouldn't be able to understand it.' Which in my mother's language meant, 'Stop and pay attention to me.' But Charley didn't seem to understand. He just went on reading the *Inquirer* to himself. As the pains would get horrible, I would squeeze his hand, and he would sort of look up, and sort of as an afterthought, squeezed my hand back. But he had no real connection with me. He wasn't really paying attention to me at all. And I didn't really have much connection with the birth. I wasn't *part* of the birth. The doctor finally had to use forceps, and I felt the tugging and suction as she was pulled out of me. And I could see it in the mirror. I could see this gorgeous magenta blood that came out. That was beautiful, just beautiful. The rest was the most awful feeling of being almost not there.

"When the baby was about six weeks old, we moved to Chicago for two years, because of Charley's work. Those were sort of lonely years, but they were partly good. They probably helped me, in a way, to actively go mad. (That's not a word I like; I really don't.) I started hallucinating when I was out in Chicago. I would look at a chair or a table or something—I had a favorite chair, a straight-backed chair, dark wood, with a very high, curved back—and I would watch it rippling into life. It would move. It would throb. I could do this any time, sitting on a bus, or anywhere.

"As far as my behavior went, though, I was almost frigid at that point. Not literally. Afternoons I would lie down, and Charley would give me an orgasm, which would take about twenty minutes. And it was always a *project*. I'd feel guilty because Charley was working so hard to do this for me, but I just sort of hated making love. We made love every single day for several years, and I was too *weak* to be able to say, 'I don't want to.' I'd start saying, 'Well, I don't feel very good.' And he'd get angry because he'd know I was turning him away. We'd have a scene for about an hour. He would get angry, really angry, and I would just turn and sulk, and then we'd always have to clear it up. So I would make love to him anyway in order to prove: 'Yes, I do love you.'

"After we got back to Philadelphia I went back to Bryn Mawr to get my degree, but I was pregnant again, and then—uh —I was seduced by the gynecologist. You see, he was in a position where he was examining me and he probably noticed or could tell the physical signs of arousal and excitement, and he just quietly manipulated me. And I didn't protest. At that time, it was beyond my ken that a woman could make love to someone other than her husband. It was not part of my moral existence. And that house of cards really came tumbling down. He probably could rightly figure out that I was vulnerable to his seduction, and the thing is that he made love to me *right* on the examining table, with my legs up in the stirrups. And it was great! That was the difficulty—he looked very much like my father, and I had an orgasm almost instantly.

"Looking at it objectively, it was totally unethical of him. He really took gross advantage, and it's outrageous what he did. I *do* mean that. But even though I didn't actively encourage him, he could see that he was going to get away with it, and for me, it was so removed from anything that I could make any connection with that it almost removed any responsibility. Then a while later, I got sick, and he made a house call, and made love. He knew he could just make love to me, and I didn't have to take the responsibility of inviting him to do so. I could pretend that it was some *deus ex machina*. A little bit like the first occasion with my father, when nothing was spoken and nothing was acknowledged. It just took place, and I wasn't responsible, officially. I remember, the next morning, I wanted to write in my diary, except that I woke up at about five in the morning, and I felt terribly sexy, so I woke Charley up and made love to him and had an orgasm with him in about five minutes, or two minutes, or one minute. He couldn't believe it.

"Toward the end of that month, January, I called this gynecologist and said, 'I'm feeling so shaky and mixed up and utterly confused, and I think I ought to see a psychiatrist.' I mean, by then the guilt had begun to set in, and I was just panicked. And part of the panic was that if *that* could fall as one point in my ethics or morals, then everything was really external to me. I had never really felt responsible for anything, and so everything I did was just trying to figure out what other people wanted me to do.

But he said, 'Oh, my dear, it's just growing pains.' I guess he wanted to protect himself, because if I told another doctor what had happened, then he might get in trouble.

"As that spring went on, Charley was away a lot, for two or three weeks running, back on weekends and then away again. We had a visitor from France, and one night when Charley was away, I called up a friend of mine, and we took the Frenchman out on the town. We picked up somebody in a bar—I don't remember just how—and we all went to a night club and had a nice time. And then—uh—I took him home with me. I wouldn't make love to him—I was just too embarrassed—but I masturbated him, apologetically. You know, I felt I had to do something for him. But I couldn't make love to him because I just couldn't face *voluntarily* committing adultery, or having sexual feelings. I was by that time feeling physically disintegrated. I do remember, in late April, sitting in the bathtub with my eyes open and watching my legs and my arms float away from me. I was so terrified. And then my head started. I held onto my head and I got out of the bathtub.

"Early in May, I finally did go to a psychiatrist, and he didn't give me any answers. He just sat and listened. And that was the *end*. I mean, if *he* couldn't do something— I met Charley at a cocktail party that week. He'd just come from something, and we met at the party, and I said, 'I went to see a psychiatrist today.' And Charley looked at me and said, 'Well, you'll have to go earn the money to do it.' That's the sort of speaking terms we were on at that point. By now I had reached a situation where I—when I couldn't think of something else to do, I found myself looking at the knives in the kitchen, and I wanted to cut my wrist. At the same time, I was writing a paper on the plays of Garcia Lorca, and when I finished, I took the paper, and a knife and some old sheets, and I got into a taxi to go out to Bryn Mawr. As we drove through town, I was trying to get the courage to cut my wrists, because I just had to do it. But at the same time, even though I was trying to kill myself, it never occurred to me that if I did cut my wrist, I might die from it.

"Then, as we drove along, I saw a man outside, in the sunlight, and he was *smiling,* and he looked joyful and happy. The freedom to smile in the sunlight. I didn't feel I had the right to do that. And I thought, That's it, brother! You know, I *f-f-f-t!* I cut my wrist, and I wrapped it up in sheets. So it didn't bleed, or I didn't see it bleed. The taxi driver didn't know anything about it. I got to Bryn Mawr, and I paid off the taxi, just as though everything were all right. I went up and delivered my paper to the teacher, and then I called the psychiatrist, and I said: 'Psychiatrist, I have cut my wrist, and what should I do now?' He said, 'Go to Such and Such Hospital.' I went to the hospital and very calmly said to the nurse, 'Well, I cut my wrist,' And she said, 'Oh, fine, take a seat over there.' So I sat there. I peeked a look at my wrist, and it wasn't bleeding very much, and I said to myself, 'Oh, well, that's very incompetent of me.' So I took out the knife and cut it again, because I didn't want to do a bad job of it. And then all I remember is that I was almost immediately being taken care of.

"But I couldn't make anyone understand what had happened. Charley came to the hospital, but he didn't seem to care at all, even then. And when I went to the psychiatrist the next day, we had a nice, rational, quiet conversation. I spoke with control, and, you know, complete sentences. I *couldn't* let my feelings go. So at the end, I said, 'Well, you know, what I feel like doing now is I want to cut off the end of my little finger and make rubber-stamp patterns with it, because I saw the patterns of flesh cut open yesterday, and they were very pretty. I liked them.' This was the only method I could use to tell him I was really crazy, absolutely out of my mind."

There have been millions of cases of husbands and wives driving one another crazy, but the ruined romance that still reverberates in our imagination is that of Scott and Zelda Fitzgerald. They seem to have been born to destroy each other, and it was a destiny that they both welcomed with an almost morbid joy. At one point, after Zelda had been confined in a mental institution, Scott wrote to her psychiatrist that "possibly she would have been a genius if we had never met." But not long after that, in one of many terrible confrontations, he told Zelda, "You are a third-rate writer and a third-rate ballet dancer. . . . I am a professional writer with a huge following. I am the highest-paid short-story writer in the world . . . and I am supporting you." Zelda's responses ranged from telling him, "My life has been so miserable that I would rather be in an asylum," to writing from the asylum, "There is no way to ask you to forgive me for the misery and pain which I have caused you. . . . You are always my darling." To a doctor, she sobbed, "I can't get on with my husband, and I can't live away from him." Scott, sinking deeply into alcoholism, told his secretary, "I am as I am because of my wife." And to the psychiatrist: "I will probably be carried off eventually by four strong guards shrieking manicly that after all I was right and she was wrong, while Zelda is followed home by an adoring crowd in an automobile banked with flowers, and offered a vaudeville contract."

Although the saga of the Fitzgeralds is one of our most popular folk tales—the brilliant young novelist and the Southern belle, spoiled darlings of the Jazz Age, outliving their time and descending into drunkenness and madness—the explanations for this saga have undergone some interesting changes. At first, at the time of Fitzgerald's death in 1940, he was considered simply a burnt-out anachronism. The *New York Times* editorial page expressed sorrow that he and some of his contemporaries "could not adjust themselves, no matter how hard they tried, to the swift and brutal changes of these times." It added that this was "a pity, for here was a real talent which never fully bloomed." That patronizing view, quite widespread, was almost single-handedly reversed by Fitzgerald's Princeton contemporary Edmund Wilson. He edited and published first the 70,000-word torso of *The Last Tycoon*, which he acclaimed as "Fitzgerald's most mature piece of work," and then the melancholy collection of articles, journals and letters known as *The Crack Up*. ("Of course all life is a process of breaking down," Fitzgerald began, "but the blows that do the dramatic side of the work . . . don't show their effect all at once. . . .").

If revisionist literary history made a hero of Fitzgerald, what could it make of his demented wife? Ernest Hemingway had an answer, and in *A Moveable Feast*, he made it cruelly explicit. "Zelda was jealous of Scott's work," he wrote, and she did her best to prevent him from accomplishing anything. "Zelda . . . smiled happily . . . as he drank the wine. I learned to know that smile very well. It meant she knew Scott would not be able to write." Zelda also told Scott that he was sexually inadequate, physically inadequate, and Scott related his embarrassment to

Hemingway. Hemingway offered to inspect him in the men's room of the restaurant where they were having lunch, then told him: "You're perfectly fine. You are O.K. There's nothing wrong with you." Fitzgerald was not satisfied. "Why would she say it?" he persisted. "Zelda is crazy," Hemingway said. "Zelda wants to destroy you." Zelda, on the other hand, had an answer of her own. To Fitzgerald's amazement and mortification, she accused him of a homosexual involvement with Hemingway. Fitzgerald never forgave that. Neither, presumably, did Hemingway.

The legend of a hero burdened with a mad wife is a romantic one—how many adolescents have quivered over the spiritual sufferings of Mr. Rochester in *Jane Eyre?*—but not necessarily a true one. Nancy Milford proved that in her biography, *Zelda,* which demonstrated that Fitzgerald's aggressions not only contributed to Zelda's madness but helped to prevent her from being cured. When Zelda managed, inside the Phipps Clinic in Baltimore, to write her novel, *Save Me the Waltz,* Scott reacted with indignation. He declared that she was trying to build a "dubitable career" with "morsels of living matter chipped out of my mind, my belly, my nervous system and my loins," and that she was trying to crash her way into literature "with the frail equipment of a sick mind and a berserk determination." He did worse. He wrote Maxwell Perkins of Scribner's, to whom Zelda's novel had been submitted, that any praise for her work should be kept "on the staid side." At the same time, he himself felt no qualms about incorporating Zelda's forlorn letters from a Swiss asylum into *Tender Is the Night.* He also seemed to have no idea that her mysterious relapse early in 1934, after more than eighteen months out of the hospital, might be connected to the fact that she had just read the galleys of *Tender Is the Night* and seen her misery exposed to the world.

From revelations such as these, some of the more intemperate feminists of our own time have argued not only that Scott drove Zelda mad but that she probably wasn't mad at all, a victim of her husband and the psychiatrists who joined in incarcerating her. Phyllis Chesler, for example, has written in *Women and Madness* that "what we consider 'madness' . . . is either the acting out of the devalued female role or the total or partial rejection of one's sex-role stereotype." She views Zelda, therefore, as a woman who was "treated and/or imprisoned by male psychiatrists—most of whom were, quite literally, agents for [her] husband's 'will.'" In actual fact, the psychological system that imprisoned Zelda, without any opposition on her part, was the network of traditions that defined the Southern belle. She was not only a social princess, whose courtiers were supposed to laugh at her jokes and hand her into carriages, but also an artistic princess, who expected applause for her renditions of Chopin waltzes or her watercolors of the rose garden. This was not a stereotype that Zelda rebelled against; it was a stereotype she profoundly believed in (as, of course, did Scott). For a newspaper interview in 1923, when asked what would represent an ideal day, she answered: "Peaches for breakfast. . . . Then golf. Then a swim. Then just being lazy . . . being quiet and hearing pleasant sounds—rather a total vacuity. The evening? A large, brilliant gathering, I believe."

The one thing completely alien to the belle was work. Not only was she unable and unwilling to do anything herself, but she resented anyone else's work depriving her of the attention she deserved. Money was supposed to come from inherited lands or trust funds or from an allowance from Daddy, the Judge (Zelda's father literally was a judge). Fitzgerald loved this game and played it as long as he could, but novelists do finally have to write their novels, during long hours of solitude; and so, while Fitzgerald labored over *The Great Gatsby* on the Riviera in the summer of 1924, Zelda spent her time swimming with a young French aviator. Then there was the crisis. Zelda talked of divorce. Scott wanted a confrontation with the aviator, who apparently had no intention whatever of marrying Zelda. Zelda swallowed lots of sleeping pills and had to be marched around the room until they wore off. When the Fitzgeralds later began telling this story to their friends, or even to strangers, they added that the aviator had tragically died—but he actually lived on to become an admiral, and to deny that there had ever been an affair. They both "had a need of drama," the admiral said. They had "made it up," and perhaps they were the victims of their own "unsettled and a little unhealthy imagination."

Scott suppressed his rage, patched up the marriage, and awaited the opportunity for revenge. It came three years later, when he was invited to Hollywood to write a screenplay for Constance Talmadge. He met a young actress named Lois Moran. Young—she was seventeen, and according to George Jean Nathan, "it was rumored that she still wore the kind of flannel nightie that was bound around her ankles with ribbons." Scott was charmed. Zelda was not. In the course of their quarrels about her, Scott delivered the Minnesota Irish Puritan stab to the Southern belle; he said that Lois Moran at least worked, had a job, earned money, supported herself. Later, when Scott was out dining with the girl, Zelda angrily took a heap of her own "artistic" creations, clothes that she had designed for herself, and burned them in the bathtub. From then on, her desire for a professional career—writing, dancing, painting, anything—became itself a career.

By this time, however, the madness was well advanced, Scott's as well as her own. What had once been a series of youthful pranks now became a series of not-so-youthful assaults. In Nice, encountering an old woman selling a trayful of nuts and candies, Scott delivered a stage kick to the underside of the tray and sent the old woman's goods flying in all directions. At a formal dinner in the garden of Gerald Murphy's villa, Scott inexplicably staggered to his feet and threw a ripe fig at the bare back of one of the guests, who ignored him. When another Riviera host failed to invite him to dinner at all, he threw cans of garbage over the host's garden wall. In all of this, Zelda was his willing accomplice, although their views of some scenes differed. One night when they encountered Isadora Duncan at an inn, Scott flirted with the aging dancer, but Zelda suddenly leaped across the table and flung herself down a long flight of stone steps.

Zelda seems to have believed passionately that even in her middle twenties she could find some kind of salvation in the ephemeral transfigurations of the dance. "The only message I ever thought I had," she wrote some years later, "was four pirouettes and a foueté." She worked long hours and presented her dancing teacher with bouquets of flowers every day, but there were some who received no message from her pirouettes. Gerald Murphy, invited to watch her at the dance studio, commented later that "there was something dreadfully grotesque in her intensity—one could see the muscles individually stretch and pull; her legs looked muscular and ugly. It was really terrible. One held one's breath until it was over. Thank God, she couldn't see what she looked like."

In a way, of course, she could, and so, in the spring of 1930, slightly drunk, she entered the Malmaison hospital on the outskirts of Paris. Pacing up and down in her room, she let her anxieties overflow, saying, "It's dreadful, it's horrible, what's to become of me, I must work, and I won't be able to, I should die, but I must work." Scott described it as "a sort of nervous breakdown from overwork," but it was not that. The feverish work was less a cause than a symptom. She heard voices, she had fainting fits, she suffered from eczema and colitis, she attempted suicide. Scott had her transferred to a sanitarium in Switzerland.

Zelda had no doubt about the reality of her breakdown. "It's ghastly losing your mind," she wrote Scott, "and not being able to see clearly, literally or figuratively—and knowing that you can't think and that nothing is right, not even your comprehension of concrete things like how old you are or what you look like." The doctors seem to have had very little idea of how to treat her, except for the usual remedies—rest, exercise, and a lot of questions. They called in Bleuler, the great Bleuler, Freud's first major follower and first major apostate, Bleuler who had originally invented the term (and thus the concept): schizophrenia. This resulted in the usual mystifications. Zelda was suffering from "neither a pure neurosis (meaning psychogenic) nor a real psychosis," her doctor wrote to Scott. "I consider her a constitutional, emotionally unbalanced psychopath—she may improve, never completely recover." Zelda, regarding Bleuler as "a great imbecile," recognized the futility of the situation. "*Please* help me," she wrote Scott. "Every day more of me dies with this bitter and incessant beating I'm taking. You can choose the conditions of our life and anything you want if I don't have to stay here miserable and sick at the mercy of people who have never even tried what it's like. . . . The longer I have to bear this, the meaner and harder and sicker I get. . . . *Please* Please let me out now."

Zelda was never completely sane during the eighteen years that remained to her, but during most of that time, she was not really insane either. She wrote a novel that was published, painted pictures that were exhibited, and her letters are coherent and even eloquent. Nor was she ever legally committed to any of the institutions in which she lived. All of her confinements and releases were the result of elaborate negotiation. When she was in the hospital, she wanted to get out, but when she was at home with Scott, she began crumbling and yearning for the artificial security of the hospital. Scott, too, wanted her at home, then wanted her away. Afflicted by alcoholism and self-doubt, he felt increasingly unable to provide for Zelda's caprices, or their daughter's upbringing, or his own needs, increasingly unable to produce the flood of stories that supported the Fitzgerald menagerie. He kept drinking, endlessly, and he kept arguing with Zelda, who fought back as best she could. She didn't even begin to realize that Scott himself was going crazy.

Like all couples, they quarreled about who was to blame for what had gone wrong in their lives, about Zelda's need for independence, about Scott's need to make money to support her lack of independence, about Zelda's irrationality, about Scott's drinking. Unlike most couples, though, their quarrels took the strange form of a struggle over the literary rights to each other's lives. Scott had been working since 1926 on a novel variously called *Our Type* and *The World's Fair* and *The Boy Who Killed His Mother*. It was originally, according to a letter to his editor, to have been partly about "an intellectual murder on the Loeb-Leopold idea" and partly "about Zelda and me and the hysteria of last May." As he worked on it over the years, rewriting one version after another, the murder idea was eliminated, and the novel became more and more the story of his life with Zelda during her periods of breakdown. That story kept changing. Zelda emerged from the Swiss clinic in the fall of 1931 and returned with Scott to see her family in Alabama. Scott went on to Hollywood to work on a screenplay. He learned only by mail that Zelda's father was dying, and that her familiar symptoms were recurring: insomnia, eye trouble, eczema, asthma. Scott took her on a vacation to Florida, but there were several hysterical scenes, and Zelda said she wanted to go back into a hospital.

Once inside, she finished *Save Me the Waltz* in less than a month. Scott angrily wrote to her psychiatrist that while he had been delayed in his own work "because of the necessity of keeping Zelda in sanitariums," she had now stolen parts of his unfinished book. "Literally one whole section of her novel is an imitation of [mine], of its rhythms, materials." It was, of course, simply Zelda's own story—a belle who is actually named Alabama marries a famous painter, lives the high life for a time, seeks independence as a ballerina but suffers a foot injury that ends her career—but Scott now insisted that Zelda's own story belonged to him alone. He demanded, as a matter of principle, the right to make a lot of changes in the manuscript. "Everything we have done is my [property]. I am a professional novelist, and I am supporting you. That is all my material. None of it is your material."

Zelda accepted Scott's changes—she was pitifully surprised and upset at his anger—but not his demand that she abandon all fiction forever. She wanted to write a novel about insanity, and she warned him that "the material which I will elect is legitimate stuff which has cost me a pretty emotional penny to amass and which I intend to use when I can get the tranquillity of spirit necessary to write the story of myself versus myself. That is the book I really want to write." By the time she did achieve that tranquillity of spirit, Scott was dead, and Zelda was so deeply involved in religion that the unfinished manuscript of *Caesar's Things* is little more than a series of visions and hallucinations.

Save Me the Waltz was a total failure. The most favorable review referred to Zelda as "a peculiar talent," and the most unfavorable referred to her as "a laughingstock." The sales were 1,392 and the royalties $120. Two years later, in the spring of 1934, Fitzgerald finally published *Tender Is the Night,* and the reception, in terms of his early success, seemed almost as bad. The reviews of this marvelously romantic novel were mixed, patronizing. Sales ended at about 13,000 copies. And Ernest Hemingway wrote with his customary grace: "Of all people on earth you need discipline and instead you marry someone who is jealous of your work, wants to compete with you and ruins you. . . . I thought Zelda was crazy the first time I met her and you complicated it even more by being in love with her and, of course, you're a rummy. . . ."

Fitzgerald had staked everything on *Tender Is the Night,* and on the morning after, he could see nothing but gray skies and doctors' bills, and now he learned that he had tuberculosis, and he could not stop drinking. *Tender Is the Night* ends with Nicole

Diver remarrying and Dick Diver fading further and further into obscurity. For a time, Fitzgerald seemed to be pursuing a similar destiny. We do not know exactly how his breakdown occurred, but in February of 1935 he suddenly fled to the little mountain resort of Hendersonville, North Carolina, where he hoped to "think it over," and to drink nothing stronger than beer. "I took a dollar room in a drab little town where I knew no one and sunk all the money I had with me in a stock of potted meat, crackers and apples." Every night, he washed his shirt and two handkerchiefs.

Fitzgerald's own account, in *The Crack Up*, is moving but not quite convincing. There are too many metaphors. It is never clear whether he does not understand his own crisis or whether he is trying to avoid the embarrassment of full confession or whether he is simply being literary. Searching back for the beginnings of the crackup, he attaches great importance, probably too much importance, to an early attack of tuberculosis that delayed him a year at Princeton, and to the obstacles in his courtship of Zelda. "A man does not recover from such jolts," he said, "he becomes a different person and, eventually, the new person finds new things to care about."

The immediate cause of the flight to North Carolina had been the revelation of a new attack of tuberculosis ("I had a strong instinct that I must be alone. I didn't want to see any people at all"), but the tuberculosis mysteriously disappeared again. Fitzgerald wrote that he "cracked like an old plate as soon as I heard the news." Only then, he said, did he begin to "realize that for two years my life had been a drawing on resources that I did not possess, that I had been mortgaging myself physically and spiritually up to the hilt." Or, in yet another metaphor, "so there was not an 'I' any more—not a basis on which I could organize my self-respect—save my limitless capacity for toil that it seemed I possessed no more. It was strange to have no self—to be like a little boy left alone in a big house, who knew that now he could do anything he wanted to do, but found that there was nothing he wanted to do."

And yet he recovered. He felt himself to be a permanently cracked plate, one that "will not be brought out for company, but . . . will do to hold crackers late at night," and he felt that his only hope for survival would be to "cease any attempts to be a person—to be kind, just or generous. . . . There was to be no more giving myself—all giving was to be outlawed henceforth under a new name, and that name was Waste." This is not, of course, a solution—that is the message of the loaves and fishes. It would not have worked even if Fitzgerald had committed himself to it, and he did not really do so. Instead, he labored on, partly for Zelda, mostly for their daughter, until his death. Having never had any treatment for his breakdown, however, no psychoanalysis, no rest cures, no wonder drugs, he did die a free man, in the apartment of his mistress in Hollywood. Zelda received, for almost twenty years, the best psychiatric treatment that money could buy, in the most progressive psychiatric clinics in the Western world. And it was because the last of these clinics was designed to be pleasantly homelike, without steel fire escapes or automatic alarms or sprinkler systems, that when the place accidentally caught fire, Zelda finally burned to death.

The crackup known as divorce is so commonplace nowadays that many people profess to regard it as no more serious than a common cold. Instead of being treated as an emotional disaster, it is viewed as some sort of liberation, freeing both husband and wife to seek new partners and new disasters. Even the children are now said to prefer divorce to "a bad marriage." I myself have never seen much evidence to support these indulgent views. Most of the divorced people I know have not fared much better with their second wives (or husbands) than with their first, and in almost every case, the children have bitterly and helplessly resented the breakup.

I remember one moderately unhappily married man, for example, who had raised his three sons in the Kennedy tradition—money, politics, football, *machismo*, and a few inspirational poems and sayings committed to memory. He eventually lined up the three adolescent boys in the dining room and began the usual speech to the effect that Daddy and Mother think it would be better if they tried living separately for a while. He was still rather shaken, when I saw him two or three days later, at the perfectly predictable result. The three sons, who all knew that their parents had been quarreling, but who had all been taught to keep cool, be tough, win—all three simultaneously burst into tears. For years, they had never once cried about anything, but now, on the very threshold of Harvard or Princeton or wherever they were going, they sobbed like babies, begged their parents to reconsider, and failed in every way to play their prescribed roles in the standard scenario of liberation. Several years have passed since then. The husband has gone through a second marriage and a second divorce, the wife has done likewise, and the oldest of the sons has had his first breakdown.

To portray such a situation in more detail, I went to seek out a man I shall have to call Sidney. He once worked in the same office with me, and I still remember the day when a colleague remarked to me, "Say, have you heard about Sidney? He says his wife is trying to murder him. He says she tried to poison his food."

"He sounds as though he's going crazy," I said, the way one always does, half jocularly, using that phrase to dismiss the problem. But it was true. Not long afterward, Sidney entered a mental hospital and stayed there for six months. Then he went to Washington and got a job with, of all things, the Peace Corps. He seemed to have recovered, so I called him up, and he invited me to come and eat some *hasenpfeffer*. He welcomed me to a spare, white-walled studio, with a fireplace at one end and a large skylight overhead. Sidney lives alone now, a man of about fifty, solidly built but not particularly athletic. He has gray hair, combed straight back, and horn-rimmed spectacles. He talks in a very low, sad voice, interrupted occasionally by a barking laugh. He remembers his wife with deep resentment.

"It all began—" he says, "it all began when I bought my wife an electric dishwasher. So she had time on her hands. The two children were growing up—they were six and eight—and housework was not enough for her. She wanted to go to school. She studied library science, which was just about the kind of thing that would enlist her full talents. She graduated from the course and got a master's degree and went to work as a librarian. At the library, she had an assistant, who was twenty-two years old. She was then thirty-six. He was a maladjusted young man who needed an older woman to teach him about life. And she was the one to do it. He was living through one summer in an apartment in a mews just a few hundred yards from where we lived—he was minding someone's cats—and they used to spend the noon hour there, in the apartment."

Sidney thought that his wife began "acting very peculiarly," but he tried for a time to avoid learning the reasons. His wife took a different tactic.

"One night, I heard her talking to my daughter, in the child's bedroom. My daughter was crying and saying, 'Will you try? Will you try?' So I finally provoked a showdown by saying, 'What in hell are you saying to her?' And then she said she couldn't live with me any longer. All this—to me, being a peasant from the state of Maine, from a family in which there had never been a divorce—all this was totally unimaginable. What's the worst thing you can imagine happening to you? For me, I'm afraid of going blind, or waking up blind and paralyzed or something like that. But in those days, to think of my family coming apart was a thought on the scale of those. The worst thing I could imagine was *happening* to me.

"So there followed three nights of—of very emotional goings on, all night long. I didn't sleep a wink. I spent my time upbraiding and abusing this female for outraging everything that held the world together. And she said it was all my own fault, for being narrow and uncomprehending. It now seems ridiculous to think of it, but I felt that I just couldn't live if my family broke up, so I went to the doctor who had done the blood tests when we got married, and I got enough sleeping pills to get me out of the situation. I went to a hotel, intending to take them there. For some reason, I made a last phone call to her, telling her what I intended to do. I'm pretty sure I did intend to do it, but I told her that I'd blink out in a more peaceful way if I knew what she was talking about—why this marriage could no longer go on, since it had gone on for twelve years, as happily as anybody else's, I guess. And it was then that she told me what it was really all about. The college student. And then I got raging mad. To think that I'd come so close to serving her purposes. It would have been lovely for her if I'd just taken the pills, faded out. But I went back to the apartment, and I said, 'I'm not getting out, you're getting out.' And she did.

"I was now alone with the two children. And the complicated thing was that one of them was very sick, the boy. In fact, he was dying. All I could do was to hire a housekeeper. In the time that I had the children, I hired three housekeepers. I couldn't manage. I had never experienced what it was like to get up in the morning and realize that a little girl needed a clean dress, or a dress that was ironed. I didn't know anything about taking care of children. I could get their breakfasts, but seeing that there were enough socks, or taking care of their other needs, that was just something that I couldn't handle very well. And at the office, in the middle of the afternoon, the housekeeper would sometimes call up and say that the children hadn't come home from school, and I would think, Oh, my God, what has happened? And I'd get on the telephone and try to trace them. This sort of thing went on and on. It was a situation that I really couldn't cope with.

"I would come to work in the morning, without much sleep, and I'd try to sit at my desk, where there would be proofs or something to work on. I'd try to work on them, but I couldn't sit still. I'd stand up and walk round and round and round until it was lunchtime. Then I went over to Sardi's East, because it was near the office. One of the particulars of this situation was that I couldn't sleep and I couldn't eat. A friend of mine told me that when it came time to eat, I should have a chicken sandwich. The waiters at Sardi's knew me, so as soon as they saw me, they'd bring three martinis and a chicken sandwich. That was lunch. Then I'd go back to the office and walk some more.

"Once at Sardi's—this is what it was like—I remember I was being taken out to lunch by a couple of press agents from one of the television networks, a man and a woman, she very glamorously and dramatically clad. I don't remember what they were trying to sell me, but we had lunch, and talked, and I stayed in the conversation, and even got off a wisecrack or two, which I thought was not bad. And all the time this was going on, in front of these two people, I was whimpering and crying, tears streaming down, face twitching and working. And even though I kept up the conversation, I kept thinking, What in God's name do they think is going on? And the funny thing was that we all pretended nothing was going on. We just sat there talking business like businesslike people.

"And other strange things began to happen. I remember walking in the streets once and thinking that the faces on the billboards were following me with their eyes, and then turning their backs on me. There was another hallucination, apparently a classic one—I later read about it in a book—where you open a desk drawer and flames come out at you. Then another time I was walking in the street, and I saw a small boy on a tricycle, and he had only one eye. I was sort of horrified by the idea of his being deformed, but I said to myself, Don't worry. There's nothing so terrible about it. It's just that one side of his face is just a plain, blank surface of skin. And then I looked up, and I saw that everybody on the street had just one eye, just like the boy. So I—I sat down on a bench until all the people on the street had two eyes again. The thing is that when you're having hallucinations, you always know you're having hallucinations, even though the hallucinations are perfectly real. It's hard to tell what's scarier, seeing things that aren't there or realizing that they aren't there.

"Anyway, just before Christmas, my departed wife, who had been living in hotels, or living in whatever rooming houses the student she took off with was living in, decided that she wanted to come back. I guess he had deserted her. And I told her that she wasn't coming back. So one night, I came home from work, and she had kidnaped the children, taken them upstate, where her family lived. I flew up there the next day, meaning to snatch them back, but they were out of the house somewhere. I only met their grandfather, a pathetic old fool, who doesn't in the least merit my hatred of him. So I came back again, defeated, and then it was the holiday season, and for some reason I had a party to go to every night, so I started drinking. I started drinking in the morning, when I got up, and when that wore off, I'd take a little more, and so on all day and all night, until I could sleep for three or four hours a night. There was a whole month when I was drunk the whole time I was awake, because it was the only way I could face things. And I never did get the children back.

"Then one January afternoon, I just left the office and went to the hospital. The reason was that I just couldn't take care of myself any more. I had a friend, the wife of my lawyer, and I was talking to her on the telephone, and it was all so—crazy—I think what she said was, 'You'd better come with me.' I think she came over in a taxi and took me to the emergency room at the hospital. That was it. At first it was a relief to think that someone was in charge, because I'd known for a hell of a while that I wasn't in charge of anything, including even getting myself fed. Now I could trust somebody else.

"All I really remember of that first day is that when bedtime came—I went in the afternoon—it was fairly early that they wanted us to go to bed. I said, 'But I can't sleep. I haven't slept in so long.' And they gave me this little shot glass full of green liquid. It was so lovely. It looked and tasted like *creme de menthe*. And I remember that as I started down the corridor to the bedroom, I started to stagger. By the time I hit the bed, I was asleep.

"The next morning, I was told that I was supposed to make my bed, so I made my bed. There came a great return of the sense of humiliation. I thought, My God, I'm a patient in an institution. And I began to blubber about that. Shortly after that the doctor came. He came to see me at least once a day. As I look back on it now, he was a nice, young, decent guy who didn't know his ass from the G clef, but who seemed so well put together himself, even though he wasn't excessively bright, that I got something out of just thinking. He's my doctor. He'll be back tomorrow. Then after about three or four weeks, he started using drug therapy, and I went on talking.

"There was a dream—and I still dream about this. And in my dreams, my former wife and my mother almost invariably change places. Now there's a Freudian thing for you. The dreams are not erotic, though. The prime point is the betrayal, the desertion. When I'm dreaming about this experience, and suffering about it in my sleep, as I no longer do when I'm awake, somewhere in the dream my wife and my mother exchange identities. And some-times, it's my mother deceiving my father, and I—do you believe in this Freudian shit?—I sort of think that some such thing really did take place in my background, and that my father came apart in a way that I knew about. I'm talking about infancy, but I mean that I think he came apart in a way that, as an infant, made me feel that the world was coming apart. He was a born come-apart, but I think he saved himself by pretending that what he knew had happened hadn't really happened. What had happened was, I think there was a point where my mother got involved with my father's father.

"A real Maine story. I come from peasants. Not just farmers —peasants. I don't say that disloyally, because they have wonderful qualities that cannot be identified with the lower class around here. Perfectly law-abiding. But ignorant. They didn't want me to go to college. They wanted me to perpetuate the kind of life that they belonged to. They thought that going to college meant that I was repudiating them, which of course it did. But there was the G.I. Bill, and so I got into Yale. But everybody I know who has passed the class barrier is a damaged individual. To make the transition over the barrier—and it's only the lower classes who believe there is a class barrier—requires that you be so maladjusted to the class that you've been born into that you're automatically a freak. You look down on your parents. And you feel guilty about that. . . .

"After I had stayed at the hospital for about six months, I didn't want to leave. I'd grown so dependent on this artificial womb. Every time I thought of the state in which I'd come in, I was scared as hell of getting out. But I had been getting better. After all, time is bound to do something for you. I'd been taken care of. That's what I really needed. I was fed. The laundry was done. Finally, I went to a thing called a halfway house, which was just a boardinghouse run by a crazy woman for people who were getting out of institutions. Then my lawyer came and got me moved to a hotel. Then an old friend asked me to come and visit him in Washington. I was still in a damn bad way, but moving around, being out, seeing people, making gestures toward going back to work—that did it. I got a job with the government just about six months after I got out of the hospital.

"That was when my son died. At first we'd thought it was leukemia, but it was a thing called dermatomyositis, a wasting disease. It worked fairly quickly in his case. He died on the anniversary of the day she snatched them. To the hour, almost. She still has the other child up in that goddamn place, and I've only seen her about three times in the past few years. One point on which I'm still totally crazy is that one, although I'm not as crazy as I was. A normal individual would say, 'It happened, it's over, let's smooth things out.' But I just can't do it. I hate her guts."

> "Any man has to, needs to, wants to
> Once in a lifetime, do a girl in."
> —Sweeney Agonistes

There was a huge party—writers, prizefighters, actors, hangers-on—more than two hundred people in all. According to one guest, they spent the whole evening "drinking and talking and ogling each other, squatting on floors and beds, jamming the living room so that you could hardly squeeze up to the bar for a drink." The host, Norman Mailer, was very nervous. One guest described him as "taut as a cat" and added: "He circulated through the rooms, briefly making his hellos, but mostly he'd get into arguments or sit in a corner playing 'starings.' He'd try to outstare somebody across the room." Another reported that Mailer got involved in two separate fistfights.

At about five in the morning, after all the guests had left, there was a confrontation in the kitchen. Adele Morales Mailer, the writer's second wife, married six years, mother of his second and third children, later told the police that Mailer suddenly attacked her with a penknife. "He came at me with a funny look in his eye," she was quoted as saying. "He didn't say a word. There was no reason. He just looked at me, and then he stabbed me."

Mrs. Mailer, critically wounded in the back and abdomen, said Mailer then left the apartment. Not until eight o'clock on that Sunday morning, November 20, 1960, did he drive her to University Hospital, where she told doctors that she had fallen on glass at her apartment. The doctors were suspicious and notified the police, but they would not let the police interrogate her, because one of the stab wounds was near the heart. The next day, while the stabbing was still secret, Mailer was interviewed by Mike Wallace on WNET, and, according to the brief account in the *Times*, "reiterated that he intended to run for mayor [of New York City]. He said that one way to alleviate juvenile delinquency would be to hold a series of jousts, in armor and on horseback [in Central Park]." Mailer elaborated on his views of criminal psychology. "The knife to a juvenile delinquent is very meaningful," he said. "You see, it's his sword, his manhood." When asked about a bruise on his own cheek, Mailer said only that he "got into quite a scrape Saturday night."

On Monday night, the police finally were permitted to question Mrs. Mailer, and as soon as Mailer came to visit her at 10:30 P.M., they arrested him and charged him with felonious assault. He denied the charge. The next day, he appeared in Felony Court before Magistrate Reuben Levy, who read into the record a report by Dr. Conrad Rosenberg, a physician at University Hospital. "In my opinion," said Dr. Rosenberg, "Norman Mailer is having an acute paranoid breakdown, with delusional thinking, and is both homicidal and suicidal. His admission to a hospital is urgently advised." Mailer himself strongly disputed this judgment. He said he had only seen Dr. Rosenberg "for thirty seconds or a minute," and he added: "I have been a little upset but I have never been out of my mental faculties. It's important for me not to be sent to a mental hospital, because my work in the future will be considered that of a disordered mind. My pride is that I can explore areas of experience that other men are afraid of. I insist I am sane." Magistrate Levy, in turn, disputed Mailer's self-judgment. "Your recent history," he said, "indicates that you cannot distinguish fiction from reality. In your interest and in the public interest, I have to commit you."

So Norman Mailer, who had once worked briefly in a state mental hospital while he was still at Harvard, and then wrote both an unproduced play and an unpublished novel about it, was now committed to the groaning wards of Bellevue Hospital, for observation. After almost three weeks of observation, the Bellevue doctors reported back to the court that Mailer was "not psychotic." General Sessions Judge Mitchell D. Schweitzer said this meant that Mailer was "able to understand the charge against him and was capable of making a defense to it." Mailer was freed on $2,500 bail and ordered to report back on December 21 to defend himself against the charge of felonious assault. In that pre-Christmas week, however, Mrs. Mailer, by now recovered, refused to sign any charges against her husband. "I have no complaint to make against anyone," she said.

Over the years, Mailer has written with an almost embarrassing candor about his various fidelities and infidelities, but he has been remarkably reticent about this particular episode. On his state of mind during the period, we can draw only limited inferences from the earlier confessions in *Advertisements for Myself:* "Bombed and sapped and charged and stoned with lush, with pot, with benny, saggy, Miltown, coffee, and two packs a day, I was working live, and overalert and tiring into what felt like death." Later, in *The Presidential Papers,* he somewhat obliquely declares: "I was in a Napoleonic mood, I had decided to run for Mayor of New York; in a few weeks I was to zoom and crash—my sense of reality was extravagant." He is reminiscing about his tenuous relationship with Jacqueline Kennedy, and he says he wrote her at about this time "that I hoped one day when work was done to do a biography of the Marquis de Sade and the 'odd strange honor of the man.'" To Mailer's chagrin, Mrs. Kennedy never answered.

There are always perils in trying to suggest any connection between a novelist's fiction and his private life, and yet it is clangorously striking that Mailer's next novel, three years after the stabbing, begins with a man murdering his wife. The hero of *An American Dream* is not Norman Mailer, of course, but rather Stephen Rojack. In the very first paragraph, however, Mailer outfits him with a collection of *machismo* status symbols of the 1960's. Rojack tells us that he not only knew Jack Kennedy, not only shared Kennedy's wartime experiences, not only was elected to Congress with Kennedy, but that he and Kennedy had gone on a "double date." Rojack sounds rather impressed; Mailer sounds rather impressed.

Rojack's girl, whom he "seduced," was the rich and bad-tempered Deborah Caughlin Mangaravidi Kelly. It was Rojack's fate to marry her, and to hate her. The two have separated by the time the novel opens. Rojack is paying his first visit in a fortnight. After some preliminary skirmishing, Deborah refers to some undefined sexual practice that Rojack has taught her and says that she will never do that again, at least not with him. He says she never did it very well anyway. She asks whether his "little girls" do it better. He says, lying, that he knows at least five who can do it better than she. She says that she hasn't had any complaints from "any new beau." He asks her, in a state of "fine horror," how many lovers she now has. She claims to have "just three," one of whom expressed surprise that she enjoyed proclivities rarely seen "outside a Mexican whorehouse."

Rojack's reaction is abrupt, not to say hysterical: " 'Shut your fucking mouth,' I said."

He slaps her, but because "my body was speaking faster than my brain," the slap turns into a blow. She reacts with unusual violence: "Like a bull she charged. Her head struck me in the stomach . . . and then she drove one powerful knee at my groin . . . and missing that, she reached with both hands, tried to find my root and mangle me." Rojack disapproves of her resistance ("she fought like a prep-school bully"), and then he begins to strangle her. Some internal voice of reason tells him to stop ("Hold back, you're going too far . . ."), but the desire to kill is uncontrollable. "I was trying to stop, but pulse packed behind pulse in a pressure up to thunderhead; some black-biled lust, some desire to go ahead . . . came bursting with rage from out of me and my mind, exploding in a fireworks of rockets, stars, and hurtling embers. The arm about her neck leaped against the whisper I could still feel murmuring in her throat, and *crack* I choked her harder, and *crack* I choked her again. . . . I was floating. I was as far into myself as I had ever been and universes wheeled in a dream."

The strange thing in this scene is not only that Rojack appears to have gone mad, but that Mailer seems unaware of it. Rojack wanders off to the maid's room, gets into bed with her, and only then returns to his wife's room to decide what to do about the body. His first thought is pure Nazism: "I had an impulse to go up to her and kick her ribs, grind my heel on her nose, drive the point of my shoe into her temple and kill her again, kill her good this time. . . ." That is too simple. He then begins to indulge in a fantasy of cannibalism. "I had a desire to take Deborah to the bathroom, put her in the tub. Then Ruta [the maid] would sit down to eat. The two of us would sup on Deborah's flesh, we would eat for days. . . . What we did not choose to devour we could grind away in the electric Disposall beneath the sink, all the impure organs and little bones. . . ."

Time is passing. Something must be done. Rojack finally decides to throw Deborah's body out the window and to claim that she committed suicide. "And I howled then in a simulation of woe, but the woe was real—for the first time I knew she was gone —and it was an animal howl." An animal howl, an animal crime— Rojack really is rather an animal, but his creator admires him. Although everyone knows that Rojack murdered his wife, Mailer never subjects him to the rigors of Felony Court or Bellevue. At the end, he walks away free.

8

Out of a Case History:
Celia Discovers Anger

Celia said she didn't want to be interviewed in her apartment because then she might not be able to get away from the questioning. So now we sit on a park bench on a windy afternoon in June. Here she is protected, in a way, by bearded joggers passing along from time to time, and women on bicycles, and bands of boys with baseball gloves. There is a distant thunder of highway traffic, and an intermittent roar of helicopters passing overhead.

Celia is a rather plump and quite attractive woman in her late thirties, a sculptress by vocation, although she has not done a great deal of it. She is somewhat pale, with freckles across her nose, and dark-blond hair parted in the middle. She is wearing blue slacks and a blue smock with a yellow fleur-de-lys pattern, with a white cardigan on top of that. Around her neck hangs a long necklace of thick wooden beads on a leather thong. As she talks, she often gives an ingratiating chuckle.

I guess I have a history of doing things very well and then collapsing. It's been—ever since I was a child, and I couldn't take tests. This goes way back to the day I entered school. I was just frightened of everything, and that's what held me back from—well, reading, and writing, and doing arithmetic. By the time I was in sixth grade, where they give you those I.Q. tests, I did so badly that my I.Q. was supposed to be 70, even though I graduated second-best in my class. I was just completely traumatized.

See, both my parents were very frightened people. They were both immigrants from Hungary. My father's parents had left him in Europe when he was six years old, with an aunt, just left him. They were very poor people, and I guess he slept in the barn most of the time. He came to Cleveland when he was eighteen, and he tried hard, learned a trade—he repaired wrecked cars—but he was very sort of cut off from people. My father was a very strong, powerful man. He never talked much to me. He always sat in a corner, quiet, and he was quiet all his life. And I think it's that silence that scared the shit out of me. You know, really, excuse the expression.

And my mother's message to me was: "Don't touch anybody, and they won't touch you." And so there was never any physical contact in our house. My older sister was a very energetic and outgoing person, and she didn't get the message that I did. She had dramas, she screamed, she yelled, and she always drove my mother right up the wall. But I didn't do anything to rock the boat. That was my role in life: Stand still and don't do anything. My mother had told me that: "Just be quiet." She never let us out of the back yard. She was always telling me, "Don't talk to strange men." But every man you meet is a strange man. So I picked up her fear of men, all men. And then I was raised as a Catholic, which screwed up everything. The confession, and the guilt—oh, all that crap that they lay on you. You know, God was always watching, and I believed it all.

I guess I took all my mother's warnings as absolute law. I was so dependent and so scared that something would happen if I didn't do what my mother said that I just didn't do anything. I spent a lot of time just sitting in the house and reading books, and very cut off, and very afraid of everything. I was too afraid to go out and meet people. But I always thought that music and art were two things I could let go with, so I got a scholarship to the Cleveland Institute of Arts. And it was a great experience for me, because there were no rules. There were finally no rules. You didn't have to sit in chairs. You could do whatever you wanted.

I met Stanley at art school—and he was already collapsing. He'd been going to Yale, studying architecture, and he'd broken down there, so they gave him a leave of absence, and he came to Cleveland. And I really enjoyed his company. He wasn't threatening, I guess because he was in as bad shape as I was. But it was good. It was really okay. So I did a lot of things that year—1958. I got a commission to do a big playground sculpture in Cleveland. And we got married. And we moved to Yale, and Stanley went back to school. And I got pregnant.

And it was too much for me, all these things happening. I just—I couldn't take it. Like the responsibility for having a child. I pretended I could do it, that it was no big deal. And I was doing my sculpture for the playground. I'd done these three dolphins that were eight feet long, and I'd decided to work in fiberglass—and of all the rotten materials to pick! Nobody was doing it then, and you had to lay it up by hand, and it stank, and I was into all kinds of bad things like acetone and styrene. And as I just kept going at this, I really started breaking down. Stanley would come home from school, and I'd be sitting in the corner and drinking. I was getting big, and the work was too much, and I just couldn't think. It really got bad.

And Stanley was beginning to drop out of school again. I didn't know he had a history of dropping out of school. We'd never talked about it when we got married. So I felt it was my fault, and I began to feel very guilty that I was doing this sculpture, and I was having the baby. And underneath, I was very scared. And I had nobody to talk to. Again the message that I got from my parents: "Don't talk to anybody, Celia. And don't tell anybody about this or they'll hurt you." Anyway, I *had* the baby, and I had a lot of mixed feelings that I never let out. Like Stanley didn't take any interest in having the baby. I always went to the doctor by myself. He was always too tired, too fagged out.

Stanley's parents were pestering him to buy a house, so one afternoon we went out and bought a rickety old house in Short Beach, about twenty miles from New Haven, and Stan set to work trying to put a furnace in, stuff like that. I started work again in my studio in an old garage. I did a huge alligator that I really wanted to do. It was a very good alligator, too, about eight feet long, in plaster, but I never finished him and cast him, and he fell apart. They accepted Stanley back at school, and then he —two months after he started, he dropped out again. And that really shook me, because I really felt that—I always thought that he was going to be a—you know, that he wasn't going to break down. I wanted him to be a husband that would go out and work and make enough money and come home and—you know. I need to be taken care of. That's one of my big things. And when he started to not be able to take care of me, that really scared me.

I began to just sort of pretend that everything was all right.

And I'm really good at pretending. I'll try anything. Anything works. I'll eat. One of my most working defenses used to be eating. If everything else fails, I'll eat, and I feel better. So I was quite overweight at that point. Another defense that I use is sleeping. I began to sleep. I never slept quite that much in my whole life. And Stanley slept, and he would sleep through classes, day and night, and I guess—it's funny, because I copied him. Because I was living with him, I just assumed his personality, sort of. I copied his defenses. Sleeping and eating were safe defenses. They were allowed in my house. Sex was bad. Sex was never allowed. So, you know, I never had to do anything about that. I never had to worry—I mean, I never, never did anything wrong, *never* had an affair with a man, *never,* before I was married, would I ever, you know, go to sleep with anybody. I had to be married.

Then we moved back to Cleveland. You can hide from things for a while, and that's what we were doing, hiding. Stanley got a job, and it seemed like a good thing, success, you know, going to work for an architect, get experience. So, like, I fed off that, and I pretended life was going great again. We didn't want to live with Stanley's parents, so we decided to live in a field about two hundred feet from their house. We had a little tent, but we didn't have much equipment for camping. We had a jeep, and I had— Jonathan was three, and I became pregnant, and I felt sunk. We bought a geodesic dome at that point, about forty feet square, just a big space, and we thought we'd try to put it up ourselves in the field. Well, they delivered the dome, and then the rains came, and Stanley and I both collapsed. One night, I was trying to work on my alligator—I had him out in the field—I had to go down for some water. I was very stubborn, and I wouldn't ask Stanley's parents for anything, like water, and so there was a river, and I'd go down and get buckets of water, and really, it was torture. I mean, if you're physically up to it, but—we didn't last. We lasted two weeks. I guess this was the first time in my life I got angry. Stanley came home late from work, and I just got hysterical. I couldn't stand it any longer. I told him I was going back to my mother's—or take me to a motel. So Stanley got angry—I remember that's the first time I saw his anger, this really violent, irrational anger. He just tore things up and threw them into the jeep, and we drove to his parents' house. And they all ran out and said, "What's wrong?" And Stan said, "We're *leaving*," and he wouldn't say anything more. And I wouldn't talk. I just said, "I've had it out there." And they said, "Come in." And we said, "No." So it was a very angry night. But once we got out of there and went to a nice air-conditioned motel, and we all took showers and had some hamburgers, it all settled down a little bit.

We decided to go to Boston at the end of that year. And again the same thing happened. Stan looked for a job, and I looked for a house, and I was seven months pregnant, so it wasn't easy to do at that point. But after two weeks, I found a little old apartment for ninety dollars, and Stan found a job, for a big firm, and he liked his work—and, like, we'd escaped again. From whatever it was. So I had the baby, Mark, and—Stan by that point was very tired. He has a habit of, when he's upset, either he sleeps or he works twice as hard. He can't say no to anybody. So the guys up in the office, they have a deadline, and they work day and night to get the job done. So he was always working overtime for them, and absolutely no help for me, and I never could ask, of course. So when I went into labor, he did get home to drive me to the hospital, and then he fell asleep on the hospital bench. And I had a very long labor, and it really devastated me to have him do that. Because I needed him there, and he was absolutely no help.

But things were kind of all right for a year, and then he decided he wanted to go back to school again. Yale was sort of cool to him, so he wrote around to other places, and went for interviews, and the school that accepted him was Columbia. So we moved to this three-room apartment, and I didn't know anybody, and he started at Columbia—and two months later, he wasn't going to school any more. Couldn't go to class. And we never could talk about it. I knew something was wrong, but not having been straight with anybody all my life, or being able to talk to anybody, I just assumed that's the way things were. Stan and I were both so afraid, both of us, that we just had to keep it all away, keep all that bad stuff away. And if one time it fell through, well, we'd just pretend that tomorrow it'd be terrific. But Stan began to drink then, too. Stan began to drink heavily.

But the good thing was that the Columbia people said, "You

can't just drop out, you have to come and talk to us." So they referred him to an Adlerian clinic on Central Park West. And the therapy did help. Stan got a good job. But it always lasted about a year. All the way through our marriage, everything came—at the end of a year, things exploded, and we moved. So with these jobs, it was a pattern too. After a year, he'd get angry at somebody, or he'd want to have a raise, and he couldn't ask for it, and they were putting too much work on him, and he couldn't say no, and he'd get furious, and he'd have to quit. But he'd always get a new job, with a little bit more money, and he'd settle down, and then I found that I was talking to people on street corners, and like all my problems with Stan would come out. Like the doorman would say, "Hello," and out would come this *"Wa-a-a-a-a."* And finally this one person—I'll never forget her—down at Riverside Park—I was telling her about Stan and being in therapy, and I was really getting hysterical, and she said, "It sounds like *you* need therapy." And that was like the shock of the century. No one had ever told me—you know, I'd been waiting for those cue cards all through my life—no one had ever told me that *I* needed therapy.

So I went over to Stan's clinic, and it's kind of existential therapy, like they make you put yourself back together in order to make *now* work. I gather. You don't go back. You deal with now, and you're going to function. My therapist was an older woman, in her sixties, a nice person, a good person, and I did get a lot of things at that point. I learned to keep the house clean, useful little everyday hints like that, but as a person I got nowhere. It was like *I* had to keep my husband going, and I had to raise my family, and they were all-important, and all I had to do was keep them going. That was the message. So I was in that therapy for eight years—until my total collapse.

Little by little, it got harder and harder. Stan went into business with a friend of ours, and for a while they had three or four good jobs, and we began enjoying life, going out to dinner. Then gradually there was less work at the office, so Stan decided to do some consulting work for the city, on renovating slums, but he didn't get paid for this work unless he demanded money, and he couldn't demand money. So we were economically falling apart. We couldn't pay the bills. And we began to sleep.

Then the city finally offered him a salaried job, and that's when I collapsed. I began to hate Stan. I began to really hate him.

Collapse is when I can't make any sense out of anything. Up to this point, something had always come along, something new, to rescue me. At this point, there was nothing. I had a job teaching art at Riverside Church at night, and I liked that, but it was getting very, very hard. I would come home, and I was so *cold* that I'd have to sit in the bathtub for half an hour, with hot water. And this was in the summer. I was beginning to get scared, and it was building up. I don't know quite what did it, except I got angry at Stan, and my marriage was threatened. I kept telling Stan to move out—"Leave, if you don't like it!" And he is just as dependent on me as I am on him. Nobody moved. And it got worse, to the point where Stan started getting angry, and he'd throw things and smash things in the house. Mostly against the wall, but occasionally he'd aim things at me. And he began drinking a lot, and that brought up his anger. I'd never had any kind of violence like that, so it really began scaring me.

I went into an incredible depression, for about a year. Sometimes I'd be very high, and then just sink, so I'd sleep all day long. If I could just get the kids' meals—I was always on the couch, reading, pretending to read, falling asleep, couldn't drag myself around. I got to the point where I could hardly make it out from my bed. My legs wouldn't work. My hands—I couldn't do any art work. I could barely write my name. And when I did go out at all, I had funny accidents. Like, I'd fall down the subway stairs. I'd trip on stuff. I fell down our stairs, from the second floor into the lobby. I must have fallen four or five times on the sidewalk. I broke a toe. I sprained an ankle. And I couldn't stand noises, street-corner noises, because there was this tremendous noise inside of me, like the sound of chaos. And I thought, Well, okay, if this is how my life is going to be, okay, I'll have to be bedridden. I'll be like those invalids in the eighteenth century, and I'll have to be carted around in a little rickshaw or something.

Well, one day, a friend stopped by for a visit, and I was in very bad shape. I was crying, and I was just trying to hold myself together. And he said, "Hey, you should meet Johanna. She's terrific. I went into therapy with her, and she helped me a lot.

Why don't you call her?" So I said, "Okay." And he said, "Do it right now, while I'm here." That's a real friend, you know, not letting me get away with it. So I called her and made an appointment. And she said, "You know, I'm in primal therapy. So before you come, I want you to read *The Primal Scream,* Arthur Janov's book, so you'll know a little bit about it." Well, I didn't know primal therapy from, you know, cereal. So I picked up that book, and God, it was like feeding right into my veins. It just took me by storm. I knew what he was talking about, and I could do it. Like, there was a place to let go, that's what I've been yearning for all my life, is a place to let go. You know, let go with your craziness.

So all I did for three solid months was go in and scream and cry and just—let go. You have to let off every mile of the feeling you've repressed, by letting it out, and you can't get to the good feelings until you let out all the bad feelings, because the bad feelings are blocking the good feelings, and that's what's making you neurotic. I went four times every week, for an hour or an hour and a half. And I found what I need. I need to talk to people. I need to tell them what's wrong. I need to tell them what I want. And I need to get angry. It's very hard for me, even now. But I'm learning to cry. When I feel bad, I can cry. And I cry and I cry and cry and cry. And eventually, I'll work through all the terror and the rage.

I got Stan into primal therapy too, last August, and one night we started having an argument. We had never fought before, never in our whole married life. We'd been sarcastic—you know, sort of "Nyah, nyah"—jabbing. But this time we had a primal argument. We stood in the kitchen, like five feet apart, and he shouted at the top of his lungs, and I did too. Every single horrible thing we could say to each other, we did. And we blamed each other for every single thing, in the most vile language you can imagine, and we really laid each other out. And the neighbors called the police. And I was so devastated by that! That they'd dared call the police! See, we live in a building that's primarily black, and all kinds of things go on in that building— screaming, knife fights, prostitution, dope, you name it. And we lived with it. But when we had one quarrel, they didn't knock on the door and say, "What's happening?" They called the police. It just blew my mind.

That brought up rage. For two weeks, I pretended it was—I was mad at the neighbors, I thought, Damn them, but I didn't think it was a big thing. Then one day I woke up—and something changed. I started playing music. I started playing heroically— *ta-ta!*—on the piano. I'm not very good, but I can make some good sounds once in a while. And I started getting angry. Stan had left for work, and the kids were in school, and I started stomping around the house, yelling at the top of my voice, "God-damn those bastards! How could they do that to me?"

Then I took a shower. And as I was in the shower, I started— it was the only time I have really been on the edge—I almost flipped out—it was like I was on the brink, and it would be so easy to go over, really go nuts, insane. As I was in the shower, I was singing, and this song came to me, and it was: "You better watch out! You better watch out!" I was singing this at the neighbors, and it was horrible, diabolic—you know, kill, murder—I'm going to kill you bastards. And I kept getting madder and madder. I finally got out of the shower, and I knew the only thing to do—and I knew I had to do this, this is what's so crazy—I had to go downstairs, and I had to stand in the hall and *scream*. Get everybody out and tell them how these rotten bastards next door —"They will screw you, they're dangerous, because they'll call the police on you, and they're horrible." And then if they didn't listen to me, I was going to go out in the street and start shouting the same thing. It was such a—I was red in the face, and I was scr—and then something clicked in my mind, and I thought, Oh, I'd better tell Johanna. Just, you know, that little click. So I called her and said, "Johanna, I'm in a rage, and I just want you to know that I have to go downstairs and tell everybody that these people next door are awful. Is that okay?" And she said, "Why don't you just come over here?"

So my hair was still wet, and I put all my old clothes on, and I stomped down the stairs—I was furious—and I slammed the door and almost broke the glass in the door. And I saw a man on the sidewalk, and I started raging at him. "Bastard!" And all the way up Amsterdam Avenue, every black man, every Puerto

Rican, anybody, every man, only men, I was raging at. "You goddam stupid asses, you goddam bastards!" I just looked them in the eye and started shouting at them. And I, who had never said "Boo" to anyone! It was such a—I couldn't control it. When I got to Johanna's, there was a mailman in the hallway, a Negro mailman, and he looked at me as though to say, "Hello," and I looked at him and shouted, "Goddam stupid asses, all of you, stupid asses!" And he just went *wfft!*—every man just went *wfft!* —cleared out of the way.

So Johanna didn't say anything. I just sat in her room, and I screamed, and it's like I was really—you know, I was drooling, and I was hitting pillows, and I was just growling—*gr-r-r-r*— that kind of thing. Just like an angry beast. And that went on for two hours, solid. It didn't stop. And at the end of it, I said to Johanna, "Was that insanity?" And she said, "No, that was anger."

PART THREE

COMING APART

God's Foot upon
the Treadle of the Loom

Nearly one hundred feet under the hills and prairies of the Dakotas, at the bottom of a network of concrete silos, nests of Air Force officers stand guard over this country's one-thousand-odd Minuteman missiles. Each of the missiles carries a nuclear warhead with a destructive power equal to more than one thousand tons of TNT. Each of them could ravage the center of the Soviet city at which it is aimed. Each of them could, if fired by a madman, attract a ferocious retaliation that would mean the beginning of the third and last world war.

This familiar disaster scenario is unthinkable, absolutely impossible, according to all the Air Force spokesmen who have talked about such things through the years. First, of course, the underground officers have to undergo a lot of elaborate tests to check their psychological stability. And then, within the green-walled control capsules, everything has been planned to remind the two officers on duty, generally a captain and a lieutenant, of their responsibilities. There must be no slackness. The red leather chairs next to the computer consoles have been designed to resemble the seats in a bomber cockpit. And both of the officers, profoundly nervous but profoundly idle, carry .38-caliber pistols at their belts.

Then the famous keys, which are worn on a chain around the neck and passed on from shift to shift. The missile cannot be fired unless the two officers simultaneously insert their keys into the unlocking mechanism (so one officer can't coerce or overpower the other), and if the keys are not inserted simultaneously, they can't be removed and tried again. Furthermore, all orders are relayed by both loudspeaker and teleprinter, and they can be heard or read by the eight other officers in four other control posts that make up a missile squadron (fifty missiles). If any of these eight other officers thinks that an order to fire might be unauthorized, he can push a button that cancels the order and stops the launching. And finally, even if a missile is launched by mistake, its warhead will not explode until seventeen different electrical circuits have been completed. The last two of these require that the computer on board the missile tell the warhead that it is over its destined target and descending at a rate of seventeen G's. The two officers who send the missile on its way, incidentally, never see the fifty-five-foot white shark leave its berth, which is seven to ten miles from their underground capsule. Nor do they ever know the name of the target at which they have fired the missile. Only the computer knows that. If everything goes as planned, according to the statistics proclaimed in 1967 by Defense Secretary Robert McNamara, and probably as true now as they were then, a Soviet missile strike and a retaliatory strike by the United States would leave approximately one hundred twenty million people dead on each side.

"But when I was working for the Navy," says Professor Chester M. Pierce of the Harvard Medical School and the Graduate School of Education, "the problem they wanted us to think about was not how to stop somebody from launching a missile by mistake, or because he'd gone insane. What they wanted us to figure out was what to do if the order came to fire those Polaris missiles, and the Polaris sub commander couldn't or wouldn't do it."

He smiles. When I first knew Chet Pierce, he was a sturdy lineman on the Harvard football team, and, if I recall rightly, the only black student in Lowell House. Now he is slim and suave and elegant, with just a few touches of white in his mustache, and he has become a specialist in what he described to his twenty-fifth class report as the psychology of "how men adjust in extreme environments." The environment here is fairly ordinary. We are eating scrambled eggs in a deserted New York hotel dining room at eight o'clock in the morning. Pierce is about to start serving as chairman of a day-long conference on various educational problems. But he is reminded of the Navy. What the Navy wanted to know was, first, what kind of stress would the Polaris commander undergo when he saw the order to fire? How much time would be spent trying to figure out whether the order was genuine, or doubting his own responsibility to carry the order out? And second, what kind of test might be devised to screen out anyone who might suddenly refuse to fire his missiles?

"In other words," I say, "they wanted to know how to screen out anybody who might prove to be sane."

"Well," says Professor Pierce, "they figure that the whole point of the command structure is to function in a crisis, and if it isn't going to function when it's needed, there's not much point in having the submarine out there at all."

"So what did you tell them?"

"We couldn't give them any hard answers. It was just a brainstorming session."

There is no doubt that the military authorities have gone to great trouble to combat the threat of some berserk lieutenant at a missile station disobeying his orders, but it is more difficult to predict and counteract the effects of madness in some General Jack D. Ripper who has the power to give the orders for the disaster of *Dr. Strangelove*. Nor is this a purely hypothetical problem, for there hovers over it the half-forgotten ghost of our first Secretary of Defense James V. Forrestal, a passionate and driven man, and mad as King Lear.

He had been a sickly child, but his mother raised her three sons sternly, beating them with a strap whenever she considered it necessary. She wanted James, her youngest, to become a priest. He rebelled against that, and against the Catholic Church itself. He dedicated much of his time to body-building, boxing, wrestling, weight-lifting. He went into journalism, then business, and worked his way up to the presidency of Dillon Read, the investment bankers. When he began to get rich, he bought his widowed mother a fur coat and a New York apartment with a fireplace. She never wore the coat or lived in the apartment.

Throughout World War II, when Forrestal was Undersecretary and then Secretary of the Navy, he maintained a kind of clearing house for tales of Communist subversion. He received regular reports on the subject from J. Edgar Hoover, and such militant clerics as Francis Cardinal Spellman and Monsignor Fulton J. Sheen, as well as a number of less reputable "experts" who produced various newsletters on the mysterious connections between Communism and "International Jewry." With his strong connections in the business and military worlds, Forrestal apparently began thinking of himself as President Truman's successor. He even wrote himself a strange memorandum on "Specifications for a Presidential Candidate: 1. Looks. 2. Height. 3. Legal or political background. 4. Desire for job. 5. Political experience. . . ." He seems to have thought that if Thomas Dewey won the 1948 election, he would be able to stay on as Secretary of Defense (Dewey was noncommittal when Forrestal broached the subject), but Truman began hearing of his eccentricities. The Defense Secretary continually dipped his fingers into a glass of water and then moistened his lips with them. He was also suffering from loss of appetite, stomach trouble and insomnia.

When Truman heard reports that Forrestal believed he was being followed and wiretapped, he assigned Secret Service Chief U. E. Baughman to make a quiet investigation. Baughman discovered, he wrote later, that "Mr. Forrestal had become so overly suspicious that whenever the front door was opened or the bell rang, he would go out to the area and peer out secretly to see who was there. And only the week before, Mr. Forrestal had come into the kitchen while the butler was there. The Defense Secretary was wearing his hat around the house, apparently forgetting that he had it on, or that he had decided to go out. On this occasion he looked right at the butler and asked, 'Where's my butler?' When the butler said, 'I'm here, sir,' Mr. Forrestal looked confused and could not remember what he wanted." Baughman reported to President Truman that Forrestal was suffering "a total psychotic breakdown . . . characterized by suicidal features."

Since Forrestal apparently expected to remain in charge of the Pentagon indefinitely, he was shocked when Truman summoned him to the White House, on March 1, 1949, and asked him to submit a letter of resignation. He stayed up most of that night, dithering over various drafts, and finally sent off the resignation the next day. It was not until the end of that month, though, that Forrestal finally attended the formal swearing-in of his successor, received a Presidential citation for "meritorious and distinguished service," and flew off to a vacation in Hobe

Sound, Florida. Robert Lovett, who had only recently resigned as Undersecretary of Defense, was on hand to greet him there. Forrestal appeared to Lovett, according to Arnold Rogow's biography of the Defense Secretary, "so changed in appearance that it was not at all easy to recognize him. In addition to looking haggard and much older than his years (he was then fifty-seven), Forrestal's always thin mouth was so tightly drawn that neither the upper nor the lower lip could be seen. His eyes, which appeared sunken in an ashen face, searched suspiciously among the small group of friends that had gathered." Lovett, trying to sound cheerful, said, "Jim, I hope you've brought your golf clubs, because the weather here has been perfect for golf." Forrestal answered: "Bob, they're after me."

It is not entirely clear who "they" were—personal enemies, of course, but apparently also Communists, foreign and domestic, whom Forrestal suspected of having infiltrated the White House, the Pentagon, and various other government agencies. He is reported to have warned that a Soviet invasion was imminent, and even to have spoken as though the invasion had already begun. There was a radio report by Drew Pearson that Forrestal at one point rushed out into the streets and shouted, "The Russians are attacking." Such reports were widely denied, dismissed, and denounced as "irresponsible." The official version was that Forrestal was simply suffering from a civilian form of what was then called "battle fatigue." The idea that Forrestal might have been insane while still serving as Secretary of Defense was criticized by the columnist Marquis Childs as "the base of a widespread Communist propaganda campaign." "Fortunately," *The New York Times* added, "with rest and proper treatment, the outlook for operational fatigue is excellent."

Just four days after his flight to Florida, Forrestal was flown back to Washington and taken to Bethesda Naval Hospital, where Captain George N. Raines, the chief psychiatrist, diagnosed his problem as "involutional melancholia." He prescribed insulin shock as well as daily sessions of psychotherapy. Forrestal seems to have improved somewhat during the seven weeks he was at Bethesda, so much so that he was allowed to wander around outside his sixteenth-floor suite, which was guarded by a Navy Medical Corpsman, and to make snacks for himself in the diet kitchen.

The screens in the kitchen, unlike those in his bedroom, were fastened only by small hooks, but Forrestal insisted to Dr. Raines that this was no danger. If he ever committed suicide, he said, it would be by hanging, not by jumping out a window. Dr. Raines saw Forrestal on the morning of May 18 and later said he "felt at that time that he was nearing the end of his illness." Dr. Raines thereupon went off to Montreal to attend a meeting of the American Psychiatric Association.

Three days later, May 21, Forrestal stayed up late at night, copying from a poetry anthology a *Chorus from Ajax* by Sophocles:

> Woe to the mother in her close of day,
> Woe to her desolate heart and temples gray,
>   When she shall hear
> Her loved one's story whispered in her ear!
> "Woe, woe!" will be the cry—
> No quiet murmur like the tremendous wail
> Of the lone bird, the querulous nightingale—

The gloomy chorus becomes ever more gloomy ("Thou shalt weep." it ends, "thou wretched father for thy dearest son,/Thy best beloved, by inward Furies torn,/The deepest, bitterest curse thine ancient house hath borne!"). But Forrestal, observing that his Navy guardian had gone off on an errand—it being now about 2 A.M.—abruptly stopped copying after the "night" in "nightingale." He neatly inserted his manuscript pages into the back of the anthology and walked across the corridor to the empty kitchen. He tied one end of his dressing-gown sash around the radiator beneath the window and then tied the other end around his neck. Then he unhooked the screen and climbed through the window. A few seconds later, a nurse heard a loud thud outside the building and sounded an alarm. Forrestal's body was found on a third-floor roof, the sash still around his neck. Back up on the sixteenth floor, the window sill outside the kitchen was found to be scratched and scraped, as if Forrestal might have tried, in his last moment of despair, to save himself.

Whether or not Forrestal was insane at the time that he commanded the fleets of American nuclear bombers, the fact that

President Truman had fired him seemed to convey the reassuring implication that Forrestal was never really in command of the bombers at all. Only the President could push the button, and if he ever decided to do so, he would act as the elected representative of all the American people. Therefore all was well. Or so it seemed, until one day in July of 1972 when a mysterious telephone call to the Knight newspapers' *Detroit Free Press* reported that Senator Thomas F. Eagleton, the newly nominated Democratic candidate for Vice-President, had once been treated in a St. Louis hospital for "mental disorders." Two reporters for the Knight newspapers took their information to the headquarters of Presidential nominee George McGovern and asked for confirmation, whereupon McGovern belatedly checked the story and then decided to make the whole matter public. Even if he had known of his partner's hospitalization, McGovern said at a press conference, Eagleton "would still have been my choice for Vice-President. . . . I think Tom Eagleton is fully qualified in mind, body and spirit to be the Vice-President of the United States and, if necessary, to take on the Presidency at a moment's notice."

Many people were less confident. While Forrestal had been a lonely man, more or less disinherited by his parents, Eagleton turned out to be, on closer examination, a creature driven by the frustrated ambitions of his father. The late Mark Eagleton had been a St. Louis attorney whose highest political attempt had been an unsuccessful campaign to become mayor of the city. His sons would have to do better. At the age of ten, young Tom had been taken by his father to attend the Democratic convention in Philadelphia. When he reached high school, his father hired a tutor to give him lessons in current events and another tutor to train him in public speaking. After Amherst and Harvard Law School, he returned to St. Louis to join his father's law firm and to carry out the family's political destiny. He was the youngest St. Louis Circuit Attorney (at twenty-seven), the youngest Missouri Attorney General (thirty-one), the youngest Lieutenant Governor (thirty-five), and finally, at thirty-eight, he defeated Edward Long for a seat in the United States Senate.

The struggle had been too hard. In 1960, after the campaign for Attorney General, he voluntarily entered the Barnes Hospital in St. Louis for four weeks for what he called "exhaustion and fatigue." There he underwent electroshock therapy. In 1964, suffering from depression, he went to the Mayo Clinic for four days, and in 1966 he returned there for three weeks. On the second visit, he again received electroshock therapy. He had never publicly admitted the reasons for these hospitalizations, and the official explanation in all three cases was that he was undergoing tests or treatments for "gastric disorders." Even at the height of the crisis in 1972, Eagleton never explained exactly what had gone wrong. He said only that he was "an intense and hard-fighting person," and that "I sometimes push myself too far." It was actually a rather common difficulty, and the American Psychiatric Association estimated that some four to eight million Americans underwent treatment for depression every year. It was remarkable, too, that Eagleton had required no further treatment for the past six years, a period during which he had served effectively in the Senate. "I have every confidence that I've learned how to pace myself," he said. But when he first gave the full details of his hospitalizations to Frank Mankiewicz, McGovern's aide observed: "This word 'shock.' Boy, that's a tough word for the public."

What the public really thinks about such things is never entirely clear. Eagleton himself found many campaign audiences sympathetic, or even enthusiastic, and a Crosley poll at the height of the crisis reported that 76.7 percent were unaffected by the disclosures, while only 5.2 percent said they were more likely to vote for Nixon. But the McGovern candidacy was so shaky at this point that even a 5 percent shift seemed ominous, and such powerful newspapers as *The New York Times,* the *Washington Post,* and the *Los Angeles Times* all solemnly intoned that Eagleton must go. McGovern, who originally had proclaimed himself "one thousand percent" behind Eagleton, was reluctant to admit that hospitalization for depression was a ground for political execution, and so there was dark talk about Eagleton's lack of judgment and candor. But *Time* magazine was probably right in observing that a Portland lawyer and Democratic party worker named Robert Duncan "spoke for many" when he said, "I think what will worry people is this stress problem. They will all see him standing eyeball to eyeball with Russia—and then going out and getting shock treatment." So the deed was done, and the impeccably sane team of George McGovern and Sargent Shriver succumbed to the worst election defeat in American history, by the impeccably sane team of Richard Nixon and Spiro Agnew.

During the uproar over Eagleton, a number of political commentators pointed out that sanity, as officially defined, had not always been a prerequisite for serving as President. John Adams had several crises that might nowadays be characterized as nervous breakdowns, Franklin Pierce was an alcoholic, and Lincoln suffered from periods of near-suicidal depression. Even in relatively recent times, Wilson and Harding shrank and shriveled under the stress of their political failures. But the President was more shielded from view in those days, a remote figure to be seen only on a flag-draped platform in the middle distance. And so there was nothing like the spectacle of watching Richard Nixon on television during the summer of 1973 and wondering whether he would go mad before our very eyes.

The spectacle began in New Orleans in August, when Nixon flew in from Florida to make a speech to the Veterans of Foreign Wars and was upset to learn that his motorcade had to be diverted because of a threat of assassination. It was in this upset state, according to officials, that he turned on Press Secretary Ronald Ziegler and gave him an angry shove, right before the recording eyes of the TV cameras. But Nixon did not appear particularly upset when he addressed the V.F.W. On the contrary, he spoke about his "peace with honor" in Vietnam with a strange mixture of belligerence, sarcasm and self-righteousness. And yet he seemed to have some physical difficulty in speaking at all. According to the *Wall Street Journal's* account of the episode, "his speech slurred. He frequently muffed pronunciation of words like 'negotiate,' 'auxiliary,' and 'occasion.' His gestures were unusual. Much of the time his eyes were closed, or were fixed on a spot at the lower left of the lectern."

From New Orleans, Nixon flew on to San Clemente, California, and possibly to counteract the comments on his appearance—reporters had begun asking whether he was getting "medication," and White House spokesmen said he was not—he convoked his first press conference in five months. The scene was almost as bad as in New Orleans. Nixon stood grinning and sweating on the sunny lawn of his San Clemente estate. The

questions were almost entirely hostile, and Nixon seemed to wel-
come their hostility, singling out reporters who he knew would
be aggressive, as though to demonstrate that he was ready for
combat. His eyes darted suspiciously among his antagonists, and
yet he kept grinning at the TV cameras, even smirking. He took
the punishment until he could take it no longer, and then he
abruptly turned and strode back to his fortress.

To the breed known as "psychohistorians," Richard Nixon
has always presented a rich subject for inquiry. His father, whom
Nixon has often eulogized as a model of diligence and respectability, was a classic example of restless and thwarted ambition.
He operated a trolley car in Columbus, Ohio, suffered frostbite,
and moved to California for his health. He opened a gas station,
planted a lemon grove, opened a general store, and ended by
reading aloud from the newspaper and raging over the corruption
of the Teapot Dome scandal. Frank Nixon also suffered most of
his life from bleeding ulcers. His wife, Hannah, was a pious
Quaker who wanted Richard to be a minister, but he told her,
at the age of twelve, that he was going to be "an old-fashioned
kind of lawyer, a lawyer who can't be bought."

In its poverty, the whole family suffered attacks of illness.
Richard had a bad accident at the age of three, which left him
with a permanent scar on his head, and at the age of four, he
nearly died of pneumonia. When he was twelve, his seven-year-
old brother Arthur suddenly suffered an attack of tubercular
meningitis and died within a week. When he was fourteen, his
older brother Harold got tuberculosis, and his mother took him
for two years to a sanitarium in the drier climate of Arizona,
leaving Frank Nixon and the three remaining sons to fend for
themselves as best they could. Young Richard followed his mother
to Arizona one summer and found her cooking and scrubbing at
the sanitarium to help pay the bills. He himself got a job cleaning out stables at the nearby Slippery Gulch Rodeo and soon
won a promotion to carnival barker. The Arizona cure failed,
however, and Harold Nixon died five years later. He was then
twenty-three, his younger brother nineteen.

Such crises undeniably helped to form the future President,
but as to the exact nature of these influences, we can only listen,

with a certain skepticism, to the speculations of the psychohistorians. One of the better-known, Bruce Mazlish, professor of history at M.I.T. and author of *In Search of Nixon,* suggests that Nixon "unconsciously perceived his beloved mother's leaving him for two years as a betrayal. Consciously, he obviously understood the necessity [but] this unconscious feeling of 'betrayal' might have affected his later attitudes on 'traitors' in high places by helping to prepare him emotionally for such a belief."

What seemed to be driving Nixon mad in the summer of 1973, however, was obviously the Watergate crisis. It must have seemed to him, at the beginning, a relatively small matter, an aberration on the part of some overenthusiastic subordinates. Hadn't Lyndon Johnson regularly bugged his enemies? Hadn't, for that matter, F.D.R.? And as for "covering up" the scandal, wasn't it perfectly normal to cover up one's misdeeds and mistakes? Was it not incomprehensible, then, that the persistent curiosity of a minor federal judge, combined with the persistent curiosity of two minor Washington reporters, should force the man who had ended the war in Vietnam and made peace with China to keep answering questions about the corruptions and coercions that he had considered standard practice in Washington ever since he had arrived there as a young Congressman a quarter of a century ago?

Yes, incomprehensible—to him at least—and unbearable as well. We learned a year later, from Nixon's own transcripts of the tapes that he mysteriously installed in his office, that he spent hours and hours in anxious conference with his adjutants on how to escape from Watergate. The tapes showed a man near the border of incoherence—confused, indecisive, appealing to various aides for understanding and support. And yet his public position during those days was that he wanted only to press forward with what he called "the larger duties of this office"—an office to which he had been elected only a few months earlier by the largest majority in history—and not to be enmeshed in "murky, small, unimportant, vicious little things." But the press, which had warmly endorsed his re-election the previous fall, kept moralizing about his fitness to govern and speculating on his mental health and even asking whether he slept regularly. ("If you're trying to get me to say that the President doesn't sleep well in the White House," an embattled spokesman said, "my reply is, he always sleeps well.")

There were reports, however, that he stayed up late at night to play the piano in solitude, and the press continued to wonder. "Others note," as *The New York Times* put it, "that at times his face appears a little puffy, that he frequently stumbles over his words, that his physical gestures seem too animated and jerky, that his tendency to ramble has increased, and that his displays of good spirit and humor seem like artificial gaiety. . . ." The President could only fight back with belligerent protestations of his own sanity. In October of 1973, when he proclaimed a worldwide alert of United States forces to counter an apparently imaginary threat of Soviet intervention in the Middle East, he went on television again to denounce the press as "outrageous, vicious, distorted," and to declare: "When many thought the President was shell-shocked, unable to act, the President acted decisively in the interests of peace." He took, as always, immense pride in his imagined ability to confront crises. "The tougher it gets, the cooler I get," he said. "I have what it takes."

A few months later, in February of 1974, Nixon went to Bethesda for his annual checkup, and his personal physician, Dr. Walter R. Tkach, pronounced him in "excellent" health. "He never overeats, he never overdrinks," said Dr. Tkach. Was he receiving any medication? "None whatsoever." Tranquilizers? "No." What about the signs of stress during the past few months? "There was no evidence whatsoever of any emotional strain," said Dr. Tkach. But as the impeachment hearings began in the spring, the emotional strain, which was visible to every television viewer except Dr. Tkach, continued. ("We're having an Aztec ceremony to clean up the mess," as Norman Mailer observed. "We won't be happy until we cut Richard Nixon's heart out and hold it high on the summit of the Presidential pyramid.")

Despite the discreet intrigues of his staff, Nixon resisted reality until the very end. Two days before his fall, on August 8, he formally summoned his Cabinet and told the assembled officials that he would not resign. Just an hour before he actually did resign, he called in forty-six Congressional supporters for a bizarre farewell. "Nixon was on the verge of emotional collapse," according to *Time* magazine's account of the affair. "He noted that it would be his last meeting in the Cabinet Room—and then he laughed loudly and incongruously. Nixon launched into a disjointed monologue. He talked of his days at Whittier College, where he had made the freshman football team, which had been so hard up for personnel that 'they even played a fellow who had a broken ankle . . .' Again the strange laugh. But as he turned to his Watergate predicament, Nixon choked up. There were long silences. 'Wait a little bit,' he would say as sobs blocked his speech. . . . As his television appointment approached, Nixon's state grew worse. He rose and started to leave the room. Weeping softly with his head down, he weaved unsteadily, then stumbled. Several aides rushed to his side, took his arms and helped him regain his balance."

Just a few minutes later, Nixon made his last Presidential speech to the nation. He seemed, by all accounts, remarkably self-possessed.

"Call me Ismal," the assassin wrote in his diary, hardly knowing what the words meant, any more than how to spell them. And again: "Ask me why I did it & I'd say 'I don't know,' or 'Nothing else to do,' or 'Why not?' or 'I have to kill somebody.' "

At the apex of Richard Nixon's power, in the spring of 1972, just a few months before his thugs were discovered inside Watergate, he was being followed across the country by a maniac determined to kill him. Maniac—the word comes easily to mind, and yet the strangest aspect of the handwritten pages found in Arthur Bremer's automobile, and published as *An Assassin's Diary*, is their complete ordinariness. Even Lee Harvey Oswald, even Sirhan B. Sirhan, had some twisted relationship to the political process, some twisted reason to hate their victims. Bremer seems to have had no political ideas at all, and no animosity toward his prospective target. The photographs that show him standing in campaign crowds show nothing but a chubby young man in dark glasses, smiling a fatuous smile.

He was only twenty-one at the time, quite average in many ways, still largely unformed. His father was a truck driver, his mother a shrew. He was the fourth of five children. He had an average I.Q. of 106, and he graduated near the middle of his class at South Division High School in Milwaukee. He enrolled for studies in photography, that voyeuristic art, at the Milwaukee Area Technical College, supporting himself with jobs as a busboy and a janitor. He lived alone in an apartment cluttered with dirty dishes, sweaty clothes, and some sex comics. He had a few dates with a plain, bespectacled girl named Joan Pemrich, but she was dismayed by the way he "would do goofy things, walk around goofy and say goofy things." She told him she didn't want to see him any more. Still a virgin, he bought a gun, quit his jobs, and drove to New York. His published diary begins with a long account of his first visit to a New York massage parlor, and his failure, even there, to lose his virginity. His story is, in all things, a mixture of lonely yearning and utter incompetence.

He began following Nixon from city to city, constantly losing his way, moving from motel to motel, and always finding Nixon too well protected, too far out of range. He raged at the fact that the President's route was repeatedly besieged by demonstrators against the Vietnam war, and that the security precautions had been organized not against him ("I'm as important as the start of WW I. I just need the little opening & a second of time"), but against them ("They're nothing. . . . To be a rebel today you have to keep a job, wear a suit & stay apolitical. Now THAT'S REBELLION!").

Seeking only fame, notoriety, a sense that he really existed, Bremer thought he saw an opportunity when he spotted Nixon's car waiting to take him out of Ottawa, and so he ran back to his hotel to "brush my teeth, take 2 asperin & I think change from a salt & pepper knit suit into my black business one"—and then ran back to find the Presidential car gone. ("Does the world remember if Sirhan's tie was on straight? SHIT was I stupid!!") "I am thruorly pissed off," he went on. "About a million things. . . . My fuse is about burnt. There's gonna be an explosion soon. I had it. I want something to happen. I was supposed to be Dead a week & a day ago. Or at least infamous. FUCKING tens-of-1,000's of people. . . . I'd just like to take some of them with me and Nixy. ALL MY EFFORTS & NOTHING CHANGED Just another god Damn failure Oh man, I a werewolf now changed into a wild thing. . . ."

Less than a month later, at a shopping center in Laurel, Maryland, Arthur Bremer was wearing a red-white-and-blue shirt when he shot down Governor George Wallace and left him crippled for life. When the judge asked him whether he had anything to say before being sentenced to prison, Arthur Bremer answered: "Looking back on my life, I would have liked it if society had protected me from myself."

The sense that one does not exist is one of the definitions of madness, and one of the traditional impulses toward assassination, but it is also one of the strongest inspirations in the yearning for power. As Professor Russel V. Lee of the Stanford Medical School put it recently, "The very qualities of egocentricity and megalomania, characteristic of many psychoses, are precisely those that lead men to aspire to high office. In fact there are those who say that the very fact of aspiration to high office is *ipso facto* proof of mental derangement." Professor Lee says he "would not go that far," but his psychiatric assessment of many of this century's leaders is withering. Of all the leaders in World War I, "not one was mentally fit." And then came Mussolini "with delusions of grandeur suggestive of paresis"; and Hitler, "a classic example of paranoia"; and Stalin, "a sociopath . . . ruthless slayer of millions of his own people." One could easily carry such descriptions on into the present: John F. Kennedy repeatedly staging military alerts as a demonstration of his toughness; Lyndon Johnson racing around his ranch in manic enthusiasm one day and sinking into depths of self-pity the next; and finally Richard Nixon. The mere listing of the symptoms reminds one of Erich Fromm's observation that "the lust for power is not rooted in strength but in weakness." And so there may be some merit in considering the relationship between power and madness not in terms of the world's great rulers but from the underview of those whom Frantz Fanon called "the wretched of the earth."

In an obscure grave in St. Michael's Cemetery in the New York borough of Queens lie the bones of Scott Joplin, dead more than half a century, hopelessly insane. He was once a child of immeasurable talent, but doomed from birth to the enraging frustrations of talent denied. He was born in 1868 in the little town of Texarkana, Texas, where his father, a former slave, worked for the Iron Mountain and Southern Railroad. His mother was a laundress. There were four other children in the family, but it was a musical household—Joplin's father played the violin, and his mother the banjo—and so they managed to find the money to buy an old piano. Young Scott not only picked out tunes but also learned the banjo and guitar. Word of the boy's ability eventually reached the town's aged German music teacher, who provided him with free lessons in piano and harmony. He also lectured him—imagine the scene—on the glories of Bach and Beethoven. Giles Joplin wanted his son to learn a useful trade. Young Scott resisted. Shortly after the death of his mother, he left home to become a wandering piano player. He was then about fourteen, but it was a period when everyone considered it quite natural for adolescents, black or white, musicians or gunslingers, to roam around. There was plenty of work to be done, and plenty of entertainment. Joplin drifted through the saloons and honky-tonks of Texas, Louisiana and the Mississippi Valley and finally settled down, at seventeen, among the gamblers and cattlemen and roustabouts in the raffish river port of St. Louis. He played the piano in the Tenderloin. He formed a band. He sang in a group called the Texas Medley Quartette.

It is difficult, indeed impossible, to reconstruct the inner life of a young black musician in the St. Louis of the 1880's. The texts of Joplin's early songs sometimes sound as though the Civil War had never been fought. Thus: "I am thinking of my pickaninny days,/And tonight my heart is filled with untold joy./They bring to me sweet mem'ries long gone bye,/When I was a pickaninny boy. . . ." Who can tell nowadays whether such a lyric represents a genuine black sentiment, or a sentiment that a black might think he was supposed to feel, or simply something that he hoped would sell? One is inclined to assume a certain element of play-acting, not to say hypocrisy, in any black nostalgia for the old plantation, but that assumption may be based on the angers of our own time. There seems to have been a somewhat easier intermingling of whites and blacks in the St. Louis of 1885 than in the St. Louis of 1975. On the other hand, this intermingling may have been based on a mutually accepted system of everyone "knowing his place," a system that the white man could enforce by shooting down any black who failed to comply.

Scott Joplin played ragtime piano in the bars and brothels of St. Louis, and then Chicago, but he was never really part of this debonair world. The portrait on the cover of "The Cascades," the marvelous rag he wrote to celebrate the fountains at the St. Louis Fair of 1904, shows a solidly built man in a black suit with a stiff white collar knifing upward into his jaw. His hair is cropped almost to the skull. The eyes are wary, defensive. Joplin was unfailingly courteous, always ready to help other musicians, either by getting their works published or by providing free room and board, but he was also a very reserved man, quiet, formal. "He was never caught smiling," his publisher once said. Instead of carousing around with the other ragtime pianists of the Mississippi Valley, Joplin struggled to write down the intricate broken rhythms that they all improvised. He enrolled in harmony and composition classes at George R. Smith College, a Methodist institution for black students in Sedalia, Missouri, and when he wrote and published the "Maple Leaf Rag" in 1899, he told one of his friends, "The Maple Leaf will make me king of ragtime composers." And so it did. As the first hit of the new ragtime craze, it sold more than a million copies, and since Joplin had the rare luck to find an honest publisher, the royalties enabled him to give up playing honky-tonk piano and to concentrate on his composing.

But ragtime composers were supposed to write honky-tonk piano pieces. Joplin's ambitions went far beyond that, and they were all destined to failure. He wrote a ballet, *The Ragtime Dance,* copied out his own orchestration and paid for one public performance, which he conducted from the piano. That performance was the last. He wrote a ragtime opera, *A Guest of Honor,* and he financed one performance of that, by the Scott Joplin Drama Company in St. Louis in 1903. By now, even the score has been lost. He continued to write beautiful piano pieces —"Leola" and "Eugenie" and "The Gladiolus" and "Scott Joplin's New Rag"—but the great passion of his later years was to write a successful folk opera. He divorced his wife, who seems to have shared the prevailing belief that ragtime pianists were a disreputable lot, and moved to New York. His second wife, Lottie, ran a boardinghouse, where unemployed musicians often lived for nothing, while Joplin devoted most of his efforts to his opera, *Treemonisha.* It was not only to demonstrate that ragtime could provide a method for a major work of art but also to preach the major thesis of the black intellectual of that era: salvation through education.

The plot consists largely of the struggle between Treemonisha, who has been educated by a white family in exchange for her parents' labor at woodchopping and laundry, and the voodoo conjurors who wander around the neighborhood and sell rabbits' feet to the superstitious blacks. "If you are eatin' food wid ease,/ And drawin' pleasant breath," sings the goofer-dust man, "Be careful you do not sneeze,/ Because 'tis a sign of death." The eighteen-year-old Treemonisha, by contrast, is a teacher. "For ignorance is criminal,/ In this enlightened day," she sings. "So let us all get busy,/ When once we've found the way." At the end, everyone joins in singing, "Marching onward, marching onward,/ Marching to the lovely tune. . . ."

It is indeed a lovely tune, entitled "A Real Slow Drag," and once again Joplin was determined to get his work on stage. In an effort to attract backers, he published the piano score at his own expense in 1911 and then set to work copying out all the orchestral parts. He auditioned a cast, he rehearsed everyone, he "worked like a dog," as one survivor recalls it, "training them." There was one performance, finally, at a hall in Harlem in 1915, and nothing happened. It was hardly the fault of Joplin's music—the opera has been successfully revived in Atlanta and Washington during the past few years—but apparently the Harlem of 1915 was not the place or time for a black folk opera. The audience wanted either to forget its past or to rebel against it.

Joplin was stricken. He had staked all his ambitions and all his money on *Treemonisha,* and the defeat shattered him. Even before that, however, he had been suffering increasingly severe attacks of depression and paranoia. His ability to work became more and more fitful. He began several new rags and songs, but could not finish them; he began orchestrating some of his older works, but he did not finish that either. He was also starting to suffer the physical deterioration caused by syphilis. He could no longer play the piano with his old flair, not even his own compositions. He would stop in the middle of a piece, correct himself, start again, stop again. When the customers at a nightclub in Washington pestered him to perform, he finally gave in, and, according to one witness, "it was pitiful to hear." In the fall of 1916, Joplin was taken to the Manhattan State Hospital, on Ward's Island in the East River. There, like Robert Schumann at Endenich, he occasionally tried to scribble music on bits of paper, but nothing has survived. The following spring, on April 1, he died. The official death certificate declared the cause to be "dementia paralytica—cerebral."

Do black men go crazy in ways that are basically different from white men's madness? "There is nothing reported in the literature or in the experience of any clinician known to the authors that suggests that black people *function* differently psychologically from anyone else," according to William H. Grier and Price M. Cobbs, two black psychiatrists at the University of California Medical Center in San Francisco, who wrote a pioneering study of the subject entitled *Black Rage* (1968). They also argue, however, that all blacks have been scarred by the lessons of slavery, handed on from generation to generation. "Whereas the white man regards his manhood as an ordained right," they say, with a certitude that might raise the eyebrows of many psychiatrists who treat white patients, "the black man is engaged in a never-ending battle for its possession. . . . In the black household [the mother] is the culture bearer. She interprets the society to the children and [she has] an ominous message for her child. . . . The child must know that the white world is dangerous and that if he does not understand its rules it may kill him. . . . Throughout his life, at each critical point of development, the black boy is told to hold back, to constrict, to subvert and camouflage his normal masculinity."

To Professor Chester Pierce of Harvard, the stress is primarily a matter of continuing white hostility. As an expert on extreme environments, he finds interesting parallels and contrasts between life in outer space and life in the ghetto.

"I think it's more extreme to live in Harlem than it is to go to space for three days," he says, "and even your chances of survival are quite different. If a man goes to space, he's time-limited, you know, six days or whatever it's going to be, and then he gets out, and he gets rewards which are unseemly for a mortal, but a man who is born in Harlem probably won't get out, and he's always in jeopardy, psychologically immobilized. His house will burn down, somebody will beat him over the head—and he knows that nobody will come to his support. I think that's a critical thing, psychologically. If a man is in space and he gets in trouble, he knows the whole world quite literally would mobilize itself to help him, but nobody helps the individual on Hastings Street in Detroit or Christian Avenue in Philadelphia. He's just there. And unlike the man coming back from space, he gets no rewards. Now the data suggests lots of ways you can prepare people to negotiate the exotic situation, so I think we could use the same data to negotiate *better* the stresses of mundane situations. One of the great needs is to make a person who is living this desperate existence in the ghetto feel more heroic. A man who goes to Antarctica, which is really more or less like going to Boy Scout camp, is made to feel that he's accomplishing a great deal, but a person getting through this day-by-day existence up in Harlem never gets any credit."

Yes, but do black people go crazy more frequently, or in different ways, than white people?

"There are textbooks," Professor Pierce says with some contempt, "that claim blacks are more susceptible to narcolepsy, say, or not as susceptible to manic-depressive states, or stuff like that, but you always get lots of cases of the opposite. The figures are not reliable because people's racism enters into even the taking of the figures. It's society that says this kind of behavior is crazy and that kind is not. And lots of psychological and sociological studies show that a doctor's diagnosis and treatment is different for any black, or any lower-class person.

"One of the things about being black means going on at two levels. You're living in the majority's world, but never, ever do you stop thinking and reacting and responding and projecting yourself in terms of your oppression, or the possibility of oppression. The two go on all the time, simultaneously, so you're registering different things all the time. That might make more stress, might make you more vulnerable to emotional difficulties, but the consequence might also be a more full life. I think that within our society, blacks get all kinds of craziness—and the remarkable thing is that there isn't more of it—just as whites get all kinds of craziness. But I really don't know the answer. I don't think we can get the answer until we have a more objective kind of evaluation, which might never be, because the state of the art is, by nature, so subjective."

The passage of time has by no means destroyed the heritage of slavery—it has brought neither integration nor equality—but it has produced important changes in the black man's role in society, and so it has produced interesting changes in the way black men go crazy. One of the most remarkable aspects of Scott Joplin's madness was the passivity with which he accepted his fate. It was taken for granted then—to some extent, it still is—that white musicians would get better jobs and more money to play white versions of the music that blacks had invented, that "Alexander's Ragtime Band" should earn a fortune while the composer of *Treemonisha* copied out his orchestrations in the basement of a Harlem boardinghouse. The anger behind Joplin's austere and unsmiling face must sometimes have been tumultuous, but there is no sign that he ever fought back or even protested. The rags of his later years are often melancholy, never belligerent.

The black hero of a generation ago appeared equally docile, but he had a different kind of gift, which enabled him to express his hidden anger in a restricted and more or less symbolic way. At the age of twenty-three, Joe Louis became the first black heavyweight boxing champion since Jack Johnson was prosecuted under the Mann Act and hounded out of the United States, more than two decades earlier. Louis, by contrast, was considered "a credit to his race." "The human race," added the sportswriter Jimmy Cannon, in what was then regarded as a *bon mot* of liberalism and racial tolerance. Louis's grandparents had both been slaves, and his father, an Alabama sharecropper named Munroe Barrow, had gone mad when the future champion was two. He was hauled away to the Searcy State Hospital for the Insane and confined there for the rest of his life. Mrs. Barrow, left with eight children, married another farmer, named Pat Brooks, a widower who had five children of his own. The thirteen children slept three in a bed, and Brooks maintained discipline with his fists. Joe was a dutiful stepson. By the time he was an adolescent, he had developed a stammer.

The reports of Henry Ford's high wages lured the family to Detroit, but the auto-factory jobs were not so easy to find. Joe ran with street gangs. When his mother arranged for him to take violin lessons, he secretly took up boxing instead. He was a prodigy. He could smash down any challenger. But the business of boxing was dominated by white men, some of them none too savory. One New York promoter called Louis's manager and proposed that the young contender throw a fight. "You understand, he's a nigger, and he can't win every time he goes into the ring," the caller said. The Owney Madden gang tried to acquire control of him. "You're a nigger manager and you got a nigger fighter," one of them said to Louis's mentor. "You ain't going to get any place without us." Louis's managers fought off such proposals, but it was in fact a white promoter, Mike Jacobs, who controlled Louis through his great years of million-dollar championship fights.

Louis understood nothing of business, and even less of taxes. In between fights, he lived high, and he borrowed freely from Jacobs to pay all the bills. And so the accounting for the second Louis-Conn fight in 1946, after four years of military service, went like this: Out of gross receipts of $1,925,564, Louis got the winner's purse of $591,116. The federal government took $115,992 in taxes, and New York State took another $28,692. Louis's managers took $140,492, Jacobs and other creditors took $204,000, and his ex-wife Marva got an alimony payment of $66,000—leaving Louis with a net loss of almost $65,000 after a victorious two million-dollar fight. It was enough to drive a man mad, and it did. Louis tried to retire in 1949, but debts and taxes forced him to attempt a comeback, which ended in a humiliating knockout by Rocky Marciano in 1951. His second retirement went equally badly. Business deals failed. He was reduced to refereeing wrestling matches. The government still demanded $1,250,000 in back taxes, and Louis's view of the world grew increasingly paranoid.

He became convinced that he was being followed—sometimes by the Mafia, sometimes just by "them"—and he took to flying around the country to escape his pursuers. Early in 1969, he holed up in a Los Angeles hotel, unable to sleep, drenched in sweat, and convinced that a mysterious Texan was trying to murder him. He told his doctor that the walls of his bedroom were talking to him. "I gotta get a blackjack or a pistol," he said. "I gotta protect myself." One day that spring, at dawn, he turned up at the doctor's house in Detroit and pleaded for asylum. The doctor agreed. By day, Louis spoke rationally, but at night, the whole household was awakened by his screams of terror. He went to New York that June to appear on some television shows and collapsed in a friend's car. He was sweating heavily and complained of pains in his stomach. He was taken to a hospital, and his stomach was pumped out. (Only later did he admit that a strange woman "gave me bad cocaine. She must be in with the Mafia.") Not long afterward, Louis was in Las Vegas with his third wife, Martha, and she found him pasting masking tape over some decorative scrollwork outside their hotel room. "I'm stopping up those cracks where those assholes are putting that poison stuff in on me," he said.

By now, Louis could hardly sleep at all, and he took extraordinary measures to protect himself from the pursuing furies. In Florida, Martha Louis found the ceiling of their hotel room covered with grease spots. "I said, 'Joe, what on earth is that on the ceiling?' . . . Joe said, 'I was stopping up the cracks. The poison gas is coming through them.' I said, 'What do you mean?' He said, 'I got this mayonnaise out of the refrigerator and smeared it over the cracks. They can't get the gas through there.'" Even at home in his apartment in Los Angeles, Louis took desperate measures to protect his sleep. "He would build a cover for the bed," according to Martha Louis. "First he would pull the bed over to the dresser and build up a thing and put something at the head of the bed and take the headboard and put it across. Then he would take another object—like he'd go into our living room and get a big gold-leaf mirror and lay it across everything to weigh it all down. Then he'd take the shade from the window and use it as a backdrop, like the top of a tent. Then he'd crawl up under it in his clothes and lay under it. Only one side of the bed wouldn't be covered, where he'd crawl in. Here he was with his shoes and everything laying under this tent. It was the most pathetic thing in the world."

Martha Louis finally decided in May of 1970 that her husband had to be hospitalized, and since he resisted all psychiatric treatment, she went to the authorities and signed a commitment order, as did Louis's two children. Three uniformed and armed deputy sheriffs and a probate court liaison officer drove up to Louis's home in Denver to take the former champion away. Louis said he would not leave unless he could call the White House. "I know Nixon," he said. "I want to tell the President what you are doing." The deputy sheriffs agreed, but when Louis called the White House, he was told that he could not speak to the President, only to a staff assistant. "Okay, then I got to call all the newspapers and radio and TV stations," Louis told the deputies. "I want everybody to know what you are doing to me." The deputies agreed to that as well, and soon the house was swarming with reporters and photographers, but Louis still had to go. He was taken to the Colorado Psychiatric Hospital and then to the nearby Veterans Administration Hospital, where the doctors agreed on a diagnosis of "involutional depressive reaction, paranoid type." A visitor went to see Louis in the hospital that summer and found him fairly relaxed, although still "thinking about them assholes blowing gas in on me." By fall, the psychiatrists released him with a daily prescription for 250 milligrams of Thorazine and a program for outpatient psychotherapy twice a week. Louis lost little time in getting himself to Las Vegas, beyond the jurisdiction of the Colorado authorities, and they never got him back.

Time brings still further changes, and Joe Louis, once a "credit to his race," is less universally admired nowadays. "When Joe Louis cleaned out Max Schmeling in their second fight," according to one angry old black man, "Schmeling stood for the very thing the white man nursed and worshiped in his own heart. But the whites applauded Joe for crushing Schmeling. Why? Because Joe's victory over Schmeling symbolized the triumph of capitalistic democracy over nazism? No! There may have been a little of that to it, but on a deeper level they applauded Joe [because] Joe's victory over Schmeling confirmed . . . the white man's image of the black man as the Supermasculine Menial, the personification of mindless brute force, the perfect slave." This angry man, described as "an old fat Lazarus . . . a chocolate Santa Claus," is the creation of Eldridge Cleaver, in *Soul on Ice,* and it is only reasonable to assume that his denunciation of Louis represents Cleaver's own view, and thus the view of the militant black radical of the late 1960's.

It is a little difficult now to remember that Cleaver was actually campaigning for the Presidency in 1968 as the official candidate of a left-wing coalition calling itself the Peace and Freedom Party, but he was very much the creature of his times. He was born near Little Rock to a nightclub piano player and a school teacher. His parents brought him to Phoenix, where he earned nickels for shining shoes, and then to Los Angeles, where the parents separated and their son began hustling marijuana. He was duly arrested and sent to reform school, then released, then rearrested and sent to prison. In prison, he became obsessed with the mystique of the white woman, that inanimate blond object that is portrayed on television as the unattainable goal of desire. The young Cleaver tacked a white pin-up girl on his wall and saw it torn down by a guard, who told him to "get yourself a colored girl for a pin-up." But in the prison yard, when he asked a number of other inmates whether they preferred white or black women, nobody chose black. "I don't want nothing black but a Cadillac," said one.

Cleaver himself admitted to the same prejudice, and then "I flew into a rage at myself, at America, at white women, at the history that had placed those tensions of lust and desire in my chest. Two days later, I had a 'nervous breakdown.' For several days I ranted and raved against the white race, against white women in particular, against white America in general. When I came to myself, I was locked in a padded cell with not even the vaguest memory of how I got there. All I could recall was an eternity of pacing back and forth in the cell, preaching to the unhearing walls."

Cleaver believed that he had been driven crazy by the alternating enticements and rejections of white society, but he apparently fell into the hands of a psychiatrist of the classical school. "His conclusion was that I hated my mother. . . . He deliberately blocked all my attempts to bring out the racial question. . . . Each time he interviewed me, he deliberately guided the conversation back to my family life, to my childhood." When Cleaver finally quieted down, he was released from the prison hospital, just as if nothing had happened, and when he finished his term, he reemerged into the public. "I became a rapist," he said. "To refine my technique and *modus operandi*, I started out by practicing on black girls in the ghetto, where dark and vicious deeds appear not as aberrations or deviations from the norm, but as part of the sufficiency of the Evil of a day—and when I considered myself smooth enough, I crossed the tracks and sought out white prey. I did this consciously, deliberately, willfully, methodically— though looking back I see that I was in a frantic, wild, and completely abandoned frame of mind. Rape was an insurrectionary act. It delighted me that I was defying and trampling upon the white man's law, upon his system of values, and that I was defiling his women. . . ."

Cleaver's confession was an expression of black madness in our time, but by the late 1960's, this particular kind of madness became almost shudderingly fashionable. The black rapist was no longer lynched; he wrote books, and the books became bestsellers. A white woman lawyer fell in love with Cleaver and got him paroled from San Quentin, and he soon became, among other things, an editor of *Ramparts*, the "information minister" of the Black Panthers, and a Presidential candidate. There was one odd aspect to all this, and that was that Cleaver had been in prison not for rape but for assault. Indeed, none of the stories about Cleaver the rapist ever specified who had been raped, or under what circumstances. Was it possible that Cleaver's celebrated rapes occurred largely in his imagination? That just as every celebrated murder case attracts people who try to make spurious confessions, Cleaver might be confessing nothing more than fantasies—and then finding, perhaps to his amazement, that the once-loathed crime was now masochistically admired as what he called "an insurrectionary act"? The actual police report on the crime for which Cleaver was arrested and imprisoned appears less insurrectionary than pitiable. A hospital nurse, sitting in a car with a friend, declared that a black man had beaten his fists against the locked windows and shouted threats and imprecations. He had run around the parking lot like someone berserk. A roving police car had rescued her and captured the wild man. Of all the boasts about actual rape, everything remains conjecture.

As a media celebrity, Cleaver spoke furiously about his manhood, describing it as though it were some kind of mystical object of which the white world had deprived him. "We shall have our manhood," he wrote. "We shall have it or the earth will be

leveled by our attempts to gain it." Such rhetoric sounded splendid in the atmosphere of the late 1960's, when both blacks and
whites seemed to consider gunplay and assault an assertion of
manhood—and the assertion of manhood a self-evident virtue. If
the Black Panthers were proving themselves by parading around
with rifles, so were the swaggering California police, who delighted in the challenge to combat. Cleaver was wounded in one
such battle, sent back to jail and bailed out again, and then he
fled to Algiers. But as we look back from the perspective of the
middle 1970's, the boast of rape seems somewhat less admirable.
After a few years of feminist propaganda, it is more clear that
such assaults, regardless of race, are not insurrectionary but simply
psychotic and brutal.

Just as time changes our perceptions, so it changes some of
our judgments on the powerful and the powerless. In the spring
of 1974, when one of my daughters graduated from college, the
Columbia brass choir, which normally performs the stately works
of composers like Sir Edward Elgar, suddenly burst forth with
the music of Scott Joplin's "The Entertainer." It had recently acquired a vast popularity because a Hollywood producer had decided to make it the theme of an Academy-Award-winning movie,
The Sting, and nobody could argue that a Hollywood hit redeems
more than a half-century of neglect. Still, at a time when Eldridge
Cleaver, once the hero of the campus, had drifted into obscure
exile somewhere in France, the gentle charm of Joplin's music
finally acquired, in the chorus of young trumpeters and trom-
bonists, an unmistakable quality of triumph.

Of all the Saint Joans who have appeared on stage and screen
—Ingrid Bergman, Julie Harris, even Hedy Lamarr—the most implausible actress ever to attempt the role was Jean Seberg. She
was selected in 1956 by Otto Preminger after a much-publicized
"nationwide talent search," because the producer claimed that he
wanted the Maid of Orleans to be portrayed not by any familiar
actress but by an unknown girl. And so the pink-cheeked, seventeen-year-old star of the high-school dramatic society in Marshalltown, Iowa, became one of the youngest and most celebrated
flops in Hollywood history. She eventually retreated to Paris, re-
made her career in Jean-Luc Godard's *Breathless*, and married

the French novelist Romain Gary. She also maintained a wide-open household that was frequented by various indigent film directors, radical poets, Black Panthers. "I guess I am a fellow traveler, at a distance, with what you might call 'leftist causes,'" she told an interviewer not long ago. "When people are in a jam, they sleep here or hide here."

Her activities troubled Gary, and in 1969 they separated. Jean was pregnant with his child, but there were rumors that the real father was black. Jean was in Switzerland, seven months pregnant, when the rumors appeared in the newspapers. "The following day, my contractions began," she recalled. "The third day I was flown to Geneva in a helicopter, and they did an emergency Caesarian. A little girl was born. She lived three days.

"I began cracking up then, without knowing it. I decided to bury my baby in my home town. I did the whole deal. We opened the coffin and took a hundred and eighty photographs, and everybody in Marshalltown who was curious what color the baby was got a chance to check it out. A lot of them came to look."

After the funeral, Jean Seberg flew to New York to consult a lawyer about suing for libel. "He said suing for libel would cost a million dollars and take ten years, and he asked if the bitterness was worth it. That's when I cracked up. I had a very, very bad mental breakdown. I wound up being locked up. . . . But part of me has become more realistic. I'm going to live this year as if it were my last."

The ultimate sense of powerlessness comes not from any confrontation between black and white, rich and poor, men and women, but from the confrontation with God. The search for one's self finally leads, therefore, to an effort to acquire God's power, either as his servant or as his antagonist. And it is one of the most striking aspects of madness that men on the brink of insanity begin to think, often for the first time, in terms of God's omnipotence.

Thus Gogol—trying to demonstrate the redemption of Chichikov in the second part of *Dead Souls,* and failing, and burning his manuscript, and setting out on a pilgrimage for the Holy Land, and finally starving himself to death, with leeches at his nose. Thus, Nietzsche demanding, "Could it be possible? This old saint

in the forest has not yet heard anything of this, that God is dead!"
Thus, Captain Ahab ("They think me mad [but] I am madness
maddened!") calling for the blood of his crew and then using it
to baptize the harpoons: "*Ego baptizo te . . . in nomine diaboli!*"
Thus, Pip, the *Pequod's* cabin boy, driven mad by the terror of
having fallen overboard, "saw the multitudinous, God-omni-
present, coral insects, that out of the firmament of waters heaved
the colossal orbs. He saw God's foot upon the treadle of the loom,
and spoke it; and therefore his shipmates called him mad. So
man's insanity is heaven's sense. . . ."

Or perhaps the opposite. Allen Ginsberg, the poet, saw his
mother go crazy through the paranoid fantasies of the Communist
jungle—"The enemies approach—what poisons? Tape recorders?
F.B.I.? Zhdanov hiding behind the counter? Trotsky mixing rat
bacteria in the back of the store?" But toward the end, she found
a kind of serenity. "Yesterday I saw God," she said, as the poet
quoted her in *Kaddish for Naomi Ginsberg:*

"What did he look like? Well, in the afternoon I climbed up
a ladder—he has a cheap cabin in the country, like Monroe, N.Y.,
the chicken farms in the wood. He was a lonely old man with a
white beard./I cooked supper for him. I made him a nice supper
—lentil soup, vegetables, bread & butter—miltz—he sat down at
the table and ate, he was sad./I told him, Look at all those fight-
ings and killings down there. What's the matter? Why don't you
put a stop to it?/I try, he said—That's all he could do, he looked
tired. He's a bachelor so long, and he likes lentil soup."

One of the origins of man's sense of God has traditionally
been his awe at the universe—"the starred heaven above me and
the moral law within me," as Immanuel Kant put it—and so, having contemplated the moral law with a deepening sense of despair, man finally decided—actually John F. Kennedy decided,
as a propaganda response to the first Soviet triumphs in space
flight—that it was time to start bringing technology and trash
and plastic American flags to that traditional storm-center of lunacy, the moon. The crew of Apollo 11—Neil Armstrong, Buzz
Aldrin and Mike Collins—duly planted the plastic flag near the
Sea of Tranquillity and then flew home, landing upside down in
the Pacific. One of their myriad gadgets set them upright again,
and then a shoal of frogmen helped them onto a raft and handed

them some scrubbing cloths and detergent with which to wipe off any contamination from the moon. Then a helicopter hauled them aboard the aircraft carrier *Hornet,* where they were locked into a large plastic box, yet another protection against possible contamination from the moon.

And there, outside their plastic box, stood President Nixon. "[He] was clearly enthusiastic," Aldrin recalled later. "He danced a kind of jig when he greeted us through the window." The President's first message—it was a strange set of priorities—was that "over one hundred foreign governments, emperors and presidents and prime ministers and kings," had sent words of praise for the astronauts. His second was that he brought "love and congratulations" from the astronauts' wives, "three of the greatest ladies and most courageous ladies in the whole world today," and that he was inviting all the astronauts and their wives to a banquet as soon as the quarantine was over. Third, he asked the astronauts whether they were seasick. They were not. Fourth, he asked them whether they knew the result of the annual all-star baseball game. They did. Then he said he would "close off" by telling them that "this is the greatest week in the history of the world since the Creation. Because as a result of what happened in this week, the world is bigger infinitely. . . ." Aldrin, inside his plastic box, observed that "it was only a matter of time before he would be reminded that there once was a fellow named Jesus Christ."

Norman Mailer, having been paid a reported one million dollars by *Life* magazine to play St. Matthew during the greatest week in the history of the world, voyaged to the astronaut bases in Houston and Cape Kennedy and then raised an interesting question: Did God want man to explore the virgin territory of the moon, and if so, why?

"To believe in God and to believe in progress—what could that mean but that the desire for progress existed in the very creation of man, as if man were designed from the outset to labor as God's agent, to carry God's vision of existence across the stars. If this were true then the intent of the Lord could hardly be to reveal His goodness to us; rather He must employ us to reveal His vision of existence *out there.* . . . A large and uncomfortable thought, for if it were so, then the flight of Apollo was a first revelation of the real intent of History. . . . In the light of God's need for supermen to negotiate His passage through the heavens, then how much more value might He give to courage than to charity. . . . Yes if speed were of the essence then Hell's Angels were possibly nearer to God than the war against poverty."

Mailer went on to denounce his own hypothesis as "disruptive to a liberal philosophical system [but on the other hand, it did offer] a reason why the heroes of the time were technologists, not poets. . . . It was because the power guiding us had desired nothing less. He was looking to the day when all of mankind would yet be part of one machine, with mechanical circuits, social flesh circuits, and combined electro-magnetic and thought-transponder circuits, an instrument of divine endeavor put together by a Father to whom one might no longer be able to pray since the ardors of His embattled voyage could have driven Him mad."

Most of the astronauts are more simple souls, but it has been remarkable how many of them returned from outer space with some sense of having been touched by a supernatural finger. These were not, after all, flower children playing with the *I Ching*, but rather the flower of the armed forces, men trained to command and to obey, to believe unquestioningly in the orthodoxies of patriotism and engineering. One would expect them to settle down afterward as airline executives or industrial consultants, and yet Ed Mitchell, the lunar module pilot on Apollo 14, came back to organize the Mind Science Foundation for the study of extrasensory perception, and James Irwin, one of the moonwalkers on Apollo 15, founded a missionary organization called High Flight to spread word of the mystical epiphany that he himself had experienced.

"I felt an overwhelming sense of the presence of God on the moon," he said. "I felt His spirit more closely than I have ever felt it on the earth, right there beside me—it was amazing. . . . When a key string broke and I couldn't get the science station up, I prayed. Immediately I had the answer. . . . God was telling me what to do. . . . I am not talking about some vague sense of direction. There was this supernatural sensation of His presence. If I needed Him I could call on Him, call on His power."

Buzz Aldrin came prepared. Onto the first space ship to reach the moon, he brought a cupful of wine and a wafer. Not long after the craft landed, he took communion, reading to himself an excerpt from the Book of John. He had intended to perform this ceremony before the television cameras that portrayed to a watching world all the trivia of space flight, but NASA had already been embarrassed by the onslaughts of Madalyn Murray O'Hair the militant opponent of official religions, who had protested vehemently against an earlier Apollo crew reading from Genesis while circling the moon. And so, at NASA's request, Aldrin's only public ceremony was to "invite each person listening in, wherever or whoever he may be, to contemplate for a few moments the events of the last few hours and to give thanks in his own individual way." If God is, as many suspect, not an interdenominational figurehead, He is capable not only of cataclysms but of mild revenges. As soon as Aldrin set foot on the moon, "my kidneys, which have never been of the strongest, sent me a message of distress. Neil might have been the first man to step on the moon, but I was the first to pee in his pants on the moon. I was, of course, linked up with the urine-collection device, but it was a unique feeling."

Aldrin was one of the most skilled of all the astronauts, a professional combat pilot who also had earned a doctorate at M.I.T. "All meat and stone," as Mailer described him, Aldrin was "a man of solid presentation, dependable as a tractor, but suggesting the strength of a tank, dull, almost ponderous, yet with the hint of unpredictability. . . . He had big features and light-brown hair, almost gold. His eyes took a turn down like samurai eyes, the corners of his lips took a right-angle turn down—it gave him the expression of a serious man at home on a field of carnage." Not the sort of man to be overwhelmed by either the dangers or the eerie mysteries of descending on the moon. "If there was any emotional reaction to the lunar landing," Aldrin said later, "it was so quickly suppressed that I have no recollection of it." Armstrong, of course, was laconic to the point of taciturnity, but when stolid Buzz Aldrin returned from his mission, he mysteriously began to crack up.

The first symptoms appeared, according to Aldrin's own account, in the hostility of his adolescent son, Mike, who became "openly argumentative [and] would develop intense headaches." The Aldrins took their son to a local psychologist, who then wanted to interview the parents and kept working on them even after he had pronounced the son cured. The psychologist finally discharged the wife as well and "zeroed in on me." Aldrin was suffering from acute depression, which became worse after he embarked on an affair with a divorcee whom he met in New York. He was told to take Ritalin as an antidepressant, but the condition got steadily worse.

"I'd go to my office in the morning, determined to work a full day and then go home to more work. I'd sit down at my desk and stare out the window. A few hours would go by and I'd drive to the beach at Galveston and walk. Then I'd go home for dinner, turn on the television, and get a bottle of Scotch. Or I'd not go home at all until everyone was in bed. . . . Several times I resolved to get help, but I could not believe that I was now incapable of getting myself going. Every time I decided to get help I began to cry."

Aldrin did finally turn to the Air Force medical authorities, who initiated a long treatment of antidepressant drugs and psychotherapy. In the course of this, Aldrin began to re-evaluate his past, his relations with the stern but often absent father who had guided him toward West Point, his fear of the melancholy that had driven his grandfather, and perhaps his mother, who had died through an "accidental" overdose of sleeping pills, to suicide. His fear of the moon, too.

"I was idly discussing books I had read as a youngster when I remembered . . . one story about a voyage to the moon during which a great deal of trouble was encountered and once the moon had been reached the space travelers departed for earth, returning home insane. It had given me nightmares as a youngster, and had secured an odd corner in my psychic life."

The doctors kept administering drugs—thioridazine and then imipramine—and they finally worked out a psychiatric explanation for the trouble, as they usually do.

"It emerged that my life was highly structured and that there had always existed a major goal of one sort or another," Aldrin recalled. "I had excelled academically, being at the top of the schools and classes I had attended during my life. Finally, there had been the most important goal of all, and it had been realized —I had gone to the moon. What to do next? What possible goal could I add now? There simply wasn't one, and without a goal I was like an inert Ping-Pong ball being batted about by the whims and motivations of others. I was suffering from what poets have described as the melancholy of all things done."

But is it not a strange idea—even after everyone has rendered due respect to the extraordinary technological feat of flying to the moon—that the idea of making that flight could somehow represent "all things done"? Poor Buddha, poor Einstein, poor Mozart, to have been so far surpassed during the greatest week since the Creation. In the summer of 1974, on the fifth anniversary of the moon landing, an NBC reporter sallied out into the streets of New York to ask a few citizens, "Who are Armstrong, Aldrin, and Collins?" The first victim, a portly, middle-aged man in a business suit, thought for a moment before he figured out the answer. "It's a stock-brokerage house," he finally said. "It's a law firm," said a second. The third also stopped to reflect a minute, and then he said, "I don't know."

Out of a Case History:
Billy Plays Dead

Billy is a television producer, and a good one, which means that his telephone rings constantly. Even though each telephone call brings new crises, and even though it is late on Friday afternoon and he is trying to clear his desk for a three-day trip to Chicago, Billy remains un-ruffled. He is a short, cherubic man with thinning, sandy hair. He once studied music, but that was long ago. He is now forty-nine and has two adolescent sons. He wears a blue-and-yellow-striped shirt and a black knitted pullover and no necktie. The walls of his office are dark gray, and on one of them, over the leather sofa, hangs a painting of a target, an oval target.

I had just passed my nineteenth birthday, and I was one of the last draftees of the war. I had gone in as a college student, as an A.S.T.P. [Army Specialized Training Program], but then the A.S.T.P. was dissolved, just in time to supply a reserve of about 200,000 infantrymen for D day. They wanted us to fill in all the undermanned divisions, so I was assigned to the Yankee Division, which was the New England National Guard division. We were the first American division to go directly from the States to France, to Cherbourg, in August of 1944. We camped in the Normandy peninsula, in pup tents in the apple orchards, and it was an absolutely blissful period. The war was by then around Paris and moving very quickly into Alsace. Everybody had a terrifically exhilarated feeling that it was going to be over next week.

One day when we came back from our usual daily hike through the countryside, we were told to assemble in this apple orchard. Our company commander was trembling with excitement, and he said that the Yankee Division had been picked to move up and join the Third Army, Patton's army. We were going to replace the Fourth Armored Division, which had been the spearhead of the Third Army's drive. It had overextended its supply lines and run out of gasoline and was then stalled or stopped. Nobody knew what the trouble really was. Anyway, they had been on the move for months, and we were going into the front line to replace them.

We were out of there in two hours. Packed up and on those trucks and on our way. It started to rain the minute we got on those trucks, and it rained—it rained for ten years. By now it was early September, and we moved up to about fifteen miles east of Nancy and made one of those nighttime exchanges. We got there at about midnight, and they left at about dawn, and there we stayed, for weeks and weeks, in the autumn rain. It was nearly like trench warfare in World War I, that's really what it was, except there were no trenches. It was a line of foxholes, about one every five yards, and in every foxhole two men lived. There was no hope of making a trench, in which case you could make dugouts and have some kind of a life with other people. You could even walk a mile a day in a trench. But here you just had a very, very limited space to share with one other man, whom you quickly grew to hate, in some kind of way.

And this would be relieved by artillery bombardments. There were perhaps three or four regular artillery barrages every day. At dawn, in the evening, and then two unexpected attacks. There was also a certain amount of strafing from the air, but not much of it. Then there were the special chores. I mean, for example, right after dark, one man would have to go back to the company command post, which was perhaps 300 to 500 yards in the rear, and bring back supplies, bring back water, bring back K rations, C rations, ammunition, grenades, what have you. And everybody on the whole front, their front and your front, knew when that was going on, so you were always sort of a sitting duck for mortar fire, which you would just have to zigzag to escape.

Every third night or so, you had to go out to outposts between the German and American armies. You sat in a gravelike hole, really a slit trench, with your head just above ground level, like this, your eyes just above ground level. In these outpost positions, you really could hear the Germans. You could hear them speaking to each other. You could occasionally see them moving, if it was a particularly bright night. I guess it was a perfectly commonplace situation, but the enemy becomes very real because he's always *there*, just as you are always "there" to him.

Occasionally, there would be attempts by the Germans to take our line—I mean, sporadically. I think it was like calisthenics for them. They would come over at five o'clock in the morning, say, and they would be terrible—I mean, it would leave—you know, they would leave one dead and three horribly wounded— and for what? I had been ideologically committed to the war, I believed in the war, but as soon as I got into combat and faced an authentic living German there, all my ideology washed off my back instantly. I don't mean that I didn't shoot at them. I did shoot. But all that stuff that had been drummed up just vanished. The war became something else to me. It was a matter that I had to shoot them or they would shoot me, that was all, that was what it was.

In any case, it was a very static fall, and very wearing on the nerves. We all lived in a constant state of dampness, cold, a kind of hunger, and *fear*, always that fear. I mean, artillery barrages, surprise attacks, and the reality of corpses all the time. Very unpleasant.

One night, after we'd been there about a month, the word went out that C Company was going to move out and take a ridge to our right, up ahead, no farther away than that fence over there. It seemed—you know—lunatic, but who the hell ever knows? Sometimes you have the feeling that maybe the whole war depends on this little move. So at about five in the morning, maybe four-thirty in the morning, we were all told to move out, in diamond formation. That's an infantry formation with a head and—well, it's shaped like a diamond. There were three squads in the platoon, maybe thirty-five or forty men in all. I was in the last part of the diamond, with a Browning automatic rifle. It was just before dawn, that teetering moment just before dawn, and very wet, muddy.

We started up over that ridge. And the first part of the diamond went over the ridge. And we continued to move. And the last part of the diamond was almost at the top of the ridge when it suddenly happened that the front part discovered that it was caught in a kind of German horseshoe, a U. That's how they were dug in on the other side of the ridge. And they let most of the diamond get over the ridge before they started in on them. It was a slaughter. Machine-gun fire, and Mausers, and then mortars.

We were all flat on our faces. Well, anyway— Two thirds of the platoon, I think, was wounded or killed within a half hour, because they were totally exposed. And I—well, I just played dead. There were others in my BAR team about eight or ten feet away, and it was my *sense* that everybody on that side of the ridge was dead or wounded, except for me. Which was just about the literal truth. And that is how the whole day went. The Germans didn't come out to counterattack, but they harassed us all day long with rifle fire and machine-gun fire and hand grenades and mortar fire.

And the worst part—I mean, while the terror of being killed was horrible, and the fear of being recognized as a living soldier on the hillside, it was the screaming of the wounded that was in the end the worst. Because that was constant. That just never let up. And they were all people I had trained with, lived with, and shared a foxhole with, for a long time. So there were real bonds there. And guilt began forming very early on. I mean, it was clear to me that I was going to act the most—what is the word? not callow—*craven* role. I mean, I was going to stay on that hill and play dead while at least four of five soldiers I had lived with for a year or more were either going to die of their wounds or be cut up by bullets, and I was not going to make a move to help them. I mean, when they screamed for water, I didn't make a move to take out my flask and throw it to them. I couldn't.

And as I said, that is how the whole day went. With terror and guilt and dawning self-knowledge about one's cowardice. You know, I was sure that anybody else would have behaved exactly the same way, except that I had until that moment maintained a whole set of illusions about myself. I had wanted to be— you know—tough. And when somebody's ten feet away and screaming for water, you do think you should be helping them, even if it's useless. And it is a horror. I mean, it is an aspect of living that's very difficult to deal with. Maybe you never deal with it. I don't know. I was just terrified. I was, being Jewish, terrified of being captured by the Nazis, and I was terrified of not being captured, and I was terrified of being wounded, and of not being wounded. There was nothing I wasn't scared of. I just spent the whole day like that, and nothing wounded me. I was not hit. I wasn't touched. Much to my lifelong regret.

Just after dark, finally, three medics showed up, with a Red Cross flag and all the rest of it. They had come across a pasture with two stretchers. And I began to help them look for wounded. I at least stood up. And once I stood up, I knew I was never going to lie down there again. I didn't care what happened to me—I had a feeling of such exhilaration when I stood up on my feet, I could hardly *bear* it. And I helped them to carry, I think, three wounded back across the pasture to the company command post. Maybe there were only two, maybe three or four. I don't even remember.

When we got back to the company command post, the commander, who was an ex-football player from one of the Middle Western universities, was in a state of absolute hysteria over what had happened. Because he had not made a move. I mean, he had done nothing all day except watch a platoon disappear—and he had not been able to act or had not made a decision to act. He was a sweet, dumb man, and I wasn't surprised when I saw him in this state. I mean, he was so helpless. But I just didn't care. I mean, *part* of me had—I had a terrific desire to crawl into a cave and never see another person for the rest of my life. If somebody had offered me that, I would have made that deal on the spot. But part of me was also dying for some action. So I said to him, "I'm going back with the medics and see if we can find any more wounded." And he said—he was hysterical—he said, "No, you're not, you've done all you have to, you're going to get a Silver Star for this." I just said, "Oh, come on." So I did go back with the medics, and we got one more wounded guy out.

And then we got—what happened then was that we loaded one of the wounded on a stretcher onto a Jeep. We got in the Jeep—there was the driver, and a medic and myself—and we started back to the divisional command post, where the hospital was, and we got caught in a ladder barrage. You know what that is? That's when an artillery unit will try to zero in on a target by just going closer and closer like rungs on a ladder. You know—thump, thump, thump. And you can see it coming at you. And we saw it coming at us. And off we jumped from that Jeep into a ditch on the side of the road—leaving, of course, our wounded exposed, on the Jeep, in the stretcher. Which was something that he didn't need, and I surely didn't need. It was another action— another craven action on my part, although what the hell I was supposed to do, I don't know. But the wounded guy was untouched. We were all untouched. This barrage went off all around us and nobody was harmed by it.

By this time it must have been about ten o'clock at night— nine-thirty—who the hell knows?—and we got to the hospital at the divisional command post. And the first thing that happened was that a chaplain greeted our Jeep and made the sign of the cross over me. I must have looked as though I really needed it. But when he did that—you have to understand that I had an Orthodox Jewish upbringing—that was kind of the ultimate irony, and I just burst into tears. And I really cried for a long time. I mean, I cried for a whole week.

So they processed me right there at the hospital. They gave me sodium amytal, or sodium pentothal, I'm not sure which it was. It was something that put me to sleep for something like fourteen hours. And when I came to, I couldn't wait to talk to the psychiatrist. I remember telling him about my experience on the hillside, over and over again. I think that I couldn't believe what had happened to me. I think that I simply could not assimilate the idea that it had happened. I felt that I must never go back to the front lines, never again in my life, but I also felt sorry for myself for not having been wounded. If I had been wounded, it would have justified the experience, so I would have come out of it with the conventional badge of honor. This way I came out of it with "psychoneurotic" stamped on my record, and a growing awareness of certain sensitivities in myself that I really did not want to accept. I wanted to be one of those guys who could handle situations like that. I was too dumb to know that nobody could. And I really hated myself for not being wounded, for being the only one who wasn't hit.

I also had to talk to the divisional historian, who wanted a record of what had happened on that ridge, for the divisional history that would inevitably be prepared. And every time I would tell him something about what happened, he would say, in effect, "That's not what happened." For three hours, he was asking me what happened and at the same time telling me what happened. Maybe he wanted a dressed-up account, because the account I was giving was really not very pretty. I don't know. He made me feel like a liar. He made me feel as though I were trying to create something, you know, but I didn't give a damn.

I must have spent two weeks in the hospital, seeing the psychiatrist every day and being shot with this drug every day, alternately weeping and being manic, and so happy to be out of the whole front that I could hardly stand it. Simultaneously guilty about that good feeling. I was really in a very crazy state for that whole period, but then slowly I began to emerge from all the craziness and to go through a long, slow healing process.

They put me on special duty in the city of Nancy, guarding a warehouse where all the divisional duffel bags were stored. I guarded this warehouse with eight other guys, but the only thing we really had to do was to take the duffel bags of the casualties. There would be casualty lists every day, and we had to find those duffel bags of the guys that had been killed and—get rid of them. They were taken away by truck or something. I think they were eventually destroyed, or the equipment would be redistributed. I don't even know what they did with it. And I felt guilty about that, too, of course. They were dead, and there I was— But by now the army considered me okay, hunky-dory. I was fine. If there had had to be an infantry invasion of Japan, I'm sure I would have been there in the infantry. But the war was ending, and they began discharging people on the points system, so I never went back to combat again.

I Have Conceived Everything but I Am Not a Criminal

Most crimes are quite unimportant. Sometimes there is a victim, grieving or dead, and then the reporters get angry quotes from angry relatives, but often there is not even a victim. The outburst of madness is scarcely worth space among the department-store ads in the local newspapers. Here are a few examples that occurred during the past year or two:

"We responded," said Sergeant Kenneth McGuire, in the wonderful language of police reports, "to a call about a berserk male at 6:30 A.M." The scene is Amityville, New York, which, despite its name, is a rather tough working-class town with a large black population on the south shore of Long Island. "On the way we received reports of firing, and when we arrived, there were gunshots from the rear of the house. We surrounded the house." The besieged man was Daniel F. Walker, an unemployed workman who, according to his mother, had recently been hospitalized for "L.S.D. addiction" but "hadn't been taking his medicine, and lately he was very nervous and frustrated." Now the police found Walker hiding behind the kitchen door with a rifle under one arm and one of his three young sons under the other. "I am God," Walker shouted at them. "I can hurt you but you can't hurt me." After two hours of bargaining, some twenty police stormed the house, and the "berserk male" was captured.

"Kill Lies All" was the mysterious message that an Iranian-born painter named Tony Shafrazi determined to spray in foot-high blood-red letters across the face of Picasso's *Guernica*. "We couldn't move, we were all stunned," said Gregory Lopasio, sixteen, who was touring New York's Museum of Modern Art with his classmates from Scarsdale High School when Shafrazi launched his attack with an aerosol spray can. "A man started to move toward the guy when he turned around, cursed, and said,

'I'm an artist.' Then everybody started yelling and a guard came."
The guard seized Shafrazi, who repeated his protests: "Call the
curator, I'm an artist." And again at the West 54th Street police
station: "I'm an artist and I wanted to tell the truth." *Guernica* is
covered with a coat of varnish, however, and within an hour the
restorers had expunged Shafrazi's "truth." "There's no damage at
all," said the museum's director of painting and sculpture.

In Detroit, young Howard Kohn, aged twenty-five, was the
Free Press's star investigator of organized crime. He and another
reporter had publicly identified eleven of the city's major heroin
dealers. He had provided a grand jury with the names of thirty
policemen connected with the drug traffic, and twelve of them
were subsequently indicted. Then, according to Kohn, he was
kidnaped by a gunman with a shaven head and surgical gloves,
who took him to a motel where he was tied up with his own
necktie and a torn pillow case. "My man wants to meet you,"
Kohn quoted the kidnaper as saying. "You been messing with him,
you know? He's going to mess with you." Kohn said he ran for his
life and received a shot in his coat before the kidnaper's gun
jammed. "REPORTER ESCAPES DEATH IN KIDNAPING,"
the *Free Press* headline cried, but after some further questioning
by his editors, Kohn admitted he had made up the whole story.
Then he checked into the psychiatric wing of the Henry Ford
Hospital.

In Washington, there was a man named Jesse Burgess
Thomas, aged fifty-three, a graduate of Andover and Harvard,
who had spent much of his life as a roving seaman. During his
wanderings, he collected things, valuable things, worthless things.
"He was a pack rat," according to one of his neighbors. His little
apartment on Washington's northwest side was cluttered with
piles of old newspapers, shell-inlaid Japanese boxes, century-old
postage stamps, dozens of cottage-cheese containers, volumes of
shipping charts, more than thirty broken umbrellas. He eked
out a living by writing articles on nautical history for the Navy
Department, and by working as a part-time taxi driver, but he
fell months behind in his rent. "Thomas just said God would take
care of him and didn't seem to care," one neighbor recalled.

The landlord went to court and won an eviction proceeding.
Around noon on a day when Thomas was away, a deputy United

States marshal and about a dozen workmen went to the apartment and carted all of Thomas's treasures out onto the street. A crowd of thirty or forty people gathered to watch. "Several witnesses said there was a 'block party' atmosphere to the eviction initially," according to the *Washington Post's* account of the affair. "Then the mood turned ugly, witnesses said. Looting, at first surreptitious and then blatant, began. A teen-ager threw some hand-tinted Japanese slides to the ground and stamped on them, destroying them. A woman accompanied by several children systematically picked through the stacks and the filing cabinets and, when she found something she liked, held it up triumphantly. Children, teen-agers, young adults, older people grabbed off everything they could."

When Jesse Burgess Thomas returned to his house and saw the crowds picking over the wreckage of his life, he collapsed with a congestive heart failure, and half an hour later, the George Washington University Hospital pronounced him dead.

The relationship between crime and insanity is—what shall I say?—symbiotic. Every major crime can be defined as an act of insanity, hence punished by incarceration; all major insanity can be defined as a crime, hence punished by incarceration. I must use the qualifying word "major," since society cannot incarcerate everyone. To drive a car carelessly is a sign of mere neurosis, so the speeder is fined rather than imprisoned, as long as he doesn't hit anyone. The suburban housewife who is caught shoplifting a leg of lamb may go free if she agrees to pay the bill. Even in questions of serious crime, the courts apply a kind of *triage*, by which one murderer is pronounced fit for trial while a second one is sent to the insane asylum.

It is society, of course, that defines what crime is, just as it defines what insanity is. Crime is the use of society's methods by people whom society has not authorized to use those methods. When the government charges money for unwanted "defense" forces, that is taxation; when the underworld does the same, that is called "the protection racket." When banks demand that their customers pay back substantially more than they borrowed, that is interest; when the underworld does the same, it is "loan-sharking." When the government enforces its decisions by coercion, such as imprisonment or even execution, people speak proudly of the rule of law; when the underworld does the same, there is excited talk of "hoods" carrying out "hits." The very word "contract," which has acquired sinister connotations of gangster gunplay, is, of course, the same word that denotes society's most fundamental legal relationship. And vice versa.

What is true for organized crime is all the more true for the individual criminal, which is to say, just about all of us. The truth, as always, emerges by night. Who, in his dreams, has not stabbed or strangled his parents, his brothers, his employers, or his girl friends? Who, for that matter, has not hidden the body somewhere and then returned over and over again to the hiding place to make sure that the secret was safe (was Poe's "Telltale Heart" written by accident, or Faulkner's "The Hound"?). Society lives by daylight, however, and every day at dawn, it renews its offer of the basic social contract: Obey the rules, and you may walk free. Break the rules, and you will be punished.

But crime and madness both represent a total rejection of the rules. The criminal rarely thinks about being caught; nor does the madman. They both live by their own rules, both the Mafia *capo* and the homicidal maniac—and, for that matter, the White House aide-de-camp. Within those rules, they are all quite law-abiding, but they constantly feel that the outside world is threatening them. As indeed it is. For we who wake up and get on the train to work every day manage to forget in the morning all the crime and madness we experienced during the night. And for those who do not forget, who live by day in our world of night, we demand punishment.

The classic figure in whom the lines of insanity and criminality intersect—whose name, in fact, is synonymous with the atrocities of every demented murderer—was illegally confined for years in the dungeons of the Bastille. A fortnight before the Paris mobs finally stormed the place, the street disorders became so tumultuous that the prison governor arrayed all his cannons on the towers of his fortress and barred all prisoners from access to strategic areas. His most celebrated prisoner, a man whom the governor described as "a person whom nothing can subdue," refused, once again, to be subdued. He seized a long drain-pipe, attached to a funnel, and, according to the testimony of a warder, he used the pipe as "a sort of megaphone which he stuck up at his window, which overlooked the Rue St. Antoine." From this vantage point, the angry prisoner "yelled till he gathered quite a crowd, then poured out vituperation of the governor and called on the citizens to come to his aid as he meant to cut his throat."

That very night, the prison governor sent a message to the royal palace at Versailles, demanding permission to transfer his fractious prisoner from the Bastille to the insane asylum at Charenton, "or to some such establishment, where he could not disturb order, as he constantly does here." The next day, the governor's request was granted, and so, at 1 A.M., six men with pistols burst into the prisoner's cell, routed him out of bed and carted him off to the insane asylum at Charenton. There, the record-keepers of the monastic order known as Petits Pères noted that His Lordship Louis Aldonce Donatien, the Marquis de Sade, was to be confined for a "period without limit" because of "his extreme immorality, indulging in much debauch and with periods of loss of sanity to which he is subject and which give his family cause to fear that in one of his attacks he may in the end disgrace them."

He did, of course, disgrace them, as well as ultimately honoring them, but was he a criminal—or insane? I have heard of major corporate executives whose self-indulgences were not dissimilar to those of the Marquis, and who were never prosecuted or committed. He was, in his way, mad, but it was largely the madness of sexual license, which is rarely punished nowadays, and the novels on which his evil reputation rests were mostly written behind the chaste walls of the various institutions in which he was imprisoned.

He had been born into one of the most distinguished aristocratic families of Provence, but a family of eroded wealth. His father was a marshal, an ambassador, a governor of four provinces; his mother was related to the Bourbons. Neither parent showed much affection for the boy, or saw much of him. He spent his adolescence as a military cadet and then as a cavalry officer during the Seven Years' War. His father found him a rich and homely bride, Renée Pélagie de Montreuil, daughter of the president of the Paris Taxation Court. Both before and after the wedding, the twenty-three-year-old Marquis, like most aristocratic cavalry officers, engaged in liaisons with various girls. Sade, however, had a remarkable mother-in-law, strong-minded, influential, and with access to the judicial authorities. She set spies on the young man, and six months after the marriage, she had him arrested for "excesses" committed in a brothel. She then got the king to release him on condition that he remain under her supervision at her estate in Normandy. For almost a year, he did so.

Sade was not to be confined, however. He got permission to go to Paris. He acquired a new mistress. He was arrested for beating an unemployed seamstress and escaped sentencing only because the girl was paid to drop charges. He seduced his wife's sister, Anne, and kept her almost a year in a bucolic *ménage à trois* at his château in La Coste. Then, taking a vacation from his two women, he went to Marseilles to collect a debt and promptly sent his valet Latour out to hire some young prostitutes for an orgy. Two of the five girls got sick, apparently from an overdose of cantharides, and went to the police to tell of the various indignities that the Marquis had performed. One of these was sodomy, which was then a capital offense, and so, although Sade had already fled to Italy, the criminal court of Aix-en-Provence tried him *in absentia*. It found him guilty and directed that both Sade and his valet should be made to "repent publicly in front of the cathedral." Then, it declared, "the said Monsieur de Sade shall be beheaded on the guillotine and Latour shall be hanged on the gallows, after which both corpses shall be burned and the ashes scattered to the wind."

Sade's mother-in-law, who had paid his debts and bribed his accusers, could probably have accepted even this new scandal. She had long ago begun referring to him as "a madman." What she could not accept was that Sade, in fleeing to Italy, had fled not with his wife but with her pretty sister. That made the girl, regardless of her wealth, unmarriageable (and indeed, when she died of smallpox ten years later, she died single). From that point on, Madame de Montreuil was relentless in her pursuit of her son-in-law. As soon as her spies told her which of the Italian principalities Sade was living in, and under what pseudonym, she persuaded the King of Sardinia to have him arrested and confined in a fortress in Savoy. "All that matters," she wrote the

Sardinian authorities, "is that [he] remains in captivity. . . . Everything else is of secondary importance."

In due time, the Marquis bribed his jailers and escaped. With a confidence that may have been either lunatic or simply aristocratic, he returned to his château at La Coste, and since King Louis XV had suddenly died, Madame de Montreuil had trouble in organizing her connections at the new court for a new assault on Sade. Once again, the Marquis resumed his old ways, hiring adolescent servant girls to take part in orgies at the château. "Yes, I admit I am a libertine," he once wrote to his wife. "I have conceived everything imaginable in this sphere, but I have by no means done everything I conceived, and shall never do so. I am a libertine, but I am neither a criminal nor a murderer."

It was the death of Sade's mother, of all things, that led to his destruction. Although he had been at war with her for years, he went to Paris for her funeral in February of 1777, and there he was arrested and imprisoned in the Château de Vincennes on a royal *lettre de cachet*, a decree that required no trial nor even a presentation of charges. "My mind is now at rest," said Madame de Montreuil. She urged the prisoner to have himself declared insane, a move that would have nullified the death sentence at Aix but would also have kept him in confinement and cost him all his property. Sade refused, demanding a new trial instead. After more than a year in prison, Sade actually won a new trial, and even more surprising, an acquittal. But although he now stood cleared of all legal charges against him, the *lettre de cachet* remained in effect, and so he was sent back to an indefinite term in prison.

For almost five years, Sade remained in Vincennes, angrily petitioning for his freedom, and beginning, finally, to write the fantasies of lust and rage that were to win him a kind of immortality, *Les Infortunes de la Vertue, Les 120 Journées de Sodom . . .* When Vincennes was closed down, the prisoner was transferred to the Bastille for another six years, suffering now from an eye disease called keratitis, growing bloated from age and confinement, still doggedly creating, in notebook after notebook, a universe in which everything was permitted. "God is wicked, evil, unjust," Sade wrote. "It was in evil that he created the world; it is by evil that he maintains it; it is for evil that he perpetuates it. . . ."

Ten days after the governor of the Bastille ordered Sade removed to the insane asylum of Charenton, the maddened Parisian mob stormed the Bastille, hacked off the governor's head, and destroyed, among other things, most of the manuscripts and books that remained in Sade's cell. The revolution was not, of course, simply a series of riots. It also brought the beginnings of parliamentary government, and a resounding declaration of the rights of man, and in the huge mental hospital of Bicêtre, a new director named Philippe Pinel revolutionized the treatment of the insane by literally striking off their chains. Denouncing the traditional institutions in which "domestics and keepers are permitted to use any violence that the most wanton caprice or the most sanguinary cruelty may dictate," Pinel argued that "the maxims of enlightened humanity" provided the best hope of "a speedy and unexpected cure."

The Marquis de Sade, after nine months of what he called "vegetating among idiots and epileptics," finally heard the news that all *lettres de cachet* had been declared invalid. "I said to the shepherd of the insane," he later recalled, " 'Monsieur, I demand that you open the gates for me immediately!' The confused man did not have the courage to refuse, the iron gates were opened, and I wished him good evening and departed." Having emerged from the insane asylum at the age of fifty, "almost robbed of my sight [and having] an enormous corpulence so that I can hardly move," Sade found the outside world a joyless place. "All my sensations are faded," he wrote, "nothing gives me pleasure any more, I love nothing. The world that I desired so madly now seems so dull—and sad."

Citizen Donatien Sade, as he was now known, became a member and then the chairman of one of those people's tribunals that had begun to rule the revolution. As such, he had the ironic satisfaction of receiving a petition denouncing his malevolent mother-in-law—and he ruled in her favor. The Marquis de Sade was not, at heart, a sadist. The howls of the mob at each clang of the guillotine only filled him with sorrow. As the terror mounted, Sade himself was arrested again, charged with being a former noble and "a very immoral man . . . unworthy of society." In the confusion of that period, however, he was moved through so many different prisons that when it came time for Sade and twenty-seven others to be executed, five of the condemned men could not be officially found, and so the remaining twenty-three were guillotined only five hundred yards from the cell where Sade stood watching. The next day, Robespierre himself was guillotined, and the terror was over. Sade was freed.

For the next few years, Sade struggled to survive by writing. His château in the south had to be sold (ransacked by neighboring peasants in 1793, its ruins survive to this day, a kind of Frankenstein castle perched at the summit of a stone-walled village on a wind-swept plateau overlooking the fields of Provence). At one point, he was reduced to living on vegetable soup at a charity hospital in Versailles. But he did finish *La Nouvelle Justine,* his extravagant double novel on the good and bad sisters, Justine and Juliette. It is, of course, a disreputable work—the virtuous Justine killed by divine lightning while Juliette goes on to savor every depravity (as one of her friends describes his ecstasy of simultaneous wickednesses: *"Je parricidais, j'incestais, j'assassinais, je prostituais et je sodomisais!"*). It was published anonymously, and when the forces of respectability began to denounce it, Sade publicly repudiated his own work: "It is not true that I am the author of *Justine!*"

With the coming of Napoleon, the Church and the bourgeoisie acquired new authority in the imposition of public morals, and in the spring of 1801, Sade was denounced to the authorities by his own publisher, one Nicolas Massé. Having been illegally imprisoned by two kings and the republic, Sade was now illegally imprisoned by the emperor. After two years, the authorities finally decided that a trial would cause a scandal, so they simply transferred him to Bicêtre, the Paris mental institution run by Pinel, and then, after six weeks, back to Charenton. Napoleon's minister of police, Joseph Fouché, joined the Paris prefect in declaring Sade to be "incorrigible" in his state of "incessant licentious insanity." Under the relatively lenient regime at Charenton, Sade persuaded the authorities that it would be "a curative method for the mentally deranged" if he could train the patients to perform in plays of his own composition, a bizarre arrangement that Peter Weiss dramatized a few years ago in his own play *The Persecution and Assassination of Jean-Paul Marat as Performed by the Inmates of Charenton under the Direction of the Marquis de Sade.*

Weiss permits Sade to describe his aberrations first as a revolutionary gesture and then as an expression of disillusionment. While being beaten by Charlotte Corday, he declares that "under the blows of my own whip . . . I created in my mind/ monstrous representatives of a dying class / who could only exercise their power/ in spectacularly staged orgies." And that he originally saw the revolution as "a chance/ for a tremendous outburst of revenge/ an orgy greater than all my dreams/ But then I saw . . . I wasn't capable of murder/ although murder/ was the final proof of my existence. . . . And when I vanish/ I want all trace of my existence/ to be wiped out."

This was indeed Sade's last wish. He was to spend the last eleven years of his life in the insane asylum at Charenton, and there he made a will, "in a condition of sanity and health," asking that his body be buried "without any ceremony" in a specifically designated grove of trees on some land he owned near Malmaison. "As soon as the grave is filled in," he said, "acorns should be planted over it, so that new trees will grow out of it later, and the wood will be as thick as it was before [and] all traces of my grave shall vanish from the face of the earth, as I flatter myself that my memory will vanish from the minds of men." When Sade died on December 2, 1814, his will was ignored, and he was given a Catholic burial in the cemetery at Charenton. Fifty years later, the cemetery was dug up, and one of the Charenton doctors who admired Sade's work "acquired," as he put it, the skull of the skeleton. He hoped to make some phrenological studies of the skull. He did in fact make some preliminary measurements which implied, according to the theories of the day, neither cruelty nor abnormal sensuality but rather a character that "resembled in every respect that of a clergyman." This expert then received a visit from a friend, a distinguished phrenologist, who borrowed the skull for some studies of his own.

The friend subsequently went on a lecture tour of England, Germany and the United States, and then suddenly died, so the severed skull of the Marquis de Sade vanished forever.

Edmund Emil Kemper III, a shy and ungainly boy with an I.Q. of 131, was about eight years old when he first thought of murdering his mother. She was described in subsequent accounts as "a strict disciplinarian," who often banished her son to the basement. She also sent him to live for a time with his grandparents in North Fork, California. There, on an August afternoon in 1964, when he was fifteen, Kemper shot his grandmother to death with two bullets in the head. When his grandfather returned from the grocery store, Kemper shot him too. Then he telephoned his mother to confess. "I just wondered how it would feel to shoot Grandma," he said.

Kemper spent five years in the Atascadero State Mental Hospital, where, among other things, he apparently memorized twenty-eight different psychological tests and the answers that the psychiatrists considered appropriate. In 1970, when he was twenty-one, he was set free. By now, he was a huge, blubbery figure, six feet nine inches, 280 pounds, but still oddly babyish, with steel-rimmed glasses and a droopy mustache. He found work on a highway construction crew and seemed to live in a state of respectable obscurity. In September of 1972, he went back to court to ask that his record as a juvenile offender be permanently sealed. The court ordered two psychiatrists to examine him. They had no way of knowing, of course, that just four days before their examination, Kemper had picked up a fifteen-year-old girl named Aiko Koo, on her way to a ballet class, and dismembered her. "He has made an expert response to the years of treatment," one of the psychiatrists declared. "I see no psychiatric reason to consider him a threat to himself or any other member of society."

The following May, the court records having been appropriately sealed, Kemper achieved his lifelong ambition. During an argument with his mother, an administrative assistant at the University of California at Santa Cruz, Kemper hit her on the head with a hammer. Then he cut off her head and her right hand. He also strangled a friend of hers, another employee at the university. After stuffing the bodies into two bedroom closets, he drove east as far as Pueblo, Colorado, and then telephoned back to the Santa Cruz sheriff's office to confess. He also confessed that he had killed Miss Koo and five other girls during the previous year. He said that he was afraid his mother would find out about these murders, and therefore he had decided to "bear the burden of killing her as well, to avoid her suffering any embarrassment."

Why, under the circumstances, had Kemper been repeatedly examined and found harmless? "Kemper is a marvelous example of the fact that psychiatrists don't know everything," observed Dr. Herbert McGraw, a staff psychiatrist at California's Napa State Hospital. "If you're right 75 percent of the time, you're doing pretty well."

All kinds of crime are essentially the same, varying only as different kinds of madness vary. It is true that the forger or the embezzler is a milder transgressor than the bank robber or the arsonist, but the patterns of madness are all there. The criminal personality considers only itself, indifferent as a lobster to all others, and yet it has only a very misty judgment of what that self is, or what its best interests might be. The madness lies not in the criminal act—as I have suggested, a Mafia "loan shark" is not radically different from a finance company—but rather in the determination to live in opposition to society's basic rules. All crime, in other words, is a rebellion against the first society that the criminal ever knew, namely his own family. Even after years wasted in jail, the gray-haired confidence man is still trying to deceive and placate his long-dead father (or mother), just as the assassin is trying to kill him.

There is a romantic theory that the most violent criminals —the murderers and rapists and armed robbers—are men of strength, that their rebellion against society is somehow heroic, almost noble. Thus, Eldridge Cleaver and his talk of rape as "an insurrectionary act." But it is not true. Indeed, there is far more truth in the old Hollywood stereotype of the cornered gangster begging for mercy. Dr. David Abrahamsen, who has spent more than thirty years studying violent crime, offers, in *The Murdering Mind*, a list of homicidal characteristics that can be applied to any number of murderers from Edmund Emil Kemper III to Lee Harvey Oswald:

> Extreme feelings of revenge and fantasies of grandiose accomplishments. . . . Loneliness, withdrawal, feelings of distrust, helplessness, fears, insignificance, loss of self-esteem, caused by early (pre-Oedipal) childhood experiences. . . . Blurred self-image; suggestible, impressionable. Inability to withstand frustration and to find sufficient gratification for expressing hostile aggressive feelings through constructive outlets. Inability to change persistent egocentricity, self-centeredness . . . into elements of healthy ideals and conscience . . . resulting in dependency on and contempt for authority. Suicidal tendencies, with depression. . . .

This is also, of course, a picture of many people who never commit a murder. "I get psychological test results all the time that say this guy is full of hostility and aggression," one psychiatrist observed in the wake of the Kemper revelations, "so I let him go, and he goes back to college and leads a perfectly normal life. The hostility and aggression are still there, and some time, under certain circumstances, they may come out. But when?" It is because of this feeling that there are murderers among us— and that we might be murderers ourselves—that we take such a lugubrious interest in every celebrated case. And in all the literature of crime, from Erle Stanley Gardner to Dostoyevsky. Much of the tension in *The Brothers Karamazov*, indeed, derives not from the question of which of the four sons was guilty of killing old Karamazov but which was innocent of the intent. They are all mad, in their different ways—Dimitry with his destructive rages, Ivan with his "brain fever" and his encounters with Satan, Alyosha with his mystic visions, and Smerdyakov, the actual murderer, suffering from Dostoyevsky's own affliction, epilepsy. "Who doesn't desire his father's death?" Ivan asks at the trial of Dimitry. "Don't disturb yourselves. I am not mad, I am only a murderer."

All murder, let us say, is a demented effort to destroy one's self, and to destroy the parents from whom that self was created.

But instead of dealing in abstractions, let us listen for a few minutes to a woman who tried, with all the incompetence that most of us bring to our most passionate endeavors, to kill both her mother and herself. Karen, as I shall have to call her, is a rather heavy-set woman of about thirty-five. Her blue eyes are almost translucent. She wears a blue smock and sandals. She smokes constantly. She has been in and out of psychiatric treatment almost all of her life. She now works as a therapist and counselor for juvenile delinquents at a state training school. She says that her mother first sent her to a psychiatrist when she was three, "because I was beginning to say 'no' a lot." Her older brother was also seeing a psychiatrist regularly. "My mother's trip was to tell us kids that we were all crazy, and that my father was crazy, a man to be feared and stayed away from. It wasn't until I was about twenty-five that I found out that *she* was the one who was crazy. The doctor who made the diagnosis called her 'a consolidated, ambulatory schizophrenic,' and he said she was the worst case he'd ever seen."

Karen says she first attempted suicide when she was thirteen, but she dismisses this as "a regular, normal thirteen-year-old ploy." She was still seeing a psychiatrist, although he "did me no good at all." She graduated from high school, went to college in Boston, traveled for a while in Europe, returned to college, got pregnant, dropped out.

"When I first knew I was pregnant," she says, "I notified the father of the child, because I figured he had the right to have some say in the alternative I chose. I got pregnant on Friday the thirteenth of October, the last day he was in the States. I notified him by letter, because he was in Paris and I was in the Middle West. Among the alternatives I gave him, I didn't include marriage. It never occurred to me to marry the guy. Well, he decided he wanted to marry me. And I decided, 'Okay, what the hell?' So then *he* cracked up, under the idea of becoming a husband and a father all at once. So we didn't get married, thank God.

"I never told my mother about the baby. She was *mine*, nobody else's. But although it was my own decision to give her up for adoption—and this was in 1962, so the culture was very different, and that's slightly important—I felt very guilty about it. I got the bright idea in my head that I had killed her, which I knew I hadn't done, but the feeling was there. So I started being masochistic, and slashing my wrists, not really trying to kill myself, just cutting myself up. One of the things that was happening was that my head was going too fast. I was thinking too fast. And every time I'd think something, another part of me would contradict it. So I went to see another psychiatrist, and he sent me to my first hospital. I hospitalized myself—that's important.

"At this hospital, they felt that my crackup was due to my not having grieved for my father when he died—that was just before I came back from Europe—and I think that was a big part of it. My mother had taught me to hate him, and there was a lot of guilt involved when he died. I should have been there, and I wasn't. But I felt tremendous guilt about other things. I started going to bed with boys when I was thirteen, and that was a big thing for a long time. I felt useless, worthless, a piece of shit, a whore. I kept trying suicide. I've attempted suicide more than a dozen times. I stopped counting at twelve. But in this hospital, they taught me that it was okay to love my father, which sounds like a very simple thing, but let me tell you, it was one of the most tremendous things that ever happened to me in my life. It took years in therapy, though, before I could happily say, 'I hate my mother.' Then one day, I tried to kill her."

Karen had been released from the Boston hospital, so she went to see her mother in Florida, where, as she puts it, "I cracked up again and stayed cracked up for four years." Her crackups apparently consisted mainly of severe depressions, and she says that she "never had a complete psychotic break." She repeatedly entered hospitals for periods of a few days or a week, the longest stay being three months. Her recollection of the murder attempt is blurred.

"The hospital gave me a pass to go out on a drive with her. It was the most ridiculous thing. I wanted to drive, and she wouldn't let me. I don't know why it was so important that I drive, and I don't know why she wouldn't let me, but suddenly I got terribly angry. I started trying to strangle her. I had never thought I was capable of such anger, physical anger. I don't remember exactly what happened. I remember that some bystanders nearly strangled me to get me away from her. One of them got me in a headlock. . . ."

Karen was taken back to the hospital, then released again. Her mother tried to take care of her, but Karen was not easy to care for. On one occasion when Karen refused to take her medicine, her mother called in the police. "Well, you've got to be crazy to fight four men, but panic will make you do anything," Karen recalls. "So I charged and tried to get through them. Well, we had a little fight, and then they taped me to a stretcher with adhesive tape." Once again, Karen was taken to the hospital, examined, and then released.

"It wasn't long after this that I got really pissed off at my mother—I forget what it was about, exactly—and I walked into her bedroom and told her I was going to kill her. Then I caught hold of myself and said, 'No, wait, we'll talk about this in the morning.' And I walked out. I went back to my room and stewed some more—got madder and madder—and then I went back to my mother's room and took hold of her by the arm. My mother is small—about five-two, a hundred and twenty-five pounds—I could kill her with two swats, probably. And I said, 'I'm going to kill you!' Then I stopped myself again and said, 'No, we'll talk about this in the morning.' And walked out. The third time I started into her room again, she had the door barricaded with a bookcase full of books. But by then I was really mad, so I knocked over the books, marched into her room, and went through the same routine. Then I went back to my room. I was lying peacefully in bed, finally having got my anger under control, when two cops showed up.

"I got handcuffed, taken to the emergency room, manacled to a table, spread-eagled, which is not the most unembarrassing position to put a woman into. Finally, they put me into a ward, and I said to the nurse, 'I'm not going to bed until I get my wallet and my cigarettes.' She said, 'Yes, you are.' I said, 'No, I'm not.' So all of a sudden, two big, burly male attendants appeared, and I got wheeled into an elevator and down into another ward. Two more male attendants and a nurse joined them, and they all took me into a seclusion room and started stripping me. Well, when they got to my bra and pants, I started fighting. And the nurse said to me, 'For God's sake, don't you have any modesty?' And I said, 'For Christ's sake, that's what I'm trying to hold on to!' Anyway, they took away all my clothes and left me in this room with a mattress on the floor and a drain in the middle of it. I stayed there for about eighteen hours. . . .

"I used to go into these tremendous rages. I didn't know what to do with these rages except to turn them in on myself. So I'd chop up my arms and legs. I didn't like that habit. Once I decided I was going to give myself an abortion, although I *knew* that I was not pregnant. I got hold of a knife. But there was a nurse who had antennae that were *so* sharp. She came into my room and talked me out of that knife without ever objectively knowing that I even had it. Finally, I got some medication that keeps the rage under control, within limits. I'm still a person who lashes out when I get angry, but the peaks and depths aren't there any more. And when I'm feeling good, I'm generally glad I cracked up. I really don't want to die."

Not all of the most interesting criminals are murderers. Garrett Brock Trapnell, for example, has apparently never killed anybody, but he has robbed at least seven banks, hijacked a plane, forged checks for thousands of dollars, and devised a technique to escape punishment by feigning insanity. A wiry man, just under six feet, with a dark, wild look in his eyes, he was born in 1938 into a distinguished military family. (One of his uncles was decorated for heroism during the Bataan death march and later became one of the first United States commanders in Vietnam.) His father graduated from Annapolis and eventually reached the rank of commander. As a boy—do we see the young Robert Lowell?—Trapnell delighted in dressing up in his father's uniform and playing with the sword. Trapnell's mother came from an old Massachusetts family, the Brocks. She had gone to Radcliffe.

She also drank heavily. The Trapnells got divorced when Garrett was four, and Mrs. Trapnell took her son and daughter to live with her mother. Mrs. Trapnell kept on drinking, according to the daughter's recollection, and the mother and grandmother "were always fighting and pulling at each other's hair. Their arguments pulled us apart. The police were always coming to the house. We moved at least five times during a six-year period." When Trapnell was about eleven, he was sent to live with his father in the Panama Canal Zone. Commander Trapnell, who was married five times in all, ended his career in Panama under rather mysterious circumstances. A Justice Department official subsequently told a *New York Times* reporter that the commander had been forced to leave the Navy for operating a brothel in Panama, but a Navy spokesman said there was no evidence of this in the official records. In any case, the commander died about two years after his son's arrival, and the last of his wives told her stepson to depart.

He was first arrested for petty theft at the age of fifteen, but an Episcopal priest befriended him and got him sent to the St. Francis Boys School in Salina, Kansas. Despite an I.Q. of 131, however, Trapnell never finished high school. After a year at St. Francis, he enlisted in the Army. He served for a time at Fort Hood, where his uncle was commandant, but he was a disciplinary problem from the start. He accidentally shot himself in the foot, was discharged, re-enlisted, was discharged again. His serious crimes began when he picked up a hitchhiker named Edgar Flury, and the two joined in staging a series of armed robberies from New Mexico to Maryland. Flury got increasingly nervous about his partner and finally called in the police because Trapnell had threatened to kill him.

"A lawyer came up to me," Trapnell later declared, "and said, 'Trap, you are going to prison for twenty years, or you can go to the state hospital.' So I went to the state hospital, and I dug the whole action. I read more damned books on psychiatry and psychology than probably any psychology student will in any school in the world." Trapnell stayed for a year at the hospital in Spring Grove, Maryland (his partner did, as the lawyer predicted, get sentenced to twenty years), and then he returned to crime. He was arrested at least once a year throughout the 1960's —there were to be twenty arrests in all—on charges of robbery, auto theft and forgery. Each time he invoked his insanity defense. He now claimed that he was a split personality, and that an alter ego named "Greg Ross" arose within him from time to time to commit various crimes for which he himself could not be held responsible.

"It's a classic Dr. Jekyll and Mr. Hyde situation," Trapnell said later. "The temporary [insanity] shot, which is much harder and more intricate, takes a bit more finesse, but it precludes hospitalization. [I said I suffered] paranoid schizophrenia, with a surfacing and submerging nature. . . . The classic dual personality, compounded by paranoia, the sense of being persecuted. The result is an inability to differentiate between right and wrong due to this split personality. Take Gary B. Trapnell and Greg Ross. They're both the same physical person, but they are two mentally different people. If Greg Ross commits a crime and the Greg Ross aspect submerges after he is put in prison, and the Gary Trapnell aspect emerges, then Gary Trapnell is not responsible legally for what Greg Ross does. Whether it [the mental illness] exists can never be proved because psychiatry as a science is the only science in the world that deals with extreme intangibles."

Armed with this magic cloak, Trapnell set out to make his fortune. He met a topless go-go dancer near Hollywood's Sunset Strip and swept her off to Las Vegas. He promised marriage (he was already married) and got her so drunk that she thought the marriage had been performed. Instead, he disappeared with her money and credit cards. He used one of the cards to rent a plane and fly to the Bahamas, where he met another adventurer named Roger Michael Peterson. According to police, the two of them invaded a jewelry store, where Trapnell thought a clerk had been rude to him, and made off with $105,000 worth of gems. The police pursued them to the airport, only to see Trapnell and Peterson take off for Florida in the rented plane.

Safely back in the United States, they devised a new system of crime. Once a month, from March through September of 1970, they went to Canada and robbed a bank in Montreal or Toronto. Their total haul was estimated at $130,000. They thought of themselves as Butch Cassidy and the Sundance Kid, and Trapnell even signed the name Butch Cassidy on a holdup note. "We were doing the thing," he said later. "Paul Newman and Robert Redford, they were just acting." Trapnell was caught in Montreal in September of 1970, claimed insanity, and was sent to the Penelle Institute. Peterson posed as his lawyer and smuggled him a toy gun, which enabled him to escape. Trapnell got back across the border before he was arrested again, and the authorities sent him to Florida to face prosecution for the Bahamas jewel theft. There, he once again convinced the psychiatrists that he had been insane at the time of the crime, and so, after three months, in March of 1971, he was set free.

During fifteen years of crime, as a matter of fact, Trapnell spent less than two years in jail. Indeed, he lived well. He had a $40-a-day hotel room in Miami. He bought a $26,000 plane and a $10,000 Mercedes. Such tastes are expensive to maintain, and so, since skyjacking was then in fashion, Trapnell seized a TWA airliner over Iowa and held ninety-eight people at gunpoint for nearly eight hours while he demanded some $300,000 in ransom. An F.B.I. agent disguised as a pilot finally got aboard the plane in New York and shot Trapnell three times. Trapnell insisted that the hijacking was the work of "Greg Ross."

At Trapnell's trial a year later, four psychiatrists and one psychologist dutifully testified that Trapnell was mentally ill at the time of the crime. (Two other psychiatrists testified that he was sane.) What they did not know was that after his release in Florida, Trapnell had boasted to a free-lance writer named Cyrus Burluwitz of his skill in deceiving psychiatrists. The interview, although never published, came into the possession of the prosecutors. "I have committed all of these crimes," Trapnell had said, "and have never gotten a [prison] number for any of them. It's the fallacy of your legal system." Despite that confession, the trial ended with a hung jury. (Trapnell had predicted that result in advance and had even identified the middle-aged female social worker who would hold out for acquittal during the 11-to-1 jury votes for conviction.) Only after a second trial was Trapnell finally convicted of air piracy, unlawful interference with a flight crew, and possession of a gun. He was sentenced to life imprisonment. "From the outset," he said to the judge, "this case has been biased against me."

What is ironic, I think, is not just Trapnell's success in convincing so many psychiatrists that he periodically went crazy but the fact that the deceived psychiatrists were probably right —that he really was crazy. One can discover all the usual patterns, the broken family, the inadequate father, the long years of thefts and frauds and fugitive violence, but there is another process at work here. Feigning madness is a dangerous course, not only because the traditional invulnerability of the madman is a very fragile invulnerability, as Hamlet eventually learned, but because the pose of madness undermines the strength by which we resist the encroachments of madness itself. The most striking evidence of Trapnell's insanity was the very act of taping an interview for the purpose of boasting that all his madnesses were fabrications. Would any sane man ever have made such a self-destructive claim to his own sanity?

On May 29, 1970, in the town of Obninsk, about one hundred miles south of Moscow, a hospital ambulance came rolling up to the apartment house of Dr. Zhores Medvedev, a distinguished young biochemist. Five men—three police officials and two others in plainclothes—emerged from the ambulance, climbed up to Medvedev's apartment and began banging on the door. "I at once decided not to open or respond in any way," Medvedev recalled later. "When all is said and done, it was my right—the inviolability of the home is protected by the Constitution of the U.S.S.R." While Medvedev was contemplating his legal rights, the police kept clamoring to get in. One of the civilians shouted through the door that he was Dr. Y. V. Kiryushin, director of the Obninsk Psychiatric Clinic. He asked Medvedev to "please open the door." Medvedev knew Kiryushin, but he still kept silent. So the police went on banging until the plaster started cracking and the door began to give way.

"Stop," Medvedev shouted, "this is a private apartment."

"It belongs to the state," a police sergeant retorted, "and the police have the right to enter any apartment."

Medvedev then demanded to know whether the police had a warrant. "We do not intend to arrest you," the sergeant said. "We are only accompanying the doctors." Alongside Dr. Kiryushin, the other man in plainclothes turned out to be Dr. Alexander Lifshits, head physician at the psychiatric hospital in the provincial capital of Kaluga. Medvedev professed to disbelieve it and demanded to see Lifshits' identity card. Lifshits didn't have one. Neither did Kiryushin. "Since neither of you have any papers," Medvedev said, "then I have the right, in my own apartment, not to discuss anything with you."

"If you refuse to talk to us," Dr. Lifshits said with some

solemnity, "then we will be obliged to draw the appropriate conclusions."

By this time, Medvedev's wife was telephoning other scientists who lived nearby, and half a dozen of them soon came troop-
ing into the apartment to cross-examine the two psychiatrists on
why they wanted to take Medvedev to the mental hospital in
Kaluga. The psychiatrists too brought in reinforcements. A police
major of the old school stamped into the apartment, chased out
the other scientists, and shouted at Medvedev: "Get to your feet!
I order you to get to your feet!" When Medvedev didn't move,
two police sergeants "came up to me on both sides and with a
practiced movement grabbed my arms at the elbows and at the
wrist, twisted them behind my back and yanked me out of my
chair. . . . With my arms twisted behind my back they took me
down the staircase [to the ambulance], shoved me inside and
started off."

The causes of this imbroglio are still somewhat obscure. In
the Western press, it was widely interpreted as part of a sinister
new tactic by the Soviet secret police to terrorize dissidents by
confining them in mental institutions. There had already been the
case of Valeriy Tarsis, who, in 1960, had smuggled out to England
the manuscript of a protest novel entitled *The Bluebottle*. Shortly
before the book was published in 1962, Tarsis was committed to
a mental hospital in Moscow and confined there for six months.
He then wrote another novel, *Ward 7*, describing his experiences
as an unwillingly drugged psychiatric prisoner: "Everything in
Ward 7 was outwardly clean and decent, but as an institution it
was . . . immoral, since its deliberate object was to damage and
not to cure." More recently, there had been the case of Major
General Pyotr Grigorenko, who began protesting about the mistreatment of Tartar nationalists in the early 1960's and eventually
became one of Russia's most militant demonstrators for civil
rights. He marched with placards in the streets of Moscow. He
wrote open letters to the K.G.B. Stripped of his military rank
and expelled from the Communist Party, he was confined in a
mental hospital for eight months during 1964–65, then released,
then seized again and recommitted in 1969. After five years in
mental institutions, where he was assaulted by other patients

and suffered a heart attack, the sixty-seven-year-old general was, in his wife's words, "very, very tired."

If the K.G.B. had a systematic policy of putting dissenters into mental hospitals, however, it would be hard to understand how such celebrated opponents as the novelist Alexander Solzhenitsyn and the physicist Andrei Sakharov escaped the claws of the police psychiatrists. Zhores Medvedev had other difficulties. His chief "crime" seems to have been the authorship of a book criticizing Trofim Lysenko—the geneticist who had delighted Stalin by arguing that acquired characteristics could be inherited, thus implying the possibility of a "new Soviet man"— and the publication of that book in the United States under the title *The Rise and Fall of T. D. Lysenko*. There had been pro- and anti-Lysenko factions in the Soviet Union for so many years that the merits of the argument had long since become encrusted by the political implications of pro- and anti-Stalinism. Even though Lysenko had by now been scientifically discredited, there were still covert supporters in many official departments outside the K.G.B., supporters ready to counterattack against criticism of Stalin's favorite scientific theoretician.

And then there was the matter of Medvedev's seventeen-year-old son, Sasha, who, like many Russians of his generation, began behaving like what Medvedev himself said "would abroad be called a 'hippie.'" According to the father's account, "his reaction to attempts at persuasion and discipline by the school and his parents, in the summer of 1968, was to run away to the South, where for two weeks he lived at the seaside, keeping himself by selling part of his stamp collection. In the Crimea, the police are on the lookout for these numerous teen-age 'fugitives' and return them to their parents; this is precisely what happened to our son. But when this escapade was repeated with the same result, we felt compelled to turn to a psychiatrist for advice. . . ." This was the same Dr. Kiryushin who subsequently appeared at Medvedev's apartment. The psychiatrist told him, or so Medvedev says, that there was nothing wrong with the boy except "a premature hormonal development" that made it difficult for him to "restrain or control his emotions," and that "as he grew up, given the proper supervision, this uninhibited behavior would pass."

It is difficult to imagine—unless we recall the behavior of

the Chicago police during the Democratic Convention of 1968—the rage with which some Soviet authorities observe the eccentricities of the younger generation. After years of war and deprivation and compulsory conformity, all in the name of what they have long been told is the higher national good, they easily become apoplectic at the spectacle of long-haired youths sitting idly on beaches with their guitars. It is also difficult for Americans to realize that the Soviet legal system derives not from English common law, in which a specific crime has to be proven in court, but rather from the Continental procedures that empower an investigating magistrate to look into more or less whatever he chooses. Even in routine cases of drunken assault, the Soviet courts mull over the accused man's work record, his personal behavior and general reputation, which may provide mitigating circumstances, or the opposite.

And since, in Soviet society, both doctors and judges are civil servants, and all civil servants are supposed to be led by the Communist Party, there exists a kind of network that inevitably links the psychiatrist and the policeman in the examination of any unorthodoxy. Theoretically, according to various regulations, this is all for the public good (just as juvenile offenders in the United States are sometimes confined indefinitely, under laws devised by the most liberal legislators, at the discretion of judges and psychiatric social workers). So it was that Medvedev found himself summoned to the office of Nina Antonenko, chairman of the Obninsk City Soviet, to answer for the misbehavior of his son. And when he defended his son—can we not imagine the scene?—Chairman Antonenko found, according to her subsequent statements, that he "behaved strangely." The next time she summoned him on the same subject, she had a psychiatrist attending the meeting. Thus began the sequence of events that brought the five men banging on Medvedev's door.

Medvedev's twin brother, Roy, a historian with good connections in Moscow's liberal intellectual establishment, started an immense hullaballoo. He repeatedly telephoned Dr. Lifshits at his home, often after midnight, to renew his protests and to cite numerous regulations that had been violated. He sent squadrons of distinguished scientists streaming to Kaluga to visit his brother and to interrogate Dr. Lifshits. They all attested to the prisoner's sanity and sent off telegrams of protest to various authorities, up to and including Premier Alexei Kosygin. "It is time to understand that the imprisonment of sane persons in madhouses because they have minds of their own is *spiritual murder*," Solzhenitsyn declared in an open letter, "a variation of the *gas chambers* and even more cruel: the condemned suffer torments more fruitful and prolonged. Like the gas chambers, these crimes will *never* be forgotten. . . ."

The psychiatrists at Kaluga reacted like turtles, sucking in their arms and legs and hoping that the storms would pass. Despite Solzhenitsyn's hyperbolic rhetoric, Medvedev was treated reasonably well in the hospital ward, the "madhouse," as his friends insisted on calling it. No kind of "therapy" was ever imposed on him. Even that, however, inspired Roy Medvedev to new arguments. At one point, Dr. Galina Bondareva, whom Lifshits had assigned to Medvedev, protested to Roy: "You think we are not concerned about your brother . . . but I spend ninety percent of my time on him." Roy's answer was typical: "It would be better if you looked after the others who are genuinely ill. That's your duty and what you are paid for. You have no right to ignore the other patients and leave them without medical attention. . . . You have violated the regulations." Actually, the hapless Dr. Bondareva seems to have thought that Medvedev really was crazy (and possibly his brother as well). According to a medical report that she later signed, Medvedev was suffering from "incipient schizophrenia." The symptoms were "split personality, expressed in the need to combine scientific work in his own field with publicist activities; an overestimation of his own personality . . . lack of a sense of reality, poor adaptation to the social environment," and, perhaps worst of all, "paranoid delusions of reforming society."

We can assume, I think, that Zhores Medvedev is perfectly sane—even the hard-pressed Kaluga authorities, after trying hard to cover up each other's mistakes, finally released him after nineteen days—and that Dr. Bondareva's diagnosis is mistaken. Indeed, Medvedev speculates on how the same Kaluga authorities would have diagnosed the "split personality" of Josef Stalin when "suddenly out of the blue he publishes an article on the problems of linguistics and personally begins to introduce tangerines and eucalyptus trees to the Crimea." Or Nikita Khrushchev, when "suddenly he begins to make decisions about the architecture of apartment houses . . . tries to grow maize in the North, forbids the private ownership of cattle in the countryside and teaches writers the secrets of their craft." And after citing the "split" interests of Spinoza, Lewis Carroll and Leonardo da Vinci, he adds: "Happily there was not psychiatry in those days, and madmen were judged simply on the basis of common sense, and sometimes even revered."

And yet, now that we have reached a point at which the state defines both crime and madness, and at which the police and the psychiatrists in many nations are prepared to follow the state's definitions, poor Dr. Bondareva's diagnosis should perhaps not be too lightly dismissed. The basic question that she raises, in such psychiatric jargon as "poor adaptation to the social environment," is this: Is protest a sign of insanity? Or, more accurately, how much protest against social regulation is permissible before it can be defined as either criminal or insane—or both?

In the Western world, we like to tell ourselves that there are no such dividing lines, that any eccentric can harangue any audience in Union Square, and the Civil Liberties Union will go to court to defend almost any shabby newspaper of disreputable opinion. Our tolerance is not unlimited, however. Ezra Pound, for example, said over the Rome radio, during the darkest days of World War II, that "the United States has been for months and illegally at war through what I consider to be the criminal acts of a president whose mental condition was not, so far as I could see, all that could or should be desired of a man in so responsible a position." And that "simple-hearted Joe Stalin [is] not wholly trusted by the kikery which is his master." And that "for twenty years you have been fed on lies, and I don't say maybe. And Mr. Squirmy and Mr. Slime are still feeding it to you right over the BBC radio, and every one of the Jew radios of Schenectady, New York and Boston—and Boston was once an American city. . . . And how much liberty have you got anyhow . . .? Are you the arsenal of democracy or judeocracy?"

These are disgusting things to say, particularly at the time when Pound said them, but are they criminal or are they insane? According to the laws of treason, they are criminal, and if Pound had been brought to trial in 1945, he might well have been condemned to death. Pound himself wanted to be tried, so that he could gain a forum for his absurd economic views, but the psychiatrists decided, like Dr. Bondareva, that he was "egocentric . . . exhibits extremely poor judgment as to his situation . . . is abnormally grandiose, is expansive and exuberant in manner . . . He is, in other words, insane." After he had spent twelve years in St. Elizabeth's Hospital the literary establishment finally began to mobilize the kind of pressure that Roy Medvedev organized within nineteen days, and so, on the recommendation of people like Ernest Hemingway and Robert Frost, the old man was finally declared to be too insane to stand trial. And therefore, precisely because he was too insane to stand trial, he was released from the hospital and allowed to wander back to Italy.

Our psycho-legal system is, as I have said, different from that of the Soviets, but it is not without its own severities. Instead of seizing the sane critic for a psychiatric examination, it sometimes sets out to prosecute the none-too-sane critic for some infraction of the criminal code. Thus poor old Wilhelm Reich, having quarreled with Freud, having quarreled with the Communist Party, having established himself on a mountaintop in Maine and convinced himself that the sick could be healed by sitting in his orgone boxes and absorbing the benefits of astral energy, poor old Reich found himself the object of a massive legal campaign by the Food and Drug Administration, a campaign that ended only with Reich's death in prison. And poor old Timothy Leary, onetime Harvard lecturer and founder of the League for Spiritual Development, whose only crime was his passion to persuade the world that salvation lay in hallucinogenic drugs. Sentenced to twenty years in prison for the possession of a minute quantity of marijuana, he was pursued as a fugitive across half the world before the agents of Nixon's law-and-order administration finally captured him in Afghanistan and, without benefit of an extradition hearing, bundled him off on a plane to the prison awaiting him in California. And poor H. Rap Brown, onetime chairman of the Student Nonviolent Coordinating Committee, driven underground by a patently unfair prosecution in Cambridge, Maryland, and finally seized and convicted for armed robbery in New York. And even all those fierce young California blacks like Donald

DeFreeze, who had first organized themselves at the Vacaville psychiatric treatment center for the criminally insane and then called themselves the Symbionese Liberation Army, and, after extorting two million dollars in food for the poor from the coffers of Randolph A. Hearst, died in a firefight with the Los Angeles police.

It can be argued indefinitely whether such people are pursued as criminals or as rebels. But if we accept the idea that dissidence is not without its perils even in such a tolerant society as ours, we still confront the question: Is the rejection of the accepted standards of society a sign of insanity? Accepted standards change, of course. There was a time when Athanasius, the fourth-century bishop who argued the controversial doctrine that Christ was both fully divine and fully human, had to flee from his enemies to the bottom of a well, and after the powerful Arian heresy was finally suppressed, it was said that all of Christian orthodoxy was once embodied in the figure of one man hiding in the bottom of a well. Our history since then has been filled with examples of people tortured and burned for defying the prevailing wisdom. Or recanting to save themselves. It was heroic for Martin Luther, who had already had at least one nervous breakdown, to nail his theses to the door in Wittenberg and to declare: *"Hier stehe ich. Ich kann nicht anders."* But would it have been heroism or insanity if he had persisted in his heresy on the rack of the Inquisition? Galileo was perhaps simply less fortunate —politically less fortunate, since the Inquisition already had him in the grip that it never got on Luther. Thus the levels of permissible opposition—and are those not the levels of sane opposition?—were different from those in Luther's Germany. So Galileo recanted, denied his own truth, signed whatever was put before him. "Unhappy is the land that breeds no hero," says the disillusioned disciple in Brecht's *Galileo.* "No, Adrea," says Galileo. "Unhappy is the land that needs a hero."

In more recent times, when many dissidents are free to defend themselves by citing constitutional precedents and legal regulations, we can confront the basic problem most simply in the case of the Buddhist monk who set himself afire in the streets of Saigon to protest against the Vietnam war. Not one man in a million can remember his name, and yet the photographs of that horribly burning figure, sitting stoically in the street, probably did more than any other single act to undermine American support of that insane war and bring it eventually to an end. But is it not an act of madness to set oneself on fire? When an American youth, inspired by the Buddhist monk, performed the same self-immolation in front of the United Nations building a few months later, everyone seemed to agree that he was mentally ill. And nobody paid much attention.

Out of a Case History:
Eddie Pursues a Timetable

Eddie once wanted to be a trumpeter, and a composer, and a nightclub comedian, but now he is a systems engineer for one of America's biggest corporations. At home on a weekend, he skips shaving and wears blue jeans. His thin brown hair is cut Roman style, with jagged edges. He is thirty-two, short, slight, pale, with deep-set blue eyes. His living room is full of entertainment equipment—a color television set hooked up to cable TV, and to a private movie service plus a quadraphonic sound system and an electric organ. As he talks, he drinks cup after cup of iced tea.

My father had cancer for a long time, about three years. It spread through a large part of his body, and he had to be hospitalized for long periods. I used to get very angry, because all the other kids had fathers that would take them places, and I don't think I was aware that he was making enormous sacrifices to be able to provide for the family. I was five when he died.

At the hospital, my mother met this fellow named Oakley, because his wife and my father were in opposite rooms. So they came to know each other through the deaths of their respective spouses. A couple of months after that, they got married, very quickly. Actually, it was about a year. So the family remained constant as a physical group—I had an older brother, and Oakley had a daughter—but it was very inconstant as any kind of relationship.

I don't remember much about my father, but hearing about it from other people's point of view, he had been a fabulous person, an entertainer type, a singer, lots of laughs. Oakley, on the other hand, was an impossible person to like. There were people that put up with him, for one reason or another, but as far as actually liking him for himself, I don't know anyone that did, or could. He was the New York manager for one of the main car-rental companies, and all you ever heard was how dramatically important he was. He was sarcastic, overbearing, constantly putting you down. He was also an alcoholic, and through his alcoholism, and through a lot of emotional problems of his own, he would end up beating you, or whatever. He used to hit my mother a lot too.

My mother was also incredibly overbearing and an unbelievably straight type, and she was always sick. She had a hysterectomy, a breast removed, and all kinds of diseases, even malaria—just so many different kinds of diseases. Which I took upon myself, because she was always telling me, "Now look what you've done to me. Look how sick you've made me this time. Well, I'm certainly not coming out of the hospital this time." So there was an *enormous* amount of emotional pressure in growing up. It was really tight. Oakley finally died when I was a freshman in college. He had a heart attack. It was all pretty sudden.

I could get sick too. I was amazingly good at psychosomatic disorders. I have an ear infection that is chronic—I have it to this day—that I could summon up at will. Whenever I wanted an ear infection, no problem. I could just think it. My mother would take care of me then, but that was another bad thing, in a way, because her attention robbed me, in my eyes, of a certain kind of masculinity that I wanted. I mean, if you can con people into taking care of you when you're sick, but it winds up being your mother that's taking care of you—anything to do with her wound up being a self-deprecating kind of experience.

The only way to cope with her was to completely avoid her, so I moved downstairs. I lived in the basement from, I guess, my junior year in high school on. I set up a studio down there, where I could practice the trumpet as many hours a day as I wanted, or I could write, or I could do whatever I wanted. I wanted to be the greatest American composer—a relatively short-lived aspiration, but I really wanted to. I wanted to be a great trumpet player. Later on, a great comic. And as it worked out, I was really proficient in those areas, because I had to be. It was my way of survival. It was the only way I could get any kind of recognition, any kind of love, from the outside. So I was really very accomplished. My mother never liked that. She was never crazy about that idea.

She'd say, "Why don't you go into business or be an engineer?"
I could have gone to Juilliard to pursue a music career, but I was
good at mathematics, so I ended up going to Manhattan College
for idiotic engineering.

College was a very trying time for me. High school wasn't
bad, because I was very active in the band. In college, I had just
started to work in some clubs as a comic, and it was the kind of
thing where the day was hell. Just trying to get through the day
was hell. And I used to drink a lot. I would go out and drink a
lot at lunch. It was a compulsion to be loved. The way it mani-
fested itself was to have people's attention, to be number one in
this, to be number one in that, to be the ultimate entertainer. It's
such a hackneyed story, but when it happens to you, it's amazing,
the strength of such compulsions. So, going to class robbed me of
time which could have been constructively spent to obtain what I
considered important. But it was a lot more than that. It was a
culmination of a lot of things that were beginning to thread together at this time. The kind of guilt that I had about my mother,
complete hatred of my mother, yet feeling guilty that I was killing her.

I had some problems with girls. Because I always said to myself, "I am really fantastic," or "They will consider me really fantastic, because I can be whatever they want me to be, without
any real work on my part." "Oh, you don't like that? Okay, I'll
change it. I'll be this instead." But what would happen is, because
I had the need just to be loved, and not for any particular thing,
or because I had this or that particular ability, but just this abstract need for acceptance—everything would backfire. I guess
things like that start showing in your eyes, that kind of need. And
I became the National League strikeout king. Girls were a little
nervous when I was around. In fact, the loss of one or two girl
friends helped to precipitate the first crisis. They weren't *the*
cause, but they were catalysts.

See, you start going into a panic, a kind of terror, but terror
is a bad word, because it implies that you're afraid of someone in
particular. It's more an abstract fear, and I guess because you
can't admit that you're functioning that way, you've got to invent
an object for your fear. So you pick something, like my mother's
going to die, or I'm going to lose this chick. But there are so many

forces at work that you can't admit you're going under. So there were lots of things. The idiocy of school, the fear that nobody would ever care about me. It's a funny thing—it's a strange paradox, because on the one hand you do have a fairly high self-esteem in the sense of the kind of output you're capable of. You say, "My God, I can really walk into a nightclub and do an act, and I'm only nineteen years old." But that doesn't really work, because then you say, "So what? I'm miserable, and nothing's working for me. My life is terrible."

And suicide hangs over you like a pall. I *knew* I was going to do away with myself. And there was *no* question that I was going to do it before thirty. No question. This was not an anxiety, this was a solid fact. So I was dealing with a limited period of time in which I had to accomplish what I was going to accomplish. And the time frames were not being met. In other words, to get where I want to be before my tragic death, and before the world reads about it, I'm going to have to have a national reputation by the time I'm twenty. Then the exact way I would die was one of my few options. As dramatic as possible. Burying my head in the sand and waiting for the tide to come in. Doing a Harold Lloyd out of a thirty-eighth-floor window. Some tricky way, where people would say, "My God! My God!"

The crisis came in my junior year, in 1962, when I was twenty. It came in a class in Electrical Engineering 2, which was network analysis. And I loved it. It was one of my favorite courses. It was taught by this guy, Brother Joseph, who was a nice guy, white-haired guy, likable guy, and I probably saw him as a father image and probably felt failure in one form or another in front of him. I don't remember the details exactly, because I've had extensive shock treatments since then, but I apparently exploded in class and threw a desk or some books, one or the other, at Brother Joseph. And then ran out. Then they found me screaming hysterically in a closet, a kind of wardrobe closet. So they carted me off to a hospital. I was terrified of the whole idea. The hospital looked like something out of a Christopher Lee movie. It was at the top of a hill, with these trees that look Gothic, like someone really worked on them to make them look like that. It's surprising there wasn't lightning that particular night.

The early part of the stay is a little hazy. I remember waking up and being in this room with just a little mattress on the floor, and the light coming through a window that had thick wire and bars on it. You're drugged out anyhow, but you wake up with the light casting barred shadows. There's a door, but you can't really see where you are. They slide open a thing when they want to talk to you. This made me very nervous. I would get very violent, start pounding against the wall, knocking my head against the door, trying to get out. I was in a straitjacket for a couple of nights, and heavily sedated. Then they give you shock treatment and insulin therapy, primarily to get rid of the immediacy of the problem, and secondarily to make you more amenable to psychotherapy. But I kept having horrible hallucinations, like imagining that I was in hell. I'd say, "This is ridiculous, this is not happening"—like you and I are talking here now, except that the walls are on fire, and you start to run from me.

I was diagnosed as having "an acute schizophrenic episode," and I stayed there for three months. Then—some of the great Academy Award performances go on there in these hospitals, because what you have to do is, you have to convince them that through their therapy—and they're conceited enough to require— I mean, you sort of say, "Thank God that I came here!" And then they kind of feel that you're adjusted enough to be let out. So, they released me, and it was already the end of the term anyhow, so I spent the summer as a camp counselor. I liked that a lot. That summer, I ran into a girl I was very, very interested in, I mean amazingly interested in. Then that started going bad, and one of the reasons it started going bad was because I had previously been hospitalized. There was a time there—I guess it was in my eyes and in my mannerisms—that I probably came off looking like a combination of the angry young man and somebody that just might do you in. We wound up breaking up, just after I went back to school. It was a terrible scene, and I was really hurt by it, crushed by it. So it was pretty much the same situation as the first time. They ushered me back to the hospital. They said, "Don't worry, we're not going to keep you in the hospital, we just want to run a few more tests on you." So they kept me for two months, basically the same treatment, and then they said, "Don't go back to school, get a job, some kind of work, for a year or two."

The corporation was very good. Here's a guy who's a two-time loser out of a mental hospital, hadn't finished college but had good marks and good aptitude on their tests, so they took me. I was a field engineer, which is primarily maintenance but also pro-graming of equipment. I liked it, but I was still a very sick boy. And I was drinking again. There were a couple of times at work when I would break down crying. I thought, This is the terrible sickness I'm going to have to live with for the rest of my life, but thank God, there's only about another ten years to go. I was still seeing a psychiatrist twice a week, because I had the fear that if I were not seeing a psychiatrist regularly, and any incident came up, I'd really be incarcerated for a long time. The psychiatrist, if nothing else, served as a good bargaining tool to keep me out of institutions, and if anything else came out of it, wonderful.

But I started lying to him, and making up stories to make the sessions as interesting as I could. I told him that I had a dual per-sonality, and that other people would manifest themselves in me. One was the very creative, soulful type, and the other a self-destructive personality, and I described when one would be stronger than the other, and I couldn't control it. A lot of this was made up, but it was made up of half-truths, okay? And I did write a lot of music. I wrote some of the music for the World's Fair, for the Malaysian Pavilion, jazz music with an Oriental flavor. And I kept working as a comic at places like the Bitter End and the Village Vanguard. I was starting to get a following. I had a routine about a guy that was selling Manhattan Island to a very sophisticated Indian. And there was another one about a cub re-porter who works with Clark Kent and notices that there's an amazing resemblance between him and Superman: "Gee, you look just like him, same eyes, same hair, same nose . . ."

But I hated performing, actually. I only liked it after it was over, when I could look back on it. And there was no way I could get through the day without crying. I would cry out of extreme depression or I would cry out of extreme elation. For years this was true. I tried to convince myself that I was lucky to be this way, because it was in the crying jags that I was very, very cre-ative. The crying happened mostly when I was alone. If it had to be, I could bring it on. I could lie down and rock and create any kind of environment I wanted. I would tell myself, This is a shitty disease I have, but isn't it wonderful that I can control it to this extent? But the drinking got worse and worse. There was a long period of time, from about 1965 to 1968, when I was living alone in Manhattan and drinking every night. A tremendous isolation set in. I was doing okay at work, but nothing really had changed. You were still in the terrifying struggle for survival, the terrifying anxieties. The only way I can describe it is, I'm sure it's the same type of anxiety you must go through if you know that there's an assassin out to get you. Except that it's tougher, because it's more abstract—you don't know what you should avoid.

I got terrified about coming into the house alone, so I bought a kitten, and the kitten became the only friend that I had in the house. I even started getting kind of a crazy jealousy about the cat's ability just to hack it, day in and day out, and not have big ups and downs. I don't remember how it happened but—I remember waking up one morning, and knowing that I'd had a drinking blackout, and I couldn't find the cat. I looked and I looked until I didn't know where to look any more. That night, I went to the freezer to get a TV dinner, and I open the door—and the cat is in there looking back out at me. Frozen. With its neck broken.

The kind of terror that's creeping over me now is really becoming—I became a complete recluse. The anxiety, terror, everything else became incredible, just really incredible. The booze was the only thing that could get me through it. From 1964 until 1972, which is eight years, there were fifteen trips to emergency wards of various hospitals. There were only three actual hospitalizations, because very fast I learned how to con my way out of these things, but I had these terrible hangovers at work, and the feeling that I'd be discovered any day now.

In 1968, I got married. She was a singer, a very attractive woman, although she could be remarkably bitchy. It was terrific in the beginning, it really was, but then I got this idea of poisoning her. I tried little by little to give her enough drugs, certain kinds of drugs—I really can't tell you how I got them or what I did, but suffice it to say that I could slowly, slowly slow her down and probably do away with her, since she was anemic, and that kind of blood condition was amenable to this kind of therapy. I could make her wish that she was no longer able to function. She would still live with me. See, I could do away with her without being rejected by her. I could, in a sense, control the situation.

I stayed with my wife for twenty-two months, and then I got a call from this woman who was my first cousin, whom I had once been very, very close to. I had spent summers with her family when I was a little kid. We had been sort of raised together. So it was terrific to see her again, because here was, for the first time in many years, a chance for roots. Her family was remote enough so that it wasn't immediately painful, but yet there was a certain kind of nostalgia. So we started living together. I guess it was also incest and other attendant silliness. So I left my wife. I had a lot of guilt about that, and I relatively quickly became disillusioned with my cousin. That started breaking up in 1972, and in 1972, I really started drinking around the clock. I was also taking a lot of pills—phenobarbital, Nembutal, Seconal—up to thirty a day. And in 1972, I also hit the age of thirty, so it was an appropriate time for me to die.

There were fights in bars, collapses in bars, a couple of tries at suicide. There was one legitimate attempt at suicide where I locked myself in a hotel room in Philadelphia and drank a fifth of Scotch, along with an enormous amount of pills, but as with all alcoholics, my system was incredible—it gets so used to dealing with the kind of drug it's being fed. There were other kinds of violence too, like taking a brick and smashing it over my head. Crazy kinds of things. One time, I woke up, and I had a lot of cuts on me, and for a day, I couldn't figure out what the hell had happened. Then I remember seeing the scissors on the table, and there was like a little spot of red on them, and that kind of pieced it together for me, and I kind of remembered. And I had done it just to have that dramatic look. And hallucinations—one recurring hallucination I had was that I would be in a hospital ward, and there would be stretchers, and the people on them would be dead. But they would not only be dead, they would be without heads, without hands, without arms. I'd walk over, and I'd pick up the cloth, just to look, and the corpse would get up, and I would scream. Then I'd get out into a hallway of my apartment—thinking the hallucination was over—and the same thing would happen all over again. Another stretcher, and I yank off the cloth, and the same kind of body— But you know you're not sleeping, you're awake.

By August of that year, I was really in the final throes, when I knew I was drinking myself to death. I mean, I had at least become that honest with myself. Then I met Maureen. She used to go out with my brother, and she had come to this bar where they used to drink together. That's how I met her. Then we got very close, and I started cutting down. I even joined Alcoholics Anonymous, although I had cut down a lot before I ever went there. A.A. helped, but getting married to Maureen helped more. That furnished a lot of things for me. It furnished security. It also furnished, in a funny kind of way, a need to stop drinking, because I didn't like to have her two kids see me drunk. I wanted them to think I was a good stepfather, and I think they do. I haven't had a drink in more than a year now, and I've also stopped seeing the psychiatrist. I can remember very vividly what it's like to want to die, but I don't want to die now. My timetable has expired.

The Lie of a Pipe Dream
Is What Gives Life

The first time I vowed to give up drinking was about twenty-five years ago, in Paris, and the reason was that I had hit a girl in the face, and that the next day I could not remember having done it. I didn't even think I was particularly drunk. I remembered that I was driving around with a group of friends, one of whom had a yellow Jeepster, and he wanted to drive over and pick up his own girl at the Salle Gaveau, where she was attending a concert of Beethoven quartets. I insisted on going in to get her myself, so I barged into the concert hall and stood against the back wall while the musicians rattled through the last movement of Beethoven's Quartet in C Sharp Minor. After it was over, I found the girl and escorted her out to the Jeepster, cheerfully whistling the main theme of Beethoven's finale. Even now, I remember all that very clearly, but then nothing more. The next day—it was like Lon Chaney, Jr., trying to find out what he had done during the night of the full moon—I asked the friend with the yellow Jeepster whether it was true, as the girl insisted, that I had punched her in the face. "Well," he said, hesitating—one always seems to make allowances for drunkenness—"well, yes, you were pretty difficult."

So I stopped drinking, for perhaps a day or two, perhaps a week, and then I went back to it. It was part of my life. I had started in college, where the freshmen all urged each other to drink up like men, and I first got sick on a punch of bourbon, milk and nutmeg. Then I discovered gin, and loved the taste of juniper, and drank a full bottle straight in one afternoon. The walls reeled as I fell asleep on the floor, waking up only to vomit. As I grew older, and went to live in Europe, my ability to drink myself sick grew more refined. I got sick on Beaujolais, I got sick on Cointreau, I got sick on all the noblest creations of European civilization. Beer, I finally told myself, was the solution. I had never liked the taste, but it was cheap, and one could learn to drink it all night without collapsing on the café tables. "Alcohol was an acquired taste," according to Jack London (in *John Barleycorn*), who first got drunk on beer at the age of five. "It had been painfully acquired. Alcohol had been a dreadfully repugnant thing—more nauseous than any physic. . . . Twenty years of unwilling apprenticeship had been required to make my system rebelliously tolerant of alcohol, to make me, in the heart and the deeps of me, desirous of alcohol."

For this, beer will work its way as well as whiskey. I saw an advertising study not long ago that tried to explain the success of the Schaefer commercials ("the one beer to have when you're having more than one") on the ground that 15 percent of the population drinks 80 percent of the beer. This drinker, according to *The New York Times,* is "that city-dwelling, blue-collar, high-school-educated, middle-income, sports-loving guy between 25 and 42 years of age who all by himself knocks off 45 cases of beer a year—16 times the national average." By my reckoning, this supposedly sodden creature, who resembles me in none of the listed categories, is a mild social drinker. I myself consume well over a hundred cases a year, along with about a hundred gallons of red wine and a good deal of Italian Vermouth, which, among other things, costs me something on the order of two thousand dollars. "When I was young," said Brendan Behan, who was also in Paris in my time, and usually full of whiskey, which prompted him to start bellowing Irish songs at parties, "being drunk represented a great victory, like being fat." But I hardly ever get drunk any more, nor have I ever again hit a girl, and if I ever did, I don't think I would forget it.

Still, alcoholism is, as has often been said, the worst drug-abuse problem in the nation. In 1971, the National Institute on Alcohol Abuse and Alcoholism estimated the cost of drunkenness at fifteen billion dollars. In 1974, it increased this figure to twenty-five billion. How such estimates are concocted is one of the many mysteries of the federal bureaucracy, but the statisticians apparently start with the hypothesis that half of all major automobile accidents are caused by alcohol, and then they work their way through computations on the cost of absenteeism, factory acci-

dents, welfare payments, and so on. (According to equally unreliable estimates, a *Newsweek* article on Russia in 1974 said:
"One economist admits that the U.S.S.R. loses as much as eighteen
billion dollars a year from absenteeism, incompetence and accidents due largely to drinking.")

But is alcoholism really a form of insanity? I have defined
the concept very loosely throughout this book, and I think it undeniable that destructive drinking can be both a symptom of
madness and a cause of its worst consequences. In fully half the
murders committed in this country, according to police estimates,
either the killer or the victim or both had been drinking. In one
quarter of all suicides, the body contains a "significant" amount
of alcohol. And just as scientists have found that a sufficiently high
dosage of amphetamines can cause all the symptoms known as
schizophrenia, so Bill Wilson, the ruined stock broker who helped
to found Alcoholics Anonymous, began arguing in the 1960's that
nutritional deficiencies might be the cause of both alcoholism and
insanity. In any case, the poisons are not limited to barroom
shootings or assembly-line sabotage. According to the National
Council on Alcoholism, about half the alcoholics in the United
States are "professional or managerial workers," and somewhere
between 5 and 10 percent of the top corporation executives in the
country are, quite simply, drunkards.

And who, with eyes to see, has not seen them? I once was
taking part in a conference involving tens of thousands of dollars
when the executive responsible for the final decision, newly back
from his martinis at lunch, fell fast asleep and began loudly snor-
ing at the conference table. And once I was at a party where an
executive who controlled a budget of several millions got so drunk
that he could not keep his car on the road. We were all going off
to another party—Mr. X. driving a rented car, with a girl he had
picked up at the first party, and I following behind with a friend
and his wife. Mr. X's car swooped wildly along the winding roads
outside this rich suburb in Connecticut, now on the left side of
the road, now on the right, until it finally lurched into a ditch and
came to a steaming stop. We all clambered out to see what damage had been done. We found the girl flung under the dashboard,
and cowering there in terror, but Mr. X, the executive, stood,

clinging to the door, swaying, and complacently surveying the mess.

"No problem, no problem," he said thickly. "All you gotta do is give me a little push."

So we returned to my car and gave him a little push.

"Why couldn't you at least get that girl out of there before he kills her?" my friend's wife protested loudly.

"Let's just not aggravate him," my friend said.

"Masculine vanity!" his wife shouted. "Let him drive her into a tree because you don't want to hurt his feelings. Goddam masculine vanity!"

"Let's just cool it," my friend said. "He's big brass, so it's up to him to decide what he's doing."

I do not know exactly what "professional or managerial workers" are. Mostly businessmen, I suppose—engineers, technologists, vice-presidents for sales. There are studies that show, without much documentation, that alcoholism is a disease of the able and ambitious, the driven. It is a little unnerving to imagine brain surgeons living on alcohol, but they, too, are among us. I remember Ring Lardner, Jr., regaling a party with the story of a Hollywood doctor who drank so many martinis at a dinner party that he passed out right on the dining-room floor. Several other guests started to lift him onto a nearby sofa, but his wife said, "No, just let him rest there. He has to operate tomorrow."

If there is too much whiskey poured at conferences in the executive suite, there is also a fair amount consumed in Washington. During the relatively abstemious regime of Richard Nixon, who was preoccupied with more mercenary sins, Domestic Affairs Adviser John Ehrlichman brought the matter out into the open by testifying before the Senate Watergate Committee in 1973: "You can go over here in the gallery and watch a member totter onto the floor in a condition of at least partial inebriation." Ehrlichman offered this observation to justify the administration's program of spying on its critics. "Someone with a serious drinking habit," he said, "is of doubtful fitness for the kind of heavy duty that . . . any Senator bears." The Senators were shocked, not only at the idea that Congressional drinking should be considered politically relevant but that it should be looked into by White House investigators. There have, of course, been several recent examples of political figures undone by alcohol—Governor Winthrop Rockefeller of Arkansas, for instance, or Congressman Wilbur Mills—but according to what *The New York Times* called "an informal survey," the incidence of alcoholism among Congressmen was only about 4 percent, which, it added, was "slightly lower than the widely accepted estimate of 5 percent for the general population." And when the *Times* reporter went to interview Dr. Morris E. Chafetz, director of the National Institute on Alcohol Abuse and Alcoholism, Chafetz remarked, "People who live in glass houses shouldn't throw stones."

The retort is well deserved, for the legendary figure of the drunken reporter may be found not only in Jimmy Cagney movies, where he generally sobers up long enough to expose civic corruption, but also in many a newspaper city room, where he sits dazedly trying to write his story without hitting three typewriter keys at once. Even among more celebrated writers, drunkenness seems to be a kind of occupational affliction. Hemingway, Faulkner, Fitzgerald—the list can begin almost anywhere.

On October 3, 1849, Dr. J. E. Snodgrass of Baltimore received a note asking him to come to a saloon named Gunner's Hall to attend to "a gentleman rather the worse for wear." At the saloon, the doctor found the gentleman "sitting in an armchair with his head dropped forward. . . . His face was haggard, not to say bloated and unwashed, his hair unkempt. . . . His forehead was shaded from view by a rusty, almost brimless, tattered and ribbonless palm leaf hat. His clothing consisted of a sack coat of thin and sleazy black alpaca, ripped more or less at several of its seams, and faded and soiled, and pants of a steel-mixed pattern of cassinette, half-worn and badly fitting. . . . The bosom of his shirt was both crumpled and badly soiled."

The semiconscious gentleman was taken in a carriage to the Washington College Hospital and placed under the care of Dr. J. J. Moran, who later reported that he remained in a stupor until about three o'clock the following morning. "To this state succeeded tremor of the limbs, and at first a busy but not violent or active delirium—constant talking—and vacant converse with spectral and imaginary objects on the walls." On the second day, Dr.

Moran tried to interrogate him, but his answers were "incoherent and unsatisfactory." When the doctor said that friends would soon come to visit him, he "said the best thing his friend could do would be to blow out his brains with a pistol." The doctor went away briefly and then was summoned back to find his patient "in a violent delirium, resisting the efforts of two nurses to keep him in a bed. This state continued until Saturday morning [his fourth day in the hospital]. At this time a very decided change began to affect him. Having become enfeebled from exertion, he became quiet, and seemed to rest." All that night, however, he intermittently cried out the name "Reynolds," a name that nobody has ever been able to explain. At five o'clock Sunday morning, he awoke again, and, according to Dr. Moran, "gently moving his head, he said, 'Lord help my poor soul!' and expired."

It is not entirely clear how great a part alcohol played in the death of Edgar Allan Poe. He had made the grievous mistake of naming as his literary executor an envious charlatan named the Reverend Rufus W. Griswold, whose posthumous biography portrayed him as a dissolute rakehell addicted to both whiskey and laudanum. Modern scholarship has corrected many of Griswold's calumnies. Against all witnesses to Poe's inebriation—a friend named Thomas Holley Chivers once encountered him on Nassau Street in New York, "tottering from side to side, as drunk as an Indian," and one of his employers, T. W. White, warned him: "No man is safe who drinks before breakfast!"—against all this, Poe's admirers have assembled the testimony of other friends, who claim that he drank only sporadically, and not in great quantities. One theory is that he was of the type that is abnormally susceptible to alcohol, and that two or three glasses of wine would make him drunk. Another theory is that he was so susceptible because he was too poor to eat much food.

Poe's admirers are a bit too protective, however. Regardless of how much he drank, the fact is that he was often drunk, and, like the classic alcoholic, he regularly turned to liquor when some difficult situation confronted him. On his meeting with James Russell Lowell, for example, the Cambridge poet who had helped him and praised him recalled that Poe appeared "rather formal, even pompous [and] I have the impression he was a little soggy with drink—not tipsy—but as if he had been holding his head under a pump to cool it." On another occasion, he went to Washington to seek financial backing for a prospective magazine, but his drinking helped to prevent anyone from supporting him. Poe's whole life, of course, was a series of crises, starting with the disappearance of his alcoholic father, then the death of his mother when he was two, and then the stern upbringing by his foster-father, John Allan. Poe ran up drunken gambling debts at the University of Virginia to the enormous sum of $2,000, which prompted Allan to cut off his support. Having thought he was destined to inherit Allan's fortune, Poe had to spend most of his life engaged in hack work for such ephemeral periodicals as *Burton's Gentleman's Magazine, Graham's Magazine* and *The Southern Literary Messenger. Harper's* rejected his collected short stories on the grounds that they were "too learned and mystical."

The worst crisis of all was the prolonged illness and death of his fragile wife, Virginia, the cousin whom he had married when she was thirteen. "Each time [she hemorrhaged]," Poe wrote to a friend, "I felt all the agonies of her death, and at each accession of the disorder I loved her more dearly & clung to her with more desperate pertinacity. But I am constitutionally sensitive—nervous in a very unusual degree. I became insane, with long intervals of horrible sanity. During these fits of absolute unconsciousness I drank, God only knows how often or how much. As a matter of course, my enemies referred the insanity to the drink rather than the drink to the insanity."

The two conditions are often intertwined in Poe's lugubrious tales. "What disease is like Alcohol!" cries the narrator of "The Black Cat" as he reports how, under the influence of "the Fiend Intemperance," he first seized his cat and cut out one of its eyes. The schizophrenic William Wilson, similarly, has "given myself up entirely to wine [with] its maddening influence upon my hereditary temper," when he finally stabs his alter ego. The drunken king in "Hop-Frog" forces his jester to drink, even though "Hop-Frog was not fond of wine; for it excited the poor cripple almost to madness; and madness is no comfortable feeling." The half-demented narrator of "Ligeia" speaks, in addition, of "the excitement of my opium dreams (for I was habitually fettered in the shackles of the drug)."

The year after Virginia's death, Poe apparently tried to commit suicide with an overdose of laudanum, but "after the laudanum was rejected from the stomach, I became calm, and to a casual observer, sane." Although the suicide attempt may have been mostly melodrama, the ensuing calm was only a brief respite. In the following spring of 1849, heading southward to give some lectures, Poe became convinced that two men sitting near him on the train were conspiring to murder him. He got off the train in Philadelphia and disappeared from sight for an entire weekend, turning up on Monday at the home of a friend named John Sartain. He asked Sartain to shave off his mustache so that the two assassins could not identify him. Sartain evidently demurred.

Poe said that he had spent the weekend confined in prison—no Philadelphia prison records show any trace of this—and that a beautiful girl had appeared atop a stone tower and warned him of terrible punishments awaiting him: "Great caldrons of boiling liquor, steaming and fizzling in the moonlight." He said he had had a vision of flying over Philadelphia in the clutches of a huge black bird, which had told him that it was the embodiment of cholera (the disease that had killed his older brother seventeen years earlier). He had had another vision about his "mother," meaning Virginia's mother, who lived with him and kept house for him even after Virginia's death. He said that "a pack of demons" brought her to the caldron that the girl on the tower had warned him about and "chopped off her feet before my eyes, then her knees, her thighs, her arms, and at last plunged the poor, bleeding trunk into the reeking, bubbling caldron."

"I have been so ill—have had the cholera, or spasms quite as bad . . ." he wrote to his mother-in-law. "It is no use to reason with me now; I must die. . . . We must die together. You have been all in all to me, darling, ever beloved mother, and dearest, truest friend. I was never *really* insane, except on occasions where my heart was touched." He managed to get himself to Richmond, and there he wrote her again ("I am so *ill*"), confessing that the visions in Philadelphia had been a kind of delirium tremens: "For more than ten days I was totally deranged, although I was not drinking one drop, and during this interval I imagined the most horrible calamities. . . . May heaven grant that it prove a warning to me."

Poe seems to have recovered somewhat in Richmond. He joined the Sons of Temperance and took a pledge of abstinence. He gave three lectures and continued trying to raise money for a magazine. He even encountered Sarah Elmira Royster, a girl he had courted at the age of seventeen. She was now a widow, who had been bequeathed an estate of $50,000, and Poe promptly proposed to her, writing to his mother-in-law that they would all live together somewhere, and that "our troubles are nearly over." Poe went so far as to buy the wedding ring, but he suddenly decided to return to New York. He stayed up all night, drinking with friends, and then boarded the 5:30 A.M. boat to Norfolk. That was seven days before Dr. Snodgrass found him disheveled and stupefied at the Gunner's Hall saloon in Baltimore. Nobody has ever discovered where Poe was during that penultimate week, or how he got to the saloon, where he reappeared, in the words of one biographer, like someone who "had been rejected by Hell."

If Poe could not tolerate alcohol, Jack London could gulp it down like chicken soup. "The fortunate man," he wrote in *John Barleycorn* (1913), "is the one who cannot take more than a couple of drinks without becoming intoxicated. The unfortunate wight is the one who can take many glasses without betraying a sign; who *must* take numerous glasses in order to get the 'kick.'" Like most alcoholics, London denied that he was an alcoholic, but he wrote, toward the end of his life, that he had "achieved a condition in which my body was never free from alcohol. Nor did I permit myself to be away from alcohol. If I traveled to out-of-the-way places, I declined to run the risk of finding them dry. I took a quart, or several quarts, along in my grip. . . . I was carrying a beautiful alcoholic conflagration around with me. The thing fed on its own heat and flamed the fiercer. There was no time, in all my waking time, that I didn't want a drink."

He was not yet forty, immensely rich and successful (he is reported to have earned more than a million dollars from his fifty books, a prodigious sum in the pre–World War I, pre–income-tax era), but he never escaped the anxieties of his childhood. He had been born the illegitimate son of an itinerant astrologer, then taken in by a stepfather with eleven children. He was eight years old before he acquired his first store-bought undershirt, a prize he valued so highly that he refused for a long time to wear a shirt that would hide it from sight. He worked ten hours a day in a tanning factory, for ten cents an hour, and then became an oyster pirate in the waters off Oakland, California, and when the raids were done, everybody drank. Whiskey in the waterfront bars sold for ten cents a glass, beer five cents, cheaper than ice cream, and London blamed this for the beginnings of his own addiction. "The pseudo-civilization into which I was born," he wrote, "permitted everywhere licensed shops for the sale of soul-poison. The system of life was so organized that I (and millions like me) was lured and drawn and driven to the poison shops. . . . We have with great success made a practice of not leaving arsenic and strychnine, and typhoid and tuberculosis germs, lying around for our children to be destroyed by. Treat John Barleycorn the same way. Stop him."

London even voted for women's suffrage on the grounds that once women had the vote, they would outlaw liquor. As indeed they did. And was it Ring Lardner, another notable alcoholic, who remarked: "Then came Prohibition, and everybody started to drink"? No, there were other reasons for London's struggle with the specter he called John Barleycorn. He had begun drinking in his childhood out of an exaggerated desire to prove himself a man, and like all beginning drinkers, he didn't know when to stop. Everywhere he went, from the Oakland docks to the sealing ports of Japan, he found that "the saloon was the place of congregation. Men gathered to it as primitive men gathered about the fire of the squatting-place or the fire at the mouth of the cave." And so, to be a man among men, he "drank for the sole purpose of getting drunk, of getting hopelessly, helplessly drunk."

Then strange things happened. One night, when he was about seventeen, in Benicia, California, he staggered off the end of a wharf, and the outgoing tide swept him out to sea. John Barleycorn, according to London's account, persuaded him that this would be a splendid fate. "I had never been morbid. Thoughts of suicide had never entered my head. And now that they entered, I thought it fine, a splendid culmination. . . . It was a man's way to die." He wept tears of drunken joy, and sang drunken songs, and "dreamed long drunken dreams," as the tide carried him toward his death. Cold seawater has a mercifully sobering effect, however, and after four hours adrift, London was picked up at daybreak by a Greek fishing vessel cruising through the San Pablo Bay.

London insisted that he was not alcoholic because he claimed that his body never felt a physical craving for liquor. Out at sea, or during prolonged periods of writing, he abstained for months at a time. He seems to have thought that the mind's craving was somehow less serious than that of the body, but John Barleycorn knew better. In London's later years, when he had to drive himself to write a thousand words every morning, he began looking forward to the cocktail that came at the end. Then he found that he couldn't write until he had a cocktail after five hundred words. Then he needed a cocktail before he started. "The work refused to be done without drinking. I had to drink in order to do it. I was beginning to fight now. I had the craving at last, and it was mastering me."

In these later years, London also had to fight against profound depressions. "In vain do I ask myself why I should be sad," he wrote. "My nights are warm. My roof does not leak. I have food galore for all the caprices of appetite . . . I have land, money, power, recognition from the world . . . a mate whom I love, children that are of my own fond flesh. . . . [But] brain-soaked with many months of alcohol, I am oppressed by the cosmic sadness that has always been the heritage of man." London tried, as always, to philosophize. He claimed that John Barleycorn spoke to him with a "white logic" that demonstrated the vanity of all human ambitions ("for there are fatal intuitions of truth that reside in alcohol"). But the depression was really no more metaphysical than the sense of decay that oppresses most men approaching forty. "In my jaw," said the onetime oyster pirate, seal-hunter, and prophet of the Nietzschean "blond beast," are "cunning artifices of the dentists which replace the parts of me already gone." What he did not write about was the more important fear of losing his creative power. To help pay for the $100,000 Wolf Ranch, which ultimately burned down, he had already taken to hiring young writers to think up plots for his books. And when he came to write his autobiographical novel, *Martin Eden*, he ended by forcing his spiritually exhausted hero to slip out a porthole in mid-Pacific. "Down, down, he swam till his arms and legs grew tired. . . . Colors and radiances surrounded him and bathed him and pervaded him. . . ." Not until eight years later did London finally follow Eden into the depths. He was found dead in his bed, and the official verdict was uremic poisoning, but there was a writing pad on his night table that recorded the amount of morphine required for death. Two empty vials lay on the floor next to his bed.

Of all the alcoholic writers, none drank with a greater ferocity than Eugene O'Neill. Starting at fifteen, he was already addicted by the time he spent his one wasted year at Princeton, and alcohol made him more manic than Poe, more despondent than London. He drank not for pleasure, nor even for stimulation, but out of a desperate desire to get drunk. And he would drink anything— even varnish mixed with water, even camphor-flavored wood alcohol, even a sinister Prohibition concoction distilled from raisins and known as "tiger piss." For all this, he told himself, he had good reasons. His father, no mean drinker himself, was a domineering and posturing figure at home and a gaping absence during his prolonged theatrical tours (he spent a quarter of a century roving the country and giving six thousand performances of *The Count of Monte Cristo*). His mother had a difficult time in giving birth to Eugene and consequently became addicted to morphine, which used to be freely dispensed as a painkiller. O'Neill was scarcely more than ten when his mother first berated him for having discovered her injecting the drug into her arm. His older brother Jamie was a hopeless alcoholic from his schooldays until almost the last year of his life. The elder James O'Neill tried to shepherd his sons along by providing them with minor parts in his touring company, but on one occasion they were both so drunk that the performance had to be canceled.

Perhaps it was the curse of the Irish, or perhaps, as O'Neill liked to speculate in his later plays, he came from a doomed family. He once went to a psychiatrist who told him that he had "a death wish," and two of his biographers (Arthur and Barbara Gelb) have computed that a total of forty characters in his forty-four published plays suffer violent or unnatural deaths. "Of these, nine are suicides," they report. "Twenty-one of the poisoned, diseased, mangled, strangled, sliced, drowned, electrocuted, cremated, or bullet-ridden men, women and children meet their ends in full view of the audience." O'Neill himself attempted suicide as early as 1912, when he was twenty-four. He swallowed what he thought was a lethal dose of Veronal and then crawled off to his verminous bedroom over a New York waterfront saloon known as Jimmy-the-Priest's. Some friends found him there, filled him up with coffee, and dragged him off to Bellevue Hospital.

O'Neill was hardly ever sober during those prewar years. He had to have a drink as soon as he woke up, usually in midafternoon, and his hands shook so badly that he often needed help to get the glass to his lips. The bartender at the Garden Hotel on 27th Street used to serve him his whiskey and then leave a towel on the bar so that O'Neill could hold one end around the glass, then twist the rest of the towel around his neck, and then use his left hand to haul in the towel and hoist the glass to his quivering lips. He often spilled most of the drink in the process.

In his later plays, O'Neill liked to portray his alcoholism as an expression of masculine conviviality, but he himself was the kind of drinker who often turned mean, particularly toward women. "He was highly sensitive and nervous," according to one friend, "[and] when he was drinking he was black Irish. When that mood was on him, you could sense the potentialities in the man for destruction and trouble." One evening on Cape Cod, for example, O'Neill dressed himself up in a sarong and an orange wig to go to a costume ball. His second wife, Agnes, was wearing a mantilla that had belonged to O'Neill's mother, but O'Neill drunkenly tore it from her head. "Go back to the gutter you came from," he shouted. By four in the morning, O'Neill had disappeared, so a friend escorted Mrs. O'Neill to their car. "Suddenly," the friend recalled later, "from the depths of the car, something with insane, blazing eyes, a mad leer and an orange wig popped up. We recoiled. It was Gene, of course, very drunk. He and Agnes had rented a room in town for the evening, but Gene now decided he wanted to go back [home]. . . . He grabbed Agnes by the hair and tried to drag her off. She yelled but no one interfered. . . ."

Throughout all this, there was one part of O'Neill's brain that rejected its own destruction. This was the part that wanted to write, demanded to write. "Altogether too much damn nonsense has been written since the beginning of time about the dissipation of artists," O'Neill said. "Why there are fifty times more real drunkards among . . . people who never think about art at all. . . . You've got to have all your critical and creative faculties about you when you're working. I never try to write a line when I'm not strictly on the wagon. I don't think anything worth reading was ever written by anyone who was drunk or even half-drunk when he wrote it." O'Neill's estimated statistics may be debatable—after all, the number of sober people who "never think about art" probably exceeds the number of artists by a lot more than fifty to one—but his statement did apply to himself.

Unlike most writers, whose work deteriorates under the influence of alcohol, O'Neill was a skid-row derelict in his early twenties and did not get his first play produced at the tiny Wharf Theater in Provincetown until the relatively advanced age of twenty-eight. Once he discovered the theater as an outlet for his spiritual demons—between 1915 and 1925, he wrote an astonishing total of twenty-six plays, including some of his most powerful, *Anna Christie, The Emperor Jones, The Hairy Ape,* and *Desire Under the Elms*—he drank less and less, and then only on furious binges. And he grew determined to fight even those binges, perhaps inspired by the example of his brother, who ended screaming in a straitjacket in a sanitarium in New Jersey.

In 1925, O'Neill talked several times with a psychoanalyst who had already come to some definite conclusions about his work. "My privately held deduction," the doctor said later, "[was] that O'Neill was emotionally starved. I had studied his plays carefully and felt they all showed an antagonism toward women, which indicated to me that he had a deep antagonism toward his mother. I believed that O'Neill hated his mother and loved his father. He duplicated his father's profession, the theater. . . . He also imitated his father in his alcoholism. I felt that O'Neill had an unconscious homosexual attraction toward his father, which he carried over to some of his friendships for men. His antagonism toward his mother was carried over to his relationships with women; because his mother had failed him, all women would fail him, and he had to take revenge on them. All women had to be punished." Perhaps O'Neill sensed the trap of an analysis essentially complete before it had even started. In any case, he chose a different analyst, Dr. Gilbert V. Hamilton, and spent six weeks under his treatment. It was a relatively short period, and yet the system seems to have worked. For the rest of his life, the former waterfront drunk was a virtual teetotaler.

There were occasional lapses, though, not only into drunkenness but into temporary fits of madness. For alcohol, along with its capacity to ruin both mind and body, can also serve as an escape from the torments of life. It can calm anxieties, wash away guilt, make it easier to talk to people (and, despite O'Neill, to write). "What's it matter if the truth is that their favoring breeze has the stink of nickel whiskey on its breath . . ." as Larry Slade puts it in *The Iceman Cometh.* "To hell with the truth . . . The lie of a pipe dream is what gives life to the whole misbegotten mad lot of us, drunk or sober." Deprived of the escape into alcohol, O'Neill had to confront a number of unpleasant-nesses, starting with the breakup of his second marriage. (It was sobriety that led Hickey to murder his wife in *The Iceman Cometh,* or, conversely, murder that led to his sobriety. "I've been out of my mind ever since," he says as he is led away.)

O'Neill treated Agnes abominably, as he treated all his wives and children, but he tried to convince himself that everything, even his drinking, had been her fault. He himself had started an affair with a thrice-married actress named Hazel Tharsing, who called herself Carlotta Monterey. Partly to escape from reporters, they set off on a trip around the world, stopping first for a prolonged stay in France. O'Neill drank himself into a stupor one night and then suffered what Carlotta called "a bad nervous breakdown." It is not clear what the symptoms were—guilt? anxiety? depression?—and O'Neill described it only as "my present scrambled mental state." Whatever it was, it happened again in Shanghai, where O'Neill again got drunk, quarreled with Carlotta and finally hit her. "I'm not going to have an old whore telling me what to do!" he cried. A local doctor diagnosed "a slight nervous breakdown" and put him in the British hospital. "I'll never forget my experience . . ." O'Neill later wrote to a friend, "teetering on the verge of a nervous breakdown and lying awake nights listening to the night target practice of a Welsh regiment . . . and to the beating of Chinese gongs keeping the devils away from a birth or a bride or a corpse or something devils like! It nearly had me climbing the walls of my room and gibbering a bit."

After more than a year of wandering, O'Neill finally married Carlotta in 1929, and she was to spend the next quarter of a century serving as his muse, guardian, secretary, housekeeper and nurse. There was another mysterious "nervous breakdown" in 1934. The main symptom seems to have been a desperate desire to live in seclusion, and so the O'Neills moved to a country estate in Georgia. Sherwood Anderson visited them there and later wrote to a friend that "Gene is a sick man. . . . I did feel death in his big expensive house. He has drawn himself away, lives in that solitary place, seeing practically no one." Aside from his chronic depressions and nervous rages, O'Neill was prey to a pharmacopoeia of illnesses, some of which may have been psychosomatic or a consequence of his alcoholic youth. In his twenties, he had caught tuberculosis and spent some time in a sanitarium, but now he suffered, at various times, kidney trouble, a back ailment, a prostate condition, appendicitis, neuritis, an adrenal deficiency, periodic toothaches, and, according to Carlotta, impotence.

Perhaps worst of all, the trembling of the young alcoholic had become a permanent and increasingly severe affliction. It was first diagnosed in 1937 as Parkinson's disease, but apparently it was something else, a "familial tremor," of unknown cause, possibly psychological. It was apparently a degenerative disease, slowly destroying the brain cells. (Oddly enough, according to one expert, "alcohol allays a familial tremor, so that a person suffering from it will have to drink to alleviate his condition.") O'Neill had increasing difficulty in walking, even with a cane. His voice became blurred, then nearly unintelligible. As he hunched over his desk in an effort to work, his crabbed handwriting became smaller and smaller. He was unable either to type or to dictate, and so finally he was hardly able to write at all. (His last play, A Moon for the Misbegotten, was finished ten years before his death.) "I nearly went mad, and so did he," Carlotta said. "It was terrible to see him come out of his study, shaken and miserable."

During this same period, O'Neill also had to bear the consequences of his mistreatment of his children. Eugene junior, whom O'Neill had totally ignored throughout his first twelve years, seemed for a time to be a promising classics scholar at Yale, but he sank deeper and deeper into alcoholic depressions and finally cut his wrists in his bathtub. The second son, Shane, who had twice attempted suicide, wandered around Greenwich Village and became addicted to heroin. The only survivor was Oona, but O'Neill had been so outraged by her adolescent marriage to the aging Charlie Chaplin that he not only never spoke to her again but forbade anyone to mention her name in his presence.

The last years were dreadful. The Nobel Prize winner, frail and enfeebled, moved in and out of hospitals. He had to have his food cut up for him, his cigarettes lit, and his reactions to his helplessness ranged from tyrannic rudeness to suicidal despair. Carlotta became increasingly Cerberean, intercepting his mail, refusing access to many of his friends. They quarreled, separated, then reunited. They fought bitterly, threatening each other with guns and knives. One night, O'Neill came prowling around Carlotta's bed, talking to himself: "I'm going to smash her skull in, and all the blood will run down her face—I know you hear me, you're just pretending to be asleep." After one such battle, O'Neill marched out of the house on a wintry night, then slipped on the ice and broke his leg. "How the mighty have fallen!" Carlotta gloated from the doorway. "Where's your greatness now, little man?" O'Neill lay semiconscious in the snow for an hour before being rescued by a passing doctor, who took him to a hospital. Carlotta then began wandering distractedly through the streets in search of her husband, until the police found her and took her to a mental hospital.

O'Neill, from his sickbed, signed a court petition declaring that Carlotta was "an insane person incapable of taking care of herself." She, in turn, having been declared simply a victim of bromide poisoning, a consequence of the medicine she took to calm her nerves, filed a countersuit for separate maintenance, charging O'Neill with "cruel and abusive treatment." A well-known Boston psychiatrist, Dr. Merrill Moore, announced it his judgment that both the O'Neills were mentally ill and ought, among other things, to be kept apart. O'Neill by now was suffering from hallucinations—he once shrank in terror at the vision of Carlotta climbing in through his hospital window—but these faded when his medicine was changed. Then came pneumonia and a gastrointestinal attack.

O'Neill could not survive without Carlotta, and so he begged her to take him back. Toward the end, he was so emaciated, less than a hundred pounds, that Carlotta had to carry him from place to place. "My back still aches from lifting him," she said after his death. Shortly after his sixty-fifth birthday, in the fall of 1953, O'Neill tried to get out of bed and walk by himself. "He asked me very quietly to please not help him," Carlotta said. "I handed him his cane, and he started forward, then fell back and hit his head. He lay on the floor, and wouldn't let me help him up. Finally, he turned himself over on his stomach and pulled himself up. But that was when he gave up. . . . After that he didn't get off the bed again." A few days later, O'Neill stopped eating, and three days after that, he died.

He haunted her, of course, just as he haunted many of the people he had dominated. José Quintero, the director who staged *Long Day's Journey into Night,* even found himself pursued by Carlotta's obsessions. "Five or six times Carlotta called me in the middle of the night and said, 'He's here,' " Quintero told a reporter from *The New York Times* not long ago.

"I would visit her at the Ritz-Carlton. In a chair was Esteban, their monkey. Talking past the monkey to him, she would say to me, 'Now tell him how hard I've been working.' I was like a lawyer for the defense. She would engage me in this three-way conversation. She would tell me how they reconciled in China. She would sit on a chair as if it were a rickshaw—and it became a rickshaw. He wasn't there for me. In a way, he was. I remember the last time I went to see Carlotta in a [mental] hospital. She mistook me for O'Neill. She had done that before. She said, 'Oh, Gene, Gene, I've expiated longer than Lavinia [the doomed heroine of *Mourning Becomes Electra*], so let me go.' "

But perhaps this is all becoming too literary. Listen for a moment to a man called Harry. He is a social worker in New York, black, aged forty-four, about six feet tall, rather handsome, with close-cropped hair and moderately long sideburns. He wears brown slacks and a short-sleeved, brown-and-white-striped shirt. He speaks somewhat languidly, often gesturing with his hands.

His father was a Baptist minister in South Carolina, his mother a schoolteacher. They were determined that he was going to become a college professor. He got as far as a B.A. from Morehouse and an M.A. from Harvard, but by then he was already drinking heavily and suffering from an ulcer. Drinking, he says, gave him "a feeling of belonging, and of being at one with people." Within a few years, however, he lost a number of jobs, got arrested several times for fighting, ended in a mental hospital, began suffering hallucinations and blackouts, and ended on the Bowery.

"Finally, I couldn't even get an agency job. They would shake their heads when I came into the door, because I had gotten to the point that if you sent me out to wash dishes, by noontime I was hustling the boss for a dollar advance so I could get a bottle of wine. And after I got the bottle of wine, I wouldn't be able to wash the dishes or do anything else, so I was more or less stuck there on the Bowery. I just cut myself a-loose from everything else, because I had found—I had found a place where I could drink, because I had to drink. That was all I wanted to do, was to stay high. I was—I did all the things that people do on the Bowery. Tried to hustle drinks. Slept in the flophouses. Got sicker and sicker.

"But I kept telling myself that I drank in order to function. Even though there wasn't much functioning. You can glamorize those things. I told myself I was doing research for a book on the Bowery. What book? I'd long since stopped writing, taking notes, or anything like that. I mean, that was a farce. Now that's—you see, I call that insanity. Here I am with drawers on that I hadn't changed in maybe three months. You know, I'd vomited on myself. You can smell me a block away—but I'm still different, and I'm still better. I was the type of drunk who, if he saw somebody on the sidewalk, or somebody sitting in a doorway, with wine sores, *that* was the alcoholic, that was the person with the problem. I was not. I was doing research for a book you see. That was the ego trip I was on. Even when I finally got wine sores myself—they're part of drinking, they're somehow connected with alcoholic neuritis, and you break out in these sores that run, mostly on the legs—even then, I wouldn't admit that I needed help. If you had approached me, I would have said I could get off the Bowery any time I wanted to, and that I could stop drinking any time I wanted to. And I sort of believed this, that some miracle was going to happen.

"I also got very paranoid feelings that death was imminent, which perhaps it was, because the Bowery is a physically dangerous place to be. People get killed there about every day, get ripped off, and things like that. They beat you up. They steal your shoes. They steal your pants. I felt that I would die there, and my only hope was to be bombed out of my skull when I died. I just didn't want to know what hit me, because I knew it would be horrible. And I knew that I was losing my strength. I had gone down to about 160 pounds, which is very skinny for me. I was like skin and bones, you know, the hollow, sunken eyes, and that kind of thing. Almost unintelligible. I seldom spoke to anybody, you know, just a glassy stare in the eyes. And filthy dirty.

"One day, I fell down in the street, on the Bowery, and I don't know how long I had been out when I came to. It was drizzling rain. I couldn't tell whether it was morning or evening, but I knew it must be one or the other, because people had to be going to work or coming from work, because there seemed to be a lot of people passing by, like shadows. But nobody could help me. I was trying to cry out for help, ask somebody to help me. But I couldn't get up off the sidewalk. I couldn't cry out. It was just like death. It was just absolutely like death. And I suddenly knew very clearly that this was it. And it was just like something said to me, 'Well, here it is. You're going to die, and you're going to die on the sidewalk in the Bowery.' You know, it's just like the total feeling came over me that I *knew*. And I guess I must have passed out again. I came to a little later on, and I think it was in the evening. It was dark then. And I sort of staggered over to what they call the big room, in the Men's Shelter, where if you can't get into a hotel, you can sleep on the floor in there. . . ."

Despite the government statistics, which state not only that alcohol is our worst drug problem but that drinking is rising among the young, alcoholism still seems a rather old-fashioned sort of madness. For the past ten or twenty years, we have heard repeatedly that the young involve themselves mainly with drugs.

Thus, Allen Ginsberg: "I saw the best minds of my generation destroyed by madness, starving hysterical naked,/ dragging themselves through the negro streets at dawn looking for an angry fix. . . ." In fact, of course, people have been driving themselves crazy with drugs since the dawn of history. The Sumerians were smoking opium some six thousand years ago. They called it "the joy plant." Cocoa leaves, belladonna, hashish, peyote—wherever these sources of pleasure grew, men soon discovered their secrets. It was only in the nineteenth century that modern chemistry brought scientific efficiency to the process of self-destruction. Morphine was derived from opium in 1803, codein in 1832. Cocaine was chemically isolated in 1859, and Sigmund Freud recommended it highly, as, of course, did Sherlock Holmes. In 1898, some wizard devised a cure for morphine addiction and named it heroin. Then came the streams of synthetic drugs—the first barbiturate, barbital, in 1903, then phenobarbital in 1912. In 1938, a Swiss chemist first concocted lysergic acid.

"Somebody once said that the war between Germany and France was basically a war between beer drinkers and wine drinkers, and it sounded absurd," says George, a wiry black youth with a ring in one ear. "But there's a cultural war between pot smokers and alcohol drinkers. And that's connected to food, too. A diet of greasy, fried food gives you a very reactive consciousness, where like somebody steps on your toe in a bar while you're drinking whiskey to burn out the fat from all the greasy chicken, and the music is so tense, intensifying the strains from your workaday life—well, you know, guns come out, and people shoot each other and punch each other—just for somebody stepping on their nicely shined shoes."

George, who used to take large doses of barbiturates, lived very differently.

"I remember one day I got on a bus to go to my job, and when I closed my eyes for a minute, people outside were opening up their businesses and getting ready for the day. Then I opened them again, and it's dark, and they're all closing down. I shake my head and look around, and people are, you know, like falling asleep and everything. I'd gone through the entire day laying there with my head against the window of the bus, back and forth from one end of the line to the other. I was sort of scared, because I could have been dead, and nobody gave a shit at all. I mean, normally, if you try to ride that long, they stop you and take you off.

"So I stopped taking the pills, and my system went into shock. I lay down on the bed and just slept. The next thing I know, I'm on the floor, and I feel that I'm a lobster, and I even remember that I've been a lobster for a long time. I mean, this is really like deep under—no hands. I mean, looking down and just seeing nothing, nobody, you know. The floor is like gravel, and every little bit of anything is like a mountain. A little piece of dust is like an enormous stone to get around, or over, and not have it blow into my face and crush me. And lots of minor little terrors like that—like the D.T.'s, I suppose, but only—you're totally, physically not a person any more. And the ocean, you could hear it. You could see the sun coming up and going down, and you know it doesn't just come up and go down just like that, right? And time is passing. I'm framing all this in more or less literal terms, but it was just like this plasticky stuff all around me, but I didn't think of it as plastic. It was like some sort of diaphanous material floating around. And sort of opening my eyes wider than they were, and seeing people standing over me, with clothes in their hands, getting ready to move me out to a hospital. . . ."

Jonathan, a long-haired youth who wears steel-rimmed glasses and is now a graduate student in philosophy in Los Angeles, encountered his first difficulties with mescaline.

"One of the things I had started doing," he recalls, "was I had started throwing the *I Ching* on numerology, and comparing that with Yeats's phases of the moon—I was just checking all these things against each other, and I kept wondering, why didn't anybody do this before, with a computer, just use all these oracles on each other and find out what the hell is there? And then I suddenly saw this combination of—a face—this terrible face that came out of nowhere. It just sort of swallowed me up. What it was saying, basically, was 'You're out of your league, punk, you're going to get your ass kicked.'

"This face, I don't know whether it was a man or a woman, young or old. It was sort of green and purple warts. That sounds like it was, you know, a Halloween mask, but it was just so terribly real that you can't believe it. And totally terrifying. I couldn't sleep any more after that. I couldn't sleep for days. Three or four days later, I'd be in the cold shower, trying to get the trip to stop. It was all very disorienting. Didn't know where I was. Who I was. Forgot what my own face looked like. Didn't know who the people around me were. Couldn't tell who was looking at me, who wasn't, who was talking to me, who wasn't. Just very basic fear, nothing very elegant."

Jonathan's mescaline face eventually faded away, but then he went to live with a group of people who spent much of their time indulging themselves in what he calls "a hell of a lot of grass." The conventional wisdom nowadays is that smoking marijuana is a harmless pastime, suitable for suburban dinner parties, but it is, after all, a mildly hallucinogenic drug, and if enough of it is available, particularly to an unstable personality, it can work wonders.

"I realized that dope wasn't doing me any favors," Jonathan says, "and I told myself that I had to stop it, but, you know, if I stopped smoking grass, maybe people would think I'd started going crazy again. When in doubt, do what those around you are doing, and they were all smoking like hell.

"People were just being so cool, it pissed me off. Like people would just go on saying, 'Far out,' forever and a day, and not recognize that there was any trouble. They were just so enthusiastic about having their own private guru—because by now, I was going in for healing people, and I really did, by putting my hands on their heads—but I really didn't want the job. I remember, Joe was going 'far out, far out, far out,' and what I finally did is, I jacked off his dog. And that really shook him up. It was just a funny illustration of everybody having his limit, and that would be it. Here I was, absolutely nuts by now, doing all these crazy things, but what finally ticked Joe off was my jacking off his dog. That was the unacceptable act. That was what made them say, 'Hey, there's something wrong here.'

"Well, I tried to go to sleep, but I couldn't get to sleep. And I kept hearing voices saying, 'Jonathan, Jonathan, Jonathan.' So I got up and went into the living room, and there was Dorothy in some sort of priestess robes, and her legs are spread, and her crotch is glowing Day-Glo orange. That's unnecessary. It's not like I don't realize what sex is—that the crotch is somehow involved—but why couldn't it be her fingers, or something like that? Anyway, her crotch is sort of Day-Glo orange, and then I see that the whole house is sort of Day-Glo orange. It was all very weird. And I was just standing there, and I said, 'What?' And she said, 'Jonathan.' She was talking in a voice that was much too low for her, and she was apparently brooding about the end of the world, and she said, 'Do we have time to move to higher ground?' I didn't know what to make of that, so I said, 'Higher ground is within.' Which seemed to satisfy everyone. They were happy with that. Then I went back to bed, and the next morning, when I woke up, it just seemed like a miracle, you know, because I looked out, and there was still some green outside, and it looked like things were all right. . . ."

These are, of course, simply some recollections of young people experimenting with powerful chemicals that they do not understand. The anthropologist Carlos Castaneda has demonstrated, in *The Teachings of don Juan* and its sequels, that a systematic approach to drug-induced visions can be more rewarding. The beginnings, though, are much the same. Castaneda starts by joining a group of Mexican Indians in chewing peyote buttons. "I felt a strong, pungent bitterness; in a moment my whole mouth was numb." In due time, he starts vomiting, "an effortless sensation . . . a pleasant flow of liquid words," and then he begins seeing visions. He imagines himself in a tunnel lined with "a wall of solid tinfoil." He sees a black dog become transparent, so that when it drinks some water, he can see the water "flowing evenly through his entire length and then shooting out through each one of the hairs. I saw the iridescent fluid traveling along the length of each individual hair and then projecting out of the hairs to form a long, white, silky mane." He joins the dog in drinking water, "and I too acquired a long, lustrous, iridescent mane. I looked at the dog, and his mane was like mine. A supreme happiness filled my whole body, and we ran together toward a sort of yellow warmth that came from some indefinite place. And there we played. . . ."

But what really happened? According to the Indians, to whom Castaneda diligently returned for further interviews, he had "puked about thirty times," and then had begun having convulsions. "You began to bump your head on the floor. . . . You shivered and whined for hours, lying on the floor. . . . I saw you leaping up in the air, screaming. . . . Suddenly you jumped up again, howling, and took off after the dog. The dog got scared. . . . I think you must have gone twenty times around the house, running in circles, barking like a dog. . . . You caught up with the dog and brought it to the porch in your arms. Then . . . you pissed all over my dog. . . . My dog got even, though; he pissed on you too."

Don Juan, the aged Indian sorcerer who has undertaken Castaneda's initiation, has a different view. "Goddammit! It was not a dog!" he says. It was, he insists, an incarnation of a figure he calls Mescalito, the spirit of mescal and peyote (perhaps the same spirit that young Jonathan once saw). Don Juan considers it a good sign that the spirit felt playful, so the long process of initiation continues. In the next volume, *A Separate Reality,* Castaneda is again aflame with peyote when he begins staring at a gnat and suddenly sees it turn into a monster.

> I thought, for some reason, that it must be close to a hundred feet tall. It seemed to be standing erect, although I could not figure out how it stood. . . . Its body was covered with tufts of black hair. It had a long muzzle and was drooling. Its eyes were bulgy and round, like two enormous white balls. Then it began to beat its wings. It was not the flapping motion of a bird's wings, but a kind of flickering vibratory tremor. . . . Its wings cut closer and closer to my eyes until they hit me. I felt that its wings had actually hit whatever part of me was there. I yelled with all my might in the midst of one of the most excruciating pains I have ever had. The next thing I knew I was seated on my mat and don Juan was rubbing my forehead. . . .

The goal of all this, according to don Juan, is to learn how to see the essence of things, to see, for example, that every man is composed of "fibers, like white cobwebs. Thus a man looks like an egg of circulating fibers. And his arms and legs are like luminous bristles, bursting out in all directions." When one can finally see, one can become a man of knowledge, and a warrior, capable of commanding all the forces of nature. One can move instantly from place to place, leap waterfalls, converse with ani-

mals. Thus the charming scene in which Castaneda, having stated
the conventional view that each falling leaf is unique, has to sit
and watch while don Juan makes the same leaf fall, drifting
down on the same course, hitting the same branches, four times
in a row. "He explained that the leaf had fallen over and over
from that same tree so I would stop trying to understand. . . .
'There's nothing to understand. Understanding is only a very
small affair, so very small,' he said."

Peyote is not necessary for seeing and knowledge, according
to don Juan's fellow sorcerer, don Genaro. "People go really crazy
when they take that peyote stuff," says don Genaro. "I've seen
the Huichel Indians eating it. They acted as if they had rabies.
They frothed and puked and pissed all over the place. You could
get epilepsy from taking that confounded thing." But don Juan
insists that Mescalito serves as the best guide through the doors
of knowledge. "He teaches us the right way to live," don Juan
said. "He helps and protects those who know him."

There have been some suggestions recently that this vener-
able Indian sorcerer does not actually exist, and that Castaneda's
substantial gifts as an anthropologist are exceeded by his gifts
as a novelist. Castaneda almost acknowledges the accusation
when, in the fourth volume of the series, he quotes don Juan as
saying that he is actually his own double, and then laughing, and
adding that he was joking. Whatever his provenance, though,
don Juan has acquired the reality of all great sorcerers, of Merlin
and Klingsor, and only he (or his double) could have described
a giant gnat as "the sentry of the other world."

Heroin is considerably less exalted, according to William
Burroughs' *Naked Lunch*, but more necessary. "I tied up for a
shot, my hands trembling with eagerness, an archetype dope
fiend," says a quasi-autobiographical narrator. "'Just an old
junky, boys, a harmless old shaking wreck of a junky.' That's the
way I put it down. As I had hoped [Narcotics Policeman] Hauser
looked away when I started probing for a vein. It's a wildly un-
pretty spectacle. . . . A column of blood shot up into the syringe
for an instant sharp and solid as a red cord. I pressed the plunger
down with my thumb, feeling the junk pound through my veins
to feed a million junk-hungry cells, to bring strength and alert-
ness to every nerve and muscle."

And cocaine: "When you shoot coke in the mainline there is a rush of pure pleasure to the head. . . . Ten minutes later you want another shot. . . . The pleasure of morphine is in the viscera. . . . You listen down into yourself after a shot. . . . But intravenous C is electricity through the brain. . . . It is a need of the brain alone—a need without body and without feeling. Earthbound ghost need. . . ."

William S. Burroughs, Harvard A.B., 1936, now past sixty, an eminently respectable-looking gentleman with thinning gray hair, very pale skin, and a rather nasal voice, was for much of his life the classic addict, willing to submit to any degradation and apparently able to pay for it. At what he calls "the end of the junk line," he was living in one room in the so-called native quarter of Tangier.

"I had not taken a bath in a year nor changed my clothes or removed them except to stick a needle every hour in the fibrous gray wooden flesh of terminal addiction. I never cleaned or dusted the room. Empty ampule boxes and garbage piled to the ceiling. Light and water long since turned off for non-payment. I did absolutely nothing. I could look at the end of my shoe for eight hours. I was only roused to action when the hourglass of junk ran out. If a friend came to visit—and they rarely did since who or what was left to visit—I sat there not caring that he had entered my field of vision—a gray screen always blanker and fainter. . . . If he had died on the spot I would have sat there looking at my shoe waiting to go through his pockets. Wouldn't you? Because I never had enough junk—no one ever does."

Burroughs took, over the course of twenty years, almost every drug he could find, from heroin to nutmeg, and by every method from smoking to suppositories. His own list includes: morphine, Dilaudid, pantopon, eukodol, paracodine, dionine, codein, Demerol, methadone. He also took ten separate "cures," which involved treatment with, among other things, Thorazine, Tolserol, barbiturates, Chloral and Paraldehyde, antihistamines, cortisone, and reserpine. He argues, against considerable evidence, that there is no such thing as "a psychotic morphine addict, I mean anyone who showed psychotic symptoms while addicted to an opiate. In fact addicts are drearily sane." On the other hand, he believes that withdrawal causes an onset of paranoia. "Everything looks threatening. . . . The doctors and nurses appear as monsters of evil." Burroughs himself finally found his own cure, fifteen years ago, through apomorphine treatment in London.

Out of his years in hell, Burroughs finally wrote his repellent novel *Naked Lunch*, which is really not a novel so much as a series of fantasies and hallucinations. "This book spill off the page in all directions, kaleidoscope of vistas, medley of tunes and street noises, farts and riot yipes, and the slamming steel shutters of commerce. . . ." Some of these fantasies apparently were induced by drugs, but most of them rise like smoke from the pits of Burroughs' tormented personality—scenes of homosexual orgies, of coprophilia and cannibalism. Certain symbols of destruction keep recurring—the sadistic doctor, the huge and ravenous insect, the heap of rotting ordure. There is more than a hint of the influence of Sade, but without Sade's passion to justify and explain. Thus, two ephemeral characters named Mark and Mary, having both had sex with Johnny, join in hanging him.

> Johnny's cock springs up and Mary guides it up her cunt, writhing against him in a fluid belly dance, groaning and shrieking with delight. . . . Sweat pours down her body, hair hangs over her face in wet strands. "Cut him down, Mark," she screams. Mark reaches over with a snap knife and cuts the rope, catching Johnny as he falls, easing him onto his back with Mary still impaled and writhing. . . . She bites away Johnny's lips and nose and sucks out his eyes with a pop. . . . She tears off great hunks of cheek. . . . Now she lunches on his prick . . . her face covered with blood, eyes phosphorescent.

Such prose tends to arouse the somnolent dogs of censorship—even today, in Long Island, some librarians keep the celebrated work on special shelves out of public view—and a hopeful prosecutor in Massachusetts undertook to suppress it as obscene. This, in turn, aroused the literary establishment to a mighty chorus of praise. Terry Southern called *Naked Lunch* "an absolutely devastating ridicule of all that is false, primitive and vicious in American life." John Ciardi proclaimed Burroughs "a writer of great power and artistic integrity engaged in a profoundly meaningful search for true values." Allen Ginsberg testified that the book was "an enormous breakthrough into truthful expression." Norman Mailer saluted Burroughs as "the only American novelist living today who may conceivably be possessed of genius." The Supreme Court of Massachusetts finally washed its hands of the matter, in the summer of 1966, by declaring the novel to be "grossly offensive" but protected by the First Amendment.

Perhaps nobody was more a victim of the drug culture—or more its creation—than the "sick" comedian Lenny Bruce. Like Burroughs, he would try anything—heroin, Methedrine, Percodan, Dilaudid, morphine suppositories. He described the results by saying, "It's like a sunflower opening in my stomach." Or again, "It's like kissing God." For this, he endured all the squalor of the addict's life, the late-night searches for a connection, the bloody syringes, the vomiting, the scar tissue forming on collapsed veins. But the squalor was part of the addiction.

"All the pain and ritual and scrambling for drugs was paying dues for the fact that the drugs were the one time he could get away from it all," according to one friend's recollection. "An example: There are two main arm veins. One doesn't hurt a bit and the other hurts like a bitch. The big one going up the inside of your arm is the easiest to see and the one where the doctor usually hits you. There's another one on the top side that doesn't hurt at all. In the one vein, if you miss, you get a terrible burn. In the other, even if you spill, there's hardly any burn at all. I used to say to him, 'Hell, why don't you shoot up *that* vein?' The answer was, 'I don't know. I always go here.' What he really meant was, 'I go here because it hurts more here than anywhere else.' . . . To me, the same masochism was behind the fact that he was always such an easy touch. He was always worried about money because when you're a junkie there's never enough money and never enough pills. . . . Once he copped a huge bottle of over a thousand pills. That should have lasted him a long time. No, he gave most of them away—because he liked the feeling of panic, having to scramble. That's paying dues. Good Jewish dues."

Of all the squalors of drug addiction, none is more squalid than the addict's inevitable involvement with the narcotics police. The first time that Bruce was arrested in Los Angeles and found to have needle marks up and down both arms, the police went through the usual rituals. They had caught him because they had been tipped off by someone they had arrested the previous day. Then they made the customary offer. They would be lenient if he would cooperate—in short, betray his connections. So he did, not once but many times. His secret betrayals even became a kind of obsession. He would telephone the police late at night to provide them with his latest jokes, gossip, chatter and tips. He even sent them valentines, laboriously scissored out of magazines and Scotch-taped to pieces of paper. But the narcotics police, like the narcotics addicts, are insatiable. Bruce's next arrest came in Philadelphia, where his hotel room was full of drugs (Methedrine, Dilaudid, Tuinal and Dolophine) prescribed by a friendly doctor. The police, tipped off, ignored the prescriptions and demanded that Bruce come to police headquarters. When he refused, they strapped him onto a stretcher and even stood the stretcher on end, with Bruce head down, for the elevator ride to the street. Bruce got a well-recommended lawyer, and the lawyer informed him, according to Bruce's subsequent statements, that it would cost him $10,000 to pay off the judge and the various authorities in charge of the case. Bruce responded by publicly denouncing the fix, and the charges were eventually dropped.

Bruce was not then crazy. That was to come later, when he immured himself within his mansion atop the Hollywood hills and spent all his days poring over his legal texts and the transcripts of his various trials for obscenity. But the signs were already becoming clear. Once, for example, he tore off his shirt and blew his nose in it. On another occasion, he went to a dinner party, urinated on the floor in front of the assembled guests, and then departed. Even in his legal battles, he was often irrational. At his first obscenity trial in San Francisco, he wrote an incoherent letter to the presiding judge, which began: "The monstrous rumor Judge Horn feels the defendant takes the matter lightly motivates this letter. Odious is the matter, my arrest for obscenity has enfilmed my career with a leperous stigma that St. Francis could not kiss away at ethereal peak. . . ." The judge promptly found Bruce guilty of contempt of court.

Bruce's increasing madness lends itself to many interpretations. In his own view, and in that of his admirers, he was the victim of bourgeois morality and political repression. There is considerable truth in this, for he was harassed in one city after another by pietistic prosecutors and ignorant police (no one in his audiences ever filed a complaint against him), and his madness took the understandable form of trying to acquire a mastery of his own legal defenses. Besides, although his act regularly contained elements generally considered to be obscene—the words "cocksucker" and "motherfucker" being those most frequently cited—the courts have consistently held that such elements cannot be grounds for prosecution if they are incidental to a "redeeming social purpose." And there never was a pornographer more obsessed with redeeming social purpose than Lenny Bruce. "I'm not sick," he repeatedly said. "The world is sick and I'm the doctor. I'm a surgeon with a scalpel for false values."

Still, it is theoretically possible to act as a social satirist, or even a polemicist, without constantly using words like "cocksucker." Bruce was as much addicted to obscenity as to drugs. It gave him a fix, made him feel good, and he could not stop. He could not stop playing the role of the naughty little boy, and he could not stop wallowing in the punishment that his naughtiness would inevitably bring. The traditional psychiatric approach, therefore, would be to trace the origins of Bruce's madness to his unhappy childhood, to a self-destructive rebellion against his doting, middle-class suburban father, and against the mother who abandoned the home and refused to bring him up but never stopped babying him and flirting with him.

Drugs apparently provided an escape from all that, but drugs also poisoned him and maddened him. So we find him at three o'clock in the morning, shouting incoherently in a hotel room in San Francisco. He had been smoking marijuana soaked in a new hallucinogenic named D.M.T., and then he had injected Percodan into his biceps, and then he had injected straight D.M.T. into his arm. The noise awakened a black friend named Eric, who was staying down the hall. Eric found Bruce on his knees, sobbing hysterically and caressing a girl who was sitting on a chair. Eric tried to calm him down, but Bruce was berserk.

"Spit in my face," he commanded Eric.

"I don't wanna spit in your face," Eric protested.

"No, I want you to spit in my face."

"I don't wanna."

"*Spit in my face!*"

Eric finally shrugged and spat in Bruce's face. Bruce wiped the spit all over his face, then tore off all his clothes and climbed onto the window sill. Eric tried to get him to come down, but Bruce shouted, "No, no, no! They have to know! They have to know where it is. It's *out there!* I have to tell them . . . it's *out there!*" As he spoke, he was struggling to open the big French window. It suddenly flew open, and Bruce fell out. He plummeted twenty-five feet to the sidewalk and lay there with both ankles broken. When the police arrived, Bruce acted as though this were yet another arrest. "You motherfuckers!" he screamed at them. "You're all after me!"

The police got him into an ambulance and took him to San Francisco General, still screaming obscenities: "Cocksucker! Muff diver!" In the hospital emergency room, Bruce even stopped a nun and shouted at her, "I wanna suck a big fat nun's cunt!" A doctor finally silenced him by pasting adhesive tape across his mouth. They put both his ankles in casts, but things got worse. He began to smell putrid. The syringe he had injected into his biceps had broken there and caused an abscess. Gangrene set in. His upper arm swelled to monstrous size and then literally exploded. Two quarts of pus came pouring out. The wound would not close. Septicemia began. Bruce lay in a state of delirium for most of two weeks, his fever sometimes as high as 105, and it was a month before he emerged in a wheelchair, pale, fat, bearded, a wreck.

Only a few years before, he had been one of the most fashionable satirists in the country. He had never been particularly funny —"Let's have a big hand for the lovable Adolf Hitler" is a reasonably typical line—but he commanded five thousand dollars a week. He could fill Carnegie Hall. People like Kenneth Tynan wrote articles analyzing his improvisations. Now he hardly worked at all, and when he did, it was a moribund scene. He would appear in second-rate clubs, reading long excerpts from his trial records, adding expletives about the quality of justice. "I know that I've *had it* as an art form!" he said bitterly during a Los Angeles show in the spring of 1964. "Oh yeah, definitely! . . . You've been with me so long that my tits are sagging now. And that as much as I try to *gnavitch* things with makeup—we've been married too long! And the reason you resist that and deny it is that if that happens with me, then it's the truth with you too!"

He retreated to his hilltop castle, filled with his law books and his legal papers. There, if the police ever tried to raid him —they never did—they would find Lenny Bruce ready for them. He attached a variety of locks to all the windows, and he even installed a medieval oaken crossbar behind the front door. He built a brick wall along one side of the house, and then, fascinated by the bricklayers' talk about their work, he persuaded them to stay on a bit longer to build a brick stairway up to the side of the house, even though there was no door in the wall at the end of the steps. Aside from the fortifications, Bruce had the whole place wired to tape recorders so that every word the raiding police might utter would be preserved for the trials that would inevitably follow.

But they could still reach him. Four months before his death, he had to appear in Los Angeles Municipal Court to be sentenced on a heroin charge. Even though the case was over, he demanded the right to speak, then took out a sheaf of papers and began reading various legal arguments to the effect that his constitutional rights had been violated. The judge, who was prepared to be lenient, finally demanded that the recitation stop. "I certainly don't want your rights violated," he said, "but I say to you: You are utterly unreasonable." The judge then gave him a mild sentence of one year, suspended, and a fine of $260. Bruce, who had apparently taken both heroin and Methedrine before the hearing, was not to be pacified. With one of the characteristic literary allusions of the social satirist, he said, "I'm going to pursue this federal action and try to establish my civil rights. Violations of civil rights are questions of equity. It has nothing to do with mercy or charity. There are those who compare me with Kafka. But the difference is—he was in Russia, and there's no constitution there."

There was no saving him. He couldn't save himself. By now $40,000 in debt, he began talking of his own death, and of "after I'm gone"—this at the age of forty. He was fascinated by a book about the afterlife, in which an English lady told of receiving communications from the departed. He asked the various girls who were constantly drifting in and out of his castle to read it aloud to him. When the end came, though, he was alone. One of his friends returned from running an errand and found him face down on the floor in front of the unflushed toilet. He was naked expect for the blue jeans crumpled around his ankles. A syringe was still stuck in his right arm. The official verdict was that he had died of an accidental overdose of morphine. There was talk of possible suicide, and even wild speculation about murder, but the police preferred to consider the case closed. Except for one of them, who went to a local recording studio and sold the record-makers some photographs of Bruce's corpse for the jacket of some future album.

Out of a Case History
Henry Reichman
Contemplates His Fortunes

*Henry Reichman's name literally means "rich man,"
which is quite appropriate, because he does have a lot of
money. He is proud of the life it enables him to lead. "All
of this, the way I live . . ." he says, waving an arm toward
the red-brocade walls, the paintings, the flowers, the gray
stone fireplace in his duplex penthouse apartment, "all
comes from my work. I didn't inherit a penny. I didn't
win the Irish Sweepstakes. All came from creating new
ideas. . . ."*

*Henry Reichman is a tall, spare man in his early six-
ties. His gray hair is thinning, his complexion clear. He
wears rimless octagonal spectacles, a checked sports
jacket, a wide blue tie, brown slacks. He speaks slowly,
carefully, with a faint German accent, pausing occasionally
to sniff. He smokes a cigar in a short plastic holder. He is
affable, but he rarely smiles. He is sure of his story.*

I left Berlin in 1926, when I was nineteen, and I lived in Paris
for a while, and then in London. I came here in 1929 and got
a job as a packer in the basement of Best & Company, the department store. I didn't plan to stay here. I came to America to
get some training experience, learn the language, and then return. But when I went back to Germany in 1932, things looked
bad, and I was unhappy there, so I told my parents I wanted to
go back to America. I feel that America is still a place where
the opportunities are tremendous, if you keep your eyes and ears
open.

In 1934, in the middle of the Depression, I decided to go
into business for myself, and I never again had a job working
for somebody else. My first idea was to develop a cola syrup that
you could mix at home the way you mix Scotch. My idea was to

316

eliminate all those little bottles, just persuade the housewife to buy my syrup by the quart and then add some club soda herself. It was a terrible flop, because people are very lazy. But then I had the idea of selling this drink, in finished form, to Macy's, and that was very successful. Then I came up with a lot of other ideas in the food business. I bought the rights to the Wizard of Oz for food products. I came up with an instant ice-cream mix under the name of Oz—the wizard of ice-cream mix—and so on.

I have an extremely low opinion of most corporations. In a big corporation, the individual is nothing. I think they're mass murderers, with their retirement plans and their method of getting rid of people who have devoted their best years to the company—it's extremely cruel. I always had a tremendous drive, a feeling that I could accomplish things, much more, much better, if I were in business for myself. I'm perfectly willing to work for peanuts for myself, but I would be deeply unhappy working for a big salary for a big corporation, because I would always have the feeling that they're underpaying me. Besides, I'm a very independent person. If a big corporation would have hired me, I don't think I would have lasted a whole day. I would have annoyed so many people by being honest, in expressing my opinions. But when you're in business for yourself, you always hope that a miracle will happen some day, and then, when you are successful, you harvest everything. Whatever mistakes I have made in life, I couldn't be fired. I could suffer, but I couldn't be fired.

After about ten or twelve years, I was doing very well. I had a wife and a son—he's now a documentary film producer. I had a nice apartment on the East Side. I belonged to a country club. In 1948, I made a tremendous contract with a company which had a Triple-A rating, the highest rating you can get in business —and then they reneged. Another company, which they represented, told them they should drop me and my product because they were intending to come out with a similar product two years later. So one day I had to come home and tell my wife, "I've lost all my—we lost—I lost all my money and all your money. And as of Monday, you have to go back to work." And she did. And we moved out of our apartment, moved to a very bad section on the West Side, because the rent was only one fourth of what I'd paid before. Our social life among our so-called friends shrank to about one percent of what it had been before. And my business kept going down, down, down, to nothing.

One night, we were at a dinner party—to be exact, it was December 22, 1948—we were at a dinner party, and when the hostess asked us to get up and go to the adjoining room, I couldn't get up. I had no power in my legs. I had no power in my arms. And—uh—of course, I was quite embarrassed. I had to stay on at the dinner table, talking with my neighbor. I kept trying to get up. I had no idea what was happening to me, absolutely no idea. This lasted about twenty minutes. Finally, with tremendous will power, I forced myself to get up and go into the other room. I never sat down there because I was afraid I couldn't get up again. When we left, and went downstairs in the elevator, there was one step which we had to go down to reach the street level, and in going down that step, in shifting my weight, I collapsed. Literally fell down. And could not assist the other people who went down with me, in getting up. I was like a bag of flour. They finally lifted me, got me into a car, got me home. I still had no power in my arms and legs.

The day after I collapsed, I remember, we had planned a Christmas party, and it was too late to cancel it. I was in bed, and I couldn't get up, but the guests stayed until about midnight, and the uncertainty about what was wrong with me was a terrible feeling. There was a tremendous amount of panic. You could put a pin into my arms and legs and I wouldn't feel anything. My wife had called our doctor, who had called a neurologist, who had called another neurologist. I told them all that I had no money left to pay them. So my doctor, who was on the staff at Mount Sinai Hospital, recommended that I should go to the charity ward, which dealt with cases like mine. He said, "The neurologists who have examined you suspect that you have a brain tumor."

So I went to the charity ward of the hospital, which was a traumatic experience. There were forty-eight patients in one room. There were people with brain tumors, nervous breakdowns, suicide attempts, accidents. One young kid next to me, twenty-two years old, had a motorcycle accident, fractured skull, died right next to me. When you see people being removed, and you know they're going to die within the next few hours—I mean, they try to prevent that they die in the big room—all of that keeps you up at night, but it stops you from thinking so much about yourself. So I came to the conclusion that things were not so bad any more, and hadn't been so bad before.

They kept me there for seven weeks and took hundreds of tests. Then one morning, one Monday morning, the head of the ward, Dr. Israel Wechsler, came to my bed. He was one of the top neurologists. He charged tremendous fees in his office, but he devoted three days of the week to the charity ward. He said to me, "There's nothing wrong with you that a five-thousand-dollar order couldn't cure. You've had a severe nervous breakdown. I want to explain what happened to you. Your body gave up. Your muscles gave up. It was a defeat. But you're as healthy as any human being I've ever examined. Actually, you could get up and leave right now, but I'm going to keep you here for another day. Here's a pad and pencil. I want you to go from bed to bed in this ward and take down the names and addresses and telephone numbers of the other forty-seven people here. Ask them what's the matter with them—in most cases you probably know it by now anyhow. And when you feel depressed, call up two or three of them and find out how they are. Some of them will be dead, and you will find out that you're very well off. That will bring you back from your depression."

And I understood that. And I did that. I got out the next day. I didn't go to a psychiatrist. I couldn't afford that. And Dr. Wechsler didn't recommend to me that I go to a psychiatrist. I also didn't have any drugs. I went back to work in a little office. My rent was thirty-five dollars, including an answering service. No help, of course. There would be days when I would lock the door and pull down the shades and start crying. But when I left the office, I could handle myself much better. And every few weeks, for about a year, I would call up some of the people who had been on that ward. Some of them had died, some of them were dying, and very few of them could answer the phone themselves. I think I only talked with one person who answered the phone himself. It's probably a terrible statement to make, but after I found out somebody was so sick, I felt better. I could blame myself. I said, What the hell? You're home now. You have no pains. Your body is functioning beautifully. There's no reason to be depressed.

Looking back, I'm very happy and grateful that I couldn't afford to check into a private room in a hospital, with nurses around the clock, where I'd be looking at the walls all day. In a ward of forty-eight patients, I had to look at things in an entirely different manner. Money lost, nothing lost; courage lost, everything lost. I have gradually become an entirely different person, with a much better set of values. At home, after I got out of the hospital, I was never ashamed to tell my son that I had lost everything, that I was a complete failure at the present time, but that I was hoping to—that things would be better some day. And my wife never once reproached me during the time when my average income used to be about ten percent of hers, never once reproached me for being an unsuccessful person. While she may have told me that many of my so-called friends tried to encourage her to leave me, because they thought I was a hopeless case, she behaved wonderfully. Chances are that if she would have made a lot of tactless remarks, I would have just walked out. And then chances are I would never have made a comeback.

That comeback didn't come right away by any means. It took more than ten years of struggle. But then I had a new idea for the supermarkets. I realized that the trading stamps had lost their power because they were not exclusively confined to one company or one area. Everybody had trading stamps, so this gimmick was neutralized. So I decided it was time for a new gimmick, and I came up with the idea of games. The first one I created was Spell Cash—S-P-E-double-L Cash. Which was a little piece of paper, two inches by three inches, which had a rather sizable inkspot on it. You had to remove the inkspot and find a letter, either C or A or S or H, underneath the spot. If you could spell the word "cash," you would win a hundred dollars.

All my ideas for the past twenty years have something to do with relieving lonesomeness, or boredom. Lonesomeness and boredom are two tremendous sicknesses, especially in this country, and they have a lot to do with breakdowns. I have made a study of lonesomeness. I have a knowledge of it, and a *respect* for it. Now my idea was not an easy idea to sell. The supermarket business is a $120 billion business. It's terribly difficult for an individual to convince these guys to back a new idea. So for two years, I visited four hundred supermarket chains without making a single sale. Finally I got a little test in six stores of the leading chain in Chicago. In this business, the ordinary increases from week to week may run 2 or 3 or 4 percent. My game produced 30 percent, and the news spread very fast. You can't patent an idea like that, but when you're first, you have a tremendous advantage. By the time other people realized—discovered my goose which laid the golden eggs—I'd already made enough money to withdraw.

So the miracle finally happened when I was fifty-four years old, which is the time when, if I worked for a big corporation, they select the watch which I'm going to get when I'm being retired. I made a tremendous comeback. I also acquired this duplex penthouse, which was written up in the newspapers. And when I came back from a business trip to move in here, I found that many of my former so-called friends and acquaintances, who had dropped me when I was poor, had sent flowers. But I have always felt that you're a lot better off if you don't hide your emotions, so I took all the flowers and threw them out the window, over the cliff, and I've never seen any of those people again.

15

Time's Winged Chariot
Hurrying Near

Who was it who said that life is a terminal illness, of which the main symptom is aging and the only cure is death? Is it the work of some embittered poet or simply a subway graffito that lingers in the memory as one grows older?

Memory, in turn, is a symptom of aging. It is a symptom to remember the silvery voice of President Roosevelt proclaiming a day that would live in infamy, or the grace with which Ted Williams swung and Tommy Harmon ran, or even the humbler symbols of a past age: the clanging trolley car, the 78-R.P.M. Caruso records, white margarine that had to be kneaded with orange powder, and the iceman laboring through the kitchen door with a great fuming block of ice held by tongs over the black rubber mat on his shoulder. Yet the loss of memory is a symptom too. The names of old friends, addresses and telephone numbers, scraps of verse, even the name of the previous night's TV movie—they bob like waterlogged driftwood at the foggy edge of the mind's shoreline, and no angry curses, no snapping of the fingers, will bring them back against the ebbing tide.

The deterioration is inexorable. The hair turns gray and grows thin at the temples, the skin dries and wrinkles, the stomach thickens, the eyes dim. For all the whiskey and cigarettes of one's youth, for all the missed lunches and lost sleep, time takes its slow revenge through mysterious back pains and internal spasms and an evaporation of the energy of life. But the deterioration of the mind is the worst. It becomes increasingly hard to concentrate, to organize one's thoughts, to think at all. There is always the lulling temptation of television and another can of beer. And then, in the middle of the night, comes the anguish. The sense of futility, and the knowledge that death has come one day closer. It once was commonplace to stay up until four in the morning, talking of

Beethoven and God, but now, even in bed, sleep often gives way to panic, until dawn arrives with the raucous sounds of the crows ravaging the garbage cans.

At work, the process of deterioration, the decay of energy, is taken for granted. Woe to any man looking for a new job after the age of forty—he expects too much money for his experience, and the company's insurance actuaries suspect that he will make too many demands on the medical fund. On the other hand, if he remains huddled within the confines of his corporation, he can anticipate being shifted, in his fifties, to some second-rate post where he can drone through the years until his mandatory retirement into poverty. He cannot protest, for then he risks being dismissed, and the company will not pay his pension. He can only remember, with a shrug, how things once were. When I worked for the New York *Daily News,* in my middle-twenties, I used to grumble at the fact that I was the only editor under thirty-five, and that there was no possibility for promotion except when my white-haired superiors occasionally had heart attacks. Now that one of my daughters is working for the *New York Post,* it seems to me that the entire press has been taken over by children. When I was in college, I thought of the Nieman Fellows as a crew of amiable codgers, far too old to be working newspapermen, but when I myself decided to apply for a Nieman Fellowship, I was startled to learn that I was barred for having passed the dreaded age of forty.

A small thing, but discrimination consists of an accumulation of small things—as does rage. Or not rage—that is too strong a term. Irritation is a more middle-aged emotion. Annoyance Exasperation. Exasperation, for example, at the now-abolished "youth fares" that required one to stay home and work while one's children flew off to Europe at special discounts. Exasperation at the advertisements by magazines boasting how many of their readers are between the ages of eighteen and thirty-four. Exasperation, for that matter, at the whole world presented on television, in which the blacks who have finally won their place before the cameras all turn out to be young blacks, while just about every man over forty is portrayed as crusty old dad with pipe and cardigan, while jolly old mom in her white apron bakes pies in the kitchen.

Small things, again, but the discrimination is real. The largest
number of poor people in this country, black and white alike, are
the old—most of them forbidden by law to earn their own living.
And unlike the other discriminations that exist from birth, to be
accepted or rejected in childhood, the discrimination against age
comes on gradually, against everyone. Indeed, part of the process
of aging is to learn and understand that process of discrimination.
"They ain't a wk. passes when you wouldn't get touched on the
raw," as Ring Lardner wrote in "Symptoms of Being 35," "if they
was any raw left." The bedridden tuberculosis patient lived to be
forty-eight, and to wish, in vain, that he could die quickly by
passing a street fight and getting a stray bullet in the back.

Let us return for a few moments to the orange-and-yellow
entry ward of Bellevue Hospital in New York. Outside, the
weather is raw and wintry, but the hospital is so hot that a fan has
to be kept spinning. On the wall hangs the sign that says: "Friendliness is free. Give today." It is 8:30 A.M., time for the regular staff
conference. One doctor and nine subordinates—nurses, social
workers, nurses' aides—gather around a shiny wooden table,
drinking coffee from paper cups. The staff gathers every morning
to interview and discuss new arrivals, a meeting that the doctor
describes as "mainly for teaching." A large Puerto Rican nurse in
a bright-red jacket consults her clipboard and reads out the symptoms of the first patient. She had walked up to the hospital gates
the night before and said she couldn't sleep. She has been here
three or four times, always in the early morning, always complaining that she can't sleep.

"Insomnia is a very funny bit," the doctor remarks. "The
hardest thing with insomnia is to convince the patient that he'll
survive. They can't sleep, they get panicky. Often, the taking of
a pill has a primarily psychological effect. Also, sleep can be very
irregular. When I went to medical school, the other kids often
slept only three hours a night and spent the rest of the time
working. I had to work in a lab until two in the morning, and
then I'd go out on a date—"

"Who'd want to go out on a date at two in the morning?" a
young black nurse wonders.

"There are always nuts around," the doctor retorts. "But this woman's insomnia was probably a symptom of depression."

"She was diagnosed as schizophrenic, in an acute state," the Puerto Rican nurse corrects him, reading from her clipboard.

"She was tearful," says another nurse, who apparently had observed her previously.

"Cheerful?" asks a third nurse, puzzled.

"No, tearful."

Suddenly the woman herself shuffles in, a Mexican, wearing a spotted brown-and-gray house dress and some worn sandals. She is short and stocky, with square, simple features and deeply mournful eyes. She is forty-four. Her name is on a plastic tag around her wrist. She smokes a cigarette, listlessly. She speaks very slowly, probably still under the effect of her sleeping pills. The doctor is kindly and solicitous as he questions her, much more kindly than the dialogue might indicate.

DOCTOR: How are you feeling?

MRS. X.: I don't feel well.

DOCTOR: What's the matter?

MRS. X: I feel shy. I feel nervous. I can't sleep.

DOCTOR: What do you mean, you feel shy? Do you feel shy at home? Outdoors?

MRS. X: Sometimes at home. Sometimes in the street.

DOCTOR: Do you mean you feel as though people were looking at you?

MRS. X: No.

DOCTOR: When you say you feel shy, what is it like? How does it feel?

MRS. X: Sometimes I'm confused. Sometimes I feel sad.

DOCTOR: Do you have a reason to feel sad?

MRS. X: My kids don't live with me any more.

DOCTOR: Where are they?

MRS. X: In New Jersey.

DOCTOR: Why are they there?

MRS. X: They're married.

DOCTOR: When did you last see them?

MRS. X: I haven't seen them for six months.

DOCTOR: Where is your husband?

MRS. X: We got divorced.

DOCTOR: When was that?

MRS. X: Long ago.

DOCTOR: Why did you get divorced?

MRS. X: We couldn't live together.

DOCTOR: Was that your idea or his?

MRS. X: My idea.

DOCTOR: What has happened to him since the divorce?

MRS. X: I don't know.

DOCTOR: Have you ever worked at a regular job?

MRS. X: I worked in assembly, putting things together.

DOCTOR: What do you do now?

MRS. X: I do my housework.

DOCTOR: Who lives with you?

MRS. X: I live alone.

DOCTOR: When you're sad, what do you think about? Do you think about the past?

MRS. X: Yes.

DOCTOR: Do you think about mistakes you made in the past?

MRS. X: No.

DOCTOR: Do you think about things you want to do over again?

MRS. X: No.

DOCTOR: Why do you come to the hospital?

MRS. X: I'm afraid to stay home.

DOCTOR: Why is the hospital better than home?

MRS. X: I don't know.

When Mrs. X shuffles away again, the doctor asks his assistants what they have learned about her. A young blonde in a ponytail replies like a college girl at some seminar. "There's a vague, empty quality about her," she says. "But what have you learned from what she said?" the doctor asks. The Puerto Rican nurse is more practical. "Nothing," she says, "and I've talked to her before."

"Right!" the doctor says. "She can't tell us what her trouble is. She probably doesn't know. She says she's 'shy,' but what does that mean? Where's the snap in her? The sense of life? She's frightened but vague. I'd bet she started getting depressed *before* the family broke up. But if she were not depressed, could she explain? I don't think so. She doesn't really have much to do, only a limited amount of movement. Being here brings certain social advantages. There are people around, activity, so she can have a sense of dependency. . . ."

In a matter of snap judgments, even the layman may take part. My own guess is that Mrs. X is not schizophrenic at all, and not abnormally depressed either. She is depressed for good and sufficient reason. Her husband has disappeared, her children have grown up and left her. She lives alone. She has no regular work, and no prospect of it. She feels herself to be ignored, help-less, and useless, and she is right. She is, in short, middle-aged.

For many middle-aged women, the voice of doom sounds in the announcement of the doctor declaring the need for a mas-tectomy. That was what happened to a woman I shall have to call Eleanor. She is a statistician in the New York Health Services Department, a neat, rather stylish brunette in a sleeveless white dress with a red belt and a red-white-and-blue scarf. She is now fifty-three. To her, the doctor's announcement sounded especially disastrous because she thought she had just created a new life for herself. She was a little bored with her husband and her four children, and so when the youngest son started school, about ten years ago, she went out and got herself a job.

"It was really not an interesting job," she recalls, "a low-level research assistant with an economic research organization, and sometimes I would fall asleep copying columns of numbers—but I was thrilled. I was just ecstatic. I thought it was so exciting to be working. I had been active in community organizations, the League of Women Voters and things like that, which allows you a great deal of ego gratification, because people think you're important, and you make speeches, and your name gets in the paper, but you're always aware that, really, it's not for real. People look at you patronizingly, because *they're* making *money*. So going back to work and making money was very thrilling. And to my great surprise, I noticed that men were paying attention to me. They were not very attractive to me, and they didn't mean anything, but the thought that somebody might be flirting with me was astounding. And amusing. I can remember taking showers and being conscious of my body in a way that I hadn't been for years.

"Up until this time, I had always thought of myself as a mother, a mother and a wife, and I would identify myself that way. But I really think that middle age is like adolescence. There's a whole new way of looking at yourself, and a self-consciousness of it, and a—I think an awakening of sexual desire. That's why I say the mastectomy was such a *shock* to me. I had the operation just three months after I started work. I adjusted to it very well, people thought, and I went on with my work and my living. But I was ashamed. I'm still ashamed. I have no pride. That's something that's gone, because I know the *truth*. And if men flirt now, it's a joke. I don't think of it at all. I just think, Well, I've done my hair nicely. . . . It's not titillating."

After the operation, Eleanor became convinced that she would soon die. Her sister had died of breast cancer, and she knew of nobody who had recovered from the disease. The sense of impending death changed a lot of her plans. When she saw that her career in economic research would not get far unless she won a Ph.D., she decided that there was no point in undertaking graduate studies, since she would not live to benefit from them. On the other hand, when her dentist recommended some elaborate "reconstruction work" on her teeth, she was pleased to decide that her death would make the expense unnecessary. She discussed none of these problems with her husband, because "he would have thought it would be more *healthful* to plan for the future," and she didn't really want anything "healthful." The prospect of death filled her with dread, but it also provided her with a kind of rescue from all the mundane problems that had oppressed her for twenty years.

"I would kind of break down from time to time," she remembers. "Mostly my depression was that I felt I was put upon—that as long as I had only a few more months or a few more years, how could people demand the same things of me that they always had? And I was resentful of that, particularly to my children. They kept demanding all the usual attentions, all the usual self-sacrifice. Sometimes, I just didn't come home from work—I went to the movies. I think it was to penalize them. I knew that they would be frantic, which they were. I didn't really want that. I just wanted them to get off my back. I wanted them to let me alone. But I kept having all kinds of problems with the children. When

I discovered that my daughter—then eighteen or nineteen, in college—was having an affair with someone, I was just thunder-struck, and terribly, terribly disappointed. I really thought that she was cheap, and stupid, and I was very sorry about it. And when I became aware that my sons were smoking marijuana, I couldn't deal with that at all. Particularly the younger one. I thought that if *he* had succumbed, then there was no hope for anybody."

Throughout all these difficulties, Eleanor kept looking to her cancer to save her.

"It wasn't a reality; it was like—it was like my *hope*. I began to nurture it. If I became frightened or something, if I didn't like what was happening in my life, I thought, Okay, I'll be out of this soon. The doctors had told me that if I didn't have a recurrence within five years, I could be considered cured. And as the time approached, the doctors would say, 'Well, that's fine, wonderful, you're marvelous.' But I began to be disappointed and resentful. I began to search for more and more symptoms that I would be taken out of this. Because there were other problems. My sex life was not satisfactory, but I couldn't think the way I had thought when I was younger—just in fantasy—of another man, either an affair or maybe another marriage. That was absolutely foreclosed, and still is. And then in my work, I had taken another job that paid a lot more money, but it turned out to be not very satisfying. My superior was very difficult to get along with. So when the five years were over, and I had a clean bill of health, I realized that I had been nurturing my illness as an escape. And I also realized that there was nothing valuable about life, nothing attractive. I had no hopes."

At that point, early in 1969, Eleanor began planning her suicide. She began, as one always does, by considering the various methods. Which would be the least painful, and in what condition would the body be discovered? She began collecting sleeping pills and hiding them in her bedroom dresser drawer, but she finally decided that such a death would make her family feel guilty, and she didn't want that. Instead, she decided to stage a traffic accident.

"So I began to practice walking in front of trucks. On the way to work, or coming home from work, I started inching up.

The first time I tried it, I stopped *well* before the truck came close. Then I started going a little bit farther. One time, I fell down in front of a truck, and the driver felt very pleased with himself that he had been so skillful in avoiding me. Sometimes, the drivers shouted at me, but they always managed to stop. The time that I thought, I'm *really* ready, I was *very* close when the truck stopped, but I came out of it, walked away, totally unshaken. All I thought was, Well, I'm not a phony; I really mean it, and I can do it, but not today. I was very interested in all this, by the way—it was on my mind all the time, for months and months—but it was as though it were happening to somebody else. I always thought of it as practicing, trying to see how you *do* it. But the rest of the time, I was getting through the days. I was keeping myself very busy, was always very busy, and seemingly cheerful. My husband must have known that I was depressed—the doctor had told him I would be depressed after the mastectomy—and he wanted me to see a psychiatrist. But I didn't want to get better; I wanted to get *out* of it. I went up to those trucks perhaps nine or ten times in all. I don't remember."

The process of salvation is often mysterious. Eleanor looked for rescue first through cancer, and then through suicide, but it finally came simply through her being fired. The research organization that she worked for needed various foundation grants that failed to materialize, and so there were staff cuts. Eleanor's patterns of self-destruction were broken, just as they might have been broken by electric shocks. She no longer had a job in downtown New York, and so she no longer commuted through the great canyons of truck traffic. She could, of course, have jumped in front of a Long Island bakery wagon, but that would have been an entirely different act, requiring a different spirit. In any case, she stayed home, and vacuumed the rugs, and found relaxation in boredom. And as time passed, some of the conditions of her madness changed by themselves. Her daughter ended her affair; her older son first found a girl friend and then married her. And Eleanor accepted all these changes as her destiny.

"I finally got a new job that January, 1971," she says. "It wasn't a terribly stimulating job, but it was very sheltered, and they thought I was very good, and that's helpful. But I didn't have any great hopes any more. You know, gone were the ambitions that I had had, or any of the hopes that I had had for the children. Now it looked like they were not ever going to *be* anything. And I feel sorry that I don't have the old dreams. I find it hard to go on without a belief that something marvelous is going to happen. But at least I'm no longer as frightened as I used to be, that the next phone call I get is going to be where somebody's in jail. I mean, I don't think that good things are going to happen any more; but I don't think so much about bad things. Just ordinary things—*that* will be okay. I think that, really, the general picture for most middle-aged women—and maybe the men too, but I haven't been that confidential with them—is a closing-down of their ambitions and their dreams. A recognition that this is the *end*. They have to face that, and they find it joyless.

"The other day, I was crossing a street, and I was daydreaming, and I almost walked in front of a truck full of furniture. And it *was* an accident. The driver had to stop so suddenly —it was one of those open-door trucks—that a chair fell out onto the street. The driver was very angry. He had to get out and put the chair back into the truck. I apologized to him, but I didn't really feel sorry. What I thought was: Why weren't you here when I needed you?"

The crisis of a woman in middle age has traditionally been a crisis of abandonment—real or imaginary—her husband dies or divorces her, and her children grow up, and she is left with a sense of uselessness. A man has many of these difficulties too, but his greatest problem is his increasing incapacity for work, or increasing doubt about the value of his work, or perhaps simply his employers' increasing unwillingness to let him do his work at all. If he is not fired, he is told—no, he is not told; the middle-aged man is never actually told much of anything—he is made to feel, to realize, that he no longer has any future. No more promotions, no more merit raises, nothing but those jocular greetings to good old Charley. The first time you have to start working for a younger man marks a kind of turning point, usually at about forty, and it is a point from which there is no return.

Percy Knauth, a veteran foreign correspondent for *Life,* wrote a rather unusual article for the magazine in 1972, entitled "A Season in Hell."

"As I awoke on an April morning a year ago, in this little

attic room in New York City, it hit me," he began. "I had been living in this world for nearly fifty-seven years, and at this moment I wanted above everything else to get out of it. Quietly, peacefully, if possible painlessly, with no fuss to anyone. The world, I was sure, had no further use for me and I had nothing to offer it. My life lay like a broken ruin around me, bits and pieces of remembered experiences which flashed into focus and out again; I could not concentrate on anything long enough to make any coherence out of it. The only consistent thought in my mind was a nonsensical word which had somehow floated to the top of my consciousness from my research of yesterday: 'tubulidentata,' the family of the aardvark. But was it 'tubulidentata' or 'tubulidentadidae'? I worried at it endlessly, while outside the rain dripped down. . . ."

Knauth's wife got him to a doctor, but he was already deeply immersed in his depression. "In that doctor's office, at first, I could only weep helplessly every time I tried to begin my story." The doctor gave him some antidepressant pills, but he warned that it would take about two weeks for them to have an effect.

"Perhaps the worst thing about depression," Knauth continued, "is the way it paralyzes the man in a man. The smallest decision, for example, absolutely floored me; I could not make up my mind about anything. Every morning I lay helpless, endlessly debating the pros and cons of arising. . . . Sexually I was impotent. I lay awake nights thinking desperately, never again, never again, while my wife breathed quietly beside me. The thought haunted me; it made me feel old. Age became an obsession with me. Was a man finished at fifty-seven? . . . The thoughts of suicide were never far away. They would come sweet and calming. The sleeping pills were at my arm, hidden behind a pile of books. And there were other means, perhaps less painful for my wife and family. Driving, it would be easy to have an accident, I could simply go out too far and let myself sink. But I could never make up my mind. Perhaps it was that deadly paralysis of the mind which saved me."

Knauth provided a vivid description of his breakdown, but he wrote only briefly about the background of the crisis. He spoke of "the horror of being alone in the world without a job, without a monthly salary, dependent entirely upon my wits to keep myself and my family going." And again:

"After a quarter of a century as a foreign correspondent, war correspondent, writer and editor, rising steadily in my profession, there had come four futile years of trying to set up a new international publishing venture for my company in Europe. . . . I was the wrong man in the wrong place at the wrong time. Couldn't this happen to anyone, at any time, in business?"

Yes, undoubtedly, but what had really happened? I decided to go to Knauth's seaside home in Connecticut and ask him. He turned out to be a very amiable, soft-spoken man with horn-rimmed spectacles and graying hair combed straight back. His doorway is watched by a snappish terrier named Mathilda, and his living room by a large tank of gleaming tropical fish. In his attic study, there is a panoramic poster of the Paris skyline, the Eiffel Tower and all that, souvenirs of days gone by.

"I had four extremely difficult years in Europe," says Knauth. "I went over there to be editor of something called the International Book Society, which was a book club—it was really a way of marketing big coffee-table books, expensive books, on a subscription basis. But almost as soon as I got there, the Time-Life book division began retreating from the whole project. In fact, they wanted me to come home in the first year that I was there, and I didn't want to, because, you know, you don't go uprooting your family, and renting your apartment and all that just to go to Europe for six months. And besides, I had a lot of what I thought were very good reasons to stay over there. I mean, this business of working together with European publishers could be a very exciting, and I think profitable thing. But it was just one frustration after another. Every time I got something cranked up to go, it was turned off at the last minute by the home office. I think they simply weren't ready to go into anything of that kind at all.

"This was very depressing—I mean, depressing in the normal use of the term. And I began to have trouble sleeping. And for nine months straight, without missing a single night, I took every night a Nembutal and two Miltowns—what my wife laughingly called a sandwich—to help me sleep. Now if you do that every night for nine months, that all by itself begins to set up chemical imbalances. When I finally got back here and saw my own doctor, he was absolutely horrified. Nembutal and Miltown are both depressants, and they're both habit-forming, and he made me stop instantly, right then and there. The result was one of the weirdest periods I can remember. I started dreaming, and I hadn't dreamed for a year. I was always out like a light. But now I dreamed the most exciting, detailed, technicolor dreams I've ever had. It really felt as though everything I had not dreamed for this long period of time was surfacing. And I think it probably *was* something like that.

"Anyway, I came back here at a time when there was a very extended cutting-down all through the company. It was in 1970. There had been a disastrous stock slide, and every division had been asked to cut its staff by fifteen percent. The only one that didn't was *Sports Illustrated,* because André Laguerre, the managing editor, refused to do it. He said, 'We're making money, and I'm not going to cut down on my staff.' So they really didn't have anything much for me to do here. I was a senior editor, and I suppose that if I'd hung around, I might have got another series to work on for the book division. But I really wanted to get out, because I was kind of fed up with the whole scene at that point. So I sort of negotiated a withdrawal from the company, completely.

"It was very scary. I was fifty-six years old, and I had never, except for one period, at the time of my divorce from my first wife—I'd never been without a pay check. And sometimes I had the cold sweats thinking about the bills to be paid. But I figured it was worth a good try. Besides, I had already negotiated a deal with another company to produce a twenty-volume illustrated encyclopedia of the animal world. It seemed like a perfectly straight-forward job, of the kind I'd been doing for eight years with the book division. As I got deeper and deeper into it, though, I found out more and more depressing things about it. The time span, to begin with, was very bad news. There was only a period of seven months allotted for the whole thing. And then I assumed that the material was all there. Well, it wasn't all there. It was supposed to be translated from an Italian publication, but a lot of the translation hadn't been done, and we didn't even have all the pictures. It was an awful job. It was a perfectly frightful job. There was nothing to do about it except to keep going and keep going and keep going. And during this whole time, I was fighting this goddam depression."

It was a fight that reached its climax on that morning in his New York apartment. Even after he got out of bed, he was helpless.

"I sat in a chair," he recalls, "and I heard the door to the apartment open, and a measured tread coming down the hallway, and all of a sudden, I knew that this was my son, one of the older boys, who was coming back from Vietnam—and I couldn't do a goddam thing about it. I sat there in my chair, feeling about a hundred and five years old, and trembling like a leaf. He came into the room, and he suddenly got scared as hell. It was just that I was totally unable to function. One of the worst aspects of depressions is this sense of worthlessness, which you get to an agonizing degree. Depression is a gradual deterioration of all the faculties with which people cope with their lives. And it's an involuted thing. It feeds on itself."

Just as Knauth's illness may have been started by the drugs that he took to get to sleep after the frustrations of a day at the office, so he found his cure mainly in drugs. A series of medicines, introduced in the middle 1950's as a treatment for tuberculosis, had been found to produce, as a side-effect, a sense of euphoria. "The mechanism of this cure is still not fully recognized," Knauth wrote later. "It takes place deep within the brain, in an area which research scientists are still busily exploring. What they do know is that at the point where impulses from the brain cells meet the receptors in the cerebral cortex, a chemical interchange takes place, and this interchange appears to be affected by the anti-depressant drugs. In depressed patients, they increase the catecholamines, the chemicals which work in the critical receptor areas. . . . Instead of lying in helpless agony, I found myself able to make plans, to project my work, to derive enjoyment from the prospect of a movie. . . . I took pleasure in the company of my wife and my children. I re-established my relationships with a world to which I had said goodbye. I began to *live* again."

There was to be no such commutation of sentence for another aging foreign correspondent, Christopher Rand. On September

26, 1968, while covering the preparations for the Olympic Games for *The New Yorker,* he fell to his death from the window of his room at the Hotel Geneva in Mexico City. He was then fifty-six. *The New York Times* obituary noted that in his wanderings, he had "befriended guerrillas in Afghanistan and lived with lepers in the Belgian Congo," and that during his Buddhist period, while covering the Korean War for the *New York Herald Tribune,* he not only ate no meat or eggs but "flew in unheated aircraft, wearing light clothing, because he would not touch leather or wear a leather jacket," and that, finally, he "had been suffering from depression and earlier attempted suicide, in Lima, Peru, by slashing his wrists."

"I went down to Peru and brought him back," Dick Rand recalls. "And in a kind of reversal of roles, I decided to get him into shape. I got him into a hospital in New York, totally against his will, first at Gracie Square and then at Bloomingdale's, out in Westchester. He went along with it, but it was perfectly clear that he was just killing time, waiting to get out. Dad had long had a disposition toward paranoia, which is a special outlook on life. How it arises, I don't know. But he'd had it for a long time, certainly back in his teens and twenties. And he'd more or less coped with it, in certain ways. The main way he coped with it was to get out of a place, when he thought he was in trouble. Still, he kept functioning pretty well, as well as you can under that kind of stress, and with five kids to support.

"He brought home the bread, and he did it in his own way. I think that when we all more or less graduated from college— college was considered the cut-off point—I think he sort of stopped fighting. He got very, very depressed. He got wildly, much more alcoholic than he had ever been. And he really lost focus. That is to say, he could do the work, and the work kept a certain amount of its integrity, but he himself went into a kind of —decline. He lost fight. And he really said, 'I don't care any more.' At one point well before he finally flipped out, he said, 'I've done my job. I don't care if I die now.'

"At that point, the seizures, the paranoid visitations became really very, very terrible. He never let me into his system, so I don't know how it worked, but he felt that the enemy was moving in, and he just couldn't fight it. Whatever defenses he had had against the enemy were no longer working. And I guess that's when suicide became the only way out. Because after all, what he was experiencing was something that I recognize—and epileptics talk about this also—and that is the anticipation of the breakdown. What he was trying to say was: 'I'm about to go crazy, I'm about to lose total control.' Now for him, that was a terrifying thing. He was a very lonely man, and he didn't have any people that he trusted.

"When he got out of the hospital—I remember when I saw him last. We had lunch in that place on 44th Street, just down from *The New Yorker*, the one that makes soufflés. La Bourgogne. It was a very strained, difficult lunch. He was about to go to Mexico. And I remember feeling that I'd never see him again alive. I remember feeling that this was a gesture of defiance on his part, because he knew that if he went to a place like Mexico, he couldn't cut it. And yet he just went. He was totally preoccupied, focused on this thing he had to do. And there was a wild panic in him. I knew it was panic. And there was nothing I could do to ease the panic. There isn't much you can do under the circumstances, because the other party isn't willing to recognize what's happening. He was on the lam again. He was always on the lam, but it wasn't working any more.

"But let's not dwell too much on the pathos of the situation. I had been trying a long time to get him to mend his ways, which children should never try to do. Fathers never mend their ways, and children are the last people to mend them. I was feeling rather peeved at my failure. Let's also say that he'd been extremely difficult during the whole experience. So I wasn't feeling very magnanimous, or very—I was just exasperated. But I also knew that this was the end. He was panicked, and I felt, you know—goddammit, why don't you just—why don't you just admit that you're terrified and do something about the terror rather than go off and kill yourself? But he wasn't able to, or willing to. I miss him, but I don't think it would make any difference, because I think he was basically always a solitary guy, and he was getting more and more that way toward the end. So it was only a matter of time. It was just a matter of time until I got a telegram from the embassy. The embassy flew up his body. The embassies are very efficient in this sort of thing. They know how to deal with it."

The final irony of middle age is not to see one's parents go crazy—one half expects that—but to see madness descend on those younger and weaker creatures whom one had hoped to protect from the world's insanity. I had the misfortune, not long ago, to watch a twenty-year-old boy breaking down before the very eyes of his bewildered parents. I happened to be spending the weekend in Connecticut with some people whom I shall call Griffin—the father is an old friend, a rather aggressive corporate lawyer, now about forty-five—and they were worried about the boy, Jason, because they had just been notified that he was being sent home from camp. The notification had provided no reason, and so the Griffins were left to speculate on all the possibilities of the middle-class imagination: Theft? Arson? A knife fight? Some sexual misbehavior?

They could believe none of their own speculations, nor could I. Jason was a gentle and affectionate boy, whom I had known since his childhood. Because of brain injuries at birth, he was slightly retarded, with an I.Q. of about 75. His retardation was serious enough to condemn him to the limbo of "special education" classes, where he was given little to do, except to watch the other boys of his age grow further and further ahead of him; at the same time, his retardation was not serious enough to prevent his suffering from their taunts and gibes. They called him a "retard" and told him "moron" jokes. But he endured, patient and good-natured, willing to help, eager to please. He took long walks, and raked leaves, and sometimes found work as a caddy at a nearby golf club. The only window in the wall he had built around himself was the screen of the television set in his second-floor bedroom. There he found strange friends of whom his parents knew almost nothing—Bob Hope, and Lawrence Welk, and all those hearty-voiced announcers who joked and babbled through the endless hours of the baseball season.

Jason was flown home from camp by one of the senior counselors, a kindly old man with a white mustache, who seemed rather shaken by the experience. Jason had been mumbling to himself for most of the past week, the counselor said. He had refused to eat or to sleep. He had wandered around the camp at night, throwing things around in the various cabins, then standing with his hands rigidly clenched on the end of his bunk for hours at a time. The previous night, he had disappeared, barefoot, and some farmer five miles down the valley had brought him back at dawn. "I don't know what's happened to him," the counselor said helplessly, "but I think you'd better get him to a doctor right away."

Outside in the back driveway, Jason was conducting an extraordinary interview with himself. He periodically made the gestures of a baseball player fielding a ball and throwing it to the nearest base, but while he fielded, he kept asking himself questions:

"What would you do if you were going to camp?

"On a bus. Gotcha.

"What would you do if it was a long trip?

"A long trip.

"What would you do if somebody said you were doing something bad?

"Yourself. Gotcha.

"What would you do if—let's see now—and there's a long base hit out to left field—what would you do if there was a fire?

"Yourself, that's all. Gotcha."

It was almost like a lie-detector test—some innocuous questions followed by innocuous answers, then some apparently dangerous questions, usually answered in the same way: "Yourself. Gotcha." While Mrs. Griffin sat in the kitchen and telephoned various psychiatrists—the only one she could reach prescribed Thorazine and offered an appointment four days later—Griffin and I sat on the back porch as guardians and watched the sad spectacle. Jason's eyes were filled with terror, and sometimes he paused in his self-interrogation to look up at the sky. At other times, when he realized that we were watching him, he would shake his head sadly from side to side, the look of the runner thrown out at first base. Then the questioning went on:

"What would you do if they said you're a troublemaker? Yourself. Gotcha."

"Jason, who are you talking to?" Griffin asked wearily.

"President Nixon," Jason said. "All the way with President Nixon."

"Why Nixon?" Griffin asked.

"He's the head man," Jason said. "He's up in my room right now."

"I see," Griffin said. Then he turned to me and said, "Jason voted for Nixon in the last election. We all used to kid him about it—he was the only person in the family who voted for Nixon. Does that mean Nixon was a symbol of authority or a symbol of rebellion?"

"I don't know," I said. "Has he ever been like this before?"

"Never."

Mrs. Griffin came out of the kitchen to report on her telephone calls. She offered Jason a glass of Fresca. He gulped it down and then started using the empty glass as a microphone for his interviews.

"Over this way, President Nixon," he said, waving his microphone as a new badge of authority, pushing his way through invisible crowds to another part of the driveway. "Right this way, over here, Mr. President."

Jason's principal method, however, seemed to be that of the sports announcer, that endless repetition of trivia to fill out the long pauses while the pitcher kicks at the mound and the batter fingers the resin. "Now over to you, Marv Albert," he said.

"Who the hell is Marv Albert?" Griffin asked.

"He's a sports announcer on NBC," I said.

"Jason!" Griffin called out.

"Now let's see," Jason was saying into the Fresca glass, "what would you do if—"

"Jason," Griffin said again, "do you know who I am?"

"Some person I used to know," Jason said. "So now let's see what two and two add up to."

Griffin shook his head. His wife came out of the kitchen again to report that a nearby hospital was willing to accept Jason for an emergency "evaluation." So we all got into Griffin's station wagon and drove there. It was a rich hospital, all white and orange, with lots of thick, red wall-to-wall carpeting, and on every corridor there were plaques identifying the donor who had paid for one "pavilion" or another. The psychiatrist was a friendly man, quite earnest. On the bookshelves above his desk stood the collected papers of Sigmund Freud, all eighteen volumes, and Erikson and

Cole and Harry Stack Sullivan. Then a nurse came to take down
the basic information.

"What is your name?" she asked Jason.

"Jerry Lewis," Jason said.

At the moment of breakdown, the hospital seems a refuge, a
sanctuary, a place where help will be found. Many times, this is
true, many times not. Young Michael Wechsler, for example,
whom we last saw crumbling at Harvard, never really recovered.
Once he was institutionalized in Cambridge, according to his own
memoir, "I started strangling myself—with ties, shirts, razor cord
—whatever I could get my hands on, which wasn't much. . . . I
tied a guitar strap pretty tight around my neck, [which] left some
large red blotches on my neck. . . ."

The boy was then eighteen. His parents found it hard to
believe what was happening. They were both good people, genuinely good people. They both believed almost unquestioningly
in the dogmas of liberalism—help for the poor and oppressed,
help for your neighbors, help even for your own children. But the
boy could not accept help. He described one typical situation in
which he regularly lay in the dark under his bedspread while
his father regularly came to visit him, found him apparently
asleep, and went away again. "I wanted to talk to him, but I just
couldn't," Michael said. "I remember one night they were playing
Shakespeare on the radio, and I was sad because I couldn't understand a lot of the vocabulary. I'd tried talking with my father that
evening, but we were in two far-apart worlds. I know I made it
pretty tough on my parents then, but not as tough as I made it for
myself. Life wasn't worth living, not one minute of it."

Having bought him a car, which he wrecked, and a motorcycle, which he wrecked, the Wechslers could think of nothing
except to keep paying the psychiatrists and obeying their various
orders and injunctions. There were to be eight in all, whom the
Wechslers are prepared to identify only as Doctor First through
Doctor Eighth. Some demanded individual therapy, some group
therapy; some demanded parental involvement, some refused
even to talk to the parents; the various therapies ranged from
Freudian analysis to insulin shock. The poor boy drifted off to

the East Village, got involved in L.S.D., played his flute with such persistence that the neighbors called the police. And he tried to write poetry:

> Oh God, why has thou forsaken all
> Us mad people who prayed again and
> Then once more; what other than madness
> Is in store. What more!

The Wechslers tried to get Michael into one of the better mental hospitals ("We hailed the news that he had been accepted with some of the same delight we had felt when Harvard had opened its doors to him"), but after he ran away eight times in a little more than a year, the hospital expelled him. And he kept getting crazier and crazier. "He was playing his flute grimly and obsessively," according to the parents' account. "In the middle of one night we found him in the driveway performing on it while standing on the top of our car. During the day he walked around the neighborhood suddenly pausing to aim his music at startled passersby and dogs."

The shifts in and out of hospitals became correspondingly more rapid and more desperate. At one point, on the eve of a return to confinement, Wechsler had to snatch his son from a ninth-floor window sill. But the hospitals could not deal with Michael, any more than his parents could, any more than he could himself. And so this bright and talented and much-loved youth finally managed, at the age of twenty-six, after the ministrations of eight psychiatrists and three mental hospitals, to kill himself.

Kurt Vonnegut's son, on the other hand, managed to survive the hospitals. During the first breakdown, when Mark Vonnegut was running around Vancouver and smashing windows, his father flew out to commit him to an institution. Mark remembers the place as "just terrible, a real hellhole." The treatment started with the usual drugs. "I'd get beaten up and have needles shoved up my ass," Mark recalls. "I was never told anything." And he loathed his psychiatrist. "He was dressed in terrible taste—really, baby-blue alligator shoes, and a pink Cadillac, Rotary Club tieclips—I don't know what more he could have done." During this initial confinement, however, Mark solved certain problems by himself.

"I felt very embarrassed, that I had very much overplayed my hand. My girl friend wasn't dead. My father hadn't killed himself. Those were some of the more realistic things I thought had happened, or might have happened."

When the psychiatrist flew off to Hawaii for a professional conference, Mark Vonnegut talked his way out of the hospital. "The orderlies seemed to be generally on my side, so I just plain split. You could walk out if you had clothes. It was sort of tricky. Getting through doors and all that stuff. But I got on the next ferry and made my way back to the farm." Back among his friends, most of them adrift on marijuana, he was welcomed as a kind of guru, returned from the lands beyond. On one occasion, he began reciting *Moby Dick* from beginning to end. "I started straight, and then I got more into—it took a hell of a long time. But I *couldn't* have recited the whole novel. There's no way. But we really lived on the *Pequod*. I lost a finger to a harpoon. Another guy lost half a foot. And, you know, we drowned in the end."

About two weeks later, there was another breakdown. The Royal Canadian Mounties took him first to a prison cell and then back to the hospital. "I also remember that there was a two-thousand-dollar bill for damages. I remember doing a lot of acrobatics, and I must have busted stuff. And I was talking—things that seemed to make a lot of sense at the time. I remember I put out my arm for shots, and I said, 'Is this going to be more like a square dance or more like a clambake?'"

He stayed in the hospital for two months, and seemed to be getting better, and then broke down again. "I knew enough about textbook psychiatry to know, in my lucid moments, that I was a paranoid schizophrenic, that I was suffering episodes of increasing severity, and that I was suffering episodes with shorter and shorter time in between. And that, as a textbook case, I was pretty much slated for this for the rest of my life. And that gave me a hell of a lot of resolve."

That resolve probably helped to save him, though he gives most of the credit to Thorazine, vitamins and electroshock. As for the possible insights of psychotherapy, he says: "That's okay, because it sounds nice—who could be against insight? Who could be against motherhood? But clinically, it has *zero* effectiveness." Now, after what he calls "a fairly stormy adolescence," a kind of peace has been established. "I mean, while my father was a good ally in my struggles, it was a bitch of a struggle for both of us, and it's nice to be plain old father and son instead of allies in a cosmic brawl. He says now that I'm his least puzzling child. He's grateful to me for that."

PART FOUR

CONCLUSIONS

16

Where We Are Now

This is the point at which I had long planned to invoke and summarize the conclusions of the experts, but I have increasingly come to believe that there really are no experts. To the basic question of who is crazy (or psychotic, if you will, or emotionally disturbed, or mentally ill), the only answer is that nobody knows. To the more difficult questions of what insanity is, and what causes it, and what can be done to cure it, the answers are even more uncertain. Again, nobody knows.

Joseph Heller summed up one form of the paradox in his famous definition of Catch 22, "which specified that a concern for one's own safety in the face of dangers that were real and immediate was the process of a rational mind. Orr was crazy and could be grounded. All he had to do was ask; and as soon as he did, he would no longer be crazy and would have to fly more missions. Orr would be crazy to fly more missions and sane if he didn't, but if he was sane he had to fly them. If he flew them he was crazy and didn't have to; but if he didn't want to he was sane and had to. Yossarian was moved very deeply by the absolute simplicity of this clause of Catch-22 and let out a respectful whistle.

" 'That's some catch, that Catch-22,' he observed.

" 'It's the best there is,' Doc Daneeka agreed."

A SCENE. A private hospital in one of New York's richest suburbs, a very respectable place, affiliated with one of the state's best universities. The psychiatric ward is brand new, just sixteen beds, swarming with uniformed nurses and vocational therapists. It costs $165 per day. This is where we last saw Jason Griffin identifying himself as Jerry Lewis in the admitting room.

The omniscient modern hospital even has a social worker specially assigned to deal with the complaints of the patients' families. She calls them in for "group sessions" every Thursday evening to ask them about their "expectations," and to keep telling them the standard excuse: "There are no easy solutions."

At her first "group session," Jason Griffin's mother is outraged, partly at the very fact of Jason's madness, partly at her own helplessness, partly at the fact that a week of hospitalization has done no good whatever. Numbed by Thorazine, Jason shuffles dazedly around the corridors or simply lies in bed, staring into space. Aside from that, he now has a fever, and the nurses will not provide any medicine, because the doctor in charge of the case has gone for the day. The staff regards Mrs. Griffin's protests largely as a symptom of her own unhappiness.

"We're all here to help each other," the bespectacled social worker says, and the other parents and wives and in-laws sitting around the bare wooden table all nod approvingly at one another.

"I don't want your help!" cries Mrs. Griffin, her face suddenly flushed with anger. "I want Jason *cured!* We brought him here to be cured. We're paying $165 a day for him to be cured."

"I understand what you're saying," the social worker says. Social workers are trained to say that they understand. "But we don't *know* any way to cure a psychotic episode."

(After a month, when the medical insurance ran out, the hospital had nothing further to suggest except electric-shock therapy, and no prognosis on how that would help. Griffin took his stupefied son out of the hospital and tried a psychiatrist who used the so-called megavitamin therapy. It worked remarkably well. A high-protein diet, supplemented by large doses of vitamins, soon restored Jason to more or less what he had been before, namely a retarded boy who had nowhere to go. Shortly before Christmas, 1974, the state authorities found him a job sweeping floors and cleaning out toilets in a supermarket. Mrs. Griffin got up at six o'clock every morning to drive him there, but at the end of a month, he was fired for incompetence. He now spends most of his time watching television. Although he speaks with a certain pride of his "nervous breakdown," he still insists that the hallucinatory voices of the previous year were all real, and that he really did have President Nixon staying in his bedroom.)

A CORRECTION. Juergen Schmidt, the banker who went mad at Harvard just after finishing his thesis on Spinoza, was dismayed by my account of the episode because I had left out an element that he considered extremely important. The reason I had left it out was that, for some reason, he had never mentioned it before. Now he wanted to explain:

"I was wandering around the stacks of Widener Library, looking for a poem by Novalis, *Schüler zu Sais*. I suddenly found myself standing within arm's reach of the book, and I opened it up, and there was the poem. It describes a student's visit to a temple in Egypt, where he sees a mysterious veiled figure. The student tears the veil away and sees—himself. As you probably know, Schiller wrote a poem on the same theme, but he treated it somewhat differently. The student flees from the temple without revealing what he has seen. I used the Novalis as the dedication for my thesis: '*Er sah, o Wunder des Wunders, sich selbst,*' or something like that. But intuitively, I shared Schiller's student's horror of self-knowledge. Like him, I fled from that knowledge, not into the desert but into madness.

"I am sure that there is an element of self-knowledge in madness. It is as though we spent most of our lives lying to ourselves about what our motivations are, about fears and guilts, pleasures and pains, the whole web of emotions with which we like to cloak ourselves. Once the web is torn, like a veil, it may reveal a truer self and a rather shocking one. That shock alone can be enough to drive some of us over the edge. For me, it all came together in the rather mysterious way that I came upon the poem by Novalis—as if someone were guiding me. And the moment I read the poem, it must have occurred to me that it held the ultimate answer: madness equals self-knowledge, and self-knowledge equals madness."

This is essentially the romantic view of insanity, particularly if we add the artistic element to the equation: self-knowledge equals creativity equals madness. The romantic view derives from the Middle Ages—the concept of the divine fool who, in his madness, can see God with a clarity that the Sermon on the Mount attributed only to "the pure in heart"—but contemporary romantics have carried this same idea on into the age of R. D. Laing and Carlos Castaneda. It is a popular view, because it establishes such an impressive hagiology of mad or half-mad artists. Gogol and Dostoyevsky, Van Gogh and Blake, Schumann and Nietzsche, Poe and Pound—who would not take pride in equating his own miseries with those of the masters? Despite the popularity of the romantic theory, however, it has very little relation to reality. Schumann wrote no music in the asylum at Endenich, and Hemingway wrote no novels at the Mayo Clinic. Indeed, if anxious artists really do have a greater susceptibility to insanity than ordinary people do—a debatable proposition—there is little evidence that their madness leads to great art or great ideas. On the contrary, the evidence is more likely to indicate that the mad artist uses all his art to fight off the wolves of the night.

For those who know it at first hand, insanity has very little romance. It is ugly, painful, frightening. And it leaves its victims in that terrible situation described by Lara Jefferson, strait-jacketed in one of the Midwestern asylums of a generation ago: "Here I sit—mad as the Hatter—with nothing to do but either become madder and madder or else recover enough of my sanity to be allowed to go back to the life which drove me mad."

A DEFINING OF DEFINITIONS. The people I interviewed for this book have all recovered enough of their sanity to return to the life that drove them mad, so they probably do not represent a scientific sample of the insane, or of anything else. Nor have I made any effort to divide them into quasi-scientific categories. I simply started out with friends who I knew had suffered break-downs, and then I proceeded through widening circles of friends of friends. So there is an obvious imbalance toward people who live in the Northeast, toward writers and artists, and even, I'm afraid, toward graduates of Harvard. But it seemed to me more important to find people who would and could talk articulately about their crises than to attempt any sort of demographic bal-ance, to match a Boston physics professor with a Seattle truck driver, or even to make sure that the number of schizophrenics was kept in proper proportion to the manic-depressives.

Indeed, I have hardly attempted to make any distinctions at all among the various official categories of madness. Listening to my subjects' stories, I never tried to diagnose their anxieties, never argued with them. I was only trying to find out what they themselves thought had happened to them. And I was struck by the candor with which they spoke. They hardly ever used the euphemistic language of psychiatrists and social workers. They scorn such terms as "inappropriate behavior" and "character disorder." They generally speak, with a kind of embarrassed honesty, of having been "nuts" or "out of my mind." When they have been confined in hospitals, they speak of their places of confinement as "the madhouse" or "the loony bin." And as for the psychiatrists, who like to think of themselves as the heirs to Hippocrates, Galen and Freud, the almost universal term for them is "shrink." In other words, those who have actually gone crazy seem to me to have a more earthy and concrete understanding of insanity than do the psychiatrists who pose as experts.

And yet I could not help feeling that a number of the people I interviewed had never really understood their own crises, that they often ignored their real problems and concentrated on other problems that were largely imaginary—and that what they thought had cured them was not the real cure at all. But I also became convinced that this *didn't matter*. What was important was that they had somehow found, in the whole pharmacopoeia of treatments, some kind of magic that had brought them back to life, because they had believed in it. And if prayer, say, can cure a man suffering from cancer ("spontaneous remission," the baffled doctors generally call it), then who are we to say that the patient must still be suffering from cancer because we the healers do not believe in the efficacy of whatever it was that cured him?

A QUESTION OF DEVILS. If we leave aside for a moment the question of cures for madness, which seem to be as immensely varied as the causes, we can see obvious patterns in those causes. At the beginning, there is always an unhappy childhood. Not necessarily what used to be called "a broken home," though that is common enough, but rather a home in which the child feels, for one reason or another, imprisoned, thwarted, mutilated. And how, one might ask, could it ever be otherwise? Every child must somehow be taught, like a dog, not to run out into traffic. Must be taught, similarly, whatever else the parents consider necessary for the child's survival—and that can vary from a love of automobile engines to a love of Schubert *lieder*. Must be taught and can be taught only by a combination of seduction and coercion (behavior-ist psychiatrists have more official terms for the process), which fills the child with an incurable sense of guilt and unworthiness.

Once the child's sense of its own worth and identity has been irreparably damaged, it is sent out into the world to fulfill two essential functions, economic and biological. First, to work for other irreparably damaged people in some destructive office or factory. Second, to find and marry another irreparably damaged person, and to raise children who, in being saved from the damage that was once inflicted on oneself, will be irreparably damaged. How does anyone survive the process? Again, nobody knows. I read in the newspapers not long ago of a four-year-old boy in Harlem who hated his life with such passion that he threw himself into a gutter and began swallowing garbage and dung and trash until he nearly choked. On the other hand, I also know a man who spent much of his childhood in Auschwitz and now lives the most conventional sort of life, giving lectures and writing book reviews.

Still, there are not only patterns in the background—the unhappy childhood, the unhappy marriage, the unhappy job (*anhedonia* is the wonderful medical term for the inability to enjoy oneself)—there are also patterns in the symptoms of break-down. The most striking, I think, is the distortion of physical perceptions. One smells differently. "It was a smell something like burning rubber," said Seymour Krim, "as if my mind was smok-ing." And there are lights everywhere. Charles Mingus III re-called "hallucinating that light bulbs were talking to me," while Peter Franck said: "My head felt light inside, irradiated, as though with sunlight, and my mind was racing, in fragments and streaks." The pseudonymous Karen had a similar feeling: "My head was going too fast. I was thinking too fast. And every time I'd think something, another part of me would contradict it."

Beyond these basic physical distortions—caused by God knows what combination of psychic stress and chemical anarchy —there are other symptoms that seem to appear over and over again. The victim suddenly becomes unable to sleep, and thus the mysteriously therapeutic qualities of rest and dreaming are denied to him just when he needs them most. In a state of in-creasing anxiety, he begins telephoning to anyone he can reach, even at great distances, or, when that fails, talking aloud and endlessly to himself. This collection of symptoms seems to derive from a situation that we can explain only by that cliché: alienation. There was a time—or so we are told—when we all knew how to define our existence in terms of town and family and vocation. Now that everyone is not only decreed to be equal but compelled to compete against strange people in strange circumstances, and all for an unknown goal variously defined as success or fulfillment or self-identification, we have all more or less lost what we used to think of as our way.

And beyond these social confusions, the most interesting patterns of madness, I think, lie in the madman's sense of having finally discovered God. Thus, Juergen Schmidt felt a sensuous pleasure in the waters that he blessed in the mental hospital ("It was like breathing wind; it had become a nectar; it was like velvet"); and thus, Mark Vonnegut felt himself committed to a cosmic struggle ("I had to think the Devil was taking over, but if I could help turn things around, then the earth would be cleansed of evil"). A generation ago, at the height of the age of skepticism, such confessions would have been automatically considered proof of insanity. Nowadays, in the age of Tarot and *I Ching*, and, more generally, skepticism about skepticism, we may be less dogmatic. Is a sudden sense of God really a symptom of madness, or is it a symptom of sanity?

ANOTHER SCENE. I saw a vision, not long ago, of the entire future of psychiatry. The woman I have identified as Nancy Chaucer, the rich and elegant lady who became a lawyer for the poor, began worrying about what she had said about her private life, so she suddenly invited me to her house in Philadelphia for what she called a "potluck dinner" and a private performance of a film about the work of R. D. Laing.

It was a potluck dinner appropriate to a family that owns an entire brownstone not far from Rittenhouse Square—a whole ham, several roast chickens, trays of pizza, a vat of lentil soup, gallons of good wine and beer. Nancy Chaucer had changed somewhat since I had last seen her—she had some gray hairs that she would once have dyed, and she wore thick trousers that she never would have considered in her crazy days; and yet, by and large, she seemed much more cheerful and peaceful than in the old times. She had just finished her first day of selecting a jury for a pickpocketing case. But while she had spent several years changing from a lunatic into a lawyer, her husband, once a lawyer, had spent the same years changing into a psychiatrist. He was now studying at the University of Pennsylvania and working as a therapist at a state hospital. "Fascinating," he said, tearing a wing from one of the roast chickens and gobbling it down and licking his fingers.

But the vision I had was inspired by the other guests at the dinner party, most of whom had not only never met me (why should they?) but had never met their hostess, Mrs. Chaucer. The reason for the dinner was that Charley Chaucer, aged forty-two, having given up law and business for the sake of getting a graduate degree in psychiatry, wanted to invite some of his young classmates to dinner. So there they all were, with their amiably mindless chattering and giggling and their blue jeans and flannel shirts and their kinky hair held together by rubber bands. "You're Otto, I'm Mike," they would say, or Rita or Sam, with youth's guileless assumption of equality, like Indians exchanging salutations in front of the wigwam. I fell into conversation with one of them, a blond girl with lots of blue eye makeup, and a bearded husband somewhere in another room. I asked her, by way of professional shop talk, what she thought of megavitamin therapy, and she said she knew nothing about it. When I explained it to her, trying not to sound like a crank, she shrugged away the explanation. "I prefer," she said, "the developmental model."

I suppose that means something, and if I ransacked the textbooks of psychiatry, I could find out what it does mean, but the vision that I suddenly had was of the blue-painted girl and all her classmates eventually taking over the seats of psychiatric authority. These people were generally too plebeian to adopt Van Dyke beards or pearl necklaces and become the next generation of Park Avenue psychoanalysts, and that probably wasn't what they wanted anyway. No, that would not be sufficiently inspiring and socially relevant. Instead, they would all find jobs in ghetto schools and welfare centers, and when some poor mother was summoned to some concrete fortress at eight-thirty in the morning for an interview on why her adolescent son had been caught setting a fire in the supply room, then this girl with the blue eye makeup would explain to the newest victim what she meant by "the developmental model."

And then we all went upstairs to watch the film on R. D. Laing. We sat on the floor, staring crick-necked at a billowing sheet tacked across a door. There were actually several films. In the first of them, the cameraman simply aimed his camera at Laing and never moved it throughout the sage's monologue. Every once in a while, the sound system would groan to a halt, and the lights would come on again while the film maker tinkered with his equipment. The audience was remarkably sympathetic. At each of Laing's ponderous witticisms, everyone chuckled appreciatively, as though he actually were a new cultural hero, actually saying new things. After about twenty minutes, Laing said, "I think we'd better break off here." And so we did. The second movie was much the same. In the third movie, the camera went to Kingsley Hall and aimed at the inmates as they babbled about themselves. It was all profoundly depressing. At the intermission, I went back to the kitchen with an equally depressed woman who said she reviewed books and we drank red wine until the screening was over.

A BIAS. I must confess that I am prejudiced against psychiatry, both the traditional sort and the new variations of people like Laing. I felt that prejudice mildly when I began this book, and two years of research have only reinforced it. I do not deny that Sigmund Freud was a great scientist, a great thinker, and a great writer. Our whole view of ourselves, both as individuals and as a mass, derives in large part from what he told us we were. But after more than half a century of psychiatry triumphant, its power to cure insanity, or even the lesser torments, still seems extremely uncertain.

One reason, which is not much publicized, is that the profession, by its very nature, has attracted a lot of neurotic or simply incompetent practitioners. Even Freud's first circle of pioneers included a number of rather unbalanced people like Rank and Ferenczi who were seeking mainly their own salvation, but the psychoanalytic movement has always tried to maintain a high level of professionalism. Psychiatry is a wider field, however, and psychotherapy covers just about anybody, and nowadays we hear all too often of doctors who tyrannize their helpless patients, or sometimes place a groping hand upon the knee. Even people who have been cured by psychiatry generally report that the discovery of the right doctor came only after a long and frustrating series of interviews with psychiatrists whose counsel was either useless or actually damaging.

Another reason, also insufficiently appreciated, is cost. A true psychoanalysis takes several years and costs many thousands of dollars. (I know of one man who has dissipated his family's entire fortune in thirty years of analysis, with no end in sight.) Even a routine psychiatrist is apt to charge between thirty and fifty dollars for an hour of his time. One result is that, according to the Manhattan study cited earlier, almost three quarters of all people with serious psychiatric problems never see a psychiatrist at all. Another result is that the basic process of psychiatry has been dangerously diluted in an effort to save everyone money. From Dr. Freud sitting in stoic contemplation next to his patient's couch, we have evolved to "group therapy" sessions, often conducted not by a doctor but by a nurse, who holds a kind of *Kaffeeklatsch* with the less drugged of the hospital's patients. And beyond that lies "milieu therapy," which is an elegant euphemism for the hospital's hope that, in view of the shortage of doctors and nurses, perhaps the patients will help to cure each other.

The ultimate problem with psychiatry, though, is the state of the practice itself. Freud's followers still maintain their complex disciplines, as do such pioneering dissenters as the Adlerians, but a combination of high costs and public dissatisfaction has bred so many dissident factions that it is now largely a matter of pure chance whether somebody on the way to a breakdown ends up in the custody of a transactional therapist, a primal therapist, a Gestaltist, a marathon-encounter group, or even, for that matter, the gurus of transcendental meditation. Or a combination or variation of these and more. The more orthodox psychiatrists frown on such innovations. Considering themselves scientists, they devote much attention to taxonomy, to differentiating between schizophrenics and borderline schizophrenics, psychopaths and sociopaths, with or without paranoid tendencies. But these are just words. All that any psychiatrist can really do is to listen to unhappy people and try to help them deal with their difficulties. Which means that even a wise psychiatrist is not very different from a wise priest or a wise parent or a wise friend. It also means that even a wise psychiatrist often can't do very much to solve the victim's problems.

A PROGNOSIS. So they give drugs. And drugs work. They work in different ways on different people, and some work better than others. Thorazine works. Haldol works. They worked originally because they kept the insane in a state of torpor, thus obviating the supposed need for straitjackets, ropes, cold baths. But although a ward filled with stupefied patients may be more harmonious than a ward filled with screaming maniacs, it is hardly an enlightening spectacle.

Thorazine and the rest of the phenothiazines work in other ways, however. Nobody knows quite how, but the prevailing theory is that the symptoms of schizophrenia are caused in large part by an overflow of sensory and perceptual stimuli, and that the phenothiazines can control this by regulating the supply of dopamine and norepinephrine in the synapses of the brain.

To be specific, I know of one sternly conservative family in which the youngest daughter, who seemed to attach great importance to family holidays, went quite mad, just after her eighteenth birthday, in the midst of the elaborate preparations for Christmas. She began chopping up her clothes with scissors, then packing the tatters into a suitcase, then running off into the dark in her mother's nightgown. A psychoanalyst could have spent years studying the implications of these desperate gestures, but when the aghast parents went to a psychiatrist, he told them that if they took the girl to a hospital, she would get mainly Thorazine, and that they might as well give it to her at home. So they did, and the girl remained in her bed for several weeks, breathing heavily, staring into space—but she did get better. In fact, she returned to school and behaved fairly normally. After a year, the parents decided to stop the Thorazine, which, as one of its side effects, was making the girl quite fat. And on each succeeding day without Thorazine, they could see the madness returning as inexorably as a rising tide inundating a rotten jetty. After a year's torpor, the girl suddenly began talking more and more rapidly, more and more incoherently. She slammed dishes into the kitchen sink, shouted at the family beagle, and generally showed so many symptoms of another breakdown that the parents reluctantly reached for the half-empty bottle of Thorazine. Whereupon everything returned to what they had come to accept as normality.

And the new megavitamin therapy—massive doses of, among other things, niacin, ascorbic acid, and calcium, combined with a very high-protein, low-carbohydrate diet—that also works. Nobody knows exactly how it works, but it does work. Its advocates are still on the defensive, remaining very cautious about their claims of success. But they are skillfully organizing themselves (the American Schizophrenia Association), and they do claim significant improvement in about three quarters of the cases they treat. I myself have met perhaps half a dozen people who were cured of severe breakdowns by this treatment; I have never met one who was not the better for it.

All of this fills many psychiatrists with a mixture of anger and despair. The drug therapists, protecting their flanks, often argue that drugs and psychotherapy should be combined, but they know quite well, as do the psychotherapists, that if drugs can cure insanity, as they often can, then the whole process of psychiatry may be just another episode in the long history of quackery. That is, in effect, the "conceptual crisis" that now dominates the whole field. The psychiatrists are not, of course, without defenses. "Sure it's possible that insanity is caused by chemical imbalances," says one. "But what causes those imbalances? Stress, mainly. And what causes the stress?" "We keep trying out these new wonder drugs, but half the time, we don't know what we're doing," says another. "We don't really know whether they work, or how they work, or why they work. It's all trial-and-error. I use them—we all do—but I still think I know a hell of a lot more about people than I know about drugs."

If we know that people do go crazy but we cannot define their madness, if we cannot really understand what insanity is or what causes it, if we recognize that political leaders and corporate executives often behave as irrationally as old men shouting to themselves in the streets or women crying in supermarkets, then what are we to do about it?

I don't know. There are, as the social workers keep saying, no easy answers. In fact, there are no hard answers either.

Try psychiatry first. And since most psychiatrists now dispense powerful pills as freely as aspirin, there is no real contradiction between the traditional psychiatry and drug therapy. The main disagreement is about which one works. Generally, they work together.

In my talks with people who have gone crazy, I have found that about one third were cured mainly by psychiatry, about one third mainly by drugs and vitamins, and about one third (perhaps slightly more than one third) by being left alone to work out their own problems. Just as the body has immense recuperative powers, so does the mind. It can build walls to shut out pain, it can create soothing fantasies, it can even purge itself through the process of dreaming. And time heals. Some of the people I talked to got better simply through a new job or a new marriage or the fact that their children were finally making their own ways into life.

I too have gone fairly crazy fairly often, sometimes in ways that nobody ever suspected. I have never consulted the psychiatrists nor taken their drugs. But like millions of other people, I am still here to tell the tale.

NOTES ON SOURCES

Notes on Sources

The literature on insanity is beyond all reckoning. The number of people who have tried to describe their own breakdowns is exceeded only by the number of psychiatrists who have tried to describe their wizardry in bringing the mad back to sanity. I have dug only a shallow trench in this mountain of misery, perhaps only a foxhole, but since this book represents the view from the foxhole, I should like to list some of the works I have found valuable.

CHAPTER 1.

This chapter is a mixture of personal impressions, news events, poetry, and so on. The account of the death of Steve Cloud comes from the following day's *New York Times* and *New York Daily News*. The statistics on various kinds of madness can be found in the Commerce Department's 1974 edition of its *Statistical Abstract of the United States*. The Midtown Manhattan Study is officially entitled *Mental Health in the Metropolis: The Midtown Manhattan Study*, two volumes, by Leo Srole, Thomas S. Langner, Stanley T. Michael, Marvin K. Opler and Thomas A. C. Rennie, published in 1962 and 1963. The fantasy entitled *2001* is best known as Stanley Kubrick's brilliant movie, of course, but the film was based on a short story by Arthur C. Clarke, who collaborated with Kubrick on the screenplay. This screenplay is full of mysteries, and Clarke subsequently explained most of them in a paperback "novelization" published in 1968. Lance Rentzel's reaction to the movie is in his autobiography, *When All the Laughter Died in Sorrow* (1972). The lines by Robert Lowell are from "Skunk Hour" and "Waking in the Blue," both included in Lowell's collection *Life Studies* (1959). See also *The New Poets*, by M. L. Rosenthal (1967). Frances Farmer's account of her incarceration comes from her autobiography, *Will There Really Be a Morning?* (1972). David Rosenhahn's experiment was published in *Science* magazine, January 19, 1973, under the title "On Being Sane in Insane Places." Solomon Snyder's book, which deals mostly with the phenothiazines, is *Madness and the Brain* (1974).

CHAPTER 2.

On the evolution of treatment for insanity, I have relied heavily on *The History of Psychiatry*, by Franz G. Alexander and Sheldon T. Selesnick (1966). See also *Madness and Civilization, A History of Insanity in the Age of Reason*, by Michel Foucault (1965), and *5000 Years of Medicine*, by Gerhard Venzmer (1972). Thomas S. Szasz deserves some kind of separate citation for his rather exaggerated but often perceptive arguments against all the traditions of what he calls "institutional psychiatry." See particularly *The Myth of Mental Illness* (1961), *The Manufacture of Madness, A Comparative Study of the Inquisition and the Mental Health Movement* (1970) and Szasz's anthology of the writings of unwilling mental patients, *The Age of Madness, The History of Involuntary Mental Hospitalization* (1973).

The story of Lara Jefferson is from *These Are My Sisters* (1948). The story of Peter Stump may be found in *The Werewolf*, by Montague Summers (1933).

Since virtually nothing is known about Hieronymus Bosch, most books about him try simply to analyze his mysterious paintings. Among the best, I think, are *Jerome Bosch*, by Jacques Combe (1957); *Hieronymus Bosch*, by Charles de Tolnay (1966); and *Hieronymus Bosch*, by Carl Linfort (undated).

On *King Lear*, the Signet paperback edition, edited by Russell Fraser (1963), contains a very useful analysis of the sources of the play, as well as commentaries by figures like Samuel Johnson and Harley Granville-Barker. See also *Shakespeare's Tragedies*, by G. B. Harrison (1952), and *Motiveless Malignity*, by Louis Auchincloss (1969).

For the story of Benjamin Rush, I have relied mainly on *Concepts of Insanity in the United States, 1789–1865*, by Norman Dain (1964). (Szasz, however, is eloquent in his denunciations of the "father of American psychiatry.") Boswell's account of the visit to Bedlam comes, of course, from *The Life of Samuel Johnson*.

The library of scholarly works on George III is imposing. The most detailed accounts of his illness are *The Royal Malady*, by Charles Chevenix Trench (1964), which argues that the King's disorder was psychotic, and *George III and the Mad Business*, by Ida Macalpine and Richard Hunter (1969), which argues that the King suffered from porphyria. For a brief recent work, see *The First Four Georges*, by J. H. Plumb (1956; revised edition, 1975). Also *The King Who Lost America*, by Alan Lloyd (1971). The quotes from Thackeray come from his book *The Four Georges*.

I know of no really good biography of Robert Schumann. The standard old-fashioned version is *Florestan*, by Robert Haven Schauffler (1945), but it has many shortcomings. See also *Schumann*, by Joan Chissell (1948), and *The Lives of the Great Composers*, by Harold C. Schonberg (1970). In many ways, the composer appears most clearly in his own writings, *On Music and Musicians*, by Robert Schumann, ed. Konrad Wolff (1946).

The literature on Freud is almost as voluminous as that on insanity. The definitive biography is the three-volume *Life and Work of Sigmund Freud*, by Ernest Jones (1953–57). See also Freud's *An Autobiographical Study*, trans. James Strachey, originally published in 1935 but reprinted in paperback form in 1963. Then there are, of course, the *Gesammelte Werke* in 18 volumes, but most of us learned most of what we know about Freud from the Modern Library Giant, *The Basic Writings of Sigmund Freud*, trans. and ed. Dr. A. A. Brill (1938).

Kurt Vonnegut's recollections of syphilitics come from *Breakfast of Champions* (1973), and it was the publication of this novel that led me to interview him.

CHAPTER 3.

The lines about Commander Lowell are quoted, once again, from Robert Lowell's *Life Studies*.

There have been several recent books about Bobby Fischer's conquest of the chess championship, notably those by George Steiner, Bradford Darrach and Claude Cockburn, but I have relied mainly on *Grandmasters of Chess*, by Harold C. Schonberg (1973). Ernest Jones's *The Problem of Paul Morphy, A Contribution to the Psychology of Chess*, was originally delivered as a scholarly paper in 1930 but is now most readily available in Jones's collected papers, *Essays in Applied Psychoanalysis* (1951).

Sylvia Plath's denunciation of "Daddy" comes from the collection of poems entitled *Ariel* (1965).

The books by and about R. D. Laing have grown rather numerous in the last few years. I myself still like *Knots* (1970) the best, since it grows from Laing's chief strength, which is his perception of paradoxes. His main expository works, I think, are *The Divided Self* (1960) and *Sanity, Madness and the Family*, with A. Esterson (1964). See also *The Politics of Experience* (1967) and *The Politics of the Family* (1969). On the actual effectiveness of Laing's methods, the only substantial account is *Mary Barnes, Two Accounts of a Journey Through Madness*, by Mary Barnes and Joseph Berke (1971). For an admiring collection of commentaries by and about Laing's group, see *Going Crazy*, ed. Hendrik Ruitenbeek (1972). Critical commentaries are less easy to find. See "The Truth Which Dares Not Speak Its Name," by Richard

Schickel, *Harper's Magazine,* April, 1971, and "After Freud and Jung, Now Comes R. D. Laing," by Peter Mezan, *Esquire,* January, 1972.

Seymour Krim has published three collections of articles and essays, *Views of a Nearsighted Cannoneer* (1961), *Shake It for the World, Smartass* (1970), and *You and Me* (1974). The first of these contains his own account of his madness, entitled "The Insanity Bit."

Hemingway's main works are all generally available, of course. The standard biography is *Ernest Hemingway, A Life Story,* by Carlos Baker (1969), which makes heavy use of the family documents but does not provide much insight. For a personally biased but much more dramatic account of Hemingway's last years, and the first account to provide the details of his suicide, see *Papa Hemingway,* by A. E. Hotchner (1966). The best analytic study of his work, I think, is still *Ernest Hemingway, A Reconsideration,* by Philip Young (1952).

CHAPTER 4.

Charles Mingus's account of his entry into Bellevue comes from *Beneath the Underdog, His World as Composed by Mingus,* edited by Nel King (1971). In this strange autobiography, which seems to have been culled from taped interviews, Mingus speaks of himself mainly in the third person, and warns us at the start that "some of the characters and incidents are fictitious."

CHAPTER 5.

The story of Michael Wechsler, which begins here, was written by his parents and sister, *In a Darkness,* by James A. Wechsler, with Nancy F. Wechsler and Holly W. Karpf (1972).

CHAPTER 7.

James Baldwin's account of the crisis in the New Jersey restaurant comes from *Notes of a Native Son* (1955).

The Fitzgeralds have been written about by many admirers. The basic biographies are still *The Far Side of Paradise,* by Arthur Mizener (1951), and *Zelda,* by Nancy Milford (1970). See also *F. Scott Fitzgerald. In His Own Time: A Miscellany,* ed. Matthew J. Bruccoli and Jackson R. Bryer (1971), a collection of contemporary reviews and interviews.

Norman Mailer has never written in any detail about his attack on his wife, and he declined to be interviewed on the matter. My version is drawn from *The New York Times, Time* and *Newsweek* of that period.

CHAPTER 9.

There have been many accounts of what the Air Force's underground missile bases look like. I have relied mainly on *Men Who Play God, The Story of the H-Bomb and How the World Came to Live With It*, by Norman Moss (1968).

The best account of Forrestal that I know is *James Forrestal, A Study of Personality, Politics, and Policy*, by Arnold A. Rogow (1963).

My accounts of both Eagleton and Nixon come mainly from *The New York Times* and *Time* during 1972 and 1973. Of the many books attempting to analyze Nixon, I think the best is *Nixon Agonistes*, by Gary Wills (1970). For psychological studies, see *In Search of Nixon, A Psychohistorical Inquiry*, by Bruce Mazlish (1972), and *President Nixon's Psychiatric Profile*, by Eli S. Chesen (1973). The quotation by Professor Russel Lee is from an article in *The Pharos*, a publication of the Alpha Omega Alpha Honor Medical Society, for January, 1974.

There is no real biography of Scott Joplin, although his recent popularity may bring several into existence. The main source of information is Rudi Blesh, who collaborated with Harriet Janis in the pioneering study *They All Played Ragtime*, originally published in 1950 and revised twice since then. Blesh also wrote the long introduction to Vera Brodsky Lawrence's edition of Joplin's collected works (1971). In contrast to Joplin, Joe Louis has been the subject of numerous biographies, but none of them is particularly memorable. The one that gives the fullest details of his breakdown is *Brown Bomber, The Pilgrimage of Joe Louis*, by Barney Nagler (1972). Eldridge Cleaver has published several books, but the essential elements of his self-portrait are all in *Soul on Ice* (1968).

Jean Seberg's story of her difficulties is from an interview with Bart Mills in *The New York Times* of June 16, 1974.

My account of the madness of moon flight comes mainly from *Return to Earth*, by Colonel Edwin E. "Buzz" Aldrin, Jr., with Wayne Warga (1973). I am also much indebted to Norman Mailer's *Of a Fire on the Moon* (1969). It is easy to carp at Mailer's eccentricities, but after a certain passage of years, it is astonishing to see how often he has covered the central events of his time, and how blazingly well he has covered them. For another account of another flight, see *To Rule the Night, The Discovery Voyage of Jim Irwin*, by James B. Irwin, with William A. Emerson, Jr. (1973).

CHAPTER 11.

Meaningless and more or less insane crimes can be found in almost any daily newspaper. The ones I happen to have selected come from *The New York Times* of September 3, 1973, March 1, 1974, and May 26, 1973, and the *Washington Post* of March 29, 1973.

I know of no really good biography of Sade (Mailer has said that he wants to write one). For a short and simple account, see *Portrait of de Sade,* by Walter Lennig, tr. Sarah Twohig (1971). For much more detailed documentation, see *The Marquis de Sade,* by Gilbert Lély, trans. Alec Brown (1961). See also *The Life and Ideas of the Marquis de Sade,* by Geoffrey Gorer (1933; revised edition, 1963). The essential nature of Sade is probably best captured by Peter Weiss's splendid play, *The Persecution and Assassination of Jean-Paul Marat as Performed by the Inmates of the Asylum of Charenton Under the Direction of the Marquis de Sade,* translated and adapted by Geoffrey Skelton and Adrian Mitchell (1965). The classic study of Sade's influence is, of course, *The Romantic Agony,* by Mario Praz (1933).

The Kemper case was covered fairly steadily in the press from May through November of 1973. I have relied on *The New York Times, Time* and *Newsweek.* David Abrahamsen's book *The Murdering Mind* appeared in 1973. The story of Garrett Trapnell also comes from the *Times,* a long and excellent account by Robert Lindsey in the issue dated January 18, 1973.

The situation of the Russian dissidents has been much told in the press during the past few years. For firsthand details of the Medvedev case, we must rely, though not without some skepticism, on *A Question of Madness,* by Zhores A. Medvedev and Roy A. Medvedev, trans. Ellen de Kadt (1971). On the workings of the Soviet legal system, I am indebted to *Justice in Moscow,* by George Feifer (1964). The basic documents on the case of Ezra Pound can be found in *A Casebook on Ezra Pound,* ed. William Van O'Connor and Edward Stone (1959). For biography, see *Ezra Pound,* by Charles Norman (1960).

CHAPTER 13.

The most entertaining book on Edgar Allan Poe is *Poe Poe Poe Poe Poe Poe Poe,* by Daniel Hoffman (1972), but for biographical details, I have relied mainly on *Edgar Allan Poe, Visitor from the Night of Time,* by Philip Van Doren Stern (1973). See also *Edgar Allan Poe, The Man Behind the Legend,* by Edward Wagenknecht (1963). As far as drinking is concerned, I think Jack London is probably his own best chronicler. *John Barleycorn,* originally published in 1913, is available in a reprint of 1968. On Eugene O'Neill, the exhaustive (970-page) biography by Arthur and Barbara Gelb (1962) has been followed by the even more exhaustive two-volume study by Louis Sheaffer, *O'Neill, Son and Playwright* (1968) and *O'Neill, Son and Artist* (1973). Though Sheaffer's much-praised work is newer and longer, I found the

Gelbs' effort just as good on the chronicle of O'Neill's life and some-what better in its account of his mental condition. José Quintero's memoir, *If You Don't Dance They Beat You*, was published in 1974.

Allen Ginsberg's shrill complaint is, of course, the opening of *Howl and Other Poems* (1956). The four volumes of Carlos Castaneda's dialogues with don Juan are by now widely available: *The Teachings of don Juan* (1968), *A Separate Reality* (1971), *Journey to Ixtlan* (1973), and *Tales of Power* (1974). William Burroughs's *Naked Lunch* first appeared in 1959. For the story of Lenny Bruce's disintegration, I have relied almost entirely on the splendid biography *Ladies and Gentlemen, Lenny Bruce*, by Albert Goldman, from the journalism of Lawrence Schiller (1974).

CHAPTER 14.
Percy Knauth has expanded his *Life* article, "A Season in Hell," into a book of the same title, published in 1975.

And then there are the books that contain marvelous bits and pieces, for which I was determined to find a place and never did. The letters of Louise Bogan, for example, published in 1973 under the title *What the Woman Lived*, ed. Ruth Limmer. "My God, what was the crime?" she wrote to Edmund Wilson from a mental institution in 1931. "Did I deserve/Therapy, out of possible punishments?/What the betrayal, that the faded nerve/Must bloom again by means not making sense/O, I shall mend! Even now I grow quite well,/Knitting round wash-cloths on the paths of hell." And her lover, Theodore Roethke, whose *Collected Poems* (1966) include the melancholy humor of "Meditation in Hydrotherapy": "Six hours a day I lay me down/ Within this tub but cannot drown./The ice cap at my rigid neck/Has served to keep me with the quick./This water, heated like my bood,/ Refits me for the true and good./Within this primal element/The flesh is willing to repent./I do not laugh; I do not cry;/I'm sweating out the will to die./My past is sliding down the drain; I soon will be myself again."

"I'm glad that you are having good, sensible professional care . . ." Louise Bogan wrote him. "Believe me, my dear, I've been through it all. . . . And after the first feelings of revolt and rage wear off, there's nothing like the peace that descends upon one with routine, lovely routine."

On a more prosaic level, John Gregory Dunne summed up his difficulties (in *Vegas, A Memoir of a Dark Season;* 1974) in terms of his eating: "For days on end . . . I subsisted on a diet of Clark bars and Hydrox cookies and Hostess Twinkies and, when I was feeling flush, cans of macadamia nuts. . . . I ate Neccos, the little host-like candy wafers, and Oreos and Florentine Pogens. I ate cube steak and McIntosh apples and Ritz crackers with Laura Scudder crunchy peanut butter. I got fat." Equally voracious, and equally anguished about her diet, was Johanna Davis, a very attractive woman who managed to finish one short novel, *Life Signs* (1973), which contained a splendid outburst by the heroine against her psychiatrist: "How in God's name do you know? You won't let me tell you about the real things, past or present. You're not interested in the fact that I walk around paralyzed most of the time, sit in ladies' rooms for hours, can't remember what it is I've gone shopping for, scrub at my house all night, and have to drug myself to get up in the morning. I'm trying to stay alive, and you only care about what goes on when I'm not alive, when I'm asleep." The psychiatrist's answer was predictable: "Why do you blame all this on me?" Josie Davis's own fate was quite unpredictable, was, in its way, insane. She went out with her son to mail a letter in late 1974, and a taxi went out of control, roared up onto the sidewalk and killed her.

So. I am only trying to say that there are many books that never found their way into my inquiry—Ervin Goffman's *Asylums*, to name yet another one, and Alan Harrington's *Psychopaths*—simply because I could not figure out how to include them. And many people, too, who sacrificed their time and their emotions to my tape recorder, for no purpose other than to help convince a skeptical world that the experience of going crazy is an experience that most of us can share.

A word of thanks, also, for research assistance by Sally Muir, Erika Sanchez and Peter Shapiro.

Locust Valley, N.Y.
March, 1975

Index

Abbott, Maya, 101
Abrahamsen, Dr. David, 255
A.D. Club, 136
Adams, John, 211
Adler, Alfred, 73
Advertisements for Myself
    (Mailer), 188
Aesculapius, 42, 77
affect, lack of, 21
aging, 322–23, 327
Agnew, Spiro, 211
Ahab, Captain, 231
Ajax (Sophocles), 208
Aken, Jerome van (J. Bosch),
    49–52
Albert, Marv, 340
Alcmaeon of Crotona, 42–43
alcoholic liquor, 283–84, 290–93
Alcoholics Anonymous, 281, 284
alcoholism, 176, 274, 280–88,
    290–301
    and insanity, 19, 284, 288,
        295–97, 301–2
    statistics on, 24, 283, 284, 295
Aldrin, Buzz, 231–35
Alekhine, Alexander, 93
"Alexander's Ragtime Band," 223
Allan, John, 288
Allen, Nancy, 23
ambivalence, 21
Amelia, Princess, 64
Americana Hotel, New York, 34–
    36, 38

American Dream, An (Mailer),
    188
American Psychiatric Association,
    78, 210
American Schizophrenia Associa-
    tion, 358
American Tragedy, An (Dreiser),
    156
Amityville, N.Y., incident of
    madness in, 244
amphetamines, 79, 284
Anderson, Sherwood, 297
Anderssen, Adolf, 95
anger, 191–200, 259–60
Anna, 157–63
Anna Karenina (Tolstoy), 156
Anthony, Saint, 44, 48–49
antihistamines, 76–77
Antonenko, Nina, 267
Apollo 11, 231
Apollo 14, 233
Apollo 15, 233
Arieti, Dr. Silvano, 35–36
Aristotle, 42
Armstrong, Neil, 231–32, 234,
    236
Army Specialized Training Pro-
    gram, 237
assassination, 217
Assassin's Diary, An (Bremer), 215
association, lack of, 21
Atascadero State Mental Hospital,
    254

371

Athanasius, 271
Athena, 42
Auchincloss, Louis, 53
Auden, W. H., 74
Augusta of Saxe-Gotha, Princess of Wales, 60–61
Auschwitz, 352
authority, fear of, 87
autism, 21

Baker, Carlos, 113–14
Baker, Sir George, 61, 62
Baldwin, James, 108, 164
barbital, 302
barbiturates, 302
Barnes Hospital, St. Louis, 209
Bastille, 247, 248, 250, 251
Bateson, Gregory, 25
Baughman, U. E., 206
Bedburg, Germany, incident of "possession" in, 48
beer, and alcoholism, 283, 291
Begner, Howard, 18
Behan, Brendan, 283
Bellevue Hospital, New York, 30–34, 117, 187, 294, 324–327
Bell Jar, The (Plath), 76
Benedict of Nursia, Saint, 44
Benicia, California, Jack London in, 291
Bergman, Ingrid, 75
Berke, Dr. Joseph, 102
Bethesda Naval Hospital, 207–8, 214
Bethlehem Hospital (Bedlam), London, 59, 60
Beverly Hills, California, Freud's theories in, 74–75
Bible (Old and New Testaments), 40–42, 47
Bicêtre mental hospital, 251, 252
Billy, 237–43

Bird of Paradise, The (Laing), 99
birth, and memory, 85
Bischione, Thomas, 18
Black Death, 44
Black Panthers, 228, 230
Black Rage (Grier and Cobbs), 221
blacks, 23, 217, 221–29, 323
   militant radicalism and, 226–29
   mother as culture-bearer for, 221
   passive madness and, 223
   psychological immobilization of, 222
   see also Black Panthers; Cleaver, Eldridge; Louis, Joe; other black personalities
Blake, William, 350
Bleuler, Eugene, 20–21, 73, 175
blood pressure, 76–77
Bluebottle, The (Tarsis), 265
Blue Cross, 24
Bondareva, Dr. Galina, 268–70
Bosch, Hieronymus, 49–52
Boston Psychiatric Hospital, 143
Boswell, James, 60
Bovet, Daniel, 76
Bowery, New York, 300–301
Bowman, Commander [Dave], 26–27
brain, 20, 42–43, 79
   as center of consciousness, 42–43
   effect of nutrition on, 78–79
   organic damage to, 20
   see also memory
Breakfast of Champions (Vonnegut), 80
Breathless (motion picture), 229
Brecht, Bertolt, 271
Bremer, Arthur, 215–17
Bride of Lammermoor, The (Scott), 165–66

Brothers of the Common Life, 49
Brothers Karamazov, The (Dosto-
    yevsky), 116, 256
Brown, H. Rap, 270
Bruce, Lenny, 310–15
Brühl, Carl, 72
Burghölzli mental hospital, 20, 73
Burluwitz, Cyrus, 263
Burney, Fanny, 61, 63
Burroughs, William, 307–10

Cabalists, 141
Caesar's Things (Z. Fitzgerald),
    177
Café de la Régence, 95
Cagney, James, 286
Cain and Abel, 40
Cannon, Jimmy, 223
Carnaval (Schumann), 64, 67
Carroll, Lewis, 269
"Cascades, The" (Joplin), 219
Castaneda, Carlos, 305–7, 349
Cat's Cradle (Vonnegut), 116
cave paintings, 41
Celia, 191–200
Celsus, 43
Chafetz, Dr. Morris E., 286
Chaplin, Charles, 298
Charcot, Jean Martin, 72
Charenton insane asylum, 248,
    252, 253
Charlotte, Queen of England, 61–
    62, 64
Charpentier, Paul, 77
Chaucer, Nancy, 96–98, 166–70,
    353–54
chemotherapy, *see* drugs in treat-
    ment of mentally ill
Chesler, Phyllis, 172
chess, 91–96, 106–7
child abuse, 87
Childs, Marquis, 207
Chivers, Thomas Holley, 287

chlorpromazine, 37, 77, 78
Chopin, Frédéric, 67
Chronicles of England (Holin-
    shed), 53
Ciardi, John, 309
Clarke, Arthur, 25, 26, 27
Cleaver, Eldridge, 226–29, 255
Cleveland Institute of Arts, 192
Cloud, Steve, 17–19, 23, 38
Cobbs, Price M., 221
cocaine, 302
codeine, 302
Collins, Mike, 231–32, 236
Colorado Psychiatric Hospital,
    226
Columbia University, 195, 229
Communists, 205–7, 231
computers, 24–27
Conn, Billy, 224
Corday, Charlotte, 253
Cornell University, 137–38
Cornuta, 17
Corpus Hippocraticus, 43
Crack Up, The (Fitzgerald), 171,
    178
crazy, definition, 19, 20, 21
Creedmore State Hospital, 80
Crimea, 266
crime and insanity, 246–47, 255,
    260–63
crime and punishment, 246–47
Crosley poll, 210

Dali, Salvador, 75
Dalrymple, Janet, 165–66
Dangerous Summer, The (Hem-
    ingway), 114
Danzig, Sarah, 101
depression, 27, 210, 235, 292,
    319, 325, 328, 332, 335
Depression, the Great, 108, 316–
    317
Des Moines Register, 133

Detroit, Joe Louis in, 224, 225
Detroit Free Press, 209, 245
Deuteronomy, 42
Dewey, Thomas E., 206
dietary deficiencies, 78
Diver, Nicole, 98
Divided Self, The (Laing), 100
divorce, 156, 179–80
D.M.T., 312
Doctors Hospital, New York, 153
Dr. Strangelove (motion picture), 205
domineering fathers, 87
Donizetti, Gaetano, 165–66
Dostoyevsky, Feodor, 23, 116, 153, 256, 350
dreaming, 333–34
drinking, 282–83
    in U.S.S.R., 284
    see also alcoholism
drug addiction, 24, 304, 307–8, 310–15
drugs in treatment of mentally ill, 37, 76–80, 184, 235, 357–359
drug traffic, 245
drunkenness, 282–96 *passim*
    national cost of, 283
    see also alcoholism
dual personality, 261–63, 278
Dunbar of Baldoon, David, 165
Duncan, Isadora, 174
Duncan, Robert, 211
Düsseldorf, 69

Eagleton, Mark, 209
Eagleton, Thomas, 22, 209–11
Eddie, 273–81
Eden Express, The (Mark Vonnegut), 105
ego and id conflict, 36
Ehrlich, Paul, 71
Ehrlichman, John, 285

Eleanor, 327–31
electroshock therapy, 43, 76, 130, 210, 277, 343, 348
Eliot, Thomas Stearns, 20
Elizabeth I, Queen of England, 52
"Entertainer, The" (Joplin), 229
Equanil, 77
Erasistratus, 43
Erikson, Erik, 340
Ernest Hemingway, A Life Story (Baker), 114
Esterson, Aaron, 101
exhibitionism, 28
exorcism, 41

families, 90, 100–101
    influence of sex in, 86, 87, 89
Fanon, Frantz, 217
Farmer, Frances, 29–30, 75
Faulkner, William, 286
Fawkes, Guy, 52
F.B.I., 114
fear of authority (domineering father), 87
Ferenczi, Sandor, 355
Field, June, 101
Fischer, Bobby, 93
Fitzgerald, F. Scott, 98, 170–79, 286
Fitzgerald, Zelda, 21, 170–79
Flury, Edgar, 261
Ford, Henry, 224
Ford Hospital, Detroit, 245
Forrestal, James V., 205–9
    suicide of, 208
For Whom the Bell Tolls (Hemingway), 113, 114
Fouché, Joseph, 252
Franck, Peter, 156–63, 352
French Hospital, 18
Freud, Sigmund, 33, 72–76, 86–89, 99, 102, 175, 340

Freud, Sigmund, *continued*
　development of psychoanalysis,
　　72, 75–76, 355, 356
　and ego–id conflict, 36
　Oedipus-complex theory, 86,
　　89
　use of cocaine, 302
Fromm, Erich, 217
Frost, Robert, 270

Galen, 44
Galileo, 50, 271
Gandhi, Mohandas K., 102
Garden of Earthly Delights, The
　(Bosch), 50–51
Gardner, Erle Stanley, 256
Gary, Romain, 230
Gelb, Arthur and Barbara, 293
Genesis, 40
Geoffrey of Monmouth, 53
George, 302–3
George III, King of Great Britain,
　60–64
Ginsberg, Allen, 231, 302, 310
Glarus, Switzerland, 57
Glasgow Royal Mental Hospital,
　99
Glovers of Wakefield, 40
God, 192, 230–35, 349, 353
　omnipotence of, and madness,
　　230–31
　and space flights, 232–34
　see also Bible
Godunov, Boris, 164
Goethe, Johann Wolfgang von, 72
Gogol, Nikolai, 70, 230, 350
Goldberg, Calman, 17
Goldwyn, Samuel, 74
Granville-Barker, Harley, 53
Graves, Robert, 164
Great Gatsby, The (Fitzgerald),
　173
Greece, ancient, 42, 58

Greenwich Village, 33, 109
Grier, William H., 221
Griffin, Jason, 338–41, 347
Grigorenko, Gen. Pyotr, 265–66
Griswold, Rev. Rufus W., 287
Groote, Gerhard, 49
Groton School, 136
group therapy, 145, 356
Guernica (Picasso), 244
Guest of Honor, A (Joplin), 219
Gunner's Hall, Baltimore, Poe at,
　290

Haldol, 357
halfway houses, 80, 185
hallucinations, 25, 52, 67, 82, 183,
　277, 280, 352
Hamilton, Dr. Gilbert V., 296
Hamlet, 24, 35, 94, 164
Handel, George Frederick, 61, 63
Harding, Warren G., 211
Harlem, New York, 221–23, 352
Harper's, 104, 288
Harry, 299–301
Harvard Crimson, 132, 135
Harvard University, 128–47, 204,
　341, 349, 350
　suicides at, 146–47
　University Health Service at,
　　143–47
Harvey, William, 57
hashish, 302
Havana, Cuba, Krim and Hem-
　ingway in, 111
Hay Wagon, The (Bosch), 49–50
Hearst, Randolph A., 271
Heller, Joseph, 347
Hell's Angels, 121, 233
Hemingway, Dr. Clarence E.,
　112–14
Hemingway, Ernest, 111–14,
　171–72, 177, 270, 286, 350
Henry VIII, King of England, 59

heroin, 302, 307, 314
Hierophilus, 43
Hiller, Ferdinand, 69
Hippocrates, 43, 56
Hitchcock, Alfred, 75
Hitler, Adolf, 217, 313
Holinshed, Raphael, 53
Hollywood Hospital, New West-
    minster, 106
Holmes, Sherlock, 302
Holyoke Center, Harvard, 144–47
homicide, *see* murder
Hoover, J. Edgar, 205
Hôpital Général, Paris, 58
Hotchner, A. E., 114–15
"Hound, The" (Faulkner), 247
hypoglycemia, 78
hysteria, 57–58

Ibsen, Henrik, 71
Iceman Cometh, The (O'Neill),
    296
I Ching, 233, 303
Illumination (motion picture), 158
imipramine, 235
Innocent VIII, Pope, 45
In Our Time (Hemingway), 113
Inquisition, 46
insane asylums, *see* mental hos-
    pitals
insanity (madness, psychosis), 34,
    37, 38, 143–47, 162–64, 336,
    343, 347, 351
    and alcoholism, 19, 284, 288,
        295–97, 301–2
    and black men, 221–23, 228
    and crime, 217, 246–47, 255–
        263, 271
    definitions of, 20–21
    in families, 90, 100–101
    history of, 57–63
    hospitalization, 20–21
    and lust for power, 217

and memory, 85
and rebellion, 271
and self-destructiveness, 19,
    23–24; *see also* suicide
and self-knowledge, 349
statistics on, 21–23, 79–80
symptoms of, 16–17, 21, 63
treatment of, 41–44, 57–63, 79,
    80, 347, 351, 358
types of, 20–21
see also mental illness *and*
    schizophrenia
insomnia, 324–25
insulin shock, 207, 277, 341
International Book Society, 333
"International Jewry," 206
International Psychoanalytical
    Association, 73
Interpretation of Dreams, The
    (Freud), 33, 73
Ionesco, Eugene, 151
Iponiazid, 77
Irwin, James, 233

Jacobs, Mike, 224
James I, King of England, 52
Jane Eyre (C. Brontë), 172
Jefferson, Lara, 47, 350
Joachim, Joseph, 69
Joan of Arc, 46
Jocasta, Queen, 86
John Barleycorn (London), 283,
    290
Johnson, Jack, 223
Johnson, Lyndon B., 213, 217
Johnson, Samuel, 57, 60
Jonathan, 303–6
Jones, Ernest, 88, 89, 93, 94, 96
Joplin, Scott, 217–21, 223, 229
journalism, 81–82, 108
    see also Knauth, Percy; Krim,
        Seymour; Rand, Christopher
Jung, Carl, 74

Kaddish for Naomi Ginsberg (Ginsberg), 231
Kansas City Star, 113
Kant, Immanuel, 231
Karen, 257–60, 352
Kemper, Edmund Emil, III, 254–256
Kennedy, Jacqueline, 188
Kennedy, John F., 188, 217, 231
Kennedy, Robert F., 135
Kernberg, Dr. Otto F., 35, 36
K.G.B., 265, 266
Khrushchev, Nikita, 269
King Lear (Shakespeare), 44–45, 52–57, 63
Kingsley Hall, London, 102–4, 355
Kiryushin, Dr. Y. V., 264, 266
Knauth, Percy, 331–35
Kohn, Howard, 245
Koo, Aiko, 254–55
Kosygin, Alexei, 268
Kraemer, Heinrich, 45
Krim, Seymour, 75, 108–11, 352
Kubrick, Stanley, 25

Laborit, Henri, 76–77
La Coste, France, 249, 250
Laguerre, André, 334
Laing, Ronald David, 26, 99–104, 349, 353, 355
Lardner, Ring, Sr., 291, 324
Lardner, Ring, Jr., 285
Largus (doctor, first century), 43
Last Judgment, The (Bosch), 50
Last Tycoon, The (Fitzgerald), 171
Las Vegas, Nevada, 226
laudanum, 289
Laurel, Maryland, assassination attempt on Wallace in, 217
Leary, Timothy, 270

Lee, Russel V., 217
Leeuwenhoek, Anton van, 57
Leonardo da Vinci, 269
Lesson, The (Ionesco), 151
Levy, Magistrate Reuben, 187
Lewis, Jerry, 348
Lieberman, Dr. Cynthia, 36
Life magazine, 114, 232, 331
Lifshits, Dr. Alexander, 264, 267, 268
"Ligeia" (Poe), 288
Lima, Peru, Christopher Rand in, 336
Lincoln, Abraham, 211
Lindner, Robert, 76
Little Rock, Arkansas, 227
Lloyd, Harold, 276
Lolita (Nabokov), 156
London, 52, 59, 60, 74, 94–95, 102
London, Jack, 283, 290–93
London Illustrated News, 94
Long, Edward, 209
Loos, Anita, 74
Lopasio, Gregory, 244
Los Angeles, 16, 74, 224, 225
Los Angeles Times, 210
Louis, Joe, 223–25
love, a kind of craziness, 156
Lovett, Robert, 207
Lowell, Commander, 87
Lowell, James Russell, 95
Lowell, Robert, 28, 29, 87, 260
L.S.D., 104, 244, 302, 342
Lucia di Lammermoor (Donizetti), 165–66
Luther, Martin, 271
Lysenko, Trofim, 266
lysergic acid, *see* L.S.D.

Macbeth, 46, 52
MacLeish, Archibald, 29
Madden, Owney, 224

Madness, *see* insanity
Mailer, Adele Morales, 186–87
Mailer, Norman, 186–90, 214, 232–34, 310
Makovsky, Andrei, 132
Mallarmé, Stéphane, 138
Malleus Maleficarum (Sprenger and Kraemer), 45
Manes, Donald R., 80
Manhattan College, 275
Manhattan State Hospital, 221
manic-depressive psychosis, 20, 63
Mankiewicz, Frank, 210
"Maple Leaf Rag" (Joplin), 219
Marat, Jean Paul, 253
Marciano, Rocky, 224
marijuana, 227, 270, 304, 329, 343
Mark, Saint, 41
Martin Eden (London), 292–93
Mayo Clinic, 115, 210, 350
Mazlish, Bruce, 213
McAlpin Hotel, 18
McGovern, George, 209–11
McGraw, Dr. Herbert, 255
McGuire, Sgt. Kenneth, 244
McLean Hospital, Belmont, 145
McNamara, Robert S., 204
medical research and therapy, 42–45
    see also mental hospitals
Medvedev, Roy, 267, 268
Medvedev, Dr. Zhores, 264–70
Meistrich, Paul, 18, 23
Mel, 154–55
melancholia, 66, 69, 207
Melville, Herman, 16
memory, 85–86, 322
mental hospitals, 21–22, 29, 30, 37, 58–60, 79–80, 251, 266, 342, 343
    see also Bellevue Hospital
mental illness, 41–45, 58–59, 144

    see also insanity; nervous breakdowns
Mental Research Center, 143
meprobamate, 77
mescal, 306
Mescalito, 306, 307
Messiah (Handel), 163
Middletown State Hospital, 150
Midtown Manhattan Study, 22
Milford, Nancy, 172
Mills, Wilbur, 286
Miltown, 77, 333, 334
Milwaukee Area Technical College, 216
mind, the, 42–43
    see also brain; memory
Mind Science Foundation, 233
Mingus, Charles, Jr., 117, 125–127
Mingus, Charles, III, 117–27, 352
Minuteman missiles, 203
Mirror of Salvation (Ruysbroek), 50
Mitchell, Ed, 233
Moby Dick (Melville), 343
Monte Cassino, 44
Montreuil, Madame de, 248–50
moon, 231–33, 235, 236
Mooney, Michael, Jr., 33–34
Moon for the Misbegotten, A, (O'Neill), 297
Moore, Dr. Merrill, 298
Moran, Dr. J. J., 286–87
Moran, Lois, 174
morphine, 293, 302, 308, 315
Morphy, Paul, 93–96, 107–8
Moses, 42
Mt. Sinai Hospital, New York, 318
Moveable Feast, A (Hemingway), 114, 171
Munter, Dr. Preston K., 143–45
murder, 23, 40, 156, 217, 256–57, 284

Murdering Mind, The (Abrahamsen), 255
Murphy, Gerald, 174
Murray, Henry, 133–34
Murray, Joseph, 18
Museum of Modern Art, 244–45
Mussolini, Benito, 217

Naked Lunch (Burroughs), 307, 309
Nancy, France, World War II experience in, 238, 243
Napoleon, Emperor, 252
narcotics addiction, *see* drug addiction
NASA, 234
Nathan, George Jean, 174
National Academy of Sciences, 24
National Council on Alcoholism, 24
National Institute on Alcohol Abuse and Alcoholism, 283, 284, 286
National Institute of Mental Health, 24
National Institute for the Psychotherapies, Inc., 34
Nawroth, Robert, 17
Nembutal, 333, 334
nervous breakdowns, 175, 271, 296–97, 318–19, 332–33, 341–43, 348, 358
    U.S. Presidents and, 211
    see also mental illness
Neue Zeitschrift für Musik, 67, 69
Neumann, John von, 25
Neuropsychiatric Institute of U.C.L.A., 23
Newcastle, Duke of, 61
New German Society of Psychotherapy, 74
New Orleans, 16, 96, 211
New Orleans Chess Club, 94

Newsweek, 284
New York City, 16, 74, 80, 87, 95, 216
    Manhattan Study, 22–23
New York *Daily News*, 109, 323
New Yorker, The, 336, 337
New York Herald Tribune, 336
New York Post, 323
New York Times, The, 19, 80, 93, 96, 171, 186, 214, 261, 336
    on Forrestal resignation, 207
    on Eagleton as Vice-Presidential nominee, 210
    on drinking, 283, 286
    Carlotta O'Neill interview, 299
niacin (nicotinic acid), 78
Nieman Fellowship, 323
Nietzsche, Friedrich, 70, 350
Nijinsky, Vaslav, 71
1984 (Orwell), 51
Nixon, Frank, 212
Nixon, Richard M., 210–16, 226, 232, 270, 285, 339–40, 348
Novalis, 349

Oedipus, 36, 86
Oedipus complex, 72, 86, 87, 89
Oedipus Rex (Sophocles), 89
O'Hair, Madalyn Murray, 234
O'Neill, Agnes Boulton, 294, 296
O'Neill, Carlotta Monterey, 296–299
O'Neill, Eugene, 293–99
    his children, 298
Ophelia, 164
opium, 77, 288, 302
organic brain damage, 20
orthomolecular psychiatry, 78
Orwell, George, 51
Oswald, Lee Harvey, 215, 256

Panama Canal Zone, 260–61
paranoia, 336, 343
    see also insanity; mental illness

Paris, 58–60, 95, 96, 247, 251
Pauling, Linus, 78
Peace and Freedom Party, 227
Pearson, Drew, 207
Peck, Gregory, 75
Pennsylvania Hospital, 58, 59, 60
Pennsylvania, University of, 58, 354
Perkins, Maxwell, 172
Peru, early brain surgery in, 42
Peterson, Roger Michael, 262
peyote, 302, 305–7
phenobarbital, 302
phenothiazine, 77, 79, 357
Phipps Clinic, Baltimore, 172
physicians, 57–58
    see also psychiatrists
Pierce, Chester M., 204–5, 221–222
Pierce, Franklin, 211
Pinel, Philippe, 251, 252
Pitt, William, the Elder, 61
Pitt, William, the Younger, 64
plague, 44, 52
Plaitakis, Emanuel, 16–17
Plath, Sylvia, 76, 98, 130
Plimpton, George, 135
Poe, Edgar Allan, 287–90, 350
Poe, Virginia, 288–89
Polaris submarine, 204–5
Polybus, King of Corinth, 86
Porcellian Club, 136
Pound, Ezra, 29, 269–70, 350
Prado Museum, Madrid, 50
Prefaces to Shakespeare (Granville-Barker), 53
Preminger, Otto, 229
Presidential Papers, The (Mailer), 188
Prial, Frank J., 19
Primal Scream, The (Janov), 198
primal therapy, 198–200
promethazine, 76–77

protection racket, 246
proteins, 78
Provence, Sade in, 248, 252
Provincetown, Massachusetts, 295
psychiatrists, 36, 77, 266, 267, 354–59
    and drug therapy, 79
    fallibility of, 255, 256, 263, 351
    self-doubt of, 37, 79
psychiatry, 37, 76–79, 135, 353, 355, 359
    dubious efficacy of, 37, 76, 356
psychoanalysis, 33, 72–77, 295, 341, 356, 357
    limitations of, 37, 75, 76
psychodrama, 151
psychohistorians, 212–13
psychotherapy, 37, 145, 196, 207, 226, 343, 358
    cost of, 37, 76
    see also group therapy;
        psychiatry; psychoanalysis
psychotic, definition of, 20
Puritani, I (Bellini), 165

Quakers, 58
Quetzalcoatl, 141
Quintero, José, 299

racial equality, 221–23
    see also blacks; individual
        names of black personalities
Radcliffe College, 144
Ragtime Dance, The (Joplin), 219
Raines, Capt. George N., 207–8
Ramparts magazine, 228
Rand, Christopher, 89–92, 335–37
Rand, Mary, 91
Rand, Richard Aldrich, 89–92, 135–138, 140, 336
Rank, Otto, 355
rape, 227–29, 255

Rauwolfia serpentina (snakeroot), 77

Rebel Without a Cause (motion picture), 76

regicide, 35–36

Reich, Dr. Robert, 80

Reich, Wilhelm, 270

Renaissance, instability during, 52

Rentzel, Lance, 27, 28

reserpine, 77

retarded child, 338, 348

retirement age, 323

Richelieu, Armand Cardinal, 140

Ritalin, 235

Riverside Church, New York, 197

Robbins, Dr. Ed, 32

Robespierre, Maximilien, 252

Rockefeller, Winthrop, 286

Rockland State Hospital, 109

Rogow, Arnold, 207

Rojack, Stephen, 188–90

Roman Catholic Church, 45, 48, 50

Roman Empire, 44

Romantic Age, 70

Romeo and Juliet (Shakespeare), 156

Roosevelt, Franklin D., 213

Rosenberg, Dr. Conrad, 187

Rosenhahn, Prof. David, 37

Rosenthal, Dr. David, 24

Rostov, Nikolai, 47

Royal Canadian Mounties, 343

Royster, Sarah Elmira, 290

Rush, Benjamin, 58–59

Rush, John, 59

Ruysbroek, Jan van, 49, 50

Sade, Marquis de, 164, 188, 248–254, 309

St. Elizabeth's Hospital, Washington, D.C., 29, 270

St. Louis, Missouri, 209, 218, 219

St. Louis World's Fair (1904), 219

St. Luke's Hospital, New York, 154

St. Michael's Cemetery, 217

Salpêtrière, La, 59

Salzburg, 73

Sams, Erich, 68

San Clemente, California, 211

Sanity, Madness and the Family (Laing and Esterson), 101–2

Sardinia, King of, 249

Sartain, John, 289

Save Me the Waltz (Z. Fitzgerald), 172, 176–77

Savonarola, Girolamo, 50

Saul, King, 41

Schiller, Friedrich von, 349

schizophrenia, 35, 100–104, 117, 175, 268, 284, 343

definition of, 20–21

genesis in family, 100–102

treatment of, 77–79, 102

women victims, 164

Schmeling, Max, 226

Schmidt, Juergen, 140–43, 349, 353

Schonberg, Harold C., 93

Schumann, August, 65–66

Schumann, Clara, 65, 66, 68–70

Schumann, Robert, 64–70, 163, 221, 350

Schweitzer, Mitchell D., 187

Scott, Sir Walter, 166

Scott, Gen. Winfield, 94

Searcy State Hospital for the Insane, 223

Seberg, Jean, 229–30

self-destructiveness, *see* suicide

senility, 20

Separate Reality, A (Castaneda), 307

Serpasil, 77
Seven Years' War, 61
sexual license, 248–49
Shafrazi, Tony, 244–45
Shakespeare, William, 52–57, 94
Shanghai, O'Neill in, 296
Sheen, Msgr. Fulton J., 205
Sherry-Netherland Hotel, 112
's Hertogenbosch, 49
Short Beach, Connecticut, 193
Sidney, 180–86
Sinatra, Frank, 137
Sirhan, Sirhan B., 215
skyjacking, 263
slavery, heritage of, 223
Smith, George R., College, 219
Smith, Kline and French, 78
Smith College, 130
snakeroot (*serpentina*), 77
Snodgrass, Dr. J. E., 286, 290
Snyder, Dr. Solomon, 37
Solzhenitsyn, Alexander, 268
Sophocles, 86, 89
Soul on Ice (Cleaver), 226
Southern, Terry, 309
Spassky, Boris, 93
Spear, Harold, 129
Specia drug company, 77
Spector, Harry, 17, 23
Spee Club, 136
Spellbound (motion picture), 75
Spellman, Francis Cardinal, 205
Spinoza, Baruch, 140, 269
Sports Illustrated, 334
Sprenger, Johann, 45
Stalin, Josef, 217, 266, 268, 269
Standish Hall, Harvard, 128
Stanley, 192–99
*Statistical Abstract of the United
    States*, 21, 23
Staunton, Howard, 94–95
Steinitz, Wilhelm, 93
Sting, The (motion picture), 229

S.T.P. (hallucinogenic), 33–34
Strakhovsky, Dr. Leonid I., 131,
    132
Stump, Peter, 48
suicide, 24, 81, 146, 208, 271,
    276, 278, 302, 330, 336, 337
  attempted, 24, 31, 139, 280,
    289, 291, 293, 294
  love and, 156
  madness and, 19
  statistics, 23–24, 147, 284
  women, 23, 235, 257–58
Sullivan, Harry Stack, 90, 341
Sun Also Rises, The (Heming-
    way), 113
Sweeney Agonistes (Eliot), 186
Sydenham, Thomas, 57
Symbionese Liberation Army,
    270
syphilis, 68, 70–71

Tarsis, Valeriy, 265
Tate, Nahum, 57
taxation, 246
Teachings of Don Juan, The (Cas-
    taneda), 305
"Telltale Heart, The" (Poe), 247
Tender Is the Night (Fitzgerald),
    98, 172, 177–78
Thackeray, William Makepeace,
    64
Thebes, 36, 86
thioridazine, 235
Thomas, Jesse Burgess, 245–46
Thorazine, 78, 150, 154, 226, 339,
    343, 357, 358
Time-Life book division, 333
Time magazine, 210, 215
Times Square, 15
Tkach, Dr. Walter R., 214
Tolstoy, Leo, 132, 157
tranquilizers, 77, 79, 139
transcendental meditation, 356

Trapnell, Garrett Brock, 260
Treemonisha (Joplin), 220, 223
trepanning, 42
Truman, Harry S, 206, 209
Tuke, William, 58
Tuttle, Anthony, 148–55
Tuttle, Peter, 148–50, 152
TWA, 263
2001 (motion picture), 25–27
Tynan, Kenneth, 313

U.C.L.A., 23, 28
United States, Freud's tour of, 73
United States Air Force, 203, 235
United States Army, 237, 261
United States Department of
    Commerce, 21, 23
United States Navy, 204
United States Secret Service, 206
United States Senate, 285
University Health Service, Har-
    vard, 143–45
University Hospital, New York,
    186–87
U.S.S.R., drinking in, 284

Van Gogh, Vincent, 70, 163, 350
Venice, California, 150
Veronal, 294
Versailles, 252
Vesalius, 44
Veterans of Foreign Wars, 211
Vienna, Freud in, 74
Vienna Medical Society, 72
Vienna Psychoanalytic Society,
    73
Vietnam war, 216, 271–72
Vincennes, Château de, 250
vitamins, 78, 79, 150, 343, 348,
    358, 359
Vonnegut, Kurt, 71, 80–82, 106,
    107, 115–16, 342

Vonnegut, Mark, 104–7, 115–16,
    342–43, 353

Wales, Prince of, 61–62, 64
Walker, Daniel F., 244
Wallace, George, 217
Wallace, Mike, 186
Wall Street Journal, 211
Ward 7 (Tarsis), 265
Warren, Devereux, 98
Warren, Dr. Richard, 62, 63
Washington College Hospital,
    286
Washington Post, 210, 246
Watergate affair, 213, 215
Wechsler, Dr. Israel, 319
Wechsler, Michael, 135, 138–39,
    341–42
Weinberg, Leonard, 18
Weinstein, Bernard M., 31
Weiss, Peter, 253
werewolf, 48
West, Louis Jolyon, 28
Wharf Theater, Provincetown,
    295
*When All the Laughter Died in
    Sorrow* (Rentzel), 28
White, T. W., 287
Wieck, Clara, *see* Schumann,
    Clara
Wieck, Friedrich, 66–68
Williams, Montgomery, 19, 23
Williams, William Carlos, 159
Wills, Dr. Francis, 62
Wilson, Bill, 284
Wilson, Edmund, 171
Wilson, Woodrow, 211
witchcraft and witches, 17, 45–
    47, 57, 164
Wittenberg, Germany, Luther in,
    271
women, 23–24, 59–60, 164, 166,
    227

Woolf, Virginia, 71
World War II, 237–43, 269

Yale University, 185, 192, 195
York Retreat, 58

Zelda (Milford), 172
Ziegler, Ronald, 211
Zinkin, Dr. Joseph, 30–31
Zurich, 73